Advances in Pattern Recognition

Springer-Verlag London Ltd.

Advances in Pattern Recognition is a series of books which brings together current developments in all areas of this multi-disciplinary topic. It covers both theoretical and applied aspects of pattern recognition, and provides texts for students and senior researchers.

Springer also publishes a related journal, **Pattern Analysis and Applications**. For more details see: http://link.springer.de

The book series and journal are both edited by Professor Sameer Singh of Exeter University, UK.

Also in this series:

Principles of Visual Information Retrieval
Michael S. Lew (Ed.)
1-85233-381-2

Advanced Algorithmic Approaches to Medical Image Segmentation
Jasjit Suri, Kamaledin Setarehdan and Sameer Singh (Eds)
1-85233-389-8

Šarūnas Raudys

Statistical and Neural Classifiers

An Integrated Approach to Design

With 68 Figures

Springer

Šarūnas Raudys
Data Analysis Department, Institute of Mathematics and Informatics,
Akademijos 4, Vilnius 2600, Lithuania

ISBN 978-1-4471-1071-2 ISBN 978-1-4471-0359-2 (eBook)
DOI 10.1007/978-1-4471-0359-2

British Library Cataloguing in Publication Data
Raudys, Šarūnas
Statistical and neural classifiers : an integrated approach to design. - (Advances in pattern recognition)
1. Pattern recognition systems 2. Neural networks (Computer science)
I. Title
006.4

Library of Congress Cataloging-in-Publication Data
A catalog record for this book is available from the Library of Congress

Originally published by Springer-Verlag London Berlin Heidelberg in 2001
Softcover reprint of the hardcover 1st edition 2001

Typesetting: Camera-ready by author
34/3830-543210 Printed on acid-free paper SPIN 10762565

In memory of my Father
and in memory of my mathematics teacher –
who was like a real father to me at school.

Foreword

Automatic (machine) recognition, description, classification, and groupings of patterns are important problems in a variety of engineering and scientific disciplines such as biology, psychology, medicine, marketing, computer vision, artificial intelligence, and remote sensing. Given a pattern, its recognition/classification may consist of one of the following two tasks: (1) supervised classification (also called discriminant analysis); the input pattern is assigned to one of several predefined classes, (2) unsupervised classification (also called clustering); no pattern classes are defined *a priori* and patterns are grouped into clusters based on their similarity. Interest in the area of pattern recognition has been renewed recently due to emerging applications which are not only challenging but also computationally more demanding (e.g., bioinformatics, data mining, document classification, and multimedia database retrieval).

Among the various frameworks in which pattern recognition has been traditionally formulated, the statistical approach has been most intensively studied and used in practice. More recently, neural network techniques and methods imported from statistical learning theory have received increased attention. Neural networks and statistical pattern recognition are two closely related disciplines which share several common research issues. Neural networks have not only provided a variety of novel or supplementary approaches for pattern recognition tasks, but have also offered architectures on which many well-known statistical pattern recognition algorithms can be mapped for efficient (hardware) implementation. On the other hand, neural networks can derive benefit from some well-known results in statistical pattern recognition. Issues related to the training and test sample sizes, feature space dimensionality, error rate estimation, and the discriminatory power of different classifiers have been extensively studied in the statistical pattern recognition literature. It often appears that some of the neural network researchers attempting to solve pattern recognition problems are not aware of these results.

Professor Raudys' book is a timely addition to the literature on pattern recognition. Professor Raudys is eminently qualified to write a monograph which presents a balanced view of classifier design and promotes an integration of statistical pattern recognition and neural network approaches. Even though his early work, published in Russian, was not easily accessible to the pattern recognition community, he is now well-known and recognised for his early contributions on the topic of "curse of dimensionality" and its practical implications in designing a pattern recognition system. His intuition and knowledge of the performance of various classifiers has enabled him to show the interrelationships among them. The book contains detailed descriptions of various classifiers which, to my knowledge, are not readily available in other textbooks. In addition to deriving analytical results concerning the relationship between sample size, dimensionality and model parameters, he also reports simulations results. These results are not available in other well-known textbooks on pattern recognition and neural networks.

In most pattern recognition books and review papers, it is the statistical approach which is used to compare and analyse classification and regression methods based on neural networks. Šarūnas Raudys was the first to show that ANN based classifiers and regression evolve into, and realise, a number of popular statistical pattern recognition methods. These findings, together with his earlier results, enable him to propose a way to utilise positive attributes of both approaches simultaneously in classifier design. His extensive coverage of the curse of dimensionality and related topics, together with a new approach to introduce statistical methodology into the neural networks design process, constitute the novelty of this book.

In summary, this book is an excellent addition to the literature on statistical pattern recognition and neural networks. It will serve as a valuable reference to other excellent books by Duda, Hart, and Stork, Ripley, Bishop and Haykin.

September 19th, 2000, East Lansing, Michigan Anil K. Jain

Preface

– Les hommes de chez toi, dit le petit prince,
cultivent cinq mille roses dans un même jardin...
et ils n'y trouvent pas ce qu'ils cherchent...
– Ils ne le trouvent pas, répondis-je...
Et cependant ce qu'ils cherchent pourrait être
trouvé dans une seule rose ou un peu d'eau...
– Bien sûr, répondis-je.
Et le petit prince ajouta:
– Mais les yeux sont aveugles. Il faut chercher
avec le coeur.

Antoine de Saint-Exupery "Le Petit Prince",
Chapitre XXV

In his book Antoine de Saint-Exupery wrote: "... In your country, people plant five thousand roses in the same garden ... and they do not find what they are searching for. Meanwhile, they could find everything they are seeking for in a single rose, or in a drop of water... However, eyes are blind. You have to seek by your heart." I am fond of Antoine de Saint Exupery. I like his books and I believe in these words.

When, after 25 years of research work in multivariate statistical analysis and statistical pattern recognition, I became interested in Artificial Neural Networks (ANN), I remembered de Saint-Exupery's words about the single rose. Instead of investigating multilayer perceptrons with thousands of neurones, I at first began to use statistical methods to analyse a single neurone – a single layer perceptron (SLP) and plain back-propagation (BP) training algorithm. The SLP and BP training are simplified mathematical models of complex information processing phenomena that take place in nature. I discovered that a single neurone can explain much about complex brain-learning behaviour.

After several years of research work, I learned that during the training phase, the single layer perceptron's weights are increasing and, therefore, the statistical properties of the cost function that is minimised during the training process are also changing. In its dynamical evolution, the SLP classifier can actually become one of several statistical classifiers that differ in their complexity.

At first the SLP classifier behaves as a simple Euclidean distance classifier. In this situation each pattern class is characterised by a sample mean vector. In further training, the SLP classifier begins to evaluate correlations and variances of features and almost becomes the standard linear Fisher classifier. Further, the SLP begins to behave as a robust classifier that ignores atypical training patterns. Later on in the training phase the SLP behaves as a classifier that minimizes the number of incorrectly classified training patterns. If there are no training errors, the SLP maximizes the margin between the decision boundary and the closest training-pattern vectors. Thus, the decision boundary is halfway between the training patterns and behaves as a support vector classifier where a fixed number of training patterns determine a position of the decision boundary. Thus, the SLP classifier begins as the simplest possible statistical classifier designed under the assumption of Gaussian pattern classes and ends as a complex classifier that can perform well with non-Gaussian pattern classes.

One more interesting peculiarity of the SLP classifier is that the performance (the generalization error) of the perceptron depends on the initial conditions. If the starting perceptron weight vector is almost optimal, the SLP classifier initially contains much useful information. This information can be utilized to determine the final weight vector. To preserve and use the information in the initial weights, one must not overtrain the SLP. This is a very valuable property of adaptively trained neural networks.

The more I work in the ANN discipline, the more I marvel at the remarkable qualities of neural networks. Specifically, I am amazed that the SLP classifier dynamics progress from the simplest algorithms to the most complex algorithms in a natural manner. Statisticians and engineers have long understood that in designing decision-making algorithms from experimental data one needs to progress from simple algorithms to complex algorithms. The artificial neurone accomplishes this complexity progression in a natural manner. Statisticians required several decades to develop a number of statistical classification and regression rules: Fisher (1936) proposed his linear discriminant function more than six decades ago and Vapnik devised his support vector machine (Vapnik, 1995) only recently. The neurone, however, implements this algorithm design progression in a logical sequence. One can think of this progression as nature's method.

There is a plethora of useful information currently available in the field of statistical pattern recognition. The main element of statistical pattern recognition is the assumption that the pattern vectors are random vectors that can be modelled as observations from multivariate distributions. In the parametric approach, the classifier designer assumes he knows this multivariate distribution precisely. In order to determine the classification algorithm, one needs to estimate the unknown multivariate density function parameters using the training data. Researchers have found that the more complex the multivariate density model assumed, or equivalently, the greater the number of parameters to be estimated, the greater the number of training vectors that must be employed to adequately determine the classifier. Therefore, a large number of parsimonious multivariate distribution densities have been formulated for this purpose.

One of the most interesting and important facts utilized in parametric classification is that if some of the pattern-class densities' parameters are in common, these parameters have a negligible influence on the increase in the generalization error. This is a very favourable property of the statistical parametric classifier approach. On the other hand, incorrect assumptions about the type of the probabilistic distribution assumed for the pattern vectors lead to an increase in the classification error. This is one of the main shortcomings of the parametric statistical classifier approach.

Being interested in both statistical pattern recognition and artificial neural network theory, I perceived a certain conflict between these two classification paradigms, and sometimes even a dissonance among proponents of these two classification methods. Statisticians generally have good mathematical backgrounds with which to analyse decision-making algorithms theoretically. They have proven many rigorous results concerning the optimality of statistical classification algorithms. However, they often pay little or no attention to the applicability of their own theoretical results and generally do not heed practical or even theoretical results obtained by ANN researchers.

ANN scientists advocate that one should make no assumptions concerning the multivariate densities assumed for the pattern classes. They, instead, propose that one should assume only the structure of the decision-making rules, for example a linear discriminant function in the space of original or transformed features, and then estimate the unknown rule coefficients (weights) directly from the training data. For this they suggest one minimize the number of errors incurred while classifying the training vectors (empirical error). Many such algorithms have been suggested to solve practical problems. Some of these algorithms have a theoretical justification and some have no theoretical elucidation yet.

Known properties and deficiencies of both statistical and neural classification algorithms hints that one should *integrate* the two classifier design strategies and utilize their good qualities. There are three key aspects of this integration. The first key is the fact that the correct initial weights of the perceptron contain information that can be saved for use in future training processes. Thus, we can utilize pattern classifiers based on statistical methods to define the initial perceptron weight vector. The second key is the fact that, during training, the perceptron changes its statistical properties and evolves from simple classification algorithms to more complex classification algorithms. The third key is the fact that, one can use the diversity of statistical methods and the multivariate models to perform different whitening data transformations, where the input variables are decorrelated and scaled in order to have the same variances. Then while training the perceptron in the transformed feature space, we can obtain the Euclidean distance classifier after the very first iteration. In the original feature space, the weight vector of this classifier is equivalent to the decision making rule found by utilizing the statistical methods and the multivariate models just mentioned. Further training can diminish the negative aspects of approximately correct or incorrect statistical assumptions.

Thus, it is possible to merge the statistical and neural approaches. Specifically, instead of using statistical methods and the multivariate models directly to design the classifier, we can use them to whiten the data. We can then train the perceptron paying special attention to the optimal stopping time. The data whitening reduces the generalisation error and simultaneously speeds up the training process. This approach merges the qualities of both statistical and neural classification algorithm design strategies. Investigations of the visual cortex in biological systems, however, have shown that the input decorrelation technique is already realized in natural systems. This is one more piece of evidence that the data decorrelation and scaling technique performed prior to perceptron training is a natural method of information processing.

An objective of this book is to explain the details necessary to understand and utilise the integrated statistical and neural net approach to design the classification rules. We, therefore, present a discussion of the diversity of linear and non-linear statistical pattern classification algorithms that can be utilised in an advanced neural network analysis. Special attention is paid to the assumptions used to design the algorithm, the generalisation error, and the training-set size relationships. Knowledge of these relationships allows one to analyse and compare the amount of information obtained from the training data, the assumptions, or from the educated guesses utilised to construct the decision-making algorithm. This is perhaps the central question that arises in machine learning and classifier design theory.

Performance, complexity, and training-set size relationships in the nonparametric neural net approach have been discussed in a number of books (Vapnik, 1982, 1995; Wolpert, 1995; Cherkassky and Mulier, 1996; Vidyasagar, 1997, etc.). According to Wolpert, "the statistical and neural net approaches have their own jargon, their own mathematical models, their own concern, and their own results. And, for the most part, they don't interact". This book primarily takes a statistical point of view but does not ignore other approaches. Alternative texts are Raudys (1976), Aivazian *et al.* (1988), Fukunaga (1990), McLachlan (1992), Devroye, Gyorfi and Lugosi (1996), Duda, Hart, and Stork (2000). The present book, however, is more focused on the integration of statistical and neural approaches to design the classification algorithms. In order to focus on performance, complexity, and design set size relationships more deeply in this book, I employ a simple formulation of the pattern recognition problem. For more general formulations of the pattern recognition problem and related questions I refer interested readers to broader texts such as Fukunaga's book. To make the book accessible to more readers, I adopt Fukunaga's notation.

The book is targeted to graduate students and research workers in data modelling, pattern recognition, and artificial neural networks. No special background beyond a good working knowledge of probability and statistics, elements of linear algebra, and calculus at the undergraduate level is required. However, one will benefit by having a popular pattern recognition or neural networks book (e.g., Fukunaga (1990) or Haykin (1998)) close at hand.

The book is organized somewhat like a reference book. At the same time I pay particular attention to the ideas used to design and analyse statistical classification algorithms that can be useful for understanding artificial neural network classifiers. For analysis of neural networks and statistical algorithms, the most important aspect is assumptions utilised in the algorithm design process. Therefore, in order to have a comprehensive point of view of the problem, I omit a part of the details concerning the estimation of parameters of well known statistical algorithms that can be found in the popular literature. To make understanding the main ideas easier, I provide a number of simple illustrative examples.

In the first chapter, I present the main definitions and terms and review the effects of finite training-set size on classifiers. In the second chapter, I review principles of the statistical decision theory, review important statistical multivariate data models, and give a taxonomy of pattern classification algorithms that can be obtained or improved while training ANN classification systems. In the third chapter, I present known results concerning the performance and generalisation error relationships for a number of parametric and nonparametric classification algorithms. In the fourth chapter, I consider training peculiarities and the generalisation and complexity of neural classifiers. In the fifth chapter, I explain the integration of the statistical and neural classification approaches. In the sixth and final chapter, I consider the topic of model selection, paying special attention to the accuracy of solutions to this important topic.

The main contents of this book crystallised during my work as a tenured researcher at the Institute of Mathematics and Informatics in Vilnius. However, other parts of the book were generated while visiting and collaborating with researchers, professors and graduate students at several institutions. These include the Department of Computer Science at Michigan State University; the Department of Information Systems at the Hankamer School of Business, Baylor University, USA; the Departments of Electrical Engineering and Applied Physics, Delft University of Technology, The Netherlands; LAFORIA, Institute Blaise Pascal, University Paris 6; Department of Electrical and Electronic Engineering, Bogazici (Bosforus) University, Istanbul; Laboratory of Information Representation, RIKEN, Tokyo; Ford Motor Company Scientific Research Laboratories. Many ideas and solutions were developed while closely collaborating with researchers of A. N. Kolmogorov Laboratory of Statistical Methods in Moscow State University. In particular I wish to thank Yurij Blagoveschenskij, Lev Meshalkin, Vladimir Vapnik, Gennadij Lbov, Anil Jain, Dean Young, Eric Backer, Bob Duin, Françoise Fogelman-Soulie, Patrick Gallinari, Bulent Sankur, Shun-ichi Amari, Andrzej Cichotski, Gintaras Puškorius and many others for useful and encouraging discussions and their hospitality and aid.

I would also like to thank my colleagues and former and present graduate students at the Institute of Mathematics and Informatics (Vilnius), Kaunas Vytautas Magnus University and Vilnius University for their challenging discussions and for their assistance in simulation studies. Special acknowledgement is expressed to Professor Laimutis Telksnys, Vitalijus Pikelis, Marina Skurichina, Tautvydas Cibas, Valdas Dičiūnas, Aistis Raudys, Aušra Saudargienė and Arūnas Janeliūnas. Exceptional thanks are expressed to Roy Davies, Edvardas Povilonis, Dean Young and Laura Thompson for their useful discussions and their aid in editing this book.

The author acknowledges the financial support from the Lithuanian State Science and Studies Foundation.

Vilnius, August 2000 *Šarūnas Raudys*

Contents

Abbreviations and Notations

ANN	artificial neural network
BP	back-propagation
DF	discriminant function
GCCM	Gaussian with common covariance matrix
EDC	Euclidean distance classifier
FS	feature space
k-NN	*k*-nearest neighbour
LDF	linear discriminant function
LOOM	leaving-one-out method
LVQ	learning vector quantisation
MEE	minimum empirical error
MLP	multilayer perceptron
PMC	probability of misclassification
PW	Parzen window
QDF	quadratic discriminant function
RBF	radial basis function
RDA	regularised discriminant analysis
RM	resubstitution method to estimate a training-set (empirical) error
SLP	single layer perceptron
SG	spherical Gaussian
SV	support vector
VC	Vapnik-Chervonenkis
ZEE	zero empirical error

$X = (x_1, x_2, \ldots, x_n)^T$ is an n-variate vector to be classified; a subscript ^{T} denotes a transpose operation

n is a dimensionality of the feature vector X

L is a number of pattern classes (categories, populations), $\omega_1, \omega_2, \ldots, \omega_L$

$p_i(X)$ is the class conditional probability density function (PDF) of vector X belonging to class ω_i

P_i is the a priori probability that observation X belongs to class ω_i

Ω is a feature space

One part of the design set is called *a training (learning) set*, while the other one is called *a validation set*. A set used to evaluate performance of the final variant is called *the test set*

N_i is the number of training vectors from class ω_r

$N = N_1+N_2$ if $N_2=N_1$, we denote $\bar{N} = N_1=N_2= N/2$

$\boldsymbol{M}_r$ is a mean vector, of the pattern class ω_r

$\hat{\boldsymbol{M}}_r$ is an arithmetic mean of the training-set of the class ω_r

$$\hat{\boldsymbol{M}}_i = \frac{1}{N_i} \sum_{j=1}^{N_i} \boldsymbol{X}_j^{(i)}$$

$\boldsymbol{X}_j^{(i)}$ is the j-th training set observation from ω_i

$\hat{\boldsymbol{M}} = ½ (\hat{\boldsymbol{M}}_1 + \hat{\boldsymbol{M}}_2)$ is a centre of the training set (if $N_2=N_1$)

Σ_i is an $n \times n$ covariance matrix (CM) of the of category ω_i. It is a function of n variances of all n features and $n(n-1)$ correlations between them. When both pattern classes share the same CM, we denote it by $\bar{\Sigma}$

$$\begin{bmatrix} \Sigma_1 & 0 & \cdots & 0 \\ 0 & \Sigma_2 & \cdots & 0 \\ \cdots & \cdots & \cdots & \cdots \\ 0 & 0 & \cdots & \Sigma_H \end{bmatrix}$$ is the block diagonal covariance matrix

$\hat{\Sigma}_i = \frac{1}{N_i - 1} \sum_{j=1}^{N_i} (\boldsymbol{X}_j^{(i)} - \hat{\boldsymbol{M}}_i)(\boldsymbol{X}_j^{(i)} - \hat{\boldsymbol{M}}_i)^T$ is a sample estimate of Σ_i

$\hat{\bar{\Sigma}}$ is a sample estimate of $\bar{\Sigma}$. $\hat{\bar{\Sigma}} = N_1/(N_1+N_2)\,\hat{\Sigma}_1 + N_2/(N_1+N_2)\,\hat{\Sigma}_2$

$\hat{\Sigma} = \Phi\Lambda\Phi^T$ is a singular value decomposition of matrix $\hat{\Sigma}$

$\hat{\Sigma}^+ = \Phi \begin{bmatrix} \lambda^{-1} & 0 \\ 0 & 0 \end{bmatrix} \Phi^T$ is a pseudoinversion of $\hat{\Sigma}$

$\hat{\Sigma} + \lambda\mathbf{I} = \Phi\,(\Lambda + \lambda\mathbf{I})\Phi^T$ is a ridge estimate of the sample covariance matrix $\hat{\Sigma}$

$\delta^2 = (\boldsymbol{M}_1 - \boldsymbol{M}_2)^T\, \bar{\Sigma}^{-1}(\boldsymbol{M}_1 - \boldsymbol{M}_2)$ is a squared generalised (Mahalanobis) distance between two pattern classes

$n^* = \dfrac{(\boldsymbol{M}^T\boldsymbol{M})^2(tr\,\bar{\Sigma}^2)}{(\boldsymbol{M}^T\bar{\Sigma}\boldsymbol{M})^2}$ is an effective dimensionality of EDC for GCCM data

$\|\boldsymbol{X} - \hat{\boldsymbol{M}}_r\|^2 = (\boldsymbol{X} - \hat{\boldsymbol{M}}_r)^T(\boldsymbol{X} - \hat{\boldsymbol{M}}_r)$ is an Euclidean distance between $\boldsymbol{X}$ and $\hat{\boldsymbol{M}}_r$

$h(X) = \boldsymbol{X}^T\boldsymbol{V} + v_0$ is a linear discriminant function (DF)

v_0, $\boldsymbol{V}^T = (v_1, v_2, \ldots, v_n)$ are weights of the discriminant function

$N_X(\boldsymbol{M}_i, \Sigma_i)$ is an n-dimensional Gaussian distribution density

$N_X(\boldsymbol{X}, \boldsymbol{M}_i, \Sigma_i) = (2\pi)^{-n/2}|\Sigma_i|^{-1/2}\, e^{-1/2\,(\boldsymbol{X} - \boldsymbol{M}_i)^T\, \Sigma_i^{-1}\,(\boldsymbol{X} - \boldsymbol{M}_i)}$

$cost_t = \dfrac{1}{N_1 + N_2} \sum_{i=1}^{2} \sum_{j=1}^{N_i} (t_j^{(i)} - f(\boldsymbol{V}^T\boldsymbol{X}_j^{(i)} + v_0))^2$ is a cost function

$f(\boldsymbol{V}^T\boldsymbol{X}_j^{(i)} + v_0)$ is an activation function

$t_j^{(i)}$ is a desired output (a target) for $\boldsymbol{X}_j^{(i)}$, the j-th training vector from ω_i

$\Phi\{a\} = \int_{-\infty}^{a} (2\pi)^{-1/2}\sigma^{-1}\exp\{-½\, t^2/\sigma^2\}dt$ is a standard Gaussian cumulative distribution function

$\varepsilon_B = \Phi\{-½\,\delta\}$ is a Bayes error for two Gaussian populations with common CM

ε_∞^A is an asymptotic error for the classifier A

ε_N^A is a conditional probability of misclassification (PMC), a conditional generalisation error

$\bar{\varepsilon}_N^A$ is an expected probability of misclassification or simply an expected generalisation error

tr is a trace of the matrix (a sum of diagonal elements)

$\mathbf{I}_r$ is an $r \times r$ identity matrix (ones on the diagonal and zeros outside)

1. Quick Overview

The main objective of this chapter is to define the terminology to be used and the primary issues to be considered in depth in the chapters that follow. In the first section, I present three of the simplest and most popular classification algorithms, and in the second section, I describe single and multilayer perceptrons and the training rules that are used to obtain classification algorithms. I give special attention to the most popular perceptron-training rule, back-propagation (BP). In the third section, I show that the three statistical-based classifiers described in Section 1.1 can be obtained via single-layer perceptron (SLP) training. The fourth section deals with performance, complexity and training-set size relationships, while the fifth section explains how to utilise these relationships while determining the optimal complexity of the decision-making algorithm. In the final section, I explain the overtraining effect that can arise while training artificial neural networks. Some bibliographical and historical remarks are included at the end of the chapter.

1.1 The Classifier Design Problem

The simplest formulation of a pattern classification task is to allocate an object characterised by a number of measurements into one of several distinct pattern classes. Let an unknown object (process, image) be characterised by the D-dimensional vector

$$\boldsymbol{S}_D = \begin{bmatrix} s_1 \\ s_2 \\ \\ s_D \end{bmatrix},$$

and let $\omega_1, \omega_2, \ldots, \omega_L$ be labels representing each of the potential pattern classes.

Then in allocatory pattern recognition, the objective is to construct an algorithm that will use the information contained in the components $s_1, s_2, \ldots, s_D$ of the vector $\boldsymbol{S}_D$ to allocate this vector to one of the L distinct categories (pattern classes) listed. Typically, the pattern classifier calculates L functions (similarity measures) $o_1, o_2, \ldots, o_L$ and allocates the unlabeled vector $\boldsymbol{S}_D$ to the class with the highest similarity measure.

In order to design such a classification algorithm one needs to fix the list of potential pattern classes. The measurements are chosen by their degree of relevance to the pattern classification problem at hand. The D measurements are obtained to formalise the large amount of information containing various a priori, unknown relationships among the pattern classes, among components of the vector S_D, etc.

Many useful ideas and techniques have been proposed during 50 years of research into the field of pattern recognition. In order to simplify the design process, researchers have proposed that one split the pattern recognition problem into two stages: the feature extraction stage and the pattern classifier design stage. In the feature extraction stage, a comparatively small number of informative features (n) are obtained from a large number of initial measurements by means of linear or non-linear transformations (typically, $n \ll D$). Then one develops an algorithm to classify an n-variate vector

$$X = (x_1, x_2, \dots, x_n)^T$$

into one of L pattern classes, where $x_1, x_2, \dots, x_n$ are components of the unclassified vector X and ^{T} denotes the transpose operation.

Example 1. Let $s_1, s_2, \dots, s_D$ contain D values of an acoustic signal. Suppose $s_1, s_2, \dots, s_D$ are realisations of a stationary random process described by the autoregression equation $s_t = x_1 s_{t-1} + x_2 s_{t-2} + \dots + x_n s_{t-n}$, where $n \ll D$. Then we can estimate the unknown coefficients $x_1, x_2, \dots, x_n$ from each segment of the signal and use $x_1, x_2, \dots, x_n$ as the components of the feature vector X.

We discuss feature extraction methods in Chapter 6. In this book, we restrict ourselves to specific classifier design tasks and we assume that the n features are already extracted so that we can perform the classification of the n-dimensional vectors X. For simplicity, we mostly consider only the two category case ($L = 2$) throughout the book.

Typically, in designing the classifier, one selects a number of n-dimensional vectors with known class membership and uses this data set as the main information source to develop a pattern recognition algorithm. This data set is called *a design set.* Often, while designing the pattern recognition algorithms, one develops a number of classifier variants differing in the feature system, in the methods used to design the classifier, in the parameter estimation methods, etc. A problem arises in determining which classifier variant to use. In order to obtain a reliable unbiased estimate of the performance of different variants for the recognition algorithm, one should use part of the design set for estimation of the algorithm's parameters (training) and another part for performance evaluation. The first part of the design set is called *a training (learning) set*, while the second part is called *a validation set.*

There exist different modifications for the data-splitting strategies. One of them is to perform the second test where the design and the validation sets are interchanged. We consider other strategies in Chapter 6. In order to evaluate the performance (generalisation error) of the final variant, we must use a new data set that have not been used for either training or for validation. This *test set* should be used only once.

An important source of "information" in developing a pattern classification algorithm involves assumptions and hypotheses concerning the structure and configuration of the pattern classes and the type of classifier decision boundary desired. One of the most popular hypotheses is that the n-dimensional vectors of distinct pattern classes are situated in different areas of a multivariate n-dimensional pattern space. One validation of this assumption is that these areas are "compact". Going further, one can assume that the arithmetic mean $\hat{\boldsymbol{M}}_r$ represents the pattern class ω_r sufficiently well. Then one can allocate an unknown vector $\boldsymbol{X}$ according to its Euclidean distance to the means $\hat{\boldsymbol{M}}_1, \hat{\boldsymbol{M}}_2, \ldots, \hat{\boldsymbol{M}}_L$ of the L distinct categories. The Euclidean distance between two vectors is defined as

$$\|\boldsymbol{X} - \hat{\boldsymbol{M}}_r\|^2 = (\boldsymbol{X} - \hat{\boldsymbol{M}}_r)^T (\boldsymbol{X} - \hat{\boldsymbol{M}}_r), \tag{1.1}$$

where $\boldsymbol{a}^T\boldsymbol{b}$ denotes a scalar product of vectors $\boldsymbol{a}$ and $\boldsymbol{b}$.

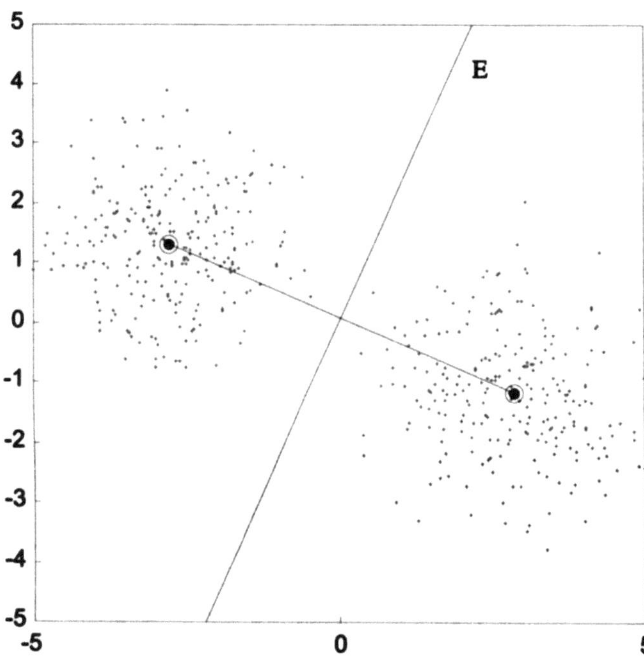

Fig. 1.1. Bivariate vectors sampled from two pattern classes, the sample means of the classes (circles), and the linear decision boundary of the Euclidean distance classifier.

This classifier is called the Euclidean distance classifier (EDC) or the nearest means classifier (Sebestyen, 1962). To design the EDC, one assumes that the pattern vectors of each class are similar among themselves and close in proximity to a "typical member" of this class (the centre represents the sample mean vector of this class). In Figure 1.1, we have depicted 300 bivariate vectors belonging to each of two pattern classes and the linear decision boundary of the EDC. The sample means of the classes, $\hat{M}_1$ and $\hat{M}_2$, are denoted by circles.

In the two pattern-classes case, we perform allocation of the vector X according to the difference

$$\|X - \hat{M}_1\|^2 - \|X - \hat{M}_2\|^2,$$

and the classification algorithm can be written as a linear discriminant function (DF) $h(X) = X^T V^E + v_0$ with

$$V^E = \hat{M}_1 - \hat{M}_2 \quad \text{and} \quad v_0 = -½(\hat{M}_1 + \hat{M}_2)^T V^E. \tag{1.2}$$

The allocation of the unclassified vector X to one of the two pattern classes is performed according to the sign of the discriminant function. This classification rule can also be obtained from the statistical decision theory if one assumes that the vector X is random and its distribution is the spherical Gaussian distribution $N_X(M_r, \sigma^2\mathbf{I})$. Here, M_r denotes the n-dimensional mean vector of the r-th pattern class and $\sigma^2\mathbf{I}$ is the covariance matrix (CM). For this pattern-class data model the CM is equal to the identity matrix $\mathbf{I}$ multiplied by the scalar σ^2 (the variance of each feature). For this theoretical data model, the EDC is an asymptotically (when the number of training vectors $N \to \infty$) optimal classifier, according to the criterion of classification error minimisation.

In the general case, the $n \times n$ covariance matrix Σ of a multivariate pattern-class distribution is a function of n variances and $n(n-1)$ correlations. If one assumes that both pattern classes share *the same* CM, we denote this assumption by $\bar{\Sigma}$. Otherwise, Σ_r represents the associated CM for the pattern-class ω_r. Generally, $\bar{\Sigma} \neq \sigma^2\mathbf{I}$, and the EDC is no longer an asymptotically optimal classification rule in terms of minimising the classification error.

Example 2. In Figure 1.2, we have a graph of 300 bivariate correlated vectors (×-marks and small pluses) of two Gaussian pattern classes $N_X(M_r, \bar{\Sigma})$ and the linear decision boundary of the EDC, depicted as line E. The sample means of the classes are denoted by circles, parameters of the data model are:

$$M_1 = -M_2 = (-2, 2)^T, \text{ and } \bar{\Sigma} = (2, 1; 1, 9)).$$

Obviously, for this data model the EDC is not the best classification rule. To design an appropriate classifier, one needs to take into account the fact that the feature variances are unequal and that the features are correlated. For such a data model one can use a linear discriminant function of the form $h(X) = X^T V^F + v_0$ with

$$V^F = \hat{\Sigma}^{-1}(\hat{M}_1 - \hat{M}_2) \quad \text{and} \quad v_0 = -½(\hat{M}_1 + \hat{M}_2)^T V^F, \tag{1.3}$$

where $$\hat{\Sigma} = \frac{1}{N_1 + N_2 - 2} \sum_{i=1}^{2} \sum_{j=1}^{N_i} (X_j^{(i)} - \hat{M}_i)(X_j^{(i)} - \hat{M}_i)^T \tag{1.4}$$

is the pooled sample covariance matrix, and allocation of the unlabeled vector $\boldsymbol{X}$ is performed according to the sign of the discriminant function (1.3). This is the first classification rule proposed in the statistical classification literature (Fisher, 1936) and it is now called the standard Fisher DF. The decision boundary corresponding to the Fisher DF is depicted by line F in Figure 1.2.

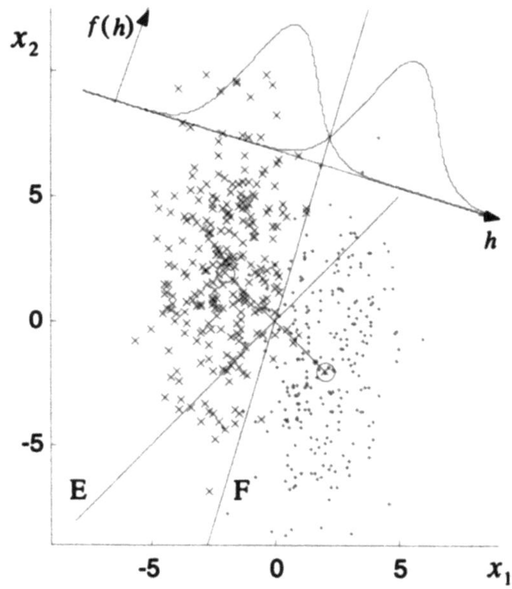

Fig. 1.2. A plot of 250+250 bi-variate vectors (×-marks and small pluses) sampled from two Gaussian pattern classes, sample means of the classes (circles), and the linear decision boundaries: the Euclidean distance classifier E, and the Fisher linear DF. Above is a plot of the two pattern-class densities $f(h)$ in the direction h of their best separability.

To obtain the Fisher rule, we project the training vectors onto a straight line h perpendicular to the decision boundary F. In the upper part of Figure 1.2, we have depicted the distribution densities $f_1(h)$ and $f_2(h)$ of the discriminant function values $h(\boldsymbol{X})= \boldsymbol{X}^T \boldsymbol{V}^F + v_0$ on a projection line h. In the new univariate space, both pattern classes are almost nonintersecting. This projection is the best linear projection possible onto a line.

In the classification literature, a large number of other parametric classification rules have been proposed. In the statistical approach, we postulate that $\boldsymbol{X}$, being the vector to be classified, is random. To obtain the classification rule (1.3), we can assume that the multivariate density of the vector $\boldsymbol{X}$ is Gaussian. Then we can estimate the unknown parameters of the Gaussian densities from the data and apply statistical decisions theory.

There is another approach to designing classification rules. Advocates of this alternative approach believe that one is unwise to make assumptions about the type of multivariate pattern-class density model and its parameters. Also, advocates of this approach insist that one should not estimate the classification-rule parameters in an indirect manner. Instead of constructing a parametric statistical classifier, these classifier designers suggest that a much better classifier-design method is to make assumptions about the classification rule structure (for example a linear discriminant function) and then estimate the unknown coefficients (weights) of the classification rule directly from the training data. As a criterion of goodness, they propose that one minimise the number of classification errors (empirical error) while classifying the training vectors. This is a typical formulation of the classifier design problem utilised in artificial neural network theory. One of several possible approaches to determining the unknown weight vector V is to adapt its components in an iterative manner. This weight-determination method is explained in the following section. Another entirely hypothetical way to estimate the weights is to generate M (a large number) random vectors V_1, V_2 ... , V_M, and to estimate the empirical errors for all M variants and then to choose the best set of weights. However, this random search procedure is utilised only in theoretical analyses.

The EDC is an asymptotically optimal classification rule for spherically Gaussian pattern classes with unequal mean vectors. Here, the word "asymptotically" means that the training-set size N tends to infinity. The standard linear Fisher DF is asymptotically optimal for Gaussian pattern classes that share a common covariance matrix $\bar{\Sigma}$ but have unequal mean vectors. However, this rule is no longer asymptotically optimal when the CMs of different classes are unequal or when the data is not Gaussian. For such types of data, the minimum empirical error (MEE) classifier is a good alternative to the EDC and Fisher's DF, which are parametric statistical classifiers.

Example 3. In order to see the differences among the classifiers in Figure 1.3, we present their decision boundaries and the data from two bivariate Gaussian classes $N_X(\boldsymbol{M}_r, \bar{\Sigma})$ contaminated with 10% additional Gaussian noise $N_X(\mathbf{0}, \mathbf{N})$.

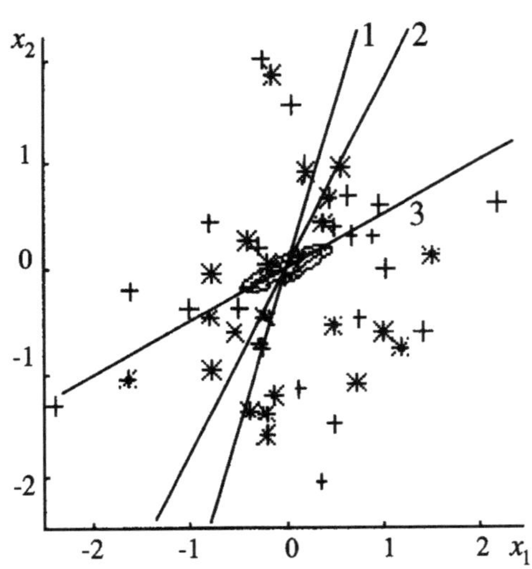

Fig. 1.3. Decision boundaries of the Euclidean distance classifier (1), the Fisher linear DF (2), and the MEE classifier (3). The noise patterns are denoted by "*" and "+".

The pattern class models have different means $M_1 = - M_2 = M$ and share a common covariance matrix $\bar{\Sigma}$. The Gaussian components are represented by two small ellipses. Parameters of the data model are

$$M = \begin{bmatrix} 0.10 \\ 0.05 \end{bmatrix},\ \bar{\Sigma} = \begin{bmatrix} 0.040 & 0.018 \\ 0.018 & 0.01 \end{bmatrix},\ \mathbf{N} = \begin{bmatrix} 1.0 & 0.5 \\ 0.5 & 1.0 \end{bmatrix}.$$

In this book, we refer to this data configuration as data model **A**.

1.2 Single Layer and Multilayer Perceptrons

The **non-linear single layer perceptron** (SLP) is a simplified mathematical model of an elementary information processing cell in living organisms – a neurone. Animal and human brains are composed from billions of such cells, which are interconnected. The standard belief is that the neurones are organised into layers, and neurones in one layer are interconnected with neurones in the next one. The complexity of connections between the neurones resembles nets. In an analogous model, the information processing units, i.e. artificial neurones, are also structured into layers. The units in one layer are interconnected with units in the adjacent layer. Thus the term *artificial neural nets* appeared.

According to Rumelhart *et al.* (1986) the SLP has several inputs (say n), $x_1, x_2, \ldots, x_n$, and one output, o, that is calculated according to the equation

$$o = f(V^T X + v_0), \tag{1.5}$$

where $f(net)$ is a non-linear activation function, e.g. a sigmoid function:

$$f(net) = 1/(1+e^{-net}) = f^{sigmoid}(net), \tag{1.6}$$

and v_0, $V^T = (v_1, v_2, \ldots, v_p)$ are the weights of the discriminant function (DF).

The output of the SLP can be used to perform classification of the unclassified vector X. When the sigmoid function (1.6) is used, we compare the output o with the threshold value of 0.5. The decision boundary is linear as are the three linear boundaries depicted in Figure 1.3. To find the weights for the SLP, we minimise a certain training set's cost function. The most popular cost function is the sum of squares cost function

$$cost_t = \frac{1}{N_1 + N_2} \sum_{i=1}^{2} \sum_{j=1}^{N_i} (t_j^{(i)} - f(V^T X_j^{(i)} + v_0))^2, \tag{1.7}$$

where $t_j^{(i)}$ is the desired output (a target) for $X_j^{(i)}$, the j-th training observation from class ω_i, and N_i is the number of training vectors from class ω_i.

unimportant. As a result we obtain the Euclidean distance classifier with the weights defined by the Equation (1.2).

In this pattern recognition algorithm, the desired outputs are associated with the class label. If the sigmoid function (1.6) is used, then typically one uses either $t_j^{(1)} = 1$, $t_j^{(2)} = 0$ or $t_j^{(1)} = 0.9$, $t_j^{(2)} = 0.1$. Outputs of the activation function (1.6) can vary in the interval of (0, 1). Therefore, we refer to the target values of 1 and 0 as "boundary" values, and we refer to the values 0.1 and 0.9 as "proximal" values (the values recommended by Rumelhart *et al.*, 1986). Some authors use another activation function:

$$f^{tanh}(net) = (e^{net} - e^{-net}) / (e^{net} + e^{-net}) = 2f^{sigmoid}(2net) - 1, \tag{1.8}$$

For this function $t_j^{(1)} = 1$, $t_j^{(2)} = -1$ (the boundary values), or $t_j^{(1)} = 0.8$, $t_j^{(2)} = -0.8$ (proximal values). Both activation functions (1.6) and (1.8) are smooth and can be differentiated. Such functions are commonly referred to as "soft-limiting" functions. In extreme cases, there are times when we analyse the hard-limiting activation function

$$f^{hard}(net) = \begin{cases} 1 \text{ if } net > 0 \\ 0 \text{ if } net \le 0 \end{cases}. \tag{1.9}$$

In this case, $t_j^{(1)} = 1$ and $t_j^{(2)} = 0$. Typically, to determine the weights v_0, $(v_1, v_2, \ldots, v_n) = \boldsymbol{V}^T$, we minimise the cost function (1.7). In the gradient descent optimisation algorithm (delta rule), we calculate derivatives of the cost function and find the weights in an iterative manner. At step *t*, we update the weight vector $\boldsymbol{V}_{(t)}$ according to equations

$$\boldsymbol{V}_{(t+1)} = \boldsymbol{V}_{(t)} - \eta \frac{\partial cost_t}{\partial \boldsymbol{V}}, \; v_{0(t+1)} = v_{0(t)} - \eta \frac{\partial cost_l}{\partial v_0}, \tag{1.10}$$

where η is the learning-step and $\frac{\partial cost_t}{\partial \boldsymbol{V}}$ is the gradient of the cost function.

When the hard-limiting cost function is used, we cannot calculate the gradient. In such cases, we must use other optimisation methods. To realise the training procedure (1.10), we must first choose the initial weights, $\boldsymbol{V}_{(t=0)}$ and $v_{0(t=0)}$. For this purpose, the neural net literature recommends one use small random numbers. In this book we advocate that one use non-random weight selection methods that can often lead to classifiers with a smaller generalisation error.

If expertly used, the training rule (1.10) can produce different algorithms to design the statistical classifiers. In fact, all three boundaries depicted in Figure 1.3 can be obtained while training the non-linear single layer perceptron. In Section 1.3 and Chapter 4, we demonstrate how this is accomplished.

The **multi-layer perceptron** (MLP) is the oldest and most frequently used type of the artificial neural network (ANN). A typical MLP classifier consists of several layers of artificial neurones containing single layer perceptrons (see Figure 1.4). Input nodes of the MLP classifier correspond to the *n* components of the feature vector. The output-layer can have one or several (say *L*) output neurones. The input signals propagate from the input layer to the output layer. Such networks are called the feedforward ANN. Typically, each neurone in the output layer corresponds to a pattern class label. Inputs to L output neurones are outputs $f_1, f_2, ..., f_h$ of the h neurones that constitute a lower (hidden) layer. Complex MLP classifiers can have many hidden layers.

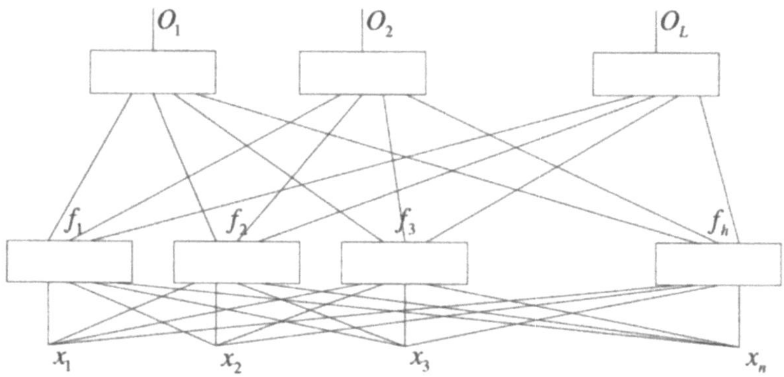

Fig. 1.4. MLP with one hidden layer.

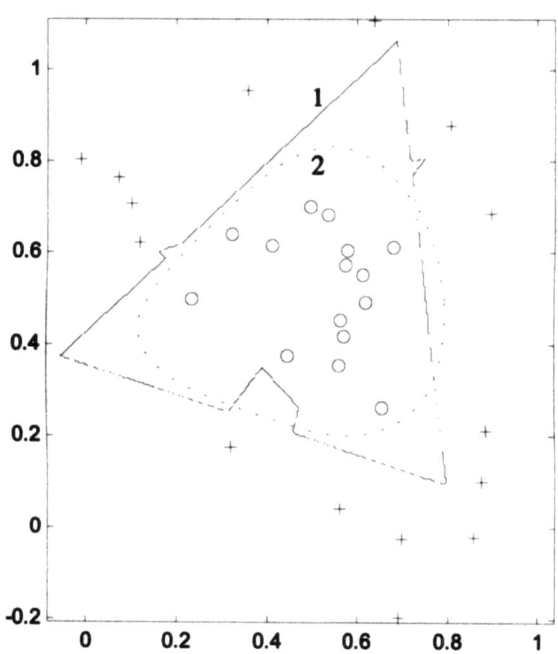

Fig. 1.5. 30 bivariate training vectors and decision boundaries of MLP with 10 hidden units and hard-limiting (1) and smooth (2) activation functions.

In order to find the classifier weights one must minimise a cost function similar to function (1.7). In the gradient descent optimisation algorithm, we need to calculate derivatives of the cost function and update the weights for all neurones in an iterative manner similar to the training of the SLP. While calculating the gradients of the hidden layer neurones, we propagate the error signal $t_j^{(i)} - f(\boldsymbol{V}^T \boldsymbol{X}_j^{(i)} + v_0)$ back to the lower layers. This technique is called *Back Propagation* (BP). The reader can find equations for the gradients of the output and hidden layer neurones in practically all artificial neural network monographs and textbooks.

When the hard limiting function is used, we obtain a piecewise-linear decision boundary. Smooth activation functions assist in obtaining smooth decision boundaries (compare boundaries 1 and 2 in Figure 1.5). The degree of non-linearity of the smooth activation function can be changed by multiplication of all components of the hidden layer weights by a certain positive constant α (Section 4.6.9). In fact, both boundaries in Figure 1.5 have been obtained by multiplying the weights of all neurones in the hidden layer of a well trained perceptron by the factor α, where $\alpha = 1000$ for the hard limiting activation function and $\alpha = 1/3$ for the soft limiting function. This bivariate data model is denoted by **SF2** and is discussed in more depth in Chapter 4. We see that the *non-linearity* of the activation function is an essential factor that affects the shape of the decision boundary. In general, the perceptron with one hidden layer, a soft-limiting activation function, and a sufficiently large number of hidden units can realise arbitrarily complex decision surfaces.

1.3 The SLP as the Euclidean Distance and the Fisher Linear Classifiers

The objective of this section is to demonstrate that in the adaptive BP training for the two-category case ($L = 2$), the SLP can realise three known statistical classifiers. In this section, we assume $N_2 = N_1 = \bar{N} = N/2$ with centred data, i.e., $\hat{\boldsymbol{M}} = ½\,(\hat{\boldsymbol{M}}_1 + \hat{\boldsymbol{M}}_2) = \boldsymbol{0}$ and analyse the cost function of the sum of squares (1.7) with activation function (1.8) and targets $t_j^{(1)}=1$, $t_j^{(2)} = -1$. Let the prior weights be zero, i.e., $v_{0(0)} = 0$, $\boldsymbol{V}_{(0)} = \boldsymbol{0}$. We train the SLP with the standard delta rule (1.10) in a batch-mode (the total gradient). Note that in the total gradient, we change the weights after calculating the gradients for *all* training vectors. For the stochastic gradient, we change the weights after calculating the gradient for *each single* training vector. During the first iteration, the weights and a scalar product, $v_0 + \boldsymbol{V}^T\boldsymbol{X}_j^{(i)}$, are close to zero. Therefore, for the tanh(*net*) activation function (1.8) we have

$$o(v_0 + \boldsymbol{V}^T\boldsymbol{X}_j^{(i)}) \cong v_0 + \boldsymbol{V}^T\boldsymbol{X}_j^{(i)}, \quad \text{and} \quad \partial\, o(v) \cong dv\,.$$

Thus,

$$\frac{\partial\, cost_l}{\partial v_{0(t)}} = -\frac{2}{N}\sum_{i=1}^{2}\sum_{j=1}^{\bar{N}} (t_j^{(i)} - v_{0(t)} - (\boldsymbol{X}_j^{(i)})^T \boldsymbol{V}_{(t)}) = 2v_{0(t)} + 2\hat{\boldsymbol{M}}^T \boldsymbol{V}_{(t)} = 0,$$

$$\left.\frac{\partial\, cost_l}{\partial \boldsymbol{V}}\right|_{V=V_{(t)}} = -\frac{2}{N}\sum_{i=1}^{2}\sum_{j=1}^{\bar{N}} \boldsymbol{X}_j^{(i)}(t_j^{(i)} - v_{0(t)} - (\boldsymbol{X}_j^{(i)})^T \boldsymbol{V}_{(t)}) = -\Delta\hat{\boldsymbol{M}} + 2\mathbf{K}\boldsymbol{V}_{(t)}, \tag{1.11}$$

where

$$\Delta\hat{\boldsymbol{M}} = \hat{\boldsymbol{M}}_1 - \hat{\boldsymbol{M}}_2, \text{ and } \mathbf{K} = \frac{1}{N}\sum_{i=1}^{2}\sum_{j=1}^{\bar{N}} \boldsymbol{X}_j^{(i)}(\boldsymbol{X}_j^{(i)})^T.$$

After the first learning iteration in the training process, we get

$$\boldsymbol{V}_{(1)} = \boldsymbol{V}_{(0)} - \eta\frac{\partial cost_l}{\partial \boldsymbol{V}} = \eta\,\Delta\hat{\boldsymbol{M}},\quad v_{0(1)} = 0. \tag{1.12}$$

This is the weight vector of the Euclidean distance (nearest means) classifier (EDC) scaled by η. In the first section, we mentioned that the EDC is the asymptotically optimal classification rule for the data model with two spherically Gaussian pattern classes. The fact that a single-layer perceptron becomes a comparatively good statistical classifier after only one iteration is a very nice property of the SLP! To demonstrate this point, we need the following conditions:

E1) the centre of the data $\hat{\boldsymbol{M}}$ is moved to the zero point;
E2) the training process starts from zero weights;
E3) if $N_2 = N_1 = \bar{N}$, we use symmetrical targets, i.e. for activation function (1.8) $t_2 = -t_1$;
E4) the total gradient training (batch mode) method is used.

Second order optimisation methods allow us to obtain the minimum of the quadratic cost function in one iteration. Equating the derivative of the cost (1.7) to zero for non-singular matrix **K**, we obtain $v_0 = 0$, and $\boldsymbol{V} = ½\mathbf{K}^{-1}\Delta\hat{\boldsymbol{M}}$.
For $\hat{\boldsymbol{M}} = \mathbf{0}$ (the centred data) we can use the representation

$$\mathbf{K} = \frac{\bar{N}-1}{\bar{N}}\hat{\Sigma} + \frac{1}{4}\Delta\hat{\boldsymbol{M}}\Delta\hat{\boldsymbol{M}}^T, \tag{1.13}$$

where $\hat{\Sigma}$ is the pooled sample covariance matrix defined in (1.4).

Using Bartlett's formula for the inversion of a symmetric positive-definite matrix,

$$(\mathbf{A} + \mathbf{V}\mathbf{V}^T)^{-1} = \mathbf{A}^{-1} - \frac{\mathbf{A}^{-1}\mathbf{V}\mathbf{V}^T\mathbf{A}^{-1}}{1 + \mathbf{V}^T\mathbf{A}^{-1}\mathbf{V}}, \tag{1.14}$$

where **A** is an $n \times n$ symmetric positive-definite matrix, we can express (1.13) in the form

$$V = k_n \hat{\Sigma}^{-1} \Delta \hat{M}, \tag{1.15}$$

where $k_n = 2/(D^2 + 4(\overline{N} - 1)/\overline{N})$, and $D^2 = \Delta \hat{M}^T \hat{\Sigma}^{-1} \Delta \hat{M}$.

If $\hat{M} = \mathbf{0}$ and the classification task is performed according to the sign of the discriminant function, then the positive constant k_n plays no role and expressions (1.15) and (1.3) are identical. Thus, in the linear SLP training process, we can obtain the standard Fisher linear discriminant function. This classifier can also be obtained using back propagation training when one uses the linear SLP (with a linear activation function, e.g. $f(net) = net$). We can approximate the Fisher classifier while training the non-linear perceptron. However, to do this we need to utilise the proximal targets.

Let us now consider the hard-limiting activation function (1.9). Then the cost (1.7) expresses the empirical classification error – the frequency of errors when the training-set is classified. Obviously, successful minimisation of this cost function leads to the minimum empirical error classifier. Unfortunately, in such a case the cost function is no longer differentiable and has many local minima. To tackle the local minima problems special discrete optimisation methods must be applied. In Chapter 4, we show how to approach the minimum empirical error classifier by the BP technique when the smooth activation function is utilised. Moreover, in zero empirical error situations, the expert training of the SLP can lead to a maximum margin classifier. For this classifier, the decision boundary is placed exactly in the middle between the closest training vectors of opposite categories. In Chapter 4, we also demonstrate that in BP training, more statistical classifiers can be obtained.

1.4 The Generalisation Error of the EDC and the Fisher DF

Asymptotic and Bayes error rates. In machine learning and classifier design theory, one of the main performance characteristics is the probability of misclassification. There are several types of classification errors or probabilities of misclassification. In order to differentiate among them, we consider the problem of classifying observations from the two Gaussian with a common covariance matrix (GCCM) pattern classes, $N_X(M_1, \overline{\Sigma})$ and $N_X(M_2, \overline{\Sigma})$.

Assume that the vectors from the first and second categories are equiprobable, i.e. the prior probabilities, P_1 and P_2, of the pattern classes are equal. Thus, $P_2 = 1 - P_1 = ½$. When all parameters are known, statistical discriminant analysis provides an optimal discriminant function that is linear, namely $h(X) = v_0 + V^T X$, with weights

$$V^{\text{optimal}} = \bar{\Sigma}^{-1}(M_1 - M_2) \text{ and } v_0 = -\hat{M}^T V^{\text{optimal}}. \tag{1.16}$$

The probability of misclassification (PMC) of this rule is

$$\varepsilon = P_1\varepsilon_1 + P_2\,\varepsilon_2,$$

where ε_1 is the probability of error of the first sort, i.e. the probability that a vector from the first class will be allocated to the second pattern class: $\varepsilon_1 = Probability\{h(X) < 0 \mid X \in \omega_1\}$, and ε_2 is the probability of error of the second sort, i.e. the probability that a vector from the second class will be allocated to the first pattern class: $\varepsilon_2 = Probability\{h(X) \geq 0 \mid X \in \omega_2\}$.

For the Gaussian data model described above, $h(X) = X^T V + v_0$ is a Gaussian random variable. Thus,

$$Probability\{\, h(X \mid X \in \omega_i) < 0 \mid X \in \omega_i \,\} = \Phi\{\, (-1)^i \frac{Eh(X \mid X \in \omega_i)}{\sqrt{Vh(X \mid X \in \omega_i)}} \,\}, \tag{1.17}$$

where

$\Phi\{a\} = \int_{-\infty}^{a} (2\pi)^{-1/2}\sigma^{-1}\exp\{-t^2/(2\sigma^2)\}dt$ is the standard Gaussian cumulative distribution function (a quick reminder: $\Phi\{a\} \to 0$ as $a \to -\infty$, $\Phi\{a\} = 0.5$ when $a = 0$, and $\Phi\{a\} \to 1$ when $a \to \infty$),

$E\,h(X \mid X \in \omega_i)$ is the conditional mean:

$$E\,h(X \mid X \in \omega_i) = E(X^T V^{\text{optimal}} + v_0) =$$

$$h(X) = M_i^T \bar{\Sigma}^{-1}(M_1 - M_2) + v_0 = \tfrac{1}{2}(-1)^{i+1}(M_1 + M_2)^T \bar{\Sigma}^{-1}(M_1 - M_2) = \tfrac{1}{2}(-1)^{i+1}\delta,$$

and $V\,h(X \mid X \in \omega_i)$ is the conditional variance:

$$V\,h(X \mid X \in \omega_i) =$$

$$E\,(M_1 - M_2)^T \bar{\Sigma}^{-1}(X - M_i)\,(X - M_i)^T \bar{\Sigma}^{-1}(M_1 - M_2)$$

$$= (M_1 - M_2)^T \bar{\Sigma}^{-1} \bar{\Sigma}\, \bar{\Sigma}^{-1}(M_1 - M_2) = (M_1 - M_2)^T \bar{\Sigma}^{-1}(M_1 - M_2) = \delta^2,$$

where $\delta^2 = (M_1 - M_2)^T \bar{\Sigma}^{-1}(M_1 - M_2)$ (1.18)

is the squared generalised distance between the two pattern classes.

When $\bar{\Sigma} = \mathbf{I}$ (the $n \times n$ identity matrix, here all n features are uncorrelated and have variances equal to one), δ^2 denotes the conventional squared Euclidean distance between the two vectors, M_1 and M_2. The generalised squared distance (1.18) was introduced by the Indian statistician P.C. Mahalanobis and, therefore, it carries his name. We use the Mahalanobis distance as a measure of the separability of two GCCM pattern classes.

Inserting the conditional means and the conditional variance into (1.17) yields

$$\varepsilon = \Phi\{-\tfrac{1}{2}\delta\}. \tag{1.19}$$

Equation (1.19) shows that, for the pattern-class models $N_X(\boldsymbol{M}_1, \bar{\Sigma})$ and $N_X(\boldsymbol{M}_2, \bar{\Sigma})$, the Mahalanobis distance uniquely determines the classification error of the optimal rule. For example, if $\delta = 2.56$, then $\varepsilon = 0.1$, if $\delta = 3.76$, then $\varepsilon = 0.03$, and if $\delta = 4.65$, then $\varepsilon = 0.01$.

Statistical decision-theory based classifiers are formulated using Bayes formula for conditional probabilities. This classifier-design method allows optimal classification rules to be obtained when all parameters are known. Thus, for the GCCM data model, the discriminant function (1.16) is a Bayes rule, and $\Phi\{-\tfrac{1}{2}\delta\}$ is its associated error rate. The minimal probability of misclassification is called the Bayes error and is denoted by ε_B. For the data model $N_X(\boldsymbol{M}_1, \bar{\Sigma})$ and $N_X(\boldsymbol{M}_2, \bar{\Sigma})$ the Bayes error coincides with the asymptotic error for the Fisher linear DF. As a reminder, the asymptotic error determines the performance of the classification rule when an arbitrarily large training-set is used to determine the classification rule's coefficients (weights). In this case, we assume we know the parameters $\boldsymbol{M}_1$, $\boldsymbol{M}_2$, and $\bar{\Sigma}$ exactly. Therefore, for the GCCM data model the asymptotic error of the Fisher classifier is $\varepsilon_\infty^F = \Phi\{-\tfrac{1}{2}\delta\}$.

Consider the Euclidean distance classifier designed for pattern classes with known parameters. The weights of the discriminant function are:

$$V^E = \boldsymbol{M}_1 - \boldsymbol{M}_2 \text{ and } v_0 = -\tfrac{1}{2}(\boldsymbol{M}_1 + \boldsymbol{M}_2)^T(\boldsymbol{M}_1 - \boldsymbol{M}_2). \tag{1.20}$$

The asymptotic error rate of this classifier is

$$\varepsilon_\infty^E = \Phi\{-\tfrac{1}{2}\delta^*\},$$

where δ^*, the effective distance between two pattern classes, is defined to be

$$\delta^* = \frac{(\boldsymbol{M}_1 - \boldsymbol{M}_2)^T(\boldsymbol{M}_1 - \boldsymbol{M}_2)}{\sqrt{(\boldsymbol{M}_1 - \boldsymbol{M}_2)^T\bar{\Sigma}(\boldsymbol{M}_1 - \boldsymbol{M}2)}}. \tag{1.21}$$

Calculations show that $\delta^* \leq \delta$. Hence, for the GCCM data model we have that $\varepsilon_\infty^E \geq \varepsilon_\infty^F$. Note that the Bayes error does not depend on the particular classifier design method. Rather, it depends on the characteristics of the data model.

Example 4. Consider the data model with GCCM pattern classes with $n = 20$, $\Delta\boldsymbol{M} = \boldsymbol{M}_1 - \boldsymbol{M}_2 = (-1.7040, 0.5244, 0.49700, \ldots, 0.0872, 0.0599, 0.0326)^T$. All correlations among the variables are equal: $\rho = 0.213$, and all n variables have unit variances. For this data model the effective and Mahalanobis distances are δ^* =3.7616 and $\delta = 4.65$, respectively, and the asymptotic classification errors are $\varepsilon_\infty^{\mathrm{E}} = 0.03$ and $\varepsilon_\infty^{\mathrm{F}} = 0.01$. In this book, we refer to this data configuration as data model **C**.

The expressions for the Mahalanobis and the effective distances, (1.18) and (1.21), respectively, as well as numerical calculation show that the asymptotic errors depend on the type of classifier design method. Both the EDC and the Fisher DF are linear classifiers. However, they use different methods to determine their respective weights. Therefore, in the general case, the asymptotic error values differ as well. We note that theoretically, for certain data models, both classifiers can have the same asymptotic errors.

Generalisation errors. Consider the *sample-based* EDC with the discriminant function (1.2). The sample mean vectors $\hat{\boldsymbol{M}}_1$ and $\hat{\boldsymbol{M}}_2$ are functions of the training vectors $\boldsymbol{X}_1^{(1)}, \boldsymbol{X}_2^{(1)}, \boldsymbol{X}_3^{(1)} \ldots, \boldsymbol{X}_{N_1}^{(1)}$, and $\boldsymbol{X}_1^{(2)}, \ldots, \boldsymbol{X}_{N_2}^{(2)}$. Therefore, $\hat{\boldsymbol{M}}_1$ and $\hat{\boldsymbol{M}}_2$ are random vectors. Thus, due to sampling error, $\hat{\boldsymbol{M}}_1$, and $\hat{\boldsymbol{M}}_2$ differ from the true population mean vectors, $\boldsymbol{M}_1$, $\boldsymbol{M}_2$, and the vector $\boldsymbol{V}^{\mathrm{E}}$ and the threshold v_0 in (1.2) differ from the ideal values determined by Equation (1.20). Hence, the decision boundary of the sample-based rule (1.2) differs from the ideal boundary of the Euclidean distance classifier (1.20). The probability of misclassification of the sample-based rule (the generalisation error) is larger than that of the ideal rule.

Example 5. The increase in the generalisation error due to estimation of the optimal classification boundary using the training data is easy to demonstrate graphically by inspecting the univariate case. In Figure 1.6, we present two Gaussian densities $N_x(m_1, 1)$ and $N_x(m_2, 1)$ with means $m_1 = -m_2 = 1.3$ and unit variances. In the univariate case, we must define only one parameter of the classification rule and that is the threshold v_0. For the ideal rule $v_0^* = ½(m_1 + m_2) = 0$. Therefore, we allocate the observation x to the first class, if $x > 0$, and to the second one, if $x \leq 0$. A part of the observations is classified incorrectly. In Figure 1.6, the probability of misclassification is proportional to the two vertically dashed areas in the centre of the figure. For a randomly chosen training-set, the threshold of the sample-based classification rule $\hat{v}_0 = -(\hat{m}^{(1)} + \hat{m}^{(2)})/2$ will always differ from v_0^* (it can coincide with the ideal threshold v_0^* only incidentally). Thus PMC

$$\varepsilon_N^{\mathrm{E}} = P_1\, Probability\{ x < \hat{v}_0 \mid x \in \omega_1\} + P_2\, Probability\{ x \geq \hat{v}_0 \mid x \in \omega_2\}, \quad (1.22)$$

which is larger than the PMC of the ideal rule.

The increase in the PMC, $\Delta\varepsilon$, is proportional to the black triangle in Figure 1.6. This increase is always positive. Thus, any shift from the ideal threshold v_0^* will always increase the classification error or PMC.

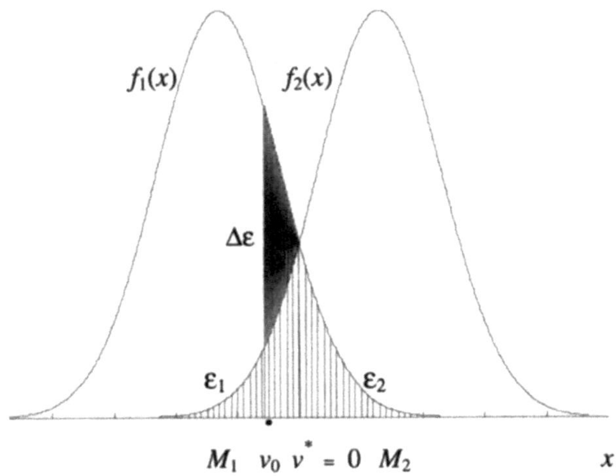

Fig. 1.6. Two univariate Gaussian pattern-class densities $N_x(M_1, 1)$ and $N_x(M_2, 1)$ and the asymptotic errors ε_1 and ε_2 (two dashed areas). The increase in the conditional error, $\Delta\varepsilon$, is marked by the solid black area.

The probability ε_N^E is conditioned on a particular training-set. Therefore, we call the probability ε_N^E the *conditional probability of misclassification* or the *conditional generalisation error.* In statistical analysis, the training vectors $\boldsymbol{X}_1^{(1)}, \boldsymbol{X}_2^{(1)}, \boldsymbol{X}_3^{(1)} \dots, \boldsymbol{X}_{N_1}^{(1)}, \boldsymbol{X}_1^{(2)}, \dots, \boldsymbol{X}_{N_2}^{(2)}$ are considered as independent random vectors. Then the sample mean vectors $\hat{\boldsymbol{M}}_1$ and $\hat{\boldsymbol{M}}_2$ may be considered to be random vectors, as well. In this context, the conditional probability of misclassification ε_N^E is also a random variable. We call an expected value, $\bar{\varepsilon}_N^E$, the *expected probability of misclassification* or, simply, an *expected (mean) generalisation error.*

For the model of two spherical Gaussian classes $N_X(\boldsymbol{M}_1, \bar{\Sigma})$, $N_X(\boldsymbol{M}_2, \bar{\Sigma})$, the sample means $\hat{\boldsymbol{M}}_1$ and $\hat{\boldsymbol{M}}_2$ are Gaussian: $\hat{\boldsymbol{M}}_1 \sim N(\boldsymbol{M}_1, \frac{1}{N_1}\bar{\Sigma})$, $\hat{\boldsymbol{M}}_2 \sim N(\boldsymbol{M}_2, \frac{1}{N_2}\bar{\Sigma})$. For this data model, and a case of equal training sample sizes, ($N_2 = N_1 = \bar{N} = N/2$), the expected generalisation error of the EDC is

$$\bar{\varepsilon}_N^E \approx \Phi\left\{ -\frac{\delta^*}{2}\frac{1}{\sqrt{T_M}} \right\}, \tag{1.23}$$

where δ^* is the effective distance between two pattern classes (defined in (1.21)),

$$T_M = 1 + \frac{4n^*}{\delta^{*2} N}, \text{ and} \tag{1.24}$$

$$n^* = \frac{((\boldsymbol{M}_1 - \boldsymbol{M}_2)^T (\boldsymbol{M}_1 - \boldsymbol{M}_2))^2 (\mathrm{tr}\bar{\Sigma}^2)}{((\boldsymbol{M}_1 - \boldsymbol{M}_2)^T \bar{\Sigma} (\boldsymbol{M}_1 - \boldsymbol{M}_2))^2} \tag{1.25}$$

is called the *effective dimensionality.*

Equations (1.23) and (1.24) show that $\bar{\varepsilon}_N^{\mathrm{E}} \geq \varepsilon_\infty^{\mathrm{E}}$. Thus, the expected error $\bar{\varepsilon}_N^{\mathrm{E}}$ approaches the asymptotic error $\varepsilon_\infty^{\mathrm{E}} = \Phi\{-\frac{1}{2}\delta^*\}$ as the training-set size N increases without bound. The increase in the expected generalisation error, $\Delta\bar{\varepsilon}_N^{\mathrm{E}} = \bar{\varepsilon}_N^{\mathrm{E}} - \varepsilon_\infty^{\mathrm{E}}$, is a function of N^{-1}.

For the moment, consider the spherical Gaussian case where $\bar{\Sigma} = \sigma^2\mathbf{I}$. Note that, for this data model, the EDC is an asymptotically optimal classifier. Also, note that $\delta^* = \delta$ and $n^* = n$ and, therefore, $T_{\boldsymbol{M}} = 1 + \frac{4n}{\delta^2 N}$. We see that the increase in the expected generalisation error depends on the asymptotic error rate and is proportional to n/N, the dimensionality divided by the training-set size. For fixed N and δ, the generalisation error increases as n increases.

Consider now the more general case with $\bar{\Sigma} \neq \sigma^2\mathbf{I}$. Then $n^* \neq n$, where $1 < n^* \leq \infty$. Thus, in theory, pattern-class densities exist where the EDC is very insensitive to the training-set size (when n^* is close to 1) and pattern-class densities exists where the EDC is very sensitive to the training-set size (when n^* is very large). This is a very important conclusion that is utilised in the further analysis of certain neural network classifiers in later chapters.

One can readily see that the Fisher discriminant function is more complex than the Euclidean distance classifier. To design the EDC one needs to estimate only the mean vectors. To design the Fisher linear DF, one needs to estimate the mean vectors μ_1 and μ_1 and the covariance matrix Σ. The sample-based estimator $\hat{\Sigma}$ causes greater fluctuations in the coefficients v_0 and V^{F} of the Fisher linear DF than in the coefficients of the sample EDC. For the GCCM data model, the estimator $\hat{\Sigma}$ is a Wishart random matrix (see e.g. Anderson, 1958). The expected generalisation error of the Fisher linear DF is

$$\bar{\varepsilon}_N^{\mathrm{F}} \approx \Phi\left\{ -\frac{\delta}{2} \frac{1}{\sqrt{T_{\boldsymbol{M}} T_{\bar{\Sigma}}}} \right\}, \tag{1.26}$$

where $T_{\bar{\Sigma}} = 1 + \frac{n}{N - n}$.

The term $T_{\bar{\Sigma}}$ arises due to the estimation of the covariance matrix $\bar{\Sigma}$. Comparison of (1.23) and (1.26) demonstrates that in the spherical Gaussian case when $\bar{\Sigma} = \sigma^2\mathbf{I}$, the more complex Fisher linear DF is more sensitive to the training-set size than the Euclidean distance classifier. The term $T_{\bar{\Sigma}}$ explicitly shows the price we pay in accuracy because we must estimate the common pattern-class covariance matrix (n variances and $n(n-1)/2$ correlations). Note that the difference between the two linear classifiers is more noticeable when N, the training-set size, is close to n.

The theoretical results considered in (1.26) are important for the design and application of neural network classifiers. In adaptive SLP training, the term $T_{\overline{\Sigma}}$ shows the cost involved in order to move the decision boundary E towards the boundary F in Figure 1.2. Also, this term shows that if N is close to n after minimising the cost function, the SLP classifier can acquire poor small sample properties (curse of dimensionality).

These two theoretical facts lead us to conclude that in the small training-set case, we need to train the SLP fewer iterations than in the large sample case. We wish to reemphasise two important facts concerning SLP training:

- after the first iteration, we can have an EDC classifier that evolves toward the Fisher classifier as training continues.
- in general, the Fisher classifier requires a larger training-set than the EDC.

1.5 Optimal Complexity – The Scissors Effect

The term T_{Σ} shows the amount of training data that is required in order to move from boundary E towards boundary F in Figure 1.2. This amount can become quite large if n, the dimensionality, is large. Thus, in the small training-set case, it is somewhat questionable as to whether or not one should attempt to move the boundary from E to F by continued training. Possibly, there are times one should stop the perceptron training process before one attempts to move the boundary through further training. The main emphasis in this book is to address these types of issues. Later, we explain that the answer to the boundary-movement question depends on the training-set size, the complexity of the problem, and the data dimensionality.

Consider the case when EDC and the Fisher DF are used to classify two equiprobable non-spherical Gaussian classes $N_X(\boldsymbol{M}_1, \overline{\Sigma})$ and $N_X(\boldsymbol{M}_2, \overline{\Sigma})$. When all parameters are known, the optimal Bayes classifier function is Fisher's linear DF

$$h(X) = (X - \tfrac{1}{2}(\boldsymbol{M}_1 + \boldsymbol{M}_2))^T \overline{\Sigma}^{-1} (\boldsymbol{M}_1 - \boldsymbol{M}_2).$$

Note that when $\overline{\Sigma}$ is not proportional to $\mathbf{I}$ (the identity matrix), the asymptotic error rate $\varepsilon_\infty^{\mathrm{E}}$ of the ideal EDC with all parameters known is larger than the Bayes error ε_{B}.

Example 6. Consider a 20-variate Gaussian data model **C** with Mahalanobis distance $\delta = 4.65$ and $\delta^* = 3.7616$ (asymptotic errors $\varepsilon_\infty^{\mathrm{F}} = 0.01$ and $\varepsilon_\infty^{\mathrm{E}} = 0.03$). For the data model **C**, the effective dimensionality $n^* = 20$. Thus, from (1.23) and (1.26), for different training-set sizes $\overline{N}$ we have:

for $\overline{N} = 15$, $\overline{\varepsilon}_N^{\mathrm{E}} \approx 0.0469$, $\overline{\varepsilon}_N^{\mathrm{F}} \approx 0.1094$;

for $\overline{N} = 25$, $\overline{\varepsilon}_N^{\mathrm{E}} \approx 0.0400$, $\overline{\varepsilon}_N^{\mathrm{F}} \approx 0.0441$;

for $\overline{N} = 40$, $\overline{\varepsilon}_N^{\mathrm{E}} \approx 0.0362$, $\overline{\varepsilon}_N^{\mathrm{F}} \approx 0.0259$;

for $\overline{N} = 80$ $\overline{\varepsilon}_N^{\mathrm{E}} \approx 0.0330$, $\overline{\varepsilon}_N^{\mathrm{F}} \approx 0.0163$.

The dependence of the generalisation error of the EDC and the Fisher DF on the training-set size $\overline{N}$ is illustrated graphically in Figure 1.7.

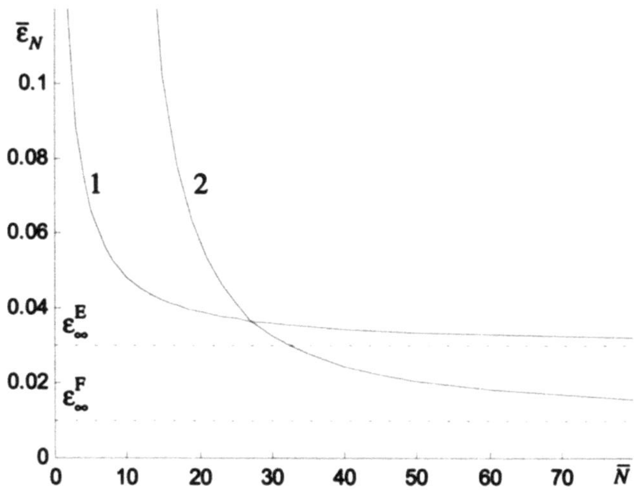

Fig. 1.7. The scissors effect – the generalisation error versus the training-set size $\overline{N}$: 1 is the Euclidean distance classifier, 2 is the standard Fisher linear classifier (adapted from Raudys, 1970).

With the given example from Figure 1.7, we see that in this case, for small training sets (up to $\overline{N} \approx 30$), one would prefer the simple-structured EDC as the classifier of choice. Furthermore, for large training sets (over $\overline{N} \approx 30$), one would prefer the more complex-structured Fisher classifier as the classifier of choice.

This phenomenon, called the scissors effect, has been known in the Statistical Pattern Recognition field for the past 30 years:

> *in small training-set cases, often it is preferable to use simple structured classification rules than the complex ones, and, vice versa, in large training-set cases, complex classifiers can be used more efficiently.*

In Equation (1.26), the generalisation error of the Fisher DF classifier indicates that when n, the number of features, is close to N, the training-set size, the generalisation error can increase considerably. In practice, the features used for classification have varying degrees of importance. Typically, there is a portion of the original set of variables that have little discriminative power. Moreover, the features are usually correlated and, with the addition of new reinforcing features, the original features can possibly have a decreasing amount of discriminative power. Thus, one may hope that a subset of the original features can be omitted with little or no loss of discriminative power. Therefore, while adding more features with decreasing importance, the generalisation error decreases at first, reaches a minimum, and then increases again. This phenomenon is known as the *peaking effect* and is well known in the field of statistical data analysis.

Example 7. Consider a 20-variate Gaussian data model **C** with correlated variables. For this data model, the Fisher linear DF is the asymptotically optimal classification rule. Let us increase the number of features sequentially, adding the features one after another. In the 20-variate data model **C**, all n features have the same discriminative power. The positive correlations between the features causes the added features to contribute less than the previous features to the Mahalanobis distance. Therefore, as the number of the features, n, increases, the asymptotic and the Bayes errors decrease quickly at first, but later, the speed of the decrease lessens (solid curves in Figure 1.8). This is a typical situation in real world pattern recognition problems.

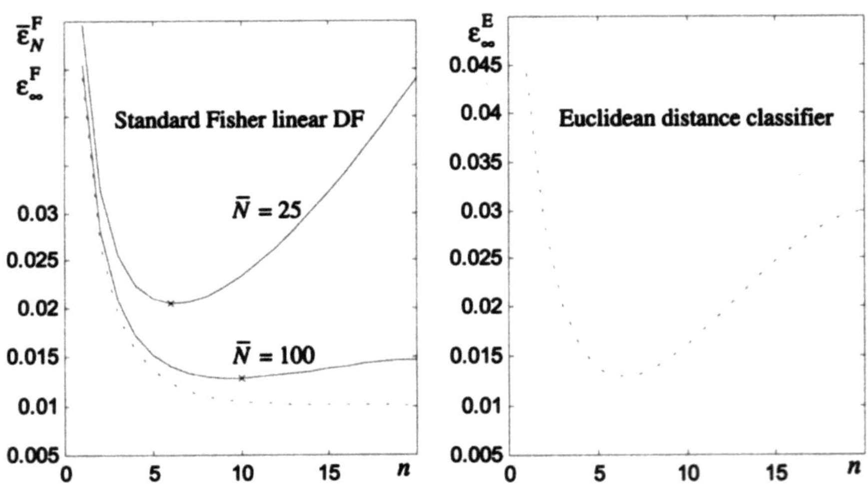

Fig. 1.8. The asymptotic (the dotted curves) and generalisation errors (solid) of the Fisher linear DF and the Euclidean distance classifier as functions of the number of the features n.

For the given dimensionality n, the generalisation error depends on both the Mahalanobis distance $\delta(n)$ and the training-set size N. When the mean vectors $\boldsymbol{M}_1$, $\boldsymbol{M}_2$ and the covariance matrix Σ must be estimated and the training-set size N is small, we introduce considerable error (noise) to the unknown components of these parameters. The statistical nature of the training-set vectors causes a certain amount of the "inaccuracy" to be included in the estimators $\hat{\boldsymbol{M}}_1$, $\hat{\boldsymbol{M}}_2$, $\hat{\Sigma}$ and, therefore, to the weight vector $V^F = \hat{\Sigma}^{-1}(\hat{\boldsymbol{M}}_1 - \hat{\boldsymbol{M}}_2)$. For a fixed training-set size N, the inaccuracy in the estimators $\hat{\boldsymbol{M}}_1$, $\hat{\boldsymbol{M}}_2$, and $\hat{\Sigma}$ increases as the number of features increase. Hence, with the addition of new features, the generalisation error decreases at first, reaches a minimum, and then begins to increase. We obtain the peaking effect early (curve for $\bar{N} = 25$) when N is small. For large N, the "noise" or inaccuracy in the estimators of $\hat{\boldsymbol{M}}_1$, $\hat{\boldsymbol{M}}_2$, $\hat{\boldsymbol{\Sigma}}$ is less. Thus, we obtain the peaking effect later (curve for $\bar{N} = 100$).

In comparison with the Fisher classifier, the less complex EDC requires the estimation of a smaller number of parameters from the training vectors because we estimate only the pattern-class means $\boldsymbol{M}_1$ and $\boldsymbol{M}_2$ and not the CM $\boldsymbol{\Sigma}$. Therefore, for the same training-set size, the "noise" level is smaller for the EDC. Usually, while utilising the EDC, we obtain the peaking effect later.

Above, we have explained the peaking phenomenon by the presence of a small training-set size. In reality, the peaking phenomenon can be observed even in the case of an infinite training-set size due to the use of a *non-optimal classifier design procedure*. A discrepancy between the true pattern-class distributions and the hypothetical pattern-class distributions induces error in estimating the parameters of the classification rule. This fact can give rise to the peaking phenomenon even in a case when the number of training samples is infinitely large.

Example 8. The Gaussian data model **C** with correlated features is not an ideal model of the pattern classes for the EDC. Theoretically, the addition of the new features can diminish the distance measure δ^* instead of increasing it. Therefore, in this data model with equally correlated features, *the asymptotic error of the EDC has a minimum* because of a peaking effect (Figure 1.8, right).

One must concede that the configuration model **C** is probably not a typical example of real world pattern-classification problems. This model, however, nicely explains one more factor that can cause the peaking phenomenon. One may conjecture that for some specific pattern classes (e.g. multimodal), a similar phenomenon can be observed in the SLP design.

The number of features where the conditional generalisation error $\varepsilon_N^{\mathsf{A}}$ reaches its minimum is called the *optimal number of features*. In practical applications, the curves $\varepsilon_N^{\mathsf{A}} = f(n)$ may have more than one minimum. The character of the curve $\varepsilon_N^{\mathsf{A}} = f(n)$ depends on the type of classification rule A (the complexity of the classifier), the pattern recognition problem to be solved, the order in which the features are presented, and the training-set size. The optimal number of features increases as the number of the training observations increases and decreases as the complexity of the classifier increases.

An important problem encountered when designing pattern classification systems is **the feature definition problem**. We have demonstrated above that in order to obtain a classifier with good generalisation performance, one needs to use a small number of effective (informative) features. A number of methods have been developed to help select the best subset of features from the totality of previously selected ones. This problem is called the feature subset selection problem and it has much in common with pruning and incremental learning algorithms for neural networks.

While selecting the best subset of features, one usually performs this type of work with a certain inaccuracy. Therefore, the order in which the features are presented may differ from the ideal ordering. Instead of having one minimum, one can have multiple minima. Moreover, if the features or, more strictly speaking, the subsets of features are ranked poorly, then we cannot observe a minimum. Statistical analysis can help evaluate these effects numerically. We consider these problems in Chapter 6.

1.6 Overtraining in Neural Networks

In perceptron training, we minimise the cost function to determine the weights. The cost value is closely related to the empirical classification error. At the beginning of the training process, the weights are small and the values of the weighted sums $v_0 + \boldsymbol{V}^T\boldsymbol{X}_j^{(i)}$ are also small. Around the zero point the activation function acts almost as a linear function. Thus the cost function approximately characterises the empirical error. When the weights are large, the weighted sums $v_0 + \boldsymbol{V}^T\boldsymbol{X}_j^{(i)}$ are also large. Then the smooth activation function acts as the hard limiting threshold function and the cost (1.7), in essence, represents the empirical classification error.

With an increase in the number of iterations, the empirical classification error customarily decreases at first. The generalisation error also initially decreases. After it reaches a minimum, it then begins to increase. This phenomenon is called overtraining or overfitting and has the same origin as the scissors and the peaking effects.

Theoretical analysis of the generalisation error and of the dynamics in the SLP classifier training reveals reasons for this phenomenon and indicates methods to utilise this fact in the best possible way. Below, we present and comment on two examples that are analysed more thoroughly in Chapter 4.

Example 9. In this example we show that in the spherically Gaussian (SG) data case, only *one iteration* is necessary to train the SLP. In order to demonstrate this fact effectively, we have chosen data with high dimensionality (n=100) and a comparatively small training-set size ($\bar{N}$ = 200 from each pattern class). Let the Mahalanobis distance be δ =3.76. The asymptotic and Bayes error rates are $\varepsilon_\infty^{\mathrm{E}} = \varepsilon_\infty^{\mathrm{F}} = \varepsilon_{\mathrm{B}}$ = 0.03. The theory (Equations (1.23) and ((1.26)) indicates that for $\bar{N}$ = 200 the EDC will yield $\bar{\varepsilon}_N^{\mathrm{E}}$ =3.48% errors on average, while the Fisher classifier will yield $\bar{\varepsilon}_N^{\mathrm{F}}$ = 5.79% errors on average. Thus, in the batch-mode, we obtain the best classifier (EDC) immediately after the first iteration. There is no need to further train the perceptron. Recall that in order to obtain the EDC after the first iteration of the training process, the training conditions E1 – E4 should be satisfied. In the present experiment, we satisfied these conditions and trained the SLP with the sigmoid activation function (1.6) and targets $t_j^{(1)} = 1$, $t_j^{(2)} = 0$.

The learning curve, the generalisation error versus the number of iterations, is presented in Figure 1.9 (curve 2). We see after the first iteration that $\varepsilon_N^{\text{SLP}} = 0.034$ is quite close to $\bar{\varepsilon}_N^{\text{E}} = 0.0348$ predicted by the theory. With an increase in the number of iterations in the training process, the decision boundary of the SLP classifier approaches that of the Fisher DF and later it approaches the maximum margin classifier. For both classifiers we have a much higher generalisation error than for the EDC.

In the second part of this experiment, we violated one of the conditions E1 – E4. Specifically, we began training from a random initial weight vector generated by a random Gaussian $N_v(0.\ 0.1)$ generator. After the first few iterations, we get a comparatively high generalisation error (it is too high to be depicted in Figure 1.9) that decreases until reaching the minimum (approximately after 50 iterations) and then begins increasing. After 100 iterations there is no difference between the two learning curves obtained for differently initialised SLPs. The expert initialisation of $\boldsymbol{V}_{(0)}=\boldsymbol{0}$ helped reduce the minimal classification error substantially.

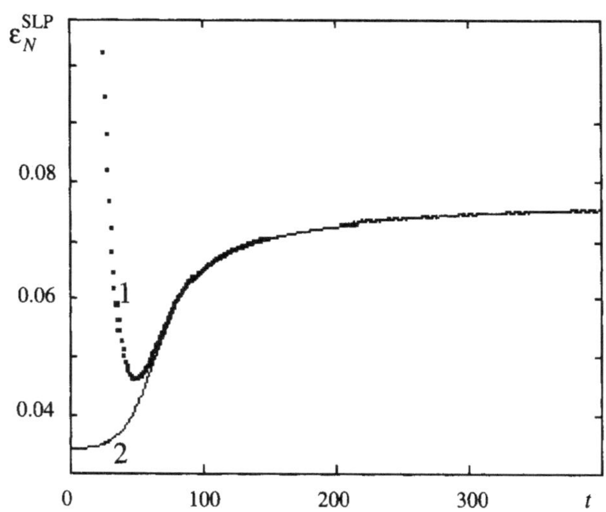

Fig. 1.9. The generalisation error versus t, the number of iterations. Spherical Gaussian classes with $\delta = 3.76$ and $n = 100$, $\bar{N} = 200$. We used the varying learning step $\eta = 1.1^t$ and random $N_x(0, \sigma^2)$ weight initialisation: 1 - $\sigma^2 = 0.1$, 2 - $\sigma^2 = 0.0$ (Reprinted from *Neural Networks*, 11:297-313, S. Raudys, Evolution and generalization of a single neurone, 1998, with permission from Elsevier Science).

Example 10. While solving real world problems, one is unlikely to encounter spherical data. One can expect that in the complex data case, one must train the perceptron more than one iteration. In order to obtain the best result we must control the training process in an intelligent way. One example of "intelligent" training is demonstrated in the learning curves depicted in Figure 1.10. Here, we have used the 20-variate artificial data **C** with correlated features and, while training SLP, we have satisfied conditions E1– E4. In this example, we have a very small training-set – only 14 vectors from each pattern class. In the previous section, we had that for $\bar{N} = 15$, $\bar{\varepsilon}_N^E \approx 0.0469$ and $\bar{\varepsilon}_N^F \approx 0.1094$. Thus, the sample size $\bar{N} = 14$ is too small to train the Fisher classifier.

For data **C** and $\bar{N} = 14$, we should avoid obtaining this classifier. We can get the Fisher classifier or a classifier close to it by controlling the magnitudes of the weights during the SLP training. If the weights are small, the activation function acts almost like a linear function. In Chapter 4, we consider several methods that can help control the weight magnitudes. One such method is the selection of proper target values. Using proximal target values, one does not allow the weights to become too large and, therefore, forces the classifier to approach the Fisher classifier. Thus, a priori, we see that proximal targets and lengthy training can lead to undesirable results. The learning curve 1 in Figure 1.10 corresponds to targets $t_j^{(1)} = 0.9$ and $t_j^{(2)} = 0.1$ (the values recommended by Rumelhart *et al.*, 1986) and confirms this presumption.

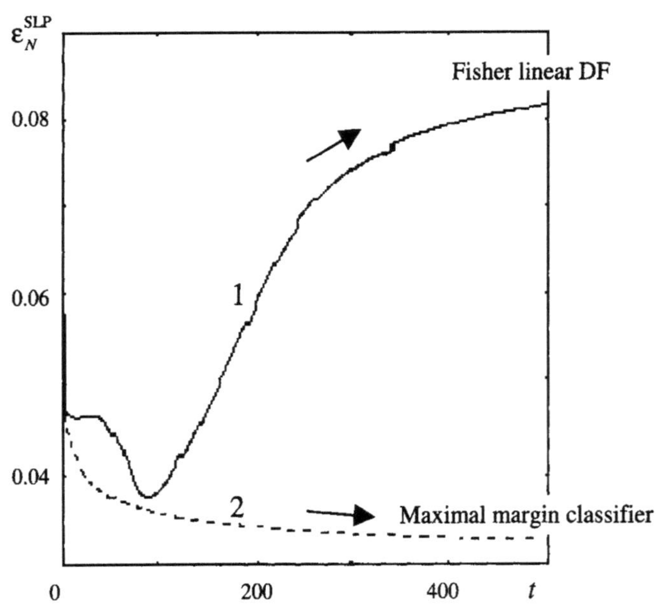

Fig. 1.10. The generalisation error versus t, the number of iterations: 1 - targets $t_1 = 0.9$, $t_2 = 0.1$, 2 - $t_1 = 1$, $t_2 = 0$. The data model **C** with a training-set size of $\bar{N} = 14$ (Reprinted from *Neural Networks*, 11:297-313, S. Raudys, Evolution and generalization of a single neurone, 1998, with permission from Elsevier Science).

In the second demonstration, we use the boundary target values $t_j^{(1)} = 1$, $t_j^{(2)} = 0$. In this case, after a few iterations the empirical error becomes equal to zero and the weights begin increasing. Initially, we are approaching the minimum empirical error classifier and then we move towards the maximal margin classifier. In this extremely small training-set size case, the minimum empirical error classifier is much better than the parametric Fisher classifier (curve 2 in Figure 1.10).

The two examples just presented illustrate that the training conditions greatly affect the resulting neural net classifier. While solving real world problems, we know neither the data model nor its parameters. Therefore, the usefulness of theoretical error estimates is less effective. Nevertheless, in some cases, we can successfully determine an appropriate classifier. In the following chapters, we demonstrate the utility of the theoretical results to the classifier design problem.

Theoretical analysis suggests that good initial weights and optimal stopping of the SLP training process are very useful in reducing the generalisation error. While working with real world data, it is worth whitening the data, i.e. initially transforming the data into spherical data. Then we have to move the data centre to the zero point and begin training with zero initial weights. So, after the first iteration we can obtain the EDC, which is a very good initial classifier for spherical data. In further training, we can utilise all the positive properties of the neural network approach. This allows us to obtain comparatively good classification rules if the training-set size is small or the pattern-class models are non-Gaussian. Therefore, we can utilise statistical methods to transform the data in the most advantageous manner. This approach is, in fact, the integration of the statistical and neural network approaches for designing pattern classification algorithms (for more details see Chapter 5).

1.7 Bibliographical and Historical Remarks

The necessity of analysing artificial neural networks using statistical methods was understood long ago. There are a number of books and review papers devoted to this problem, including: Hertz, Krogh and Palmer (1991), Sethi and Jain (1991), Haykin (1999), Michie *et al.* (1994), Ripley (1994), Cheng and Titterington (1994), Bishop (1995), Vapnik (1995), Schuermann (1996), Vidyasagar (1997), Cherkassky and Mulier (1998), Jain, Duin and Mao (2000). For a more in-depth study of statistical pattern recognition, the author recommends the following monographs: Duda, Hart and Stork (2000), Young and Calvert (1974), Tou and Gonzales (1974), Devijver and Kittler (1982), Aivazian *et. al.* (1989), Fukunaga (1990), Schalakoff (1992), Devroye, Giorfi and Lugosi. (1996). An excellent presentation of many ideas and results pertaining to statistical discriminant analysis and pattern recognition is McLachlan's monograph (1992). However, some connectionists find this book difficult to read.

The first mathematical model of a neurone was proposed as a binary threshold unit. Later this model was generalised by changing the hard-limiting threshold function to the soft-limiting function. Subsequently, multiple neurones were analysed. The neurones were then organised in layers with feedforward connections between layers. For a more detailed review, see Hertz *et al.* (1991), and Haykin (1999). Around 1960, a number of training algorithms for determining the weights of the network were proposed on the grounds of physiological analysis and ad hoc principles. Originally, the first idea was to show the training patterns sequentially and to make the weight change only if the classification error occurred. Later, Tsypkin (1966) and Amari (1967) showed that different adaptive iterative training algorithms can be obtained formally from the condition of the iterative minimisation of a certain cost function. Thus came the discovery that different cost functions and optimisation methods produce distinctly different training algorithms. The standard cost function of the sum of squares with the linear activation function was proposed by Widrow and Hoff (1960) as an adaline algorithm. The "tanh" non-linear soft-limiting function was introduced by Amari (1967) and the cost function (1.7) was suggested by Pietrantonio and Jurs (1972).

The gradient-type back-propagation training algorithm for determining the weights of the multilayer perceptron was discovered in several different research areas of information processing by Tsypkin (1966, 1973), Amari (1967), Bryson and Ho (1969), Werbos (1974), Parker (1985), Le Cun (1986), Rumelhart, Hinton and Williams (1986). A careful review of different optimisation algorithms in neural network training can be found in Van der Smagt (1994). Koford and Groner (1966) were the first to show that the adaline algorithm leads to the standard Fisher linear discriminant function. Raudys (1995*a*, 1996, 1998*b*) has shown that under certain training conditions after the first iteration the SLP leads to the Euclidean distance classifier and later to other six known statistical classifiers. For the regression task, this question has been considered by Sjoberg and Ljung (1992) and later by Raudys (2000*b*).

The small training-set properties of the EDC (formally, the Fisher linear DF with known covariance matrix) were first analysed by John (1961). Raudys (1967) was the first to suggest the analysis of the sample-based discriminant functions using a double asymptotic approach where the number of the training samples N and the number of the features n increase simultaneously (now this method is called the thermodynamic limit approach). Deev (1970, 1972) and Raudys (1972) obtained generalisation error expressions for the Fisher linear DF.

The dimensionality and fixed training-set size effect was first mentioned by Rao (1949). The optimal dimensionality problem for pattern classification was first considered by Allays (1966), Hughes (1965) and Lbov (1966). The "scissors effect" that arises in the application of pattern classification algorithms of different complexity has been formulated by Raudys (1970) and Kanal and Chandrasekaran (1971). Later, under different names, the complexity and sample size effect was rediscovered and popularised in a number of papers and books (Vapnik and Chervonenkis, 1974; Duin, 1978; Jain and Chandrasekaran, 1982; Raudys and Jain, 1991, Geman *et al.*, 1992). The graphs in Figure 1.7 for the EDC and the Fisher classifier are taken from Raudys (1970). Utilisation of the data whitening transformations prior to training the perceptron as a means of integrating the statistical and neural network classifier design approaches was first suggested in Raudys (1998*a* and 1998*c*).

2. Taxonomy of Pattern Classification Algorithms

Two or three hundred different pattern classification algorithms have been suggested in literature during the last 50 years. The main objective of this chapter is to review a selection of known statistical algorithms that can be obtained or improved by training ANN-based classification systems. The first selection contains seven statistical algorithms that can be obtained while training linear and non-linear single layer perceptrons and the second selection contains algorithms that can be approached in ANN training after deriving new non-linear features from the original ones. Particular attention is given to methods which can be used to structure the covariance matrices and describe them by a small number of parameters. This approach is not very popular in statistical pattern recognition, however, together with utilisation of neural networks, it becomes a powerful tool to solve problems in small training-set situations.

Principles of statistical decisions, plug-in and Bayesian sample based rules will be presented shortly, explaining why some of the statistical rules are not optimal. Parzen window and *k-NN* non-parametric classifiers will be described to allow radial basic functions and learning vector quantisation networks to be considered. In order to rationalise the co-operation of neural networks we discuss several classifiers for categorical (discrete valued) features. The reader can find more details regarding classification algorithms in Fukunaga (1990), McLachlan (1990), Duda, Hart and Stork (2000) and other texts on the subject.

2.1 Principles of Statistical Decision Theory

In this section, we use the statistical decision function approach and derive the optimal decision rule, which classifies unknown vectors X with the smallest probability of misclassification. Suppose we know that an n-variate observation vector X belongs to one of the two classes, ω_1 and ω_2. In the statistical approach it is assumed that the multivariate observations are random vectors (see e.g. Fukunaga, 1990). Let $p_i(X)$ be the class conditional density function of vector X belonging to class ω_i, and let P_i be the a priori probability of the class ω_i. Then using the Bayes Theorem, a posterior probability $P(\omega_i \mid X)$ of the vector X to belong to the class ω_i can be expressed as

$$P(\omega_i | X) = \frac{P_i \, p_i(X)}{p(X)} ,$$

where, in the two category case, $p(X) = P_1 \, p_1(X) + P_2 \, p_2(X)$ is an unconditional probability density function of vector X.

A decision rule based on the posterior probabilities classifies an unknown observation vector X into class ω_1 if

$$P(\omega_1 | X) > P(\omega_2 | X)) \tag{2.1}$$

and into the class ω_2 otherwise. Condition (2.1) may be rewritten by using the discriminant function (DF)

$$h_0(X) = \frac{P_1 \, p_1(X) - P_2 \, p_2(X)}{p(X)} . \tag{2.2}$$

Hence, the **a posteriori probability decision rule** is: to classify an unlabeled observation $\mathbf{X}$ into class ω_1 if $h_0(\mathbf{X}) > 0$ and into class ω_2 otherwise.

Now we can demonstrate that this classification rule is optimal in a sense of yielding the *minimum probability of misclassification* (PMC). The PMC may be expressed as

$$\varepsilon = P_1 \int_{\Omega_2} p_1(X) \, d X + P_2 \int_{\Omega_1} p_2(X) \, d X, \tag{2.3}$$

where Ω_1 and Ω_2 splits the measurement space Ω into two nonintersecting parts: if the observation $X \in \Omega_i$, then it is classified into population ω_i, $i = 1, 2$.

Since Ω_1 and Ω_2 are disjoint, and $\Omega_1 \cup \Omega_2 = \Omega$, we have that

$$\int_{\Omega_1} p_1(X) \, d X + \int_{\Omega_2} p_2(X) \, d X = 1.$$

Therefore, Equation (2.3) may be rewritten as

$$\varepsilon = P_1 \, [1 - \int_{\Omega_1} p_1(X) \, d X] + P_2 \int_{\Omega_1} p_2(X) d X$$

$$= P_1 - \int_{\Omega_1} [P_1 \, p_1(X) - P_2 \, p_2(X)] \, d X. \tag{2.4}$$

From expression (2.4) we see that the probability of misclassification will be minimised by assigning observation X to ω_1 only if discriminant function

$$h(X) = P_1\, p_1(X) - P_2\, p_2(X) \tag{2.5}$$

is positive.

Since $p(X)$ defined in (2.2) is always positive, we see that both discriminant functions, (2.2) and (2.5), are equivalent. Because $P_i\ p_i(X)$ is positive, the discriminant function which yields the minimum error rate can be expressed as

$$h^*(X) = \log p_1(X) - \log p_2(X) + \log \frac{P_1}{P_2}. \tag{2.6}$$

Figure 1.6, presented in the previous chapter, illustrates the decision making scheme. Two curves $p_i(X)$ represent densities multiplied by the prior probabilities $P_1 = P_2 = 0.5$. The total classification error consists of two parts:

> ε_1 (the error of the first kind) is the probability that any object from ω_1 is allocated to ω_2; and
>
> ε_2 (the error of the second kind) is the probability that any object from ω_2 is allocated to ω_1.

The minimum of the classification error sum is obtained when we select the "decision threshold" v_0^* at a point where $P_1\ p_1(X) = P_2\ p_2(X)$. The use of any other "decision threshold" will lead to higher sum classification error rates (in Figure 1.6, the area $\Delta\varepsilon$ appears). In the multiclass case, the minimum of the classification error sum (and the maximal probability of correct classification) is obtained if one makes the classification according to a maximum of the product $P_i p_i(X)$, $(i = 1, \ldots, L)$.

A further generalisation of the decision making process occurs, if we assume that the costs of incorrect decisions of the first kind and of the second kind are not equal among themselves. Let $C_{1/2}$ be the cost of incorrect decisions of the second kind, $C_{2/1}$ be the cost of incorrect decisions of the first kind, then the competitive losses of the two types of decisions are $C_{1/2}P_1\ p_1(X)$ and $C_{2/1}P_2\ p_2(X)$. Thus, in order to minimise the sum of losses for each X, one needs to select a solution with a minimal loss

$$\min_i \{ \sum_{j \neq i} C_{i/j} P_i p_i(X) \}.$$

It is easy to generalise the above solution for the multiclass problem and for the case when we would like to have one more decision – to refuse classification in ambiguous cases. In the latter case, one needs to introduce an additional rejection class and to take into account the additional analysis and computation costs involved (see e.g. Fukunaga, 1990, chapter 3).

In a limit case, one can choose one of the costs $C_{1/2}$ or $C_{2/1}$ to be extremely large. Then in a decision-making process, we minimise only one kind of probability of misclassifications.

Expressions (2.2), (2.5) and (2.6) are the most commonly used forms to compose the discriminant function in the statistical pattern recognition. These classification rules are optimal in the sense of yielding the minimum error rate (this is a risk function, if we use the loss instead of using the probability of misclassification).

In order to implement such classification rules, one must know a priori of probabilities P_1 and P_2 and the class-conditional densities $p_1(X)$ and $p_2(X)$. In most practical problems, the models generating the observation vectors X are unknown and the density functions $p_1(X)$ and $p_2(X)$ have to be estimated using the training sets. Both parametric (e.g., multivariate Gaussian densities) and nonparametric (e.g., Parzen window, k-nearest neighbour approach) estimation methods can be utilised for the density estimation problem.

In the **parametric approach**, a functional form of the densities $p_i(X)$ is supposed to be known up to an unknown parameter vector $\mathbf{Y}_i$, i.e. $p_i(X)= p_i(X \mid \mathbf{Y}_i)$.

Example 1. One assumes the n-variate vector X is multivariate Gaussian with independent components. Its distribution density function is

$$p_i(x_1, x_2, ..., x_n) = \prod_{j=1}^{n} (2\pi)^{-1/2} \sigma_{ij}^{-1} e^{-1/2 (x_j - m_{ij})^2 / \sigma_{ij}^2}. \tag{2.7}$$

Here, the $2n$-variate parameter vector $\mathbf{Y}_i$ is composed from $m_{i1}, m_{i2}, ..., m_{in}$ components of the mean vector, and $\sigma_{i1}, \sigma_{i2}, ..., \sigma_{ip}$ components of variances (one for each feature). Thus, $\mathbf{Y}_i = (m_{i1}, m_{i2}, ..., m_{in}, \sigma_{i1}, \sigma_{i2}, ..., \sigma_{ip})^T$. One of the possibilities for the classification rule design is to estimate vectors $\mathbf{Y}_1$ and $\mathbf{Y}_2$ from the training data and to insert the estimate obtained into the expressions for the densities $p_i(x_1, x_2, ..., x_n)$ and the discriminant function (2.6). For the Gaussian classes just discussed and $P_1 = P_2 = ½$ we obtain following quadratic discriminant function

$$h^*(X) = \sum_{j=1}^{n} [- ½ (x_j - \hat{m}_{1j})^2 s_{1j}^{-2} + ½ (x_j - \hat{m}_{2j})^2 s_{2j}^{-2} + ½ \ln \frac{s_{2j}}{s_{1j}}], \tag{2.8}$$

where $\hat{m}_{i1}, \hat{m}_{i2}, ..., \hat{m}_{in}$ are estimates of the components of the mean vector M_i and $s_{i1}, ..., s_{in}$ are estimates of variances of each single feature in the i-th class:

$$\hat{m}_{ij} = 1/N_i \sum_{t=1}^{N_i} x_{jt}^{(i)}, \quad s_{ij} = 1/(N_i - 1) \sum_{t=1}^{N_i} (x_{jt}^{(i)} - \hat{m}_{ij})^2,$$

$x_{jt}^{(i)}$ is the j-th component of training vector $X_t^{(i)}$ $i = 1, 2;$ $t = 1, 2, \ldots, N_i$ and N_i is a number of training vectors from the ith pattern class.

Utilisation of the sample estimates instead of the true parameters in Expression (2.6) is called a **plug-in approach** to designing the classification rule. It is the most widely used technique to design the statistical classifiers. In chapter 3 we will see that in case $N_1 >> N_2$ (or *vice versa*), this approach does not minimise the probability of misclassification and does not lead to optimal use of the training-set observations to design the classification rule.

An alternative to the plug-in technique is a **Bayes predictive approach** that theoretically leads to optimal classification rules. A cardinal assumption of the Bayes approach is an assumption that the classifier designer knows a priori of distributions $p_{prior}(\mathbf{Y}_i)$ of the parameter vectors $\mathbf{Y}_1$, $\mathbf{Y}_2$. It is a *very strong assumption*. Often it cannot be satisfied in practical situations. An incorrect definition of $p_{prior}(\mathbf{Y}_1, \mathbf{Y}_2)$ leads to an increase in the classification error. Hence, in statistical pattern recognition, the predictive Bayes approach did not gain a wide recognition. In recent years, this approach has obtained considerable attention in the analysis of regularisation processes in ANN training. Therefore, in Section 2.4, we present some details and a small discussion.

There exist a great variety of mathematical models to parameterise multivariate distribution density functions $p_i(X)$ and to estimate those parameters. Also there is a number of **nonparametric estimation methods** such as the Parzen window (PW) and the k-nearest neighbour (k-*NN*) rules. Each of these models or methods can be used in expressions (2.2), (2.5) and (2.6) and results in a specific classification algorithm. In principle, all of them can be called Bayes algorithms, since they are designed using the Bayes formula, and statistical decision function approach. However, it is approximately true, since all the training-set based estimates of the densities $p_i(X)$ are not the true densities.

2.2 Four Parametric Statistical Classifiers

In Section 1.2, we introduced two popular statistical classifiers, the Euclidean distance and the standard Fisher linear DF classifiers. We have shown that these classification rules can be obtained in the adaptive SLP training. Now we are able to show that these classifiers can be obtained by applying the principles of the statistical decision functions discussed in the previous section.

2.2.1 The Quadratic Discriminant Function

In statistical pattern recognition, most often the pattern vectors are supposed to be multivariate Gaussian. The multivariate Gaussian density has the form

$$p_i(X) = N_X(X, M_i, \Sigma_i) = (2\pi)^{-n/2} |\Sigma_i|^{-½} e^{-½ (X-M_i)^T \Sigma_i^{-1} (X-M_i)} \tag{2.9}$$

where M_i is an n-variate mean vector of the i-th pattern class and Σ_i is an $n \times n$ symmetric, positive definite covariance matrix (CM). The symmetric covariance matrix, $\Sigma = ((\sigma_{ij})) = ((\sigma_i \sigma_j \rho_{ij}))$, characterises variances σ_i^2, and correlations ρ_{ij} between the components of the feature vector X.

For the multivariate Gaussian vectors, the maximum likelihood estimators of M_i and Σ_i are

$$\hat{M}_i = \frac{1}{N_i} \sum_{j=1}^{N_i} X_j^{(i)}, \tag{2.10a}$$

$$\hat{\Sigma}_i = \frac{1}{N_i - 1} \sum_{j=1}^{N_i} (X_j^{(i)} - \hat{M}_i)(X_j^{(i)} - \hat{M}_i)^T. \tag{2.10b}$$

Inserting estimates (2.10*a* and 2.10*b*) into the density (2.9) and then into (2.6) yields the following sample-based plug-in *quadratic discriminant function* Q:

$$\hat{h}^Q(X) = (X - \hat{M}_2)^T \hat{\Sigma}_2^{-1} (X - \hat{M}_2) - (X - \hat{M}_1)^T \hat{\Sigma}_1^{-1} (X - \hat{M}_1) + \ln \frac{|\Sigma_2|}{|\Sigma_1|} + \ln \frac{P_1}{P_2}. \tag{2.11}$$

This rule often is called a standard quadratic DF. It forms the second-order decision boundary in the multivariate feature space. The MLP with the soft-limiting activation function also can form similar non-linear boundaries.

Example 2. In Figure 2.1, by "crosses" and "and small pluses", we depict 500+500 bi-variate vectors from two spherical Gaussian populations and the non-linear decision boundaries of the quadratic DF (boundary Q) and MLP with two hidden neurones (boundary MLP). In spite of visible difference in decision boundaries, both classifiers result in approximately 5½% error.

2.2.2 The Standard Fisher Linear Discriminant Function

Suppose both pattern classes share a common covariance matrix $\bar{\Sigma} = \Sigma_1 = \Sigma_2$, and let $P_2 = P_1$. Then inserting sample estimates of the mean vectors and the covariance matrix into Equation (2.11), and omitting the term $\ln(P_1/P_2)$, we obtain the Fisher linear discriminant function (1.3), defined in Section 1.1. This classification rule is historically the first one. It was proposed by Ronald Fisher (1936), where he mapped training vectors $X_j^{(1)}$ from class ω_1 and vectors $X_j^{(2)}$ from class ω_2 on a straight line and searched a direction of this line in order to get the best separability of the classes. To define the "separability", he used a measure

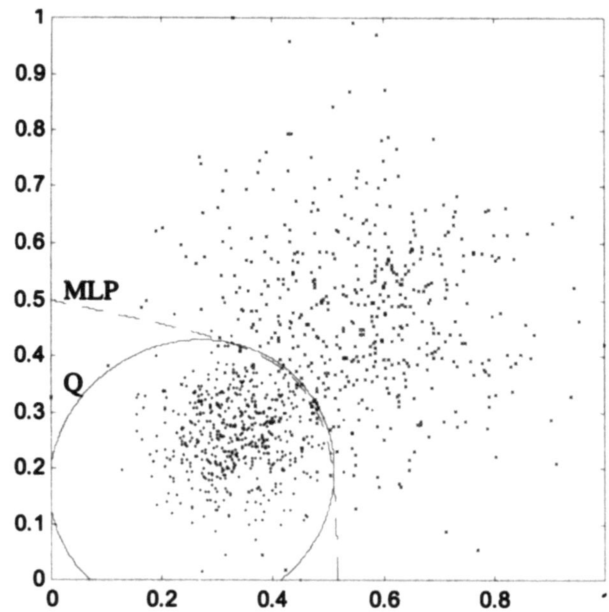

Fig. 2.1. 200 bi-variate vectors from two Gaussian classes $N_X((-1,-1)^T, \mathbf{I})$, $N_X((2,2)^T, 4\mathbf{I})$ and the non-linear decision boundaries of the quadratic DF and the MLP with 2 hidden neurones.

$$T^2 = \frac{[\bar{h}_1(\boldsymbol{X}) - \bar{h}_2(\boldsymbol{X})]^2}{\hat{V}[h_1(\boldsymbol{X})] + \hat{V}[h_2(\boldsymbol{X})]} = \left(\frac{\boldsymbol{V}^T\hat{\boldsymbol{M}}_1 - \boldsymbol{V}^T\hat{\boldsymbol{M}}_2}{\sqrt{\boldsymbol{V}^T\hat{\Sigma}^{-1}\boldsymbol{V}}}\right)^2, \tag{2.12}$$

where $\bar{h}_i = \boldsymbol{V}^T\hat{\boldsymbol{M}}_i + v_0$ is a sample mean value of DF, $h(\boldsymbol{X}) = \boldsymbol{X}^T\boldsymbol{V}^F + v_0$, evaluated from all training vectors from class ω_i, and $\hat{V}\,[\,h_i\,(\boldsymbol{X})\,]$ is a sample variance.

The measure (2.12) is a difference in the sample means of the projections divided by a standard deviation. Maximisation of (2.12) gives the weights of the standard linear Fisher DF defined in Equation (1.3). Illustration of the above mapping have been presented in Figure 1.2.

2.2.3 The Euclidean Distance Classifier

While designing the standard linear DF, it was supposed that both classes share a common covariance matrix $\bar{\Sigma}$. Suppose now that $\bar{\Sigma}$ is proportional to the identity matrix **I**, i.e. $\bar{\Sigma} = \sigma^2\mathbf{I}$ (we suppose the variables to be uncorrelated and have identical variances). For equal prior probabilities of the classes, we classify according to the sign of the discriminant function. Then the parameter σ^2 becomes unimportant. As a result we obtain the Euclidean distance classifier with the weights defined by the Equation (1.2).

2.2.4 The Anderson–Bahadur Linear DF

The linear DF is preferable when the covariance matrices of the different classes are equal among themselves. When the covariance matrices differ radically, it is preferable to use the quadratic discriminant function (2.11). There is an alternative to the quadratic DF suggested by Anderson and Bahadur (1962). In this classifier, the estimates of the covariance matrices are weighted by factors γ and $1 - \gamma$. The weight vector has the form:

$$V^{AB} = (\gamma\ \hat{\Sigma}_1 + (1-\gamma)\ \hat{\Sigma}_2)^{-1}(\hat{M}_1 - \hat{M}_2), \tag{2.13}$$

where factor γ is a certain function of $\hat{M}_1, \hat{M}_2$ and $\hat{\Sigma}_1$, $\hat{\Sigma}_2$.

We denote this classifier as AB. This rule approximates the non-linear decision boundary of the quadratic DF by a certain plane. A difference between these decision boundaries is most important in the area where the both pattern classes intersects. Often (but not always) the AB rule results in a close performance compared to the quadratic DF.

Example 3. In Figure 2.2 we depict a major part of bi-variate Gaussian training vectors and decision boundaries for four types of parametric classifiers: E – the Euclidean distance classifier, F – the standard Fisher linear DF, Q – the standard quadratic DF and AB – the *Anderson–Bahadur linear DF*. In spite of the difference in the covariance matrices of the classes, the AB and Q classifiers result in a similar classification performance. Below we present the training and test errors and their average: an estimate of the asymptotic classification error:

$$\hat{\varepsilon}_\infty^{E} = (0.027 + 0.031)/2 = 0.029,$$

$$\hat{\varepsilon}_\infty^{F} = (0.024 + 0.031)/2 = 0.027,$$

$$\hat{\varepsilon}_\infty^{Q} = (0.008 + 0.008)/2 = 0.008,$$

$$\hat{\varepsilon}_\infty^{AB} = (0.009 + 0.019)/2 = 0.014.$$

While choosing the distribution parameters for this illustration, efforts have been made to provide a large difference between ε_∞^{Q} and ε_∞^{AB}.

2.3 Structures of the Covariance Matrices

In Section 1.4, we have seen that the ratio between the number of features and the number of training examples is essential in determining the generalisation abilities of the statistical classifiers. In the two-category case, for the linear DF, we have to estimate $2n$ components of the mean vectors and $n(n+1)/2$ components of the covariance matrix. For the quadratic classifier, we have to estimate two mean vectors and two matrices, i.e. $2n + n(n+1)$ parameters. When the number of features is large, the number of parameters can become extremely large.

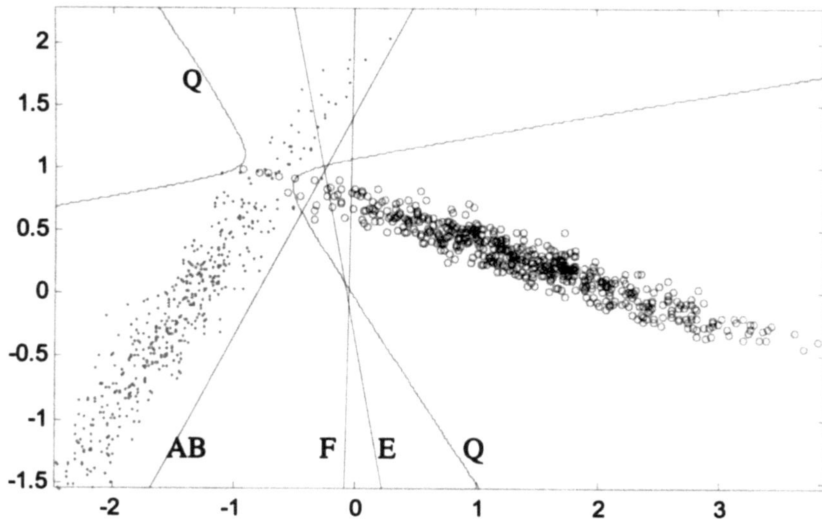

Fig. 2.2. Decision boundaries of four parametric classifiers.

Thus, to design the classifier, one needs a very large number of training examples. In many real world problems, only a finite number of examples is available. Therefore, the designer is forced to reduce the number of parameters. One way to do this is to reduce the number of features. Another way is to simplify the classifier. To do this, one needs to make some assumptions (constraints) on the structure of the covariance matrix.

2.3.1 A Set of Standard Assumptions

In Section 2.1 an example of such an assumption was already made – the covariance matrices of two classes were assumed to be identical. Further reduction in the number of parameters is available by constraining a type of dependency between the separate features. Constraints on the type of the covariance matrix help to reduce the number of parameters to be estimated from the training-set. If these constraints are not far from the true reality, then we can obtain a reduction in the generalisation error. The largest gain in reduction in the number of parameters is obtained in high-dimensional cases. In the ANN design, one can benefit from the utilisation of the constraints in following situations:

- we use the weights of the statistical classifier with the constrained covariance matrix to initialise the perceptron weights;

- we use the constrained estimates of the covariance matrix to whiten the data i.e. to rotate and scale the feature space in order to obtain pattern class distributions as close as possible to a spherical distribution. Then the Euclidean distance classifier obtained after the first training iteration of the SLP is a good classifier for the spherical pattern classes.

A set of the most powerful assumptions (constraints) is made if one assumes that:

(a) the covariance matrices of the different classes are identical;
(b) the features are statistically independent (this assumption was discussed at the end of Section 2.1);
(c) the variances of all features are identical.

If $P_2 = P_1$, the first constraint induces *the Fisher linear DF*. If all three assumptions are made, then the covariance matrix has a structure $\boldsymbol{\Sigma}_i = \mathbf{I}\,\sigma^2$. The use of this particular set of assumptions and the density (2.9) induces *the Euclidean distance classifier.*

If we use assumption (*b*), then we will have a quadratic classifier for independent features. This discriminant function (2.8) was already discussed in Section 2.1. Here, in order to design the classifier for the two-category case, one needs to estimate two n-variate mean vectors $\boldsymbol{M}_1$ and $\boldsymbol{M}_2$ and two diagonal matrices $\boldsymbol{D}_1$ and $\boldsymbol{D}_2$, with n variances in their diagonals, altogether $4n$ parameters. To invert sample based matrices $\hat{\boldsymbol{D}}_1$ and $\hat{\boldsymbol{D}}_2$, one needs to invert only the diagonal elements. We denote this as a *quadratic classifier,* $\mathrm{D_1D_2}$.

Let only assumptions (*a*) and (*b*) be made: the features are uncorrelated, and the variances of all features are identical. Then we have the linear discriminant function with following weights

$$\boldsymbol{V}^{\mathrm{D}} = \hat{\boldsymbol{D}}^{-1}(\hat{\boldsymbol{M}}_1 - \hat{\boldsymbol{M}}_2) \quad \text{and} \quad v_0 = -\,\Delta\hat{\boldsymbol{M}}^T \boldsymbol{V}^{\mathrm{D}}, \tag{2.14}$$

where $\hat{\boldsymbol{D}}$ is the sample estimate of the diagonal variance matrix composed from diagonal elements of $\hat{\boldsymbol{\Sigma}}$, the sample covariance matrix and $\Delta\hat{\boldsymbol{M}} = ½\,(\hat{\boldsymbol{M}}_1 - \hat{\boldsymbol{M}}_2)$.

We will call this classifier, the linear classifier for diagonal CM, or a *diagonal classifier* and denote it by the letter D.

2.3.2 Block Diagonal Matrices

A generalisation of the "diagonal" classifier is a discriminant function for Gaussian vectors having a block structured dependence between the variables. This DF structurally resembles the multi-layer perceptron with one hidden layer. Now, let us present more details. Let n components of random vector $\boldsymbol{X}$ be divided into H blocks $\boldsymbol{X}_1, \boldsymbol{X}_2, \ldots, \boldsymbol{X}_H$ with dimensionalities $n_1, n_2, \ldots, n_H$ ($\sum_{j=1}^{H} n_j = n$).

Inside each block, the features are supposed to be mutually dependent. The separate blocks are supposed to be statistically independent. Then the covariance matrix of vector $\boldsymbol{X}$ can be represented in a block-diagonal way:

$$\bar{\Sigma} = \begin{bmatrix} \Sigma_1 & \mathbf{0} & \cdots & \mathbf{0} \\ \mathbf{0} & \Sigma_2 & \cdots & \mathbf{0} \\ \cdots & \cdots & \cdots & \cdots \\ \mathbf{0} & \mathbf{0} & \cdots & \Sigma_H \end{bmatrix} \tag{2.15}$$

and one can use the following linear discriminant function

$$h^{\mathrm{BL}}(\boldsymbol{X}) = \sum_{j=1}^{H} [\boldsymbol{X}_j - ½(\hat{\boldsymbol{M}}_{j1} + \hat{\boldsymbol{M}}_{j2})]^T \hat{\Sigma}_j^{-1}(\hat{\boldsymbol{M}}_{j1} - \hat{\boldsymbol{M}}_{j2}) + c, \tag{2.16}$$

where $\hat{\boldsymbol{M}}_{j1}$ and $\hat{\boldsymbol{M}}_{j2}$ are n_j-variate vectors, the estimates of the mean vectors of each block of each of two classes, $\hat{\Sigma}_j$ is the sample maximum likelihood estimate of Σ_j, the covariance matrix of the j-th block, and c is a constant. Typically $c = 0$, however, in order to take into account an effect of unequal training-set sizes, N_1 and N_2, we will use a special c value (for a discussion of this problem, see Section 3.5.3).

The difference between the diagonal D and the block-diagonal classifier BL is that, instead of n independent separate variables, we have H independent blocks of variables with $n_H = \sum_{j=1}^{H} n_j(n_j+1)/2$ parameters to be estimated from the training-set. When both n and H are large, we have a drastic reduction in the number of parameters of the covariance matrix that have to be estimated from the training-set. Our experiments with a dozen of real-world data sets have shown that this model is useful.

It is very important that the parameters of the block covariance matrix are same for both competing pattern classes while analysing the influence of the number of parameters on the generalisation error (discussed in the next chapter). Here we can trace a similarity with the multilayer perceptron, where the weights of the hidden layer neurones affect all outputs, i.e. these weights are common for all outputs.

2.3.3 The Tree Type Dependence Models

An interesting and useful model which requires a small number of parameters to describe a joint dependence between all n variables is a model based on an approximation of a joint probability distribution by the first order *tree dependence*. According to the fundamentals of the probability theory, each multivariate density can be represented as

$$p(x_1, x_2, ..., x_n) = p(x_1)\, p(x_2 \,|\, x_1)\, p(x_3 \,|\, x_2, x_1) ... p(x_n \,|\, x_{n-1}, ..., x_2, x_1). \qquad (2.17)$$

In the first order tree dependence model, it is assumed that each variable is conditioned, at most, upon one other variable. One can say that each variable has only one "boss" component on which it depends. Then probability density function (2.17) can be written in the following simplified form:

$$p(x_1, x_2, ..., x_n) = \prod_{j=1}^{n} p(x_j \,|\, x_{mj}) \quad (1 \leq m_j \leq n) \qquad (2.18)$$

where a sequence $m_2, \dots, m_n$ constitutes a graph of connections (an unknown permutation of the integers 1, 2, ..., n) and $p(x_i \,|\, x_0)$, by definition, is equal to $p(x_i)$.

In a general case, the covariance matrix has $n \times n$ non-zero elements. An inverse of this matrix $\bar{\Sigma}^{-1}$, however, has $2n$-1 non-zero elements. It is a result of the assumption that each component of the vector X depends only on one other component. For complex data, one has to construct the second and higher order tree dependence models. This important model is rarely mentioned in pattern recognition textbooks and remains practically unnoticed in the pattern recognition community. Therefore in Appendix 2, we present more details of this model and provide a numerical example.

2.3.4 Temporal Dependence Models

The recognition of the temporal and spatial objects and phenomena requires working with vectors of very high dimensionality. It is an advantageous area of application for the constrained statistical classifiers. There is a number of models that allow evaluation of temporal or spatial dependence between the data points. Undoubtedly, the expertise gained in this area can be useful in ANN design.

Let the components $x_1, x_2, ..., x_{n-1}, x_n$ of the multivariate vector be measurements differing in time or in space and assume they are realisations of a *stationary random process*. Then the covariance matrix has the following structure

$$\bar{\Sigma} = \begin{bmatrix} \delta_1 & \delta_2 & \delta_3 & \dots & \delta_{n-1} & \delta_n \\ \delta_2 & \delta_1 & \delta_2 & \dots & \delta_{n-2} & \delta_{n-1} \\ \delta_3 & \delta_2 & \delta_1 & \dots & \delta_{n-3} & \delta_{n-2} \\ \dots & \dots & \dots & \dots & \dots & \dots \\ \delta_{n-1} & \delta_{n-2} & \delta_{n-3} & \dots & \delta_1 & \delta_2 \\ \delta_n & \delta_{n-1} & \delta_{n-2} & \dots & \delta_2 & \delta_1 \end{bmatrix}. \qquad (2.19)$$

We see there are only n parameters $\delta_1, \delta_2, \delta_3, \dots, \delta_n$ that describe the structure of dependence between the variables. A number of special models, such as auto-regression, moving average, ARMA and circular, allow further reduction of the number of parameters (see e.g., Appendix 3 and Fukunaga, 1990). For example, in the moving average model, we assume

$$x_t = \mu_t + b_0 v_t + b_1 v_{t-1} + \dots + b_q v_{t-q},$$

where μ_t, b_0, b_1, ... , b_q are q+2 independent parameters of the model.

2.4 The Bayes Predictive Approach to Design Optimal Classification Rules

The plug-in approach of designing the classification rule does not lead to the optimal use of the training-set observations to design the classifier. An alternative to the plug-in approach is a Bayes (predictive) approach. This method theoretically leads to the optimal classification rules.

2.4.1 A General Theory

Let $p_1(X \mid \mathbf{Y}, \mathbf{Y}_1)$, $p_2(X \mid \mathbf{Y}, \mathbf{Y}_2)$, be the conditional probability density function (PDF) of the classes. Here, we assume that the vector **Y** is common for the distribution densities of both classes. In the Bayes predictive approach, two principal assumptions are:

- parameter vectors $\mathbf{Y}$, $\mathbf{Y}_1$, $\mathbf{Y}_2$ are random;
- the designer knows their *a priori* distribution density $p^{prior}(\mathbf{Y}, \mathbf{Y}_1, \mathbf{Y}_2)$.

We use these two assumptions and derive the optimal discriminant function with a minimal generalisation error over *all possible classification problems* defined by the density $p^{prior}(\mathbf{Y}, \mathbf{Y}_1, \mathbf{Y}_2)$.

Let $X_1^{(1)}, X_2^{(1)}, \dots, X_{N_1}^{(1)}, X_1^{(2)}, \dots, X_{N_2}^{(2)}$ be the training vectors. Then according to the Bayes formula the *a posteriori* distribution of $\mathbf{Y}$, $\mathbf{Y}_1$, $\mathbf{Y}_2$ is

$$p_i^{aposteriori}(\mathbf{Y}, \mathbf{Y}_1, \mathbf{Y}_2 \mid X_1^{(1)}, X_2^{(1)}, \dots, X_{N_1}^{(1)}, X_1^{(2)}, \dots, X_{N_2}^{(2)}) =$$

$$\frac{p(X_1^{(1)}, \dots, X_{N_2}^{(2)} \mid \mathbf{Y}, \mathbf{Y}_1, \mathbf{Y}_2)\, p^{prior}(\mathbf{Y}, \mathbf{Y}_1, \mathbf{Y}_2)}{\int p(X_1^{(1)}, \dots, X_{N_2}^{(2)} \mid \mathbf{Y}, \mathbf{Y}_1, \mathbf{Y}_2)\, p^{prior}(\mathbf{Y}, \mathbf{Y}_1, \mathbf{Y}_2)\, d\mathbf{Y} d\mathbf{Y}_1 d\mathbf{Y}_2} \tag{2.20}$$

and the *a posteriori* distribution density of vector X is

$$p_i^{aposteriori}(X \mid X_1^{(1)}, X_2^{(1)}, \dots, X_{N_1}^{(1)}, X_1^{(2)}, \dots, X_{N_2}^{(2)}) =$$

$$\int p_i(X \mid \mathbf{Y}, \mathbf{Y}_1, \mathbf{Y}_2)\, p(\mathbf{Y}, \mathbf{Y}_1, \mathbf{Y}_2 \mid X_1^{(1)}, \dots, X_{N_1}^{(1)}, X_1^{(2)}, \dots, X_{N_2}^{(2)})\, d\mathbf{Y} d\mathbf{Y}_1 d\mathbf{Y}_2. \tag{2.21}$$

This predictive density is used to obtain the optimal classification rule.

2.4.2 Learning the Mean Vector

Now we will illustrate how this approach can lead to the Euclidean distance classifier. Let the vector $\boldsymbol{X}$ be Gaussian with the density in Equation (2.9). Suppose the covariance matrix $\bar{\Sigma}$ of this distribution is common for both pattern classes and known. Let the *a priori* distribution of the mean vector $\boldsymbol{M}$ be Gaussian

$$p_i^{prior}(\boldsymbol{M}_i) = N_{\boldsymbol{M}}(\mu, \mathbf{K}), \tag{2.22}$$

where μ is n-variate vector and $\mathbf{K}$ is an $n \times n$ symmetric positive defined matrix.

We will need the equality

$$\int N_X(\boldsymbol{M}, \Sigma) N_{\boldsymbol{M}}(\mu, \mathrm{K}) d\,\boldsymbol{M} = N_X(\mu, \Sigma + \mathbf{K}). \tag{2.23}$$

Use of (2.22) and (2.23) in (2.20) and (2.21) results in

$$p_i^{aposteriori}(\boldsymbol{M}_i \mid \boldsymbol{X}_1^{(i)}, \boldsymbol{X}_2^{(i)}, ..., \boldsymbol{X}_{N_i}^{(i)}) =$$

$$N_{\boldsymbol{M}}((\mathbf{K}^{-1} + \Sigma^{-1} N_i)^{-1}(\Sigma^{-1}\hat{\boldsymbol{M}}_i N_i + \mathbf{K}^{-1}\mu), (\mathbf{K}^{-1} + \Sigma^{-1} N_i)^{-1}). \tag{2.24}$$

$$p_i^{aposteriori}(\boldsymbol{X} \mid \boldsymbol{X}_1^{(i)}, \boldsymbol{X}_2^{(i)}, ..., \boldsymbol{X}_{N_i}^{(i)}) =$$

$$N_X((\mathbf{K}^{-1} + \Sigma^{-1} N_i)^{-1}(\Sigma^{-1}\hat{\boldsymbol{M}}_i N_i + \mathbf{K}^{-1}\mu), (\mathbf{K}^{-1} + \Sigma^{-1} N_i)^{-1} + \Sigma). \tag{2.25}$$

Equation (2.25) is too complex to follow the influence of the prior distribution on the estimate of probability density functions of the classes. Assume the prior mean vector μ is common for both classes. Let $\Sigma = \mathbf{I}\sigma_x^2$, $\mathbf{K} = \mathbf{I}\sigma_a^2$. Then the *a posteriori* density for vector $\boldsymbol{X}$.

$$p_i^{aposteriori}(\boldsymbol{X} \mid \boldsymbol{X}_1^{(i)}, \boldsymbol{X}_2^{(i)}, ..., \boldsymbol{X}_{N_i}^{(i)}) =$$

$$N_X(\hat{\boldsymbol{M}}_i \frac{\sigma_a^2}{\sigma_a^2 + \sigma_x^2 / N_i} + \mu \frac{\sigma_x^2 / N_i}{\sigma_a^2 + \sigma_x^2 / N_i}, \mathbf{I}(\sigma_a^2 \frac{\sigma_x^2 / N_i}{\sigma_a^2 + \sigma_x^2 / N_i} + \sigma_x^2)), \tag{2.26}$$

From Equation (2.26), we see that the more we have training vectors, the effects of the prior distribution is less noticed. When the number of training vectors is small or the covariance matrix of the prior distribution is "narrow" then the contribution of prior distribution is significant. Inserting (2.26) into (2.6), results in a quadratic discriminant function. When $N_2 = N_1$ we obtain the linear classifier (1.2) i.e. the standard EDC. We see for the spherical Gaussian distributions of $\boldsymbol{X}$ and priors for $\boldsymbol{M}_i$, the plug-in classifier (the EDC) is not optimal in the Bayes predictive sense if $N_2 \neq N_1$.

Equations (2.25) and (2.26) show that analytical expressions of the Bayes approach are much more complex than that of the plug-in approach. Moreover, in the Bayes approach, an important and very difficult problem is the determination of parameters of the prior distribution.

One of suggestions most often used in the literature is to choose a very "flat" density as a prior. For the above example, it would be a choice of a very large value of σ_a^2. When $\sigma_a^2 \to \infty$ then, from (2.26), it follows that

$$p^{aposteriori}(\boldsymbol{M}_i) = N_{Mi}(\hat{\boldsymbol{M}}_i,\ \mathbf{I}\frac{\sigma_x^2}{N_i}). \tag{2.27}$$

$$p_i^{aposteriori}(\boldsymbol{X} \mid \boldsymbol{X}_1^{(i)}, \boldsymbol{X}_2^{(i)}, \ldots, \boldsymbol{X}_{N_i}^{(i)}) = N_X(\hat{\boldsymbol{M}}_i \times 1 + \mu \times 0, \mathbf{I}(\frac{\sigma_x^2}{N_i} + \sigma_x^2)). \tag{2.28}$$

To show the similarity with (2.26), in Equation (2.28) we presented the mean as a sum of two terms. The variance in the above equation depends on N_i and indicates once more that the difference between the classifiers obtained by the plug-in and the Bayes approaches arises when $N_2 \neq N_1$.

In order to see a parallel between network training and the Bayes predictive approach, let us represent the estimate of the mean of the *a posteriori* distribution as a recurrent equation. Let us have t observations from ω_i and add a new, $(t+1)$-th, observation $\boldsymbol{X}_{t+1}^{(i)}$. As before, let $\sigma_a^2 \to \infty$. For the new observation vector $\boldsymbol{X}_{t+1}^{(i)}$, we use the *a posteriori* density (2.27) as a prior density, i.e. $\mu = \hat{\boldsymbol{M}}_i$, $\sigma_a^2 = \frac{\sigma_x^2}{t}$.

Note that $\hat{\boldsymbol{M}}_i$ is estimated from t training vectors. Then applying (2.28) with a new training-set size, $N_i = 1$, we obtain

$$p^{aposteriori}(\boldsymbol{M}_i) = p(\boldsymbol{M}_i \mid \boldsymbol{X}_1^{(i)}, \ldots, \boldsymbol{X}_t^{(i)}, \boldsymbol{X}_{t+1}^{(i)}) =$$

$$N_X(\hat{\boldsymbol{M}}_i \frac{1}{t+1} + \boldsymbol{X}_{t+1}^{(i)} \frac{t}{t+1}, \mathbf{I}\frac{1}{t+1}\sigma_x^2). \tag{2.29}$$

Thus, utilisation of the maximal value of the *a posteriori* density as the estimate of $\boldsymbol{M}_i$ after $t+1$ training vectors results in the following iterative procedure

$$(\hat{\boldsymbol{M}}_i)^{t+1} = (\hat{\boldsymbol{M}}_i)^t(1-\eta) + \boldsymbol{X}_{t+1}^{(i)}\eta, \tag{2.30}$$

where $\eta = \frac{1}{t+1}$ and $(\hat{\boldsymbol{M}}_i)^t = \hat{\boldsymbol{M}}_i$.

The reader should pay attention to the above procedure, where the parameter η is the "learning step". This parameter is derived strictly from using the statistical approach. In this training scheme, the optimal value should diminish as the number of training vectors increases. This η value is optimal for the given assumptions and performance criterion.

2.4.3 Learning the Mean Vector and CM

An iterative way to recompute the estimate of the mean (as well as the variance) can be applied to construct the iterative procedure to adapt other parameters of the classification rule. Similar equations have been derived for estimation of the covariance matrix and for the *a posteri*ori distribution of the multivariate Gaussian vector $\boldsymbol{X}$. Again, in this approach, $\boldsymbol{M}_1$, $\boldsymbol{M}_2$, and $\overline{\Sigma}$ are supposed to be random variables and the prior distribution $p^{prior}(\boldsymbol{M}_1, \boldsymbol{M}_2, \overline{\Sigma})$ to be known. Then we seek for the *a posteriori* (predictive) density of vector $\boldsymbol{X}$, and, for this density estimate, we design the classifier. Such a classifier is optimal in the sense that it yields the minimal classification error for a *set of classification problems* defined by the prior distribution $p^{prior}(\boldsymbol{M}_1, \boldsymbol{M}_2, \overline{\Sigma})$. For the uniform prior distribution of $\boldsymbol{M}_1$, $\boldsymbol{M}_2$ and $\overline{\Sigma}$, the predictive density is

$$p_i^{aposteriori}(\boldsymbol{X} \mid \boldsymbol{X}_1^{(i)}, \boldsymbol{X}_2^{(i)}, \ldots, \boldsymbol{X}_{N_i}^{(i)}) \propto$$

$$\left(\frac{N_i}{N_i+1}\right)^{\frac{n}{2}} \left(1+\frac{N_i(\boldsymbol{X}-\hat{\boldsymbol{M}}_i)^T \hat{\Sigma}^{-1}(\boldsymbol{X}-\hat{\boldsymbol{M}}_i)}{(N_i+1)(N-2)}\right)^{\frac{N-3}{2}} . \tag{2.31}$$

If one uses the above density to obtain the classification rule, a quadratic discriminant function results. When $N_2 = N_1 = \overline{N}$ and the prior probabilities of the classes are equal, the above optimal Bayes classifier is linear and becomes equivalent to the Fisher linear discriminant. Thus, the Fisher classifier is an optimal sample-based classifier in the predictive Bayes sense when the prior distribution of the mean vector and the covariance matrix are uniform and we have the same number of training vectors from both pattern classes ($N_2 = N_1$).

2.4.4 Qualities and Shortcomings

The Bayes predictive approach is the only method that formulates optimal sample based classification rules. This method allows us to analyse the optimality of the empirical plug-in approach. We have seen that EDC becomes the optimal classification rule for a uniform prior distribution of the mean vectors $\boldsymbol{M}_1$, $\boldsymbol{M}_2$. For the case N_2=N_1, the standard Fisher linear DF becomes the optimal classification rule for uniform prior distribution of the mean vectors $\boldsymbol{M}_1$, $\boldsymbol{M}_2$ and the covariance matrix $\overline{\Sigma}$. This classifier, however, is no longer optimal when $N_2 \neq N_1$. The use of the Bayes approach allows us to avoid painful problems associated with inversion of ill-conditioned sample covariance matrix in the high dimensional case.

The plug-in approach is computationally simple and intuitively understandable. The Bayes predictive approach, however, requires much more complex analytical expressions. A main drawback of the predictive Bayes approach consists of the definition of the prior distribution density of unknown parameters. The flat and almost uniform *a priori* distribution of n-variate mean vectors as well as $n(n+1)$ coefficients of an inverse of the covariance matrix, $\bar{\Sigma}^{-1}$, imposes that certain unrealistic sets of parameters $\boldsymbol{M}_1$, $\boldsymbol{M}_2$ and $\bar{\Sigma}$ can occur. Among these occurrences, one can meet situations that have almost singular distributions of pattern classes.

The almost uniform prior distribution is a suggested mathematical manoeuvre to overcome numerical difficulties. It is not based on the analysis of real-world situations. In Chapter 3, we will see that the expected PMC of such "optimal" solutions are at times even higher than that of the plug-in classifier. Therefore, the optimism that arose after suggesting this approach in the mid-sixties soon died away. Nevertheless, it is a powerful theoretical tool to analyse and design decision making rules. No doubt, in the future, this method will be elaborated further with practical models to define prior distributions of unknown parameters and should find a wider range of applications.

2.5 Modifications of the Standard Linear and Quadratic DF

If N_1, N_2 are small in comparison with the number of dimensions n, i.e. $N < n + 2$, then there arises problems associated with the inversion of the sample covariance matrix $\hat{\Sigma}$. In Section 2.3, we described a number of structures of the covariance matrix which can be useful to overcome this kind of difficulty. In this section, we will present four other techniques to deal with the dimensionality problem.

2.5.1 A Pseudo-Inversion of the Covariance Matrix

One of possibilities for dealing with singular matrices is to use a pseudo-inversion. A sense of the pseudo-inversion of the symmetric matrix $\hat{\Sigma}$ consists of a singular value decomposition of this matrix:

$$\hat{\Sigma} = \Phi\Lambda\Phi^T,$$

where Φ is an orthogonal $n \times n$ matrix such that

$$\Phi^T \hat{\Sigma} \Phi = \Lambda = \begin{bmatrix} \lambda_1 & 0 & \dots & 0 \\ 0 & \lambda_2 & \dots & 0 \\ \dots & \dots & \dots & \dots \\ 0 & 0 & \dots & \lambda_n \end{bmatrix}, \qquad (2.32)$$

and Φ is called an eigenvectors matrix and Λ is called an eigenvalues matrix of $\hat{\Sigma}$.

Note that $\mathbf{\Phi}^T\mathbf{\Phi} = \mathbf{\Phi}\,\mathbf{\Phi}^T = \mathbf{I}$ and $\mathbf{\Phi}^{-1} = \mathbf{\Phi}^T$. In order to grasp a better understanding of the pseudo-inversion, suppose for a moment that $\hat{\Sigma}$ is a positive defined matrix and can be inverted in a standard way. Following (2.32), the inverse can be written as

$$\hat{\Sigma}^{-1} = (\mathbf{\Phi}\Lambda\mathbf{\Phi}^T)^{-1} = (\mathbf{\Phi}^T)^{-1}\Lambda^{-1}\mathbf{\Phi}^{-1} = \mathbf{\Phi}\,\Lambda^{-1}\mathbf{\Phi}^T. \tag{2.33}$$

Now, let the sample covariance matrix be singular. Some of the eigenvalues are equal to zero. Suppose $\lambda_1, \lambda_2, \ldots, \lambda_r > 0$, and $\lambda_{r+1}, \ldots, \lambda_n = 0$. When $N_i < n+1$, then $r = N_i - 1$. Denote

$$\lambda = \begin{bmatrix} \lambda_1 & 0 & \ldots & 0 \\ 0 & \lambda_2 & \ldots & 0 \\ \ldots & \ldots & \ldots & \ldots \\ 0 & 0 & \ldots & \lambda_r \end{bmatrix}.$$

Thus, we can rewrite equation (2.32) in a block way

$$\mathbf{\Phi}^T\,\hat{\Sigma}\,\mathbf{\Phi} = [\mathbf{\Phi}_1\,\mathbf{\Phi}_2]^T\,\hat{\Sigma}\,[\mathbf{\Phi}_1\,\mathbf{\Phi}_2] = \begin{bmatrix} \lambda & 0 \\ 0 & 0 \end{bmatrix}, \tag{2.34}$$

where we have split the orthogonal matrix $\mathbf{\Phi} = [\mathbf{\Phi}_1\,\mathbf{\Phi}_2]$ into $n \times r$ matrix $\mathbf{\Phi}_1$ and $n \times (n\text{-}r)$ matrix $\mathbf{\Phi}_2$. Then, in analogy with the conventional inverse (2.33), the pseudo-inverse of matrix $\hat{\Sigma}$

$$\hat{\Sigma}^{+} = \mathbf{\Phi}\begin{bmatrix} \lambda^{-1} & 0 \\ 0 & 0 \end{bmatrix}\mathbf{\Phi}^T = [\,\mathbf{\Phi}_1\,\mathbf{\Phi}_2]\begin{bmatrix} \lambda^{-1} & 0 \\ 0 & 0 \end{bmatrix}[\,\mathbf{\Phi}_1\,\mathbf{\Phi}_2]^T = \mathbf{\Phi}_1\,\lambda^{-1}\,\mathbf{\Phi}_1^T. \tag{2.35}$$

In a number of mathematical program packages, there exist standard matrix pseudo-inversion subroutines. Use of (2.35) in (1.3) results in the Fisher linear DF with pseudo-inversion, or, simply, the **Pseudo-Fisher classifier PF**. Equation (2.35) shows that we invert only the positive defined eigenvalues matrix λ. Instead of classifying the vectors X in the original n-dimensional space, we classify new vectors $X_{new} = \mathbf{\Phi}_1^T X$ in an r-dimensional subspace of non zero eigenvalues of the covariance matrix. The resulting decision hyperplane is at *equal distances* from all N training vectors.

In the analysis of adaptive classification algorithms (Chapter 4), we will also meet pseudo-inversion. There, instead of the standard sample covariance matrix $\hat{\Sigma}$, the following sample covariance matrix of non-centred training vectors is sometimes used:

$$\hat{\Sigma}_{NC} = \frac{1}{N_1 + N_2 - 2}\sum_{i=1}^{2}\sum_{j=1}^{N_i} X_j^{(i)}(X_j^{(i)})^T. \tag{2.36}$$

2.5.2 Regularised Discriminant Analysis (RDA)

Another approach to the overwhelming difficulties associated with the matrix inversion in regression and discriminant analysis, apart from the standard CM estimates (1.4) or (2.10*b*), is to use a "ridge" CM estimate

$$\hat{\Sigma}_{RDA} = \hat{\Sigma} + \lambda \mathbf{I}, \tag{2.37}$$

where λ is a positive regularisation constant.

The use of representation (2.32) indicates that $\hat{\Sigma} + \lambda\mathbf{I} = \mathbf{\Phi}(\Lambda + \lambda\mathbf{I})\mathbf{\Phi}^T$. Now, it is easier to invert the matrix $\hat{\Sigma}_{RDA}$: we add positive constants λ to all eigenvalues of the matrix $\hat{\Sigma}$. The new matrix $\hat{\Sigma} + \lambda\mathbf{I}$ becomes positive defined. Inserting (2.37) into Equation (1.3) gives

$$V^{RDA} = (\hat{\Sigma} + \lambda\mathbf{I})^{-1}(\hat{M}_1 - \hat{M}_2) \text{ and } v_0 = -\tfrac{1}{2}(\hat{M}_1 + \hat{M}_2)^T V^{RDA}. \tag{2.38a}$$

If the prior probabilities of the classes are equal among themselves, we perform the classification according to the sign of the discriminant function. For further analysis and for practical applications it is convenient to rewrite Equation (2.38*a*) in a following way

$$V^{RDA} = k_\lambda ((1-\lambda_1)\hat{\Sigma} + \lambda_1\mathbf{I})^{-1}(\hat{M}_1 - \hat{M}_2), \tag{2.38b}$$

where $0 \leq \lambda_1 = \lambda/(1+\lambda) \leq 1$, and $k_\lambda = 1/(1+\lambda)$ can be ignored in classification according the sign of the discriminant function.

Representation (2.38*a*) shows that, when $\lambda_1 = 0$, we have the standard Fisher linear DF and, when $\lambda_1 = 1$, we have the Euclidean distance classifier. This classification method is known as a **regularized linear discriminant analysis** (RDA). The parameter λ controls a similarity of RDA to EDC and to the Fisher linear DF. The following modification of the linear RDA is used to design the linear classifier when the covariance matrices are different

$$V^{RDA*} = (\gamma(1-\lambda_1)\hat{\Sigma}_1 + (1-\gamma)(1-\lambda_1)\hat{\Sigma}_2 + \lambda_1\mathbf{I})^{-1}(\hat{M}_1 - \hat{M}_2), \tag{2.39}$$

where we have two regularisation parameters, λ_1 and γ.

The weight vector (2.39) resembles that of the Anderson-Bahadur procedure (Equation (2.13)). Some authors claim it to be the most powerful classification method among other parametric linear statistical classifiers. Here, the optimal values of two parameters, λ_1 and γ, should be determined in order to obtain the best generalisation. The optimal values of λ_1 and γ depend on the training-set size. It is important to know that the optimal values fluctuate with each random training-set.

The configuration of the real multivariate data is usually unknown to the designer. There is a small chance that optimal values of λ_1 and γ can be determined theoretically. It is recommended that one uses a cross-validation error rate estimation method to find the optimal values.

2.5.3 Scaled Rotation Regularisation

One more generalisation of the linear RDA is a scaled rotation (SR). In addition to the regularisation of the eigenvalues Λ in the singular value decomposition $\hat{\Sigma} = \Phi\Lambda\Phi^T$, here we regularise the orthogonal $n\times n$ eigenvectors matrix $\mathbf{\Phi}$ and estimate the covariance matrix as $\hat{\Sigma}_{SR} = \mathbf{\Phi}^{\alpha}(\Lambda + \lambda\mathbf{I})(\mathbf{\Phi}^{\alpha})^T$. The parameter α, a real valued variable, controls the degree of rotation determined by matrix $\mathbf{\Phi}^{\alpha}$ from the identity matrix $\mathbf{I}$ (when $\alpha=0$) to the eigenvectors matrix $\mathbf{\Phi}$ (when $\alpha=1$) and beyond (when $\alpha>1$). The regularisation is performed by means of two parameters, α and λ. This technique is especially effective when used with a linear data transformation, $X_{new} = \Lambda^{-1/2}\mathbf{\Phi}^T X$, performed prior to the training of the non-linear single layer perceptron (see Chapter 5).

2.5.4 Non-Gaussian Densities

The multivariate Gaussian density is the simplest statistical model for multivariate vectors with continuous components. A more general family of the distributions is

$$f_i(X) = k_e \Psi(X)\, J\{H(X,\ \mathbf{m}_i,\ \mathbf{K}_i)\}, \tag{2.40}$$

where $\mathbf{m}_i$ is a n-variate vector, $H(X, \mathbf{m}_i, \mathbf{K}_i)$ is a distance measure between the two vectors, X and $\mathbf{m}_i$, in a space transformed by matrix $\mathbf{K}_i$, $\Psi(X)$ is an arbitrary *scalar function* of X, $J\{\cdot\}$ is an arbitrary monotone decreasing uni-variate function and k_e is a normalising constant.

One of the possible metrics is $H(X, \mathbf{K}_i, \mathbf{m}_i) = (X - \mathbf{m}_i)^T\mathbf{K}_i^{-1}(X - \mathbf{m}_i)$. The function $\Psi(X)$ does not depend on the class index. Thus, using (2.40) in (2.6) results in a *quadratic* discriminant function. If matrix $\mathbf{K}_i$ does not depend on the class index i, then we have the *linear* classifier. A method of obtaining maximum likelihood estimates of the resulting discriminant function was proposed by Day and Kerridge (1967). For linear classification we have to maximise the product

$$L = \prod_{i=1}^{2}\prod_{j=1}^{N_i} \frac{[\exp(V^T X_j^{(i)} + v_0)]^{2-i}}{1 + \exp(V^T X_j^{(i)} + v_0)} \tag{2.41}$$

with respect to the weights V, v_0. Note that the same result can be obtained without any assumptions on the type of the distribution density functions of the pattern classes. In the probabilistic interpretation, a ratio

$$\frac{\exp(V^T X_j^{(i)} + v_0)}{1 + \exp(V^T X_j^{(i)} + v_0)}$$

expresses *a posteriori* probability that vector $X_j^{(i)}$ belongs to class ω_i. Like the sum (1.7), the product L is in fact a cost function to be minimised. In discriminant analysis literature, this decision-making procedure is known as a **logistic regression.** It has received considerable attention in solving medical diagnostic problems where it is important to estimate *a posteriori* probabilities that the observation vector X belongs to a certain pattern class.

Note that in the probabilistic model (2.40), the vector $\mathbf{m}_i$ is not the mean vector and the matrix $\mathbf{K}_i$ is not the covariance matrix. The model (2.40) is more general than the model of multivariate Gaussian distribution (2.9). This model contains a favourable peculiarity, having weaker assumptions on the class conditional densities. The weaker assumptions, however, require more training vectors to estimate the density and to design the classification rule. This is the unfavourable characteristic of the model.

Resemblance between the product L and the cost function utilised in the single layer perceptron training (see Equation (1.7) and Chapter 4) indicates that the logistic regression can be analysed as one of the modifications of the artificial neural networks.

2.5.5 Robust Discriminant Analysis

In many applications, we have data contaminated by "noise", i.e. the measurement vectors have many atypical observations, called *outliers*. In this case, the maximum likelihood estimates derived for the Gaussian data become ineffective. There is a branch of statistics which deals with such data and derives the parameter estimates that are robust to atypical observations: *robust statistics*. Most popular are Huber M-estimates. As an example, we present an iterative procedure to obtain a robust estimate of the mean vector M and the covariance matrix Σ.

To obtain robust estimates $\hat{M}_M$ and $\hat{\Sigma}_M$ (here we omit the index of class i), one first computes conventional sample maximum-likelihood estimates $\hat{M}$ and $\hat{\Sigma}$. Then, these estimates are used to compute initial distances H_j of each training vector X_j to a centre $\hat{M}$ of the training-set $H_j = (\mathbf{X}_j - \hat{M})^T \hat{\Sigma}_M^{-1} (\mathbf{X}_j - \hat{M})$. In the end, one replaces sample estimates by the following weighted estimates

$$\hat{M}_M = \frac{1}{N} \sum_{j=1}^{N} X_j w_j \,/\, \sum_{j=1}^{N} w_j,$$

$$\hat{\Sigma}_M = \frac{1}{N-1} \sum_{j=1}^{N} (X_j - \hat{M}_M)(X_j - \hat{M}_M)^T w_j^2 \,/\, \sum_{j=1}^{N} w_j^2,$$

where w_j is a weight (an "importance") of the observation vector X_j, e.g.

$$w_j = \begin{cases} 2/H_j & \text{if} \quad H_j > 2 \\ 1 & \text{if} \quad H_j \le 2. \end{cases}$$

In the second iteration, one uses the previously obtained estimates $\hat{\boldsymbol{M}}_M$ and $\hat{\Sigma}_M$ to find new values for H_j, and then again finds new estimates $\hat{\boldsymbol{M}}_M$ and $\hat{\Sigma}_M$. The iterative procedure is repeated several times and the influence of the distant atypical training vectors is diminished. It is suggested that the robust estimates $\hat{\boldsymbol{M}}_M$ and $\hat{\Sigma}_M$ can be used in the plug-in sample linear and quadratic discriminant functions.

One more way to get the robust discriminant function is obtained from a generalisation of the Fisher criterion (2.12). The generalisation of the Fisher criterion (2.12) can be written in following way:

$$T_{gen} = \frac{1}{N_1 + N_2} \sum_{i=1}^{2} \sum_{j=1}^{N_i} \varphi\left(\alpha \frac{t_j^i - \boldsymbol{V}^T \boldsymbol{X}_j^{(i)} - v_0}{\sqrt{\boldsymbol{V}^T \mathbf{S}^{-1} \boldsymbol{V}}}\right), \tag{2.42}$$

where $t_j^{(i)}$ is the class index of the training pattern vector $\boldsymbol{X}_j^{(i)}$: $t_j^{(1)} = +1$, $t_j^{(2)} = -1$, $\varphi(c)$ is a non-decreasing odd and non-constant function, e.g. $\varphi(c) = (-1)^{i+1} \tanh(c)$ (c is a positive constant). Parameter α controls a robustness and should be found in trial and error.

Fisher used the linear function $\varphi(c) = c$. The utilisation of the non-linear function $\varphi(c)$ generalises the Fisher criterion. It has an essential similarity with the adaptive SLP design discussed in Chapter 1. Due to saturation of the non-linear function $\varphi(c)$, the solution becomes more robust to outliers than the standard Fisher discriminant. For numerical optimisation of the above criterion, the function $\varphi(c)$ should be smooth and differentiable. It should be similar to the soft-limiting activation function (1.8) used in the ANN design.

2.6 Nonparametric Local Statistical Classifiers

The assumptions on the structure class conditional densities considered in the previous sections are based on the global structure of multivariate density functions. A large group of statistical pattern classification algorithms is founded on the utilisation of nonparametric estimates of the multivariate density functions. Here, no assumptions about the global structure of the populations are made. This group of density estimation methods allow us to consider complex multimodal distributions.

2.6.1 Methods Based on Mixtures of Densities

If we are confronted with multimodal densities, it is reasonable to assume that each class consists of several subclasses. The density function can be written as a sum

$$p_i(X) = \sum_{j=1}^{m_i} P_{ij}\, p(X \mid \mathbf{Y}_{ij}), \tag{2.43}$$

where m_i is a number of subclasses in the population (class) ω_i, P_{ij} is the *a priori* probability of the jth subclass from ω_i ($j = 1, \ldots, m_i$; $\sum_{j=1}^{m_i} P_{ij} = 1$), $p(X \mid \mathbf{Y}_{ij})$ is a probability density function of the j-th subclass, and $\mathbf{Y}_{ij}$ is a vector of parameters of the ij-th component (subclass) of the mixture.

Representation (2.43) allows one to approximate complex unimodal and multimodal distribution density functions that can be found in practical pattern recognition problems. An illustration of two univariate densities, $f_1(x)$ and $f_2(x)$, with $m_1=3$ and $m_1=2$ is presented in Figure 2.3.

In the two pattern classes case, the discriminant function (DF) obtained from representation (2.43) has the following form

$$h(X) = P_1 \sum_{j=1}^{m_1} P_{1j}\, p_1(X \mid \mathbf{Y}_{1j}) - P_2 \sum_{j=1}^{m_2} P_{2j}\, p_2(X \mid \mathbf{Y}_{2j}). \tag{2.44}$$

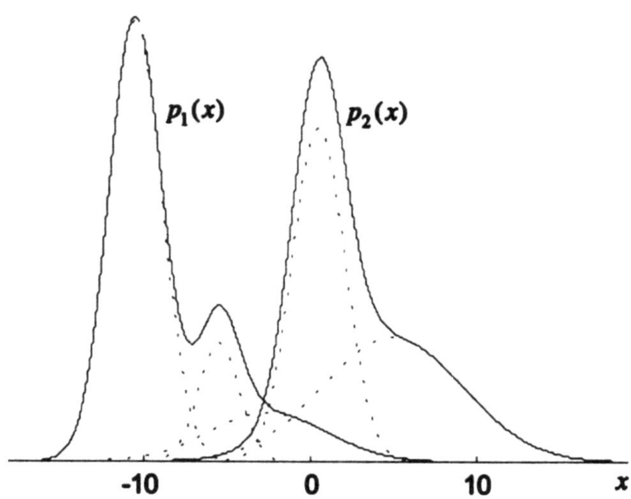

Fig. 2.3. Two multimodal uni-variate density functions represented by the mixture model: $p_1(x)$ is composed of three components and $p_2(x)$ of two.

In principle, considering representation (2.43), one can use any known parametric density function, e.g. the general multivariate density (2.40). Equation (2.43), however, requires a great number of parameters to be estimated. Therefore, in the literature, only analysis of simple cases with a small number of parameters can be found, i.e. Gaussian densities with the identity or the diagonal covariance matrices:

$$h(X) = \sum_{i=1}^{2} (-1)^{i+1} P_i \sum_{j=1}^{m_i} P_{ij}\, (2\pi)^{-n/2}\, e^{-1/2(X-C_{ij})^T D^{-1}(X-C_{ij})}, \tag{2.45}$$

where C_{ij} is a "centre", the mean vector of the j-th subclass of the class ω_i, and D is a diagonal matrix. In a simplified model, $D = I\sigma^2$.

There exist methods that use the training vectors in order to estimate unknown parameters of the mixture density. A typical example is the maximum likelihood method. An alternative is to use cluster analysis techniques, which are much faster.

The mixture model (2.43) and the discriminant function (2.44) constitute a basic model for a special type of artificial neural networks, known as radial basis functions (RBF). In the RBF approach, the statistical parameters of the mixtures Y_{1j}, Y_{2j} serve as initial values of the weights in the iterative ANN training. Typically, the cost function of the sum of the squares is used in order to estimate the network weights by means of the adaptive training process.

2.6.2 Piecewise-Linear Classifiers

A significant simplification of the calculation process during the recognition phase follows if, instead of the sum in (2.44), one analyses each of the m_i components separately as an independent new subclass. Then a piecewise-linear discriminant function can be constructed:

$$h(X) = \min_j \{ (X - C_{2j})^T D^{-1}(X - C_{2j})\} - \min_j \{ (X - C_{1j})^T D^{-1}(X - C_{1j}) \} =$$

$$\min_j \{-2 X^T D^{-1} C_{2j} + (C_{2j})^T C_{2j}\} - \min_j \{-2 X^T D^{-1} C_{1j} + (C_{1j})^T C_{1j}\}. \quad (2.46)$$

A decision making scheme which performs the above calculations is depicted below.

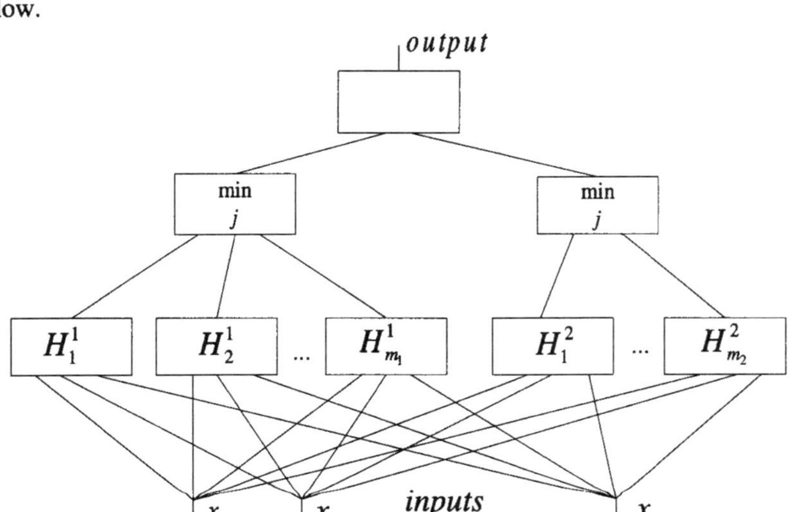

Fig. 2.4. A version of the piecewise-linear classifier designed for a mixture of spherical densities.

In the ANN literature, this kind of decision-making scheme and the discriminant function (2.46) are known as the learning vector quantisation (LVQ) network. In addition to the cluster analysis and the mixture decomposition methods, statistical analysis is traditionally used to evaluate the centres $\mathbf{C}_{ij}$. In the ANN approach, these parameters are used for initialisation of the network.

2.6.3 The Parzen Window Classifier

The mixture statistical model contains a structurisation of the multivariate densities only in local areas of the multivariate feature space, Ω. In some applications, we have no information on either the global structure or the local structure of the multivariate densities. However, we can assume:

1) the objects of one class are similar among themselves, i.e. distances between the vectors $\boldsymbol{C}_{i1}, \boldsymbol{C}_{i2}, \ldots, \boldsymbol{C}_{ir}$ and $\boldsymbol{X}_s^{(i)}$ can be small;

2) each physical measurement $\boldsymbol{X}_j^{(i)}$ (j-th training vector from the class ω_i) is performed with some error, i.e.

$$\boldsymbol{X}_j^{(i)} = \boldsymbol{X}_{0j}^{(i)} + \xi_j^{(i)}, \tag{2.47}$$

where $\xi_j^{(i)}$ is a measurement error (noise) vector: e.g., $\xi_j^{(i)} \sim N_X(\mathbf{0}, \boldsymbol{D}\lambda)$, and $\boldsymbol{X}_{0j}^{(i)}$ is a measured value of the n-variate feature vector. In principle, it might be obtained only in a case when the physical measurements are performed exactly (without errors).

The above two assumptions are not very restrictive. They impose that, in a small distance from each training vector, an other observation from the same pattern class can be found. Essentially, it is *additional prior information*. This information can be profitable if used inventively.

Assume now that to each training vector $\boldsymbol{X}_j^{(i)}$, we add an infinite number of new random vectors $\boldsymbol{Z}_1$, $\boldsymbol{Z}_2$, $\boldsymbol{Z}_3$, ... having Gaussian distribution with zero mean and the diagonal covariance matrix $\boldsymbol{D}\lambda$:

$$p(\boldsymbol{Z}) = N_z(\mathbf{0}, \boldsymbol{D}\lambda),$$

Resulting density estimates of the new vectors $\boldsymbol{X}_{sj}^{(i)} = \boldsymbol{X}_j^{(i)} + \boldsymbol{Z}_s$ can be analysed by superposition of N_i random vectors. The probability density function of a set of "noisy" vectors can be represented as

$$\hat{p}_i(\boldsymbol{X}) = \frac{1}{N_i} \sum_{j=1}^{N_i} N_X(\boldsymbol{X}_j^{(i)}, \boldsymbol{D}\lambda). \tag{2.48}$$

In the statistical literature, this estimate of the probability density function is known as a nonparametric Parzen window (PW) estimate. Use of (2.48) in (2.5), the equation for the optimal Bayes classifier, results in the following plug-in discriminant function

$$h^{PW}(X) = P_1 \hat{p}_1(X) - P_2 \hat{p}_2(X) =$$

$$\frac{P_1}{N_1} \sum_{j=1}^{N_1} N_X(X_j^{(1)}, D\lambda) - \frac{P_2}{N_2} \sum_{j=1}^{N_2} N_X(X_j^{(2)}, D\lambda). \qquad (2.49)$$

In many practical applications reported in the literature, the PW classifier appears to be one of the best classifiers and often outperforms the ANN. To illustrate the Parzen window approach, we depict the non-parametric PW estimates of the univariate densities of the two pattern classes in Figure 2.5.

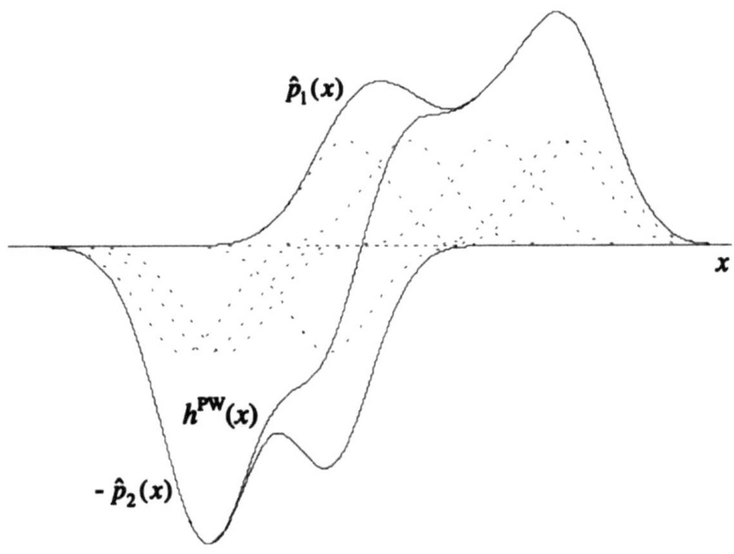

Fig. 2.5. The nonparametric Parzen window estimates of PDF of the two pattern classes and their difference – the value of the discriminant function.

A comparison of (2.49) with (2.45) shows that the two equations differ:

- in the number of elements to be summed (N_i versus m_i);
- in definition of the weighting coefficients ($1/N_i$ versus P_{ij}); and
- in the centres of Gaussian densities ($X_j^{(i)}$ versus $C_j^{(i)}$).

This means that the density estimators in (2.48) are in fact the mixture estimators when the centres of the subclasses are all vectors of the training-set. A generalisation of the Parzen window estimate with the Gaussian kernels (2.48) is:

$$\hat{p}_i(X) = \frac{1}{N_i} \sum_{j=1}^{N_i} \kappa \{H(X, X_j^{(i)})\}, \tag{2.50}$$

where $H(X, X_j^{(i)})$ is a distance between vectors X and $X_j^{(i)}$; for continuous variables usually $H(X, X_j^{(i)}) = (X - X_j^{(i)})^T \mathrm{A}_i (X - X_j^{(i)})$ and A_i is an $n \times n$ positive definite symmetric matrix, $\kappa(H)$ is an arbitrary monotonic decreasing function of argument H called a *kernel* or a *smoothing function*. It can be a bell-shaped function like the Gaussian function in Equation (2.48), a logistic function

$$\kappa\{H(X, X_j^{(i)})\} = \frac{\lambda}{H(X, X_j^{(i)}) + \lambda}$$

uniform, trapezoidal, etc. In principle, it can even be asymmetric. In the case of continuous variables, the matrix A can be the full (not constrained) covariance matrix, the diagonal matrix, $\mathrm{A} = D\lambda$, or an identity matrix, $\mathrm{A} = \mathbf{I}\lambda$ (Euclidean distance). In principle, the matrix A can be common or different for both classes. It can be dependent on each training vector, $X_j^{(i)}$, too.

The parameter λ is called a *smoothing parameter*. When λ is small, then we have weak smoothing. When λ is large, the smoothing is significant and "fulfils an empty space between the multivariate training vectors".

Peculiarities of the decision boundary. Very often the spherical Gaussian kernel $\kappa\{H(X, X_j^{(i)})\} = c_{PW} \exp(-H(X, X_j^{(i)})/\lambda)$ with $\mathrm{A} = \mathbf{I}\lambda$ and normalising constant c_{PW} is used. By using the first two terms of Taylor series expansion, $\exp(H) = 1 + H/1! + H^2/2! + \ldots$, it is easy to show that when λ is very large, function (2.49) leads to

$$h^{PW}(X) \rightarrow \frac{c_{PW}}{\lambda}\left[\frac{P_2}{N_2}\sum_{j=1}^{N_2}(X - \hat{M}_2)^T(X - \hat{M}_2) - \frac{P_1}{N_1}\sum_{j=1}^{N_1}(X - \hat{M}_1)^T(X - \hat{M}_1)\right].$$

Let $N_2 = N_1 = \overline{N}$ and $P_2 = P_1$. Then we have a linear discriminant function with weight vector $V^{PW} \equiv V^{E}$:

$$h^{PW}(X) \rightarrow \frac{c_{PW}}{\lambda^2}\left[X^T V^{(E)} - \frac{1}{2}(\hat{M}_1 + \hat{M}_2)^T V^{(E)} + \frac{1}{2}(1 - \frac{1}{\overline{N}})(\mathrm{tr}\,(\hat{\Sigma}_2 - \hat{\Sigma}_1))\right],$$

as $\lambda \rightarrow \infty$. (2.51)

Comparison of (2.51) with the weight vector of EDC (1.2) indicates that only the threshold value v_0 is different from that of the Euclidean distance classifier, i.e. the decision boundary is parallel to the discriminant hyperplane of the EDC. A distance between the two hyperplanes depends on a difference of traces (tr) of two sample covariance matrices, $\hat{\Sigma}_1$ and $\hat{\Sigma}_2$. Thus, this distance is a random variable which varies with each new training-set.

A contribution of each single training vector $X_j^{(i)}$ to the value of DF (2.49) depends on distance $H(X, X_j^{(i)})$. While using the Gaussian kernel $\exp(-H(X, X_j^{(i)})/\lambda)$, the contribution of vector $X_j^{(i)}$ diminishes exponentially with $H(X, X_j^{(i)})/\lambda$. Therefore, for very small λ, we have one nearest neighbour rule.

Example 4. In Figure 2.6, we plot a scatter diagram of $N = 100$ bi-variate vectors of two non-overlapping pattern classes. An algorithm that generates the classes is presented in subsection 2.8.3 (see Figure 2.12*a*). The straight line (1), in Figure 2.6, corresponds to the decision boundary of the Euclidean distance classifier. The straight line (2) is the decision boundary of the Parzen window classifier with Gaussian kernel and great smoothing ($\lambda = 1000$). It is parallel to line (1). For $\lambda = 2$, we have a smooth non-linear decision boundary (curve 3) and for $\lambda = 0.001$ the decision boundary is close to that of the 1-*NN* (one nearest neighbour) rule: we see the decision boundary is placed approximately in the middle of the closest training vectors of opposite classes.

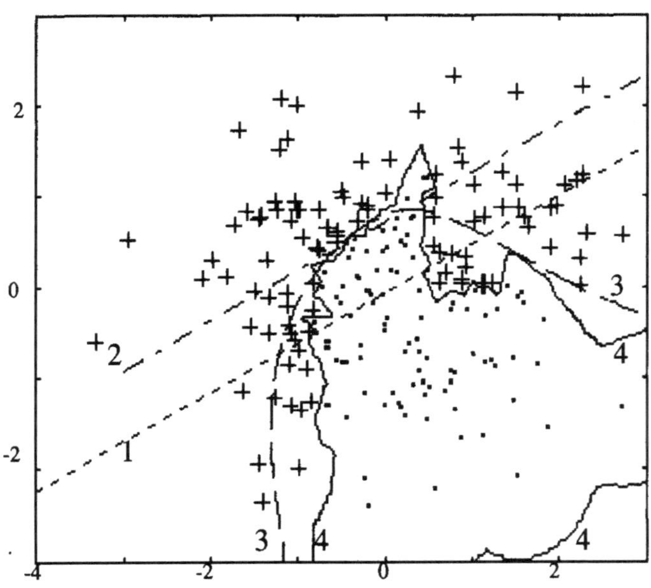

Fig. 2.6. Effect of the smoothing parameter λ on a complexity of the PW classifier: 1 is the decision boundary of the EDC; 2 is PW with $\lambda = 1000$; 3 is $\lambda = 2$; and 4 is $\lambda = 0.001$.

We see that the classification rule and complexity of the nonparametric Parzen window estimator depends severely on the value of the smoothing parameter λ. For large values of λ, we have a simple decision boundary and for small values of λ, we have a complex one. One of the main problems while designing a classifier which uses the Parzen window approach, is to choose the proper complexity of the classifier, i.e. the value of the smoothing parameter λ.

In other variants of the Parzen window classifier, a value of the parameter λ can be constant in the entire multivariate feature space Ω or may vary in it. The parameter λ can be determined *a priori*, or it can be found from the information contained in the training-set.

2.6.4 The *k-NN* Rule and a Calculation Speed

Suppose now, that in an n-dimensional sphere, S_r, the output of the kernel function $\kappa(\alpha)$ is a constant value and, outside the sphere, it equals zero. In other words, we suppose that the "measurement noise" is uniformly distributed in an n-dimensional sphere in the n-variate feature space Ω. Let a radius of this sphere vary in Ω, so that exactly k training vectors are contained in the sphere. Then $\hat{p}_1(X) / \hat{p}_2(X)$, a ratio of the two PDF estimates at the fixed point X of the space, becomes proportional to the ratio of n_1, a number of the first class training vectors in the sphere, against n_2, a number of the second class training vectors in this sphere. Thus, allocation of an unknown vector X to one of the classes should be accomplished according to class membership of the majority of training vectors in the sphere containing exactly k vectors. Such a classification rule is called a *k-nearest neighbour rule* and its shorthand definition is the *k-NN* rule.

The parameter, k, is very important: it determines the complexity of the classifier i.e. the amount of smoothing in the estimation of the multivariate density functions. Determination of an optimal number of neighbours is a very weighty problem while designing the *k-NN* classifier. When $k=1$, we have a simple nearest neighbour classifier.

The *k-NN* rules can differ in k i.e. the number of nearest neighbours. Different modifications of this classifier use different types of metrics in which the distances between the vector X and its neighbours from the training-set are measured. When training-set vectors that are classified incorrectly by the *k-NN* rule are deleted from the set, an increase in the performance of the new rule has sometimes been noticed. Various heuristics to delete "unnecessary" training observations exist. In order to reduce the number of calculations necessary to make classifications, some authors propose using only typical training vectors from each pattern class. Other authors propose excluding training vectors that are far from a decision boundary. Similar ideas are also used in the ANN design.

The *k-NN* classifier requires the calculation of distances between X, the vector to be classified, and all $N = N_1 + N_2$ training vectors. Therefore, it is slow in the classification phase. Several special calculation schemes for a fast search for the nearest neighbours have been proposed in the literature. The ideas for reducing the classification time of the *k-NN* classifier can also be used for the PW classifier.

One of the possibilities for reducing the calculation time required to make the classification is to use *multivariate histograms*. The main idea of designing the multivariate histograms is to split the multivariate space Ω into "hyper-rectangular" spaces, i.e. cells $\Omega_1, \Omega_2, \ldots, \Omega_m$, and for each class to calculate the numbers of training observations that fall in each cell. An allocation of an unknown object is performed according to class membership of the majority of training vectors of one class in the cell that contains the object to be classified. The simplest way to design the multivariate histogram classifier is to determine one or several threshold values for each variable and to remember the number of training vectors in each cell. Then the class indexes $\gamma_1, \gamma_1, \ldots, \gamma_m$, should be determined for all m cells. Such a classifier is in fact a classifier for categorical variables. We analyse this category of classification methods in Section 2.9.

We emphasise once more that the nonparametric PW and the *k-NN* classifiers are closely related among themselves, to the radial basic function and to the learning vector quantisation classifiers used in modern ANN technology.

2.6.5 Polynomial and Potential Function Classifiers

In order to reduce the classification time of the PW classifier, we can use different expansions of the kernel function. These expansions lead to *polynomial* and *potential function classifiers* where we do not need to store all of the training vectors in the computer memory at one time.

In the **polynomial classifiers**, we utilise the Taylor series expansion of the kernel function. For the kernel $\kappa\{H(\boldsymbol{X}, \boldsymbol{X}_j^{(i)})\} = c_{PW} \exp(-H(\boldsymbol{X}, \boldsymbol{X}_j^{(i)})/\lambda)$ with the Euclidean metric $H(\boldsymbol{X}, \boldsymbol{X}_j^{(i)}) = (\boldsymbol{X} - \boldsymbol{X}_j^{(i)})^T (\boldsymbol{X} - \boldsymbol{X}_j^{(i)})$, we can write

$$\hat{p}_i(\boldsymbol{X}) = \frac{c_{PW}}{N_i} \sum_{j=1}^{N_i} \exp\{(-\frac{1}{2}(\boldsymbol{X} - \boldsymbol{X}_j^{(i)})^T (\boldsymbol{X} - \boldsymbol{X}_j^{(i)})/\lambda)\} =$$

$$\frac{c_{PW}}{N_i} \exp\{-\frac{1}{2}\boldsymbol{X}^T\boldsymbol{X}/\lambda\} \sum_{j=1}^{N_i} \exp\{-\frac{1}{2}\boldsymbol{X}_j^{(i)T}\boldsymbol{X}_j^{(i)}/\lambda\} \exp\{\boldsymbol{X}^T\boldsymbol{X}_j^{(i)}/\lambda\}.$$

Having applied the Taylor series expansion $\exp\{c\} = 1 + c + c^2/2 + \ldots$ for the last term of the above representation, we obtain

$$\hat{p}_i(\boldsymbol{X}) = \frac{c_{PW}}{N_i} \exp\{-\frac{1}{2}\boldsymbol{X}^T\boldsymbol{X}/\lambda)\} \{1 + \frac{1}{\lambda}\mathbf{A}^T\boldsymbol{X} + \frac{1}{\lambda^2}\boldsymbol{X}^T\mathbf{B}\boldsymbol{X} + \ldots\}, \quad (2.52)$$

where vector column **A** and matrix **B** are certain functions of the training vectors and do not depend on $\boldsymbol{X}$, the vector to be classified.

A complexity of the decision boundary depends on a number of terms utilised in the expansion. From the other side, representation (2.52) can be used only when values $\boldsymbol{X}^T\boldsymbol{X}/\lambda$ are small, i.e., for large λ.

In the **potential functions** approach, we utilise following expansion

$$\kappa\{H(\boldsymbol{X}, \boldsymbol{X}_j^{(i)})\} = \sum_{s=1}^{r} a_s(\boldsymbol{X}_j^{(i)}) b_s(\boldsymbol{X}), \quad (2.53)$$

where $a_s(\boldsymbol{X}_j^{(i)})$ and $b_s(\boldsymbol{X})$, $(s = 1, 2, \ldots, r)$ are *a priori* selected sets of functions.

Then

$$\hat{p}_i(X) = \sum_{s=1}^{r} v_{is} b_s(X).$$

In a case where the representation (2.53) is exact, $v_{is} = \frac{1}{N_i} \sum_{j=1}^{N_i} a_s(X_j^{(i)})$.

In a case where the representation (2.53) is approximate, we can find unknown coefficients $v_{i1}, v_{i1}, \ldots, v_{ir}$ by minimising a leaving-one-out approximation error

$$\frac{1}{N_i} \sum_{l=1}^{N_i} \left(\sum_{s=1}^{r} v_{is} b_s(X_l^{(i)}) - \frac{1}{N_i - 1} \sum_{j=1\, j \neq l}^{N_i} \kappa \{H(X_l^{(i)}, X_j^{(i)})\}\right)^2.$$

The potential function approach is in fact the mapping of the input vectors X into the new r-variate space by means of an *a priori* selected set of functions. Therefore, minimisation of the above sum of squares error leads to a linear discriminant function in the new feature space. Therefore, in this classifier only new sample means and sample covariance matrices are utilised to find the coefficients of the decision rule. The artificial neural networks and the support vector approaches can give one many ideas and can lead to new algorithms which can improve solutions.

2.7 Minimum Empirical Error and Maximal Margin Linear Classifiers

Often an objective of the classifier design is to obtain a rule which minimises the probability of misclassification. For known class conditional densities, the representation (2.6) can be used to obtain the classifier with the minimal probability of misclassification. The type of the classifier depends on the assumptions about the conditional densities.

In some cases, special efforts should be made in order to obtain a simple linear classifier instead of a more complex non-linear decision rule that minimises the probability of classification. As an example, we have mentioned the Anderson–Bahadur linear DF (2.13). In the multivariate Gaussian case, this rule is asymptotically the best one among all linear classifiers.

2.7.1 The Minimum Empirical Error Classifier

In practice, the class conditional densities are unknown, however, the designer has only the training-set available. Thus, the designer should like to obtain the classifier with the minimum number of errors while classifying the training vectors. We call such types of the classification rule the minimum empirical error (MEE) classifier. To design the MEE classifier, one needs to introduce a sample based cost function and to minimise it. One of the possible cost functions which characterises the number of misclassifications among the training-set vectors is

$$Cost = \frac{1}{N_1 + N_2} \sum_{i=1}^{2} \sum_{j=1}^{N_i} \varphi\,(t_j^{(i)} - V^T X_j^{(1)} - v_0), \tag{2.54}$$

where $t_j^{(i)}$ is the class index of the training pattern vector $X_j^{(i)}$, $t_j^{(1)} = +1$, $t_j^{(i)} = -1$, and $\varphi(\varepsilon)$ is a threshold function, e.g.

$$\varphi(\varepsilon) = \begin{cases} 1 \ \text{if}\ V^T X_j^{(1)} + v_0 < 0 \ \text{ or } \ V^T X_j^{(2)} + v_0 > 0 \\ 0 \ \text{if}\ V^T X_j^{(1)} + v_0 > 0 \ \text{ or } \ V^T X_j^{(2)} + v_0 < 0 \end{cases} \tag{2.55}$$

The threshold function is not continuous. Therefore, it impossible to minimise the cost function (2.54) with (2.55) using ordinary numerical methods. To minimise the empirical error, instead of minimising (2.54) with (2.55), Do-Tu and Installe (1978) proposed using a smooth analogue of the threshold function

$$\varphi(\varepsilon,\sigma) = (-1)^{i-1} \int_{-\infty}^{\varepsilon} h(\sigma, t)dt\,, \ \text{with} \quad 0 \le h(\sigma, t) \le 1\,, \tag{2.56}$$

where $h(\sigma, t)$ is a window function, e.g., a zero mean Gaussian density with variance σ^2.

The minimisation of the cost (2.54) with (2.56) can be performed in an iterative way. The parameter σ is decreasing during the training process. Then, with an increase in the number of iterations, the function $\varphi(\varepsilon,\sigma)$ gradually approaches the threshold function (2.55) and the cost function (2.54) eventually minimises the empirical error more and more precisely. In Chapter 4, we will show that in the non-linear SLP training, we can obtain a similar effect automatically.

A number of other authors have tried to find the coefficients of the linear discriminant function that minimised the empirical classification error. Their algorithms are based on the use of a sequential random search procedure, the Kiefer–Wolfowitz stochastic approximation, linear programming, the algebraic method, linear transformations of the co-ordinate system, and a number of other bright heuristic ideas. Ad hoc principles are used to overcome numerical difficulties. Thus, in one of their algorithms, Vapnik and Chervonenkis (1974), after applying a conventional algorithm to find the weights of the linear discriminant function, sequentially excluded training pattern vectors that were at the farthest distances from a current discrimination boundary $V^T X + v_0 = 0$ and were classified incorrectly. At the end, one obtains the classifier that minimises the empirical error approximately.

2.7.2 The Maximal Margin Classifier

When the number of empirical errors is zero, the resulting discriminant function is not unique. Numerous hyperplanes can classify the training vectors without error.

Some additional criteria should be introduced in order to obtain a unique solution. Typically, a minimal distance between the discriminant hyperplane and the training set vectors is maximised. In order to find the optimal weight vector $\boldsymbol{V}$ in their "generalised portrait" linear classification method, Vapnik and Chervonenkis (1974) suggested minimising the quadratic form

$$\boldsymbol{V}^T\boldsymbol{V} \tag{2.57}$$

under the constraints $\boldsymbol{V}^T\boldsymbol{X}_j^{(1)} \geq \Delta$ and $\boldsymbol{V}^T\boldsymbol{X}_j^{(2)} < -\Delta$, ($j = 1,2, \ldots, N_i$; $i = 1,2$). Δ is a positive constant, a bound for the margin.

In reaching a unique solution, they used the quadratic optimisation techniques. This classification algorithm is called a *maximal margin classifier*. There are a fixed number of training vectors equally distant from the discriminating hyperplane. These vectors are called *support vectors* and a fixed set of the support vectors determines a position of this hyperplane (Figure 2.7).

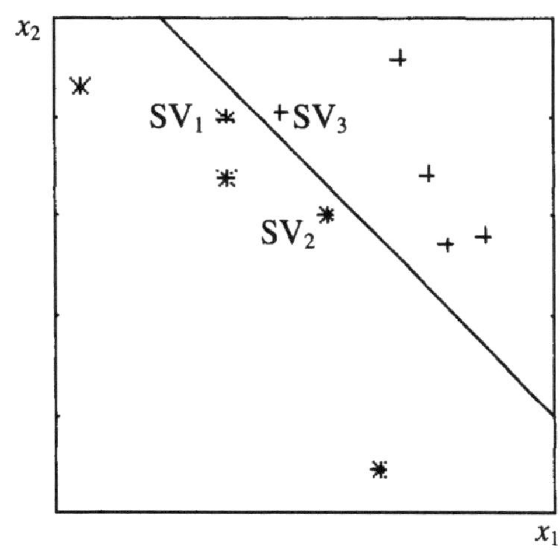

Fig. 2.7. Ten bi-variate training vectors. Only three of them (support vectors SV_1, SV_2 and SV_3) determine the position of the optimal (maximum margin) decision boundary (the dotted line).

2.7.3 The Support Vector Machine

A generalisation of the maximal margin classifier is a support vector (SV) machine that implements the following idea: it maps the input vectors $\boldsymbol{X}$ into a high dimensional feature space through non-linear mapping via a chosen *a priori*. In this space, the maximal margin separating hyperplane is constructed. To map the input vectors $\boldsymbol{X}$ into the high dimensional feature space, one can use polynomial functions, radial basic functions, outputs of the hidden layer of the multilayer perceptrons, etc.

Example 5. In Figure 2.8*a*, we depict a distribution of 15 + 15 bi-variate training vectors from two artificially generated pattern classes and the decision boundary of the SV machine designed in a five-variate space of the features $y_1 = x_1$, $y_2 = x_2$, $y_3 = x_1^2$, $y_4 = x_2^2$, $y_5 = x_1 x_2$. The two-stage decision-making scheme is presented in Figure 2.8*b*. Here the first stage maps bi-variate input vectors $\boldsymbol{X}$ into the five-dimensional feature space through the five polynomial functions. In the second stage, the linear maximal margin classifier is realised.

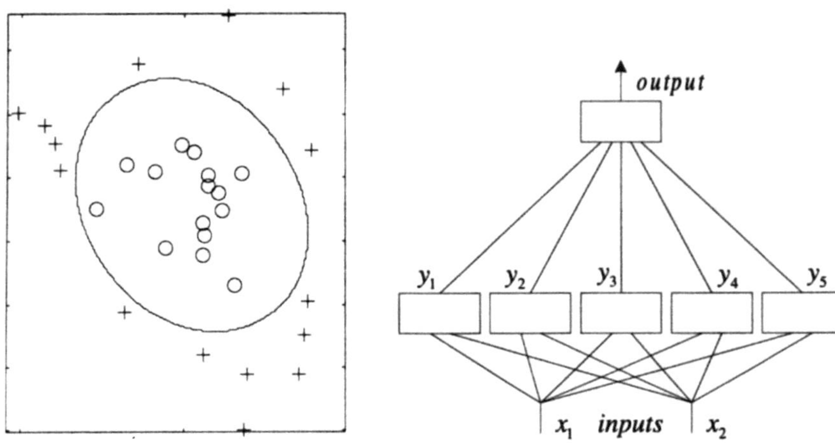

Fig. 2.8. A distribution of 15 + 15 bi-variate training vectors from two artificially generated pattern classes and the decision boundary of the support vector machine designed in five-variate space of the new features $y_1 = x_1$, $y_2 = x_2$, $y_3 = x_1^2$, $y_4 = x_2^2$, $y_5 = x_1 x_2$ (an optimal boundary is an ellipsis) and the decision making scheme (right).

The maximal margin classifier results in maximal distances of the training vectors from the resulting hyperplane. In the new high dimensional space, we also have the maximal margin. However, we cannot say that in the original n-variate space, the distances of a few of the closest training vectors to a non-linear decision boundary are equal among themselves and cannot be increased further. In order to find the optimal weight vector Cortes and Vapnik (1965) suggested a smart method to minimise the quadratic form in the original feature space. Instead of using the quadratic optimization technique to find the weights of the linear classifier in the second stage of the decision making algorithm, in principle, one can use other statistical methods, train the SLP classifier, etc.

2.8 Piecewise-Linear Classifiers

Like the nonparametric classifiers, the piecewise-linear (PWL) decision boundaries allow one to discriminate classes having complex multimodal distribution densities. The piecewise linear classifiers have gained great attention in pattern recognition theory and practice. A very large number of methods based on formal principles and bright heuristic ideas have been proposed during the last three decades. A decision making scheme of the piecewise-linear classifiers resembles that of the multilayer perceptron with one hidden layer. The learning vector quantisation neural networks also realise the piecewise-linear decision boundaries. The weights that determine the piecewise-linear classifiers can be used to initialise the weights of the hidden layer units of MLP. It is the reason why we pay special attention to these algorithms in this book.

In principle, there are two approaches to designing the piecewise-linear classifiers. In the first approach, the designer begins from the *description of the classes*. In the second, he begins from the *description of hypothetical decision boundaries* (the structural or architectural approach).

2.8.1 Multimodal Density Based Classifiers

In the first approach to designing the piecewise-linear classifiers, it has been traditional to suppose that each class is composed from a mixture of the components. Each component can be represented by the sub-population or by a single multivariate pattern vector that is close to a border between the pattern classes. Then one needs to find the linear decision sub-boundaries that classify the sub-populations, the single pattern vectors or the groups of single pattern vectors of the opposite classes. It is not difficult to do this if one chooses *exact definitions* of the sub-populations, single pattern vectors or groups of single pattern vectors of different classes. The methods used to design the linear classifiers, described already in this chapter, can be used for this purpose. In accordance with the selection of the sub-populations, single pattern vectors or groups of single pattern vectors of different classes and the classifier design method used, one can acquire a piecewise-linear or even piecewise-quadratic decision boundary.

Example 6. We have had the PWL classifier designed according to the first approach in Section 2.6.2. There we assumed that each of the m_i components of the mixture is an independent subclass. In Figure 2.9 we depict two pattern classes, one having a three-modal density with components ω_{11}, ω_{12}, ω_{13} and the other having a bi-modal density with components ω_{21}, ω_{22}. A piecewise-linear decision boundary is composed from three piecewise-linear boundaries: h_{11}, h_{22}, and h_{32}. Each of the elementary first level discriminant functions $h_{ij}(\boldsymbol{X})$ allocates an unlabeled vector $\boldsymbol{X}$ into one of subregions Ω_{ij} or $\overline{\Omega}_{ij}$. A final decision is made on the basis of elementary decisions by a special output stage classifier.

A hierarchical decision-making scheme for the "mixture" model of the piecewise-linear classifier is displayed in Figure 2.10. Decision element H_j performs a linear operation to calculate a "pseudo-distance" y_j between an unlabeled input vector $\boldsymbol{X}$ and the sub-population ω^*_j with the mean vector $\boldsymbol{M}^*_j$

$$y_j = -2\boldsymbol{X}^T\boldsymbol{M}^*_j + \boldsymbol{M}^{*T}_j\boldsymbol{M}^*_j . \qquad (2.58)$$

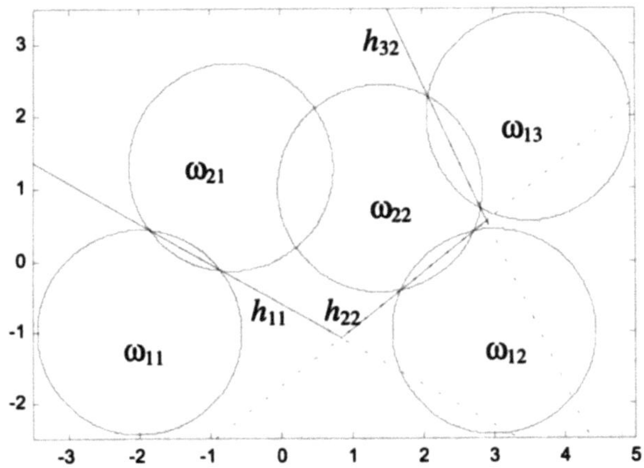

Fig. 2.9. Two bi-variate populations, one having a bi-modal density and the other having a three-modal density, and a piecewise-linear decision boundary.

In the Euclidean distance measure $H^{E}(\boldsymbol{X}, \boldsymbol{M}_j^*) = (\boldsymbol{X} - \boldsymbol{M}_j^*)^T(\boldsymbol{X} - \boldsymbol{M}_j^*)$, term $\boldsymbol{X}^T\boldsymbol{X}$ is common for all first level elements H_j. Therefore, Equation (2.58) ignores this term. Hence, the first level elements are linear. Elements "$\min_j$" in the Figure 2.10, choose a minima from each group of the first level elements. The output decision element "min" determines which minimum is the smallest one and allocates the vector $\boldsymbol{X}$ to the corresponding class.

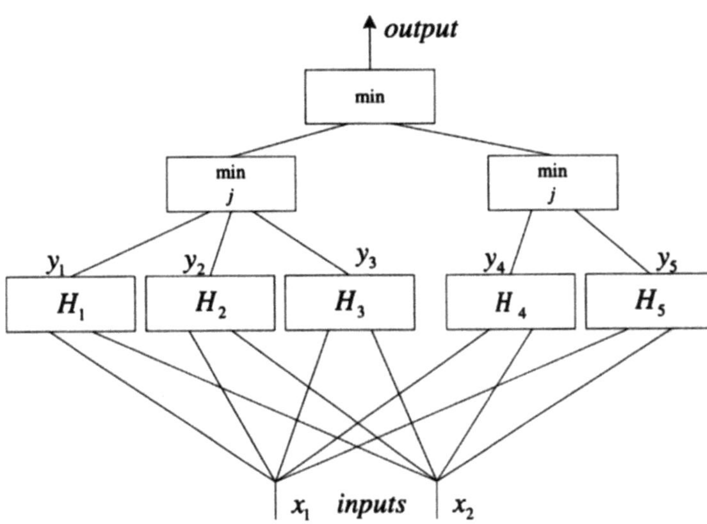

Fig. 2.10. Decision-making scheme for the "mixture model" piecewise-linear classifier.

The only training required to design the classifier is a determination of the mean vectors of the subclasses. This can be done, for example, by using one from a great amount of known cluster analysis methods. Instead of the Euclidean distance , one can use more sophisticated distance measures, e.g. the metric $H^A(X, \mu_{ij}) = (X - M_j^*)^T A (X - M_j^*)$, where A stands for an $n \times n$ matrix. In the learning vector quantisation (LVQ) network approach, unknown parameters are learned in an iterative procedure where a certain cost function is minimised.

2.8.2 Architectural Approach to Design of the Classifiers

In the multimodal density based approach, an architecture of the decision making algorithm follows from the description of the pattern classes. In the architectural approach, it is supposed that the functional form (architecture) of the piecewise-linear decision-making scheme is known *a priori*. Usually it is supposed that the piecewise-linear classification is performed in two stages. In the first stage, there is a certain number of the linear classifiers which perform classification in the n-variate feature space. In the second stage, there is an additional decision-making element that groups decisions already made in the first stage. Let the first stage's linear classifiers H_i generate outputs

$$y_i = \begin{cases} 0 & \text{if} \quad v_0 + \sum_{i=1}^{n} v_i x_i > 0 \\ 1 & \text{otherwise} \end{cases}.$$

In the second stage, a final classification is performed. In principle, one can use any known parametric or nonparametric classifiers for the categorical data. In the next section, we will consider algorithms that can be utilised while making the final decision. The simplest example for binary solutions (0 or 1) made by the second stage element can serve the linear or quadratic classifiers, e.g.

$$output = \begin{cases} 0 & \text{if} \quad w_0 + \sum_{i=1}^{h} w_i y_i > 0 \\ 1 & \text{otherwise} \end{cases}.$$

A hierarchical decision making scheme which performs such classification is presented in Figure 2.11.

2.8.3 Decision Tree Classifiers

Nowadays, decision tree classifiers are among the most powerful and most popular classification techniques used to work with complex continuous, discrete and mixed data. This technique's decision-making scheme is very similar to the feed-forward multilayer perceptron. In order to choose a proper architecture of the multilayer perceptron it is important to know the ideas used to design the decision tree classifiers. Solutions of the MLP classifier can be represented as a decision tree, and *vice versa*, i.e., the decision tree can be utilised to fix MLP architecture and its initial weights.

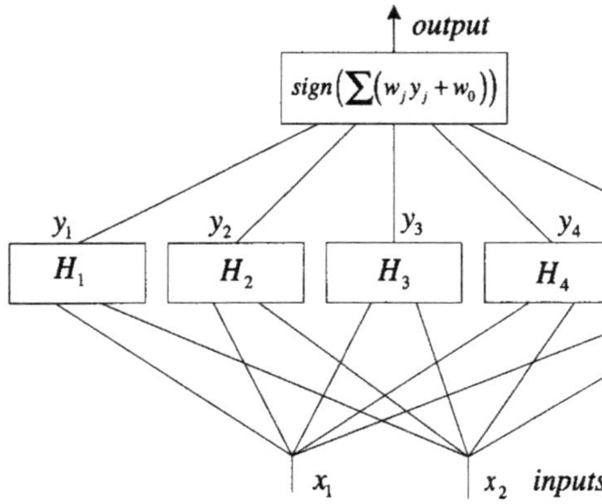

Fig. 2.11. Decision-making scheme in the "architectural" piecewise-linear classifier.

To make a solution concerning the class membership of the vector ***X***, the decision tree classifier most often uses only one feature at a time and allocates the vector ***X*** to one of the branches of the tree. Then it is sent further to the next branch, etc., until a final decision is made. In more complicated algorithms, more than one feature takes part in decision-making. Typically linear classifiers are used in each decision, however, decision tree design algorithms have been proposed where quadratic classifiers are utilised.

Example 7. In Figure 2.12, we present a scatter diagram of the artificial data and the decision tree classifier. The decision is performed by feature x_1 at first. In this stage, conditions $x_1 < a$ or $x_1 > b$ are verified. If $x_1 < a$, we have a final (terminal) node: we allocate vector ***X*** to the class "×". If $a \leq x_1 \leq b$, we go on to the second decision stage, and verify a condition: if $h(X) = v_1x_1 + v_2x_2 = < d$ (v_1=-1, v_2=1, d=1), we allocate the object ***X*** to the class "+" if $v_1x_1 + v_2x_2 \geq d$, we allocate object ***X*** to the class "×". If, at the very beginning, we have had an answer $x_1 > b$, in the second stage we verify: if $x_2 < c$, , we decide on class "+", and if $x_2 \geq c$, then class "×".

The decision tree classifier can easily be used to classify objects characterised by the features, some of which are continuous and the rest are discrete. Such variables are called *mixed* and such situations often occur in applications. There is a great number of algorithms proposed to design the decision tree classifiers. In order to design the decision tree, at each node one needs to specify the set of features, the number of classes, the type of the classifier, and its parameters. In addition, one needs to specify the complexity and the architecture of the tree: the geometry, the number of nodes, and the number of final leaves. There is a tremendous number of ways to obtain the decision tree classifiers of different configurations and different complexity. The decision trees can differ according to:

– strategies utilised to make the decisions at each single node (the type of decision made at each node; in our example, we had two types of decision made by the single features and by the linear discriminant function);
– metrics (criteria) to determine the "most powerful" feature or the subset of features in order to make a current decision in each node (e.g., the Mahalanobis distance, the empirical probability of misclassification, a divergence, etc., see Chapter 6);
– a metric used to determine parameters of the single classifiers in the nodes;
– a way to design the architecture of the tree and its complexity;
– a criterion to determine the classification performance in order to determine the complexity of the decision tree, a rule to stop splitting;
– a type of procedure to optimise the decision tree just designed.

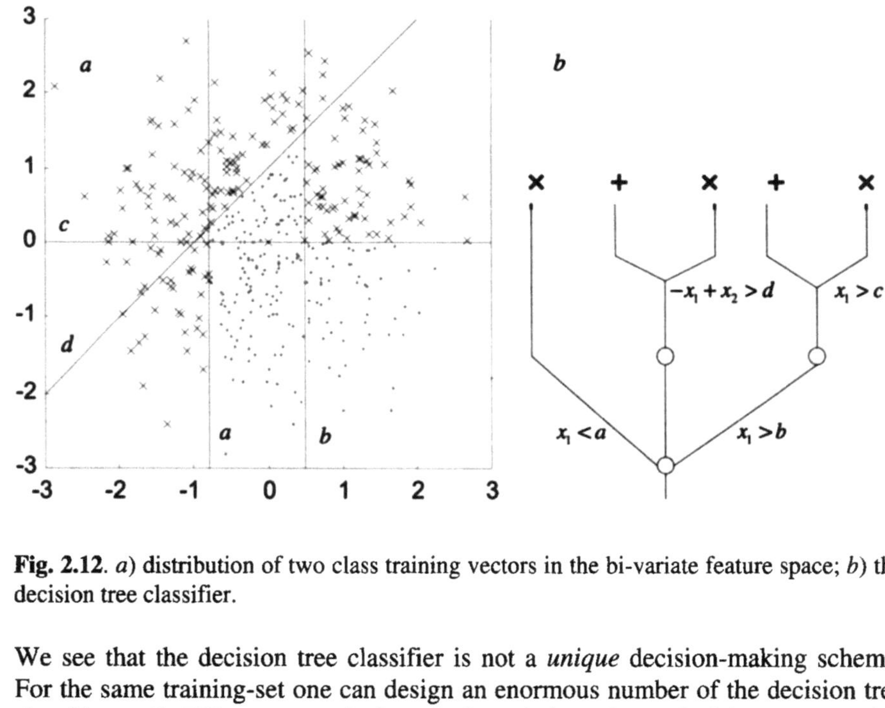

Fig. 2.12. *a*) distribution of two class training vectors in the bi-variate feature space; *b*) the decision tree classifier.

We see that the decision tree classifier is not a *unique* decision-making scheme. For the same training-set one can design an enormous number of the decision tree classifiers of different complexity. A knowledge about decision tree design strategies is very important for the ANN designers. We remind the reader that the decision-making scheme of the multi-layer perceptron can be approximated by the decision tree classifier and *vice versa*, i.e. the decision tree classifier can be represented as the MLP.

Example 8. In Figure 2.13*a*, we present a scheme of the MLP with *two hidden layers* that classify the data presented in Figure 2.12*a*. Four neurones in the first hidden layer are verifying the following conditions: $x_1 < a$ (A), $x_1 < b$ (B), $-x_1+x_2<d$ (C), $x_2 < c$ (D). Five neurones in the second hidden layer perform an operation "AND" and two output neurones, an operation "OR". At first, this MLP was composed without training, directly from the decision tree architecture and its parameters. The coefficients that describe the decision tree solution were used as the *initial values* of the MLP classifier. Then MLP was trained by using the back-propagation technique. As a result, we obtain a smooth decision boundary (curve in Figure 2.13*b*). After multiplication of all weights of the hidden layer by factor 10000 we obtain a piecewise-linear decision boundary that can be utilised to form a new decision tree where both features, x_1 and x_2, are utilised in each node. Four dotted straight lines represent the single linear decision boundaries of four hidden layer neurones.

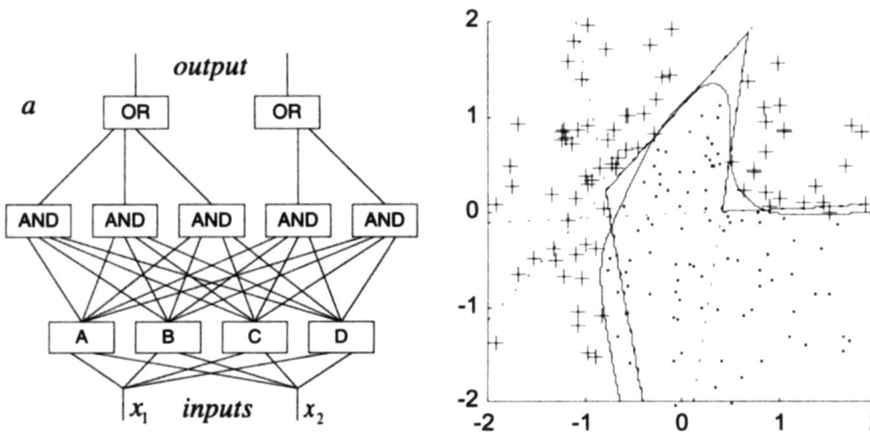

Fig. 2.13. The MLP with two hidden layers which reproduces the decision boundary of the decision tree classifier in Figure 2.12*b* (*a*) and the decision boundary of the MLP with one hidden layer, four hidden units, and the hard-limiting and smooth activation functions.

2.9 Classifiers for Categorical Data

In many applications, the features are not continuous but discrete: each measurement can assume only several possible values (states, cells or bins), such as, a profession, a sex, the type of an engine, etc. In ANN design, we are faced with categorical variables when we design a co-operative neural network composed from several expert networks and one "boss" network. The boss (a gating rule) should analyse categorical judgements of the expert networks (indexes of the pattern classes to which an unknown input vector X has been assigned by each expert network) and make a final decision.

2.9.1 Multinomial Classifiers

Let the j-th variable assume m_j possible values (states, bins). Then a total number of theoretically possible bins of n-variate vector X will be $m = \prod_{j=1}^{n} m_j$. Each particular n-variate vector $\boldsymbol{X}$ can assume only one bin from m possible ones, say, s_j-th bin (j = 1, 2, ..., m). In order to design the classification rule, we assume that n-variate vector $\boldsymbol{X}$ is a random one and use the theory of statistical decisions. Denote a probability that vector $\boldsymbol{X}$ from ω_i has assumed state s_j by $P_j^{(i)}$ (j=1, 2, ..., m). In the two category case, the conditional distribution of vector $\boldsymbol{X}$ from class ω_i is characterised by m probabilities

$$P_1^{(i)}, P_2^{(i)}, \ldots, P_{m-1}^{(i)}, P_m^{(i)}, \quad \text{with} \quad \sum_{j=1}^{m} P_j^{(i)} = 1, \quad (i=1, 2).$$

Let vector $\boldsymbol{X}$ be assumed to be the state s_j. Then Equation (2.5) results in the following optimal Bayes discriminant function

$$h(X) = P_1 P_j^{(1)} - P_2 P_j^{(2)}. \tag{2.59}$$

Probabilities of the states $s_1, s_2, \ldots, s_m$ can be described by a multinomial distribution. Therefore, the classifier in which a decision is made according to probabilities of all m cells is called a *multinomial* classifier. We index it by the letter M.

Example 9. To illustrate the above decision-making scheme, let us analyse a two category classification problem with three variables (features). Let the first and second features take only two values, 0 and 1. The third feature can take three values: 0, 1 and 2. Then a total number of possible states (bins) of the 3-variate vector $\boldsymbol{X}$ is 12 (m = 2×2×3):

s_1	s_2	s_3	s_4	s_5	s_6	s_7	s_8	s_9	s_{10}	s_{11}	s_{12}
000	001	002	010	011	012	100	101	102	110	111	112

Let the conditional probabilities of each of these 12 states (bins) be:

s_1	s_2	s_3	s_4	s_5	s_6	s_7	s_8	s_9	s_{10}	s_{11}	s_{12}
0.01	0.02	**0.07**	**0.10**	**0.17**	**0.11**	0.08	**0.17**	0.01	0.02	**0.23**	0.01
0.16	0.02	0.03	0.02	0.02	0.05	**0.16**	0.03	**0.21**	**0.13**	0.10	**0.07**

In this problem, we must allocate vector $\boldsymbol{X}$ to the first class if it will take one of the following states: $s_3, s_4, s_5, s_6, s_8, s_{11}$ (the probabilities of these bins are in bold). If vector $\boldsymbol{X}$ takes one of states $s_1, s_7, s_9, s_{10}, s_{12}$, then one needs to allocate the vector $\boldsymbol{X}$ to the second class (the probabilities of these bins are also in bold). In a case where the vector $\boldsymbol{X}$ takes the second state, s_2, and the prior probabilities of the classes are equal among themselves ($P_2 = P_1 = ½$), it is unimportant to which class it is allocated.

The asymptotic and the Bayes probabilities of misclassification are

$$\varepsilon_\infty^M = \varepsilon_B = 0.2 =$$

$$½\,(0.01 + 0.02 + 0.03 + 0.02 + 0.02 + 0.05 + 0.08 + 0.03 + 0.01 + 0.02 + 0.10 + 0.02).$$

In a general case, the asymptotic and Bayes probabilities of misclassification of the multinomial classifier are

$$\varepsilon_\infty^M = \varepsilon_B = \sum_{j=1}^{m} \min\{ P_1 P_j^{(1)}, P_2 P_j^{(2)} \}. \qquad (2.60)$$

2.9.2 Estimation of Parameters

In the L category case, the multinomial classifier is determined by $L \times m$ probabilities $P_j^{(i)}$ ($j = 1, ..., m,\ i = 1, ..., L$). To evaluate the unknown parameters one can use the maximum likelihood estimates:

$$\hat{P}_j^{(i)} = n_j^{(i)} / N_i, \qquad (2.61)$$

where $n_j^{(i)}$ is a number of observations from the i-th class training set falling into the state s_j.

Utilisation of (2.61) in (2.59) results in the plug-in rule. In order to get the Bayes predictive rule, let us assume that the prior distribution of the probabilities $P_1^{(i)}, P_2^{(i)}, ..., P_{m-1}^{(i)}, P_m^{(i)}$ follow a Dirichlet distribution

$$P_{prior}(P_1^{(i)}, P_2^{(i)}, ..., P_{m-1}^{(i)}, P_m^{(i)}) = k_{mi}\,(P_1^{(i)})^{\gamma_1 - 1}(P_2^{(i)})^{\gamma_2 - 1} \cdots (P_{m-1}^{(i)})^{\gamma_{m-1} - 1}(P_m^{(i)})^{\gamma_m - 1},$$

where k_{mi} is a normalising constant and $\gamma_1, \gamma_2, ..., \gamma_m$ are parameters of the prior distribution.

Then the Bayes estimate of $P_j^{(i)}$ is

$$\hat{P}_j^{(i)} = (n_j^{(i)} + \gamma_i)/(N_i + \sum_{j=1}^{m} \gamma_i), \qquad (2.62)$$

If we do not give preference to any particular bin, then $\gamma_1 = \gamma_2 = ... \gamma_m = \gamma$. Then instead of (2.62) we will have

$$\hat{P}_j^{(i)} = (n_j^{(i)} + \gamma)/(N_i + m\gamma), \qquad (2.63)$$

If $\gamma=1$, then we have a uniform distribution of the bin's (cell's) probabilities $P_1^{(i)}$, $P_2^{(i)}$, ..., $P_{m\text{-}1}^{(i)}$, $P_m^{(i)}$. If $N_2 \neq N_1$, the estimates (2.63) differ from estimates (2.61). Thus, we notice once more that the plug-in and the Bayes predictive classification rules are different.

2.9.3 Decision Tree and the Multinomial Classifiers

In the two category case, making a decision by the multinomial classifier one needs to remember all $2m$ conditional probabilities (essentially one needs to remember only the class memberships of each state). It is easy to do, when we have a 3-variate vector and only 12 states. In many practical cases, one can have tens and hundreds of features. When the number of features, n, is moderate or large, the number of states (bins) becomes enormously large. For example, when we have 10 variables and only one threshold (each feature can have then only two states), the number of cells $m = 2^{10} = 1024$. When we have 20 variables, then $m > 10^6$. The necessity of compressing the information arises: we need to represent a decision-making scheme by a small number of parameters.

Different algorithms for compressing this information exist. Two principal assumptions used in these algorithms are:

- many states belonging to one pattern class can be joined together, then separate states can be described by a smaller number of features;
- class memberships of the bins with zero or very small probabilities $P_j^{(i)}$ can be arbitrary.

One can also use the Boolean algebra approach and present a solution in conjunctive disjunctive form. Special algorithms to design multivariate histograms and decision tree classifiers can be used here. The multivariate histogram that splits multivariate space Ω into the "hyper-rectangular" spaces i.e., cells Ω_1, Ω_2, ... , Ω_m, is in fact, the multinomial classifier. We have met the decision tree solutions in Section 2.8.3.

Example 10. In Figure 2.14, we have the decision tree classifier for the above classification problem with three categorical variables. At the beginning, the first feature x_1 makes a decision and allocates the object $\boldsymbol{X}$ to one of the branches. If the object was allocated to the right branch, a final decision is made by the third variable x_3. If it was allocated to the left branch, then the second feature x_2 makes a subsequent decision. If $x_2 = 1$, then the object is allocated to the first class, otherwise one uses the third feature x_3. The final number of branches, i.e. leaves, of the decision tree is 5. It is significantly less than the number of bins $m = 12$. To make a decision, one needs to remember class memberships of the leaves and the architecture of the tree. It requires much less computer memory than the multinomial classifier. Moreover, assessments of the decision tree can be interpreted easily. The decision tree classifier design from the training data or from a set of probabilities $P_1^{(i)}$, $P_2^{(i)}$, ..., $P_{m\text{-}1}^{(i)}$, $P_m^{(i)}$, ($i = 1,\ldots, L$) is a combinatorial problem which, in practical cases, can be solved only with a certain accuracy (deviation from an optimal solution).

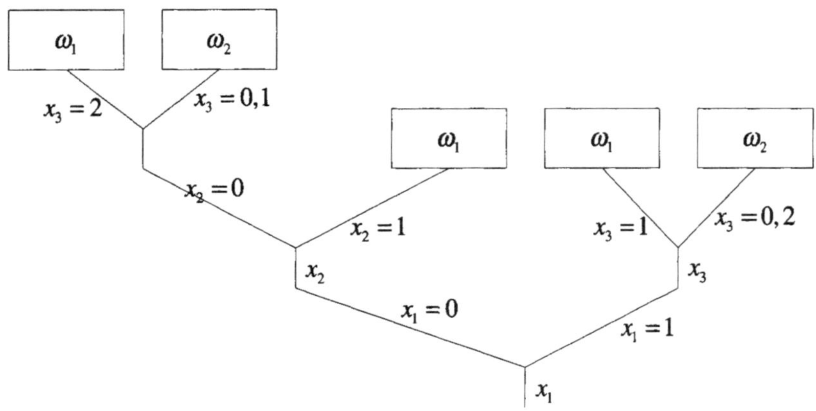

Fig. 2.14. The decision tree classifier for categorical two class data with three features.

2.9.4 Linear Classifiers

In order to overcome difficulties associated with the tremendous number of bins, the parametric methods to describe the multivariate distribution can also be used. In the statistical inference, a popular class of decision-making algorithms, when dealing with categorical data, are the latent class model and contingency tables. We mention here only one simple method.

The simplest assumption most often used to design parametric classifiers is an assumption that variables are mutually independent. Then

$$P\{x_1 = s_1, x_2 = s_2, \dots, x_n = s_n \mid \omega_i\} = \prod_{j=1}^{n} P_j^{(i)}(s_g^j), \tag{2.64}$$

where $P_j^{(i)}(s_g^j)$ is a probability that the j-th component of the multivariate vector $X = (x_1, x_2, \dots, x_n)^T$ will take the state s_g^j, $g = 1, 2, \dots, m_j$.

The number of probabilities $P_j^{(i)}(s_g^j)$ to be estimated from the training data is $\sum_{j=1}^{n} m_j - n$. Applying the general theory to design the classification rule, we have the following discriminant function:

$$h(X) = \sum_{j=1}^{n} \ln \frac{P_j^{(1)}(s_g^j)}{P_j^{(2)}(s_g^j)} + \ln \frac{P_1}{P_2}. \tag{2.65}$$

To estimate the probabilities $P_j^{(i)}(s_g)$, one can use the maximum likelihood or Bayes approach (essentially it will be the equations (2.61) and (2.63) applied for each variable separately). For independent binary (with two states only) variables, we have a linear discriminant function and, for independent ternary variables, it is quadratic. In the general case, for m-valued conditionally independent variables we have the (m-1)-th degree polynomial discriminant function (Toussaint, 1972).

The binary variables can be considered as continuous. Therefore, in this case, all classifier design techniques suitable for the continuous variables can be utilised.

2.9.5 Nonparametric Local Classifiers

To estimate the distribution of a group of dependent categorical variables and design the classification rule, one can use *the non-parametric approach*: the *k-NN* and Parzen window rules. For the categorical variables, we cannot use the conventional kernels used for the continuous variables. There is a short list of distance measures useful for this purpose:

$$\varphi(H) = (\lambda)^{n - H(X, X_j)} (1 - \lambda)^{H(X, X_j)}, \qquad (2.66a)$$

where $H(X, X_j)$ is a distance between X and X_j, e.g. a number of disagreements between these two vectors, and λ is the smoothing parameter incorporated in the distance metric already,

$$\varphi(H) = \sum_{j=1}^{n} H(x_\alpha, x_{\alpha j}), \qquad (2.66b)$$

$$\varphi(H) = \prod_{j=1}^{n} H(x_\alpha, x_{\alpha j}), \qquad (2.66c)$$

where $H(x_\alpha, x_{\alpha j})$ is a distance between the α-th components of vectors X and X_j, e.g., $H(x_\alpha, x_{\alpha j}) = 1$ if $|x_\alpha - x_{\alpha j}| < \delta$ and $H(x_\alpha, x_{\alpha j}) = 0$ otherwise.

An appropriate choice of the kernel function allows the use of this non-parametric approach when we have a *mixture of continuous and categorical variables*. While constructing the classifier, we need to choose the optimal complexity of the rule, i.e. the value of the smoothing parameter λ. We will return to this question in the next chapter.

2.10 Bibliographical and Historical Remarks

Fisher (1936) was the first to propose a method of classifying multivariate vectors into several categories. Optimal discriminant functions in the case of known distribution density functions of the pattern classes were discussed by Welch

(1939) and a theory of statistical decisions is presented by Wald (1944, 1950). Anderson (1951) proposed the plug-in approach to design sample-based classification rules. He showed that the plug-in sample based classification rule is identical to the Fisher rule if $N_2 = N_1$ and the classes are multivariate Gaussian with common covariance matrix.

Anderson and Bahadur (1962) obtained the minimal classification error linear discriminant for a case when the classes are Gaussian but the covariance matrices are different. Their result was generalised by a wider class of distributions by Patterson and Mattson (1966) and Smith (1971). Later Zhezel (1975), Lipskaya (1981) and Bunke and Fisher (1983) have shown that, for two arbitrary multivariate populations, the weight vector of the discriminant function (optimal in a sense of a upper bound of the classification error) can be expressed as

$$V_{\text{opt.}} = (\Sigma_1 + \gamma\Sigma_2)^{-1}(\boldsymbol{M}_1 - \boldsymbol{M}_2),$$

where $\boldsymbol{M}_1, \boldsymbol{M}_2$ are mean vectors, Σ_1, Σ_2 are covariance matrices, and a scalar parameter γ can be found from $\boldsymbol{M}_1 - \boldsymbol{M}_2$, and Σ_1, Σ_2.

Harley (1963), Hoerl and Kennard (1970) and DiPillo (1979) formulated the problem of regularisation of the covariance matrix in the small training-set situation. A scaled rotation regularisation was proposed by Raudys (2000*c*). For more details concerning RDA see Friedman (1989) and McLachlan (1992). A distinction of the complexity of five classification rules according to the structure of the covariance matrices was first analysed by Raudys (1972) and the block-diagonal type matrix structure was used by Goldin and Poplavskij (1970). Chow and Liu (1968) suggested the first order tree type model of the dependence between the variables for classification purposes. Zarudskij (1979, 1980) expressed the elements of the inverse of the covariance matrix as a function of elements of correlations and variances, and suggested using the Kruskal (1956) algorithm to find the graph. Different types of models of the Toeplitz matrix can be found in Anderson (1971) and Box and Jenkins (1976). Han (1970) considered the circular covariance matrix and suggested a simple way of its diagonalisation. Han (1968) and Pivoriunas (1978) considered models where all the variables are equally correlated and Kligiene (1977) has written an inverse of the covariance matrix of the autoregression stationary random process (Appendix 3).

The Bayes predictive approach to estimating the probability density function for designing the classification rule was first used by Abramson and Braverman (1962), who analysed the Gaussian case with unknown means and known covariances. Geisser (1964) and Keehn (1965) considered the case of the unknown covariance matrix. Gupta (1977) has shown that in the case where $N_2=N_1$, for uniform prior distributions of the components of the mean vector and the covariance matrix, the predictive Bayes approach results in the linear DF (1.3), in exactly the same way as the standard Fisher rule.

Schuermann (1977), Malinovskij (1979) and Duin (1995) suggested the use of the pseudo inverse of the covariance matrix while designing the sample-based classifier when $N < n$. Day (1969*b*) gave a general formula (2.40) for families of distribution densities for which the linear and quadratic classification are optimal and Day and Kerridge (1967) suggested a procedure to find unknown parameters.

Randless *et al.* (1978) proposed the use of the Huber (1981) robust M-estimates in discriminant analysis, as well as the generalised Fisher linear DF to classify contaminated populations. Other robust classification procedures for contaminated data have been considered in Kharin (1996).

Do-Tu and Installe (1978) invented the window function technique to design the classifier with smallest training-set (empirical) error. Other procedures of this group are based on the use of a sequential random search procedure (Wolf, 1966), the Kiefer-Wolfowitz stochastic approximation (Yau and Schumpert, 1968), linear programming (Ibaraki and Muroga, 1970), the algebraic method (Warmack and Gonzales, 1973), linear transformations of the co-ordinate system (Miyake, 1979) and heuristic ideas (Vapnik and Chervonenkis, 1974). When the zero empirical classification error is obtained, the resulting discriminant function is not unique. Some additional criteria have been introduced which favour an increase in the distance between the dicriminant hyperplane and the training vectors closest to it. Examples are the tolerance function (Babu and Chen, 1971), the margin function i.e. the Euclidean distance of training vector from the separating hyperplane (Glucksman, 1966; Vapnik and Chervonenkis, 1974; Boser *et al.*, 1992; Duin, 1995; and Cortes and Vapnik, 1995). The non-linear SLP classifier was first analysed as seven statistical classifiers by Raudys (1995*a*, 1996, 1998*b*).

Shlesinger (1968) and Day (1969*a*) suggested the procedure to find parameters of the mixture of multivariate Gaussian densities and proposed using this model for classification. Patrick and Shen (1971) suggested using *a priori* information on the means and covariance matrices of the subclasses. Parzen (1962) generalised the Rosenblatt (1956) histogram approach to estimate an unknown probability density function and found conditions of consistency of this estimate. Wolverton and Wagner (1969) showed that with increase in the training-set size and with decrease in the smoothing parameter, the Parzen window density estimate-based classifier tends to the optimal Bayes classifier. The nearest neighbour classification rule has been introduced by Fix and Hodges (1951) and subsequently generalised as the *k-NN* rule. Sebestyen (1962) suggested utilising the multivariate histograms for the classification. For more information about the kernel estimates see Hand (1982), Silverman (1986), Scott (1992) and Wand and Jones (1995). There are numerous references for the reduced kernel estimates, see e.g. Fukunaga and Hayes (1989) and Holmstroom and Hamalainen (1993).

The multinomial procedure to classify discrete valued vectors has been proposed in Linhart (1959) and Cochran and Hopkins (1961). Abend and Hartley (1969) suggested using the Bayes approach to estimate unknown probabilities of the states. A prototype of the decision tree classifier, i.e. a stepwise procedure to reduce the number of cells, has been proposed by Hills (1967). More information on the decision tree classifiers can be found in the monographs of Lbov (1981) and Breiman *et al.* (1984). Popular software for decision trees is prepared by Quinlan (1993). Taxonomy of the decision tree design algorithms considered in Section 2.8.3 is from Norusis (1991). A variety of different models used to design the classifiers for categorical variables and for the mixed ones can be found in Lachenbruch and Goldstein (1979).

In general, there exist several hundred algorithms to construct the classification rules. In the classical theory of statistical decision functions, an emphasis is made on the description of the pattern classes: one estimates the conditional distribution densities $p_1(X) = P(X \mid X \in \omega_1)$ and $p_2(X) = P(X \mid X \in \omega_2)$ at first and only then designs the discriminant function. We have titled this approach a *parametric* statistical approach.

A significant part of the statistical analysis performed in the field of the *structural* (artificial neural network) approach (Tsypkin (1966), Amari (1967), Levin *et al*, 1990; Amari, Fujita and Shinomoto, 1992 and Amari and Murata, 1993). In Chapter 3 we will present a short review of finite training-set size investigations obtained in a stream of this research direction. Therefore, here we present few details. In this approach, one makes assumptions on a structure of the discriminant function, i.e. *a posteriori* probability $P(o \mid V, X)$, and on the unconditional distribution density $p(X) = p_1(X)+p_2(X)$. We have named this a *constructional* statistical approach.

Typically $P(o{=}1 \mid V, X) = 1/(1+\exp(-\beta f(V, X))$, $P(o=2 \mid V, X) = 1 - P(o{=}1 \mid V, X)$. The parameter β is called a "*temperature*" parameter. When parameter $\beta \to \infty$, the function $1/(1+\exp(-\beta f)$ turns out to be the threshold function (we denote this function by $\theta(f)$), and the network is *deterministic*, emitting an answer $y=1$ when $f(V, X)>0$, and $y=-1$ otherwise. The threshold function $\theta(f)=1$, if $f>0$ and $\theta(f)=-1$ otherwise. When β differs from infinity, then the output $P(o \mid V, X)$ is smooth and the network is called *stochastic*.

For a further review of this approach, it is important to distinguish several cases. Suppose that there exists parameter V^* such that an ideal teacher network calculates $f_{\text{teacher}}(V^*, X) = f_{\text{network}}(V^*, X)$, and generates the teacher signal t based on it. In some deterministic cases, there exists a set of the parameter vectors V, all of which give the correct classification of the input vectors. In other words, there exists a neutral *empty zone* (the margin) between the vectors of two pattern classes. The teacher signal t is said to be *noiseless* if t is given by a sign of $f(V^*, X)$ and *noisy* if t is stochastically produced depending on the value $f(V^*, X)$, irrespective of the network itself being deterministic or stochastic. In many cases, $f_{\text{teacher}}(V^*, X) \neq f_{\text{network}}(V^*, X)$ which means that there is no weight vector V^* such that function $f_{\text{network}}(V^*, X)$ can reproduce the teacher's signal $t = \theta(f_{\text{teacher}}(V^*, X))$ correctly. The model $f_{\text{network}}(V, X)$ is said to be *unfaithful* (*unrealisable*) in this case. In the classical discriminant analysis approach, we have a similar situation. For example, for Gaussian classes with different covariance matrices the quadratic DF is the optimal Bayes rule. Often the quadratic DF cannot classify the training-set without error. In fact, the teacher signal is noisy. In practice, however, in order to construct the linear classifier, the designer often assumes that the covariance matrices are common in all pattern classes. Thus, in this case, the optimal solution is unrealisable by the linear rule.

In the structural approach, one can make use of the Bayes predictive approach to find the weight V. Let $p^{prior}(V)$ be a prior distribution of V. Then, for a set of statistically independent input–outputs $\chi_N = [(X_1, o_1), (X_2, o_2), \ldots, (X_N, o_N)]$, the joint probability density of n examples is

$$P(V, \chi_n) = p^{prior}(V) \prod_{i=1}^{n} P(o_i \mid V, X_i) f(X_i).$$

By using the Bayes formula, the posterior probability density is given by

$$p^{porterior}(V \mid \chi_n) = \frac{P(V, \chi_N)}{\prod_{i=1}^{n} P(X_i) \int p^{prior}(V) \prod_{i=1}^{n} P(o_i \mid V, X_i) dV},$$

and can easily be used to obtain the classification rule.

While defining the classification algorithms one ought to remember that *there is no single Bayes classification rule.* All plug-in rules are based on the Bayes formula, however they are different. The differences arise from assumptions about the structure of the distribution density function and the method utilised to estimate unknown parameters. The Parzen window classifier is also based on the Bayes formula. Asymptotically as $N \to \infty$ and $\lambda \to 0$, the PW approaches the Bayes decision rule. Consequently, in principle, it can be called the Bayes rule. One ought to distinguish the Bayes classification rule (plug-in rules) and the Bayes predictive approach where we have to make certain assumptions about the type and parameters of *a priori* distributions of the parameters.

3. Performance and the Generalisation Error

Generalisation (test set) and empirical (training-set) classification errors are meaningful characteristics of any pattern classification system. Generally, one needs to know both these error rates and their relationship with the training-set sizes, the number of features, and the type of the classification rule. This knowledge can help one to choose a classifier of the proper complexity, with an optimal number of features, and to determine a sufficient number of training vectors. While training the non-linear SLP, one initially begins with the Euclidean distance classifier and then moves dynamically towards six increasingly complex statistical classifiers. Therefore, utilisation of theoretical generalisation error results obtained for these seven statistical classifiers becomes a guide for analysing the small sample properties of neural net generated classification algorithms.

The generalisation error depends on the (unknown) characteristics of the data. To design the classifier we make also certain assumptions about the data. In applications, this hypothetical model can be violated. Thus, in order to derive formulae for the generalisation and asymptotic errors, we need to differentiate between

- assumptions about the distribution densities used to *design* the classifier; and
- assumptions about the data model for which this particular classifier is *applied.*

In this chapter, after a more precise presentation of the main types of classification errors and a short overview of competing methods for analysing the small sample behaviour, we consider a number of parametric linear and non-linear classification rules. An exceptional peculiarity of our consideration is the asymptotic analysis where both the number of inputs n and the training-set size N are increasing at a constant rate. For the simplest classifiers, we derive expressions for the generalisation error and compare the approximate generalisation error results with exact ones obtained from complex formulae. We also review asymptotic investigations for other more sophisticated classification rules. We then show the deterioration of the plug-in based classifiers when the number of training vectors in each category is very diverse and demonstrate that parameters of distribution densities that are common for the two pattern classes have a small influence on the generalisation error. Finally, we show that it is usually the intrinsic dimensionality of the data, and not the number of features, that most often determines the sensitivity of a pattern recognition classifier to the training-set size.

3.1 Bayes, Conditional, Expected and Asymptotic Probabilities of Misclassification

There are several types of probabilities of misclassification (PMC) that are helpful in characterising the quality of a pattern recognition system (an algorithm). Among these are probabilities ε_{ij} of incorrect classification of an object from class ω_i as ω_j, a general sum of probabilities of misclassification, the loss, a rejection rate (refuse from decision), etc. In many applications, however, the general sum probability of correct (or incorrect) decisions is the most important. In Chapter 1, we already introduced the *Bayes, conditional, expected* and *asymptotic* probabilities of misclassification. We now define these probabilities more precisely.

3.1.1 The Bayes Probability of Misclassification

Suppose we know the conditional probability density functions (PDF) $p_1(X)$, $p_2(X)$ and the prior probabilities P_1, $P_2 = 1\text{-}P_1$ of the pattern classes. Then, we can design the optimal Bayes classifier B which, in classifying all possible vectors from classes ω_1 and ω_2, results in the minimal probability of misclassification. This PMC is called the *Bayes error* and is denoted by ε_B.

The Bayes PMC is a function of only the true probability density functions of the classes $p_1(X)$, $p_2(X)$ and the prior probabilities P_1, P_2. One can represent the Bayes PMC as

$$\varepsilon_B = \int_{\Omega} \min \{P_1 p_1(X), P_2 p_2(X))\} d X. \tag{3.1}$$

In Figure 1.6, the Bayes error corresponds to two dashed areas.

3.1.2 The Conditional Probability of Misclassification

In each real classification problem, we use the training data to design an appropriate classifier. Usually, we need to choose one particular classifier design algorithm. In Chapter 2 we presented several of the algorithms: the EDC, the Fisher, the minimum empirical error classifiers, etc. The probability of misclassification of a classifier designed from one particular training-set using the algorithm A is conditioned on the particular classifier method and the particular training-set. The error rate for classifying the pattern vectors from the general population is called the *conditional probability of misclassification* and is denoted by $\varepsilon_N^{\mathsf{A}}$. The index A indicates that the classifier design method A was used, and the index N symbolizes that the training-set is fixed, composed of $N = N_1 + N_2$ observation vectors. The word *conditional* indicates that the classifier, and its probability of misclassification, are conditioned on one particular training-set. Thus, for $\mathsf{A} \equiv$ EDC we will obtain one value for the conditional PMC ($\varepsilon_N^{\mathrm{E}}$) and for $\mathsf{A} \equiv$ F (the Fisher classifier) we, with rare exceptions, obtain another value ($\varepsilon_N^{\mathrm{F}}$). Use of a new training-set composed from N_1, N_2 new observations will result in a new pair of conditional probabilities ($\varepsilon_N^{\mathrm{E*}}$ and $\varepsilon_N^{\mathrm{F*}}$). In order to simplify analytical formulae in this chapter, we will often assume $N_2=N_1=\overline{N} = N/2$. In the artificial neural networks literature, this error rate is sometimes referred to as the *conditional generalisation error.*

3.1.3 The Expected Probability of Misclassification

In statistical theory, one analyses sets of randomly sampled observations. Therefore, classifier's parameters and the classifier's probability of misclassification can be analysed as *random* variables. In probability theory, a random variable is characterised by its probability density function. Let $f(\varepsilon_N^{\mathsf{A}})$ be the probability density function of the random variable $\varepsilon_N^{\mathsf{A}}$ and let $\overline{\varepsilon}_N^{\mathsf{A}}$ be its expectation over all possible random training sets of size N_1 and N_2. This expectation is called the *expected probability of misclassification.*

In the artificial neural net literature, both the conditional and expected errors are often called the *generalisation error.* Often little attention is given to the differences between them. In this book, we make a distinction between these two types of error rate: the conditional PMC is referred to as the *conditional* generalisation error and the expected PMC $\overline{\varepsilon}_N^{\mathsf{A}}$ is called the *expected (mean)* generalisation error.

3.1.4 The Asymptotic Probability of Misclassification

The parameters of a classification rule are determined more and more precisely as the training sample sizes, N_1 and N_2, increase. In particular, the mean value of $\varepsilon_N^{\mathsf{A}}$, namely $\overline{\varepsilon}_N^{\mathsf{A}}$, tends to some fixed value, and the variance $V\varepsilon_N^{\mathsf{A}}$ tends to zero. At the limit, when $N_1, N_2 \to \infty$, the probability density function $f(\varepsilon_N^{\mathsf{A}})$ becomes similar to a delta function (a constant value $\varepsilon_\infty^{\mathsf{A}}$). This limit is called the *asymptotic probability of misclassification*:

$$\varepsilon_\infty^{\mathsf{A}} = \lim_{N_1 \to \infty, N_2 \to \infty} \overline{\varepsilon}_N^{\mathsf{A}}.$$

The asymptotic PMC $\varepsilon_\infty^{\mathsf{A}}$ depends on A, the method used to design the classifier, the prior probabilities P_1, P_2, and on the true pattern-class densities $p_1(X)$, $p_2(X)$. We note that the asymptotic PMC $\varepsilon_\infty^{\mathsf{A}}$ does not depend on the training-set or its size.

Example 1. To demonstrate the differences between the four types of classification errors we depict the probability density function of the random variable $\varepsilon_N^{\mathsf{A}}$ for three values of the training set size $\bar{N} = N/2 = N_1 = N_2$ in Figure 3.1.

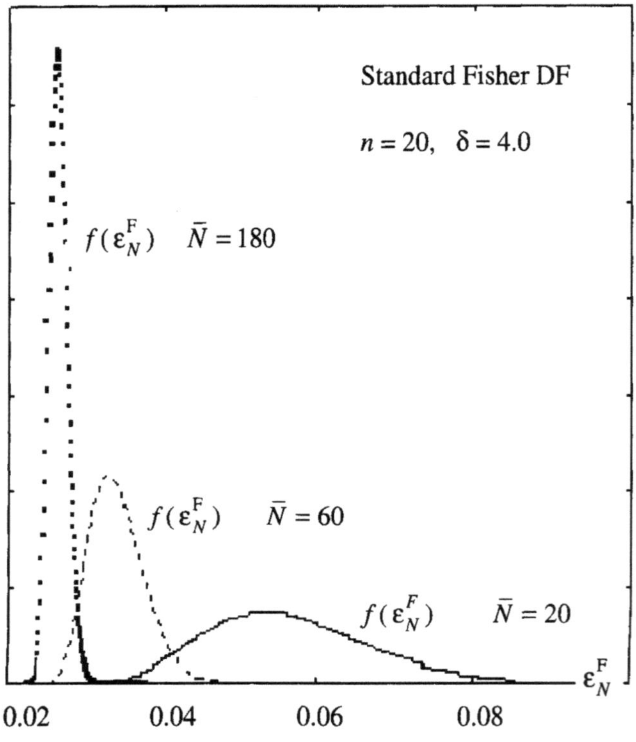

Fig. 3.1. The histograms of the conditional probabilities of misclassification of the standard Fisher linear DF for training-set sizes $\bar{N} = 20$, 60 and 180.

The probability density function $f(\varepsilon_N^{\mathsf{A}})$ of the random variable $\varepsilon_N^{\mathsf{A}}$ is always to right of the Bayes PMC ε_B. The non optimality of the classifier design procedure causes $\varepsilon_N^{\mathsf{A}} < \varepsilon_\infty^{\mathsf{A}}$ for certain training sets. However, we always have that $\varepsilon_N^{\mathsf{A}} \geq \varepsilon_B$ and $\bar{\varepsilon}_N^{\mathsf{A}} \geq \varepsilon_\infty^{\mathsf{A}}$.

3.1.5. Learning Curves: An Overview of Different Analysis Methods

In this chapter, we analyse the learning curves that decrease in the generalisation error $\bar{\varepsilon}_N^A$ as N increases. A number of approaches to studying the generalisation error in the finite training-set size case have been proposed. In our analysis, we compare the multivariate statistics approach with other approaches. For this comparison, we need certain definitions that are utilised in these other approaches. Therefore, we will present a very brief overview of these competing approaches. We give more details about these approaches in the last section of this chapter.

Above we have already stressed the importance of distinguishing between the assumptions about the distribution densities used to *design* the classifier and the assumptions about the data model for which a particular classifier *is applied.* To denote this difference, some researchers have stated that when the distribution density assumptions utilised to design the classifier coincide with the data model for which this particular classifier is applied, we have a *faithful* case. When the designer's assumptions differ from reality, we have an *unfaithful* case.

Vapnik and Chervonenkis (1968, 1974) and Vapnik (1982) developed the Cover (1965) capacity concept and obtained a number of upper bounds for the *conditional* generalisation error ε_N^A for classifiers that minimise the empirical classification error. In Sections 3.6.2 and 3.6.6, while discussing the minimum empirical error and maximal margin classifiers, we will present several of their error bounds. Amari, Fujita and Shinomoto (1992) did not specify a particular type of distribution densities. They have shown that the *expected* generalisation error $\bar{\varepsilon}_N^A$ behaves asymptotically (when $N \to \infty$) as

$$\bar{\varepsilon}_N^A \sim h/N,$$

when the network is deterministic, the teacher signal is noiseless, and the network giving correct classification is uniquely specified by the h-dimensional weight vector $\boldsymbol{V}$. In the case with an empty zone between the pattern classes ($\varepsilon_\infty^A = 0$), we have much better small sample behaviour, namely:

$$\bar{\varepsilon}_N^A \sim c/N^2,$$

for a unique deterministic network trained by the noisy teacher

$$\bar{\varepsilon}_N^A \sim c/N^{1/2},$$

and for the stochastic network

$$\bar{\varepsilon}_N^A \sim \varepsilon_\infty^A + c_1/N,$$

where c and c_1 are unknown constants.

Amari and Murata (1993) have proved fundamental universal convergence theorems for the average generalisation and training errors measured as the predictive entropic loss $\overline{H}_N^{\text{A}}$ (stochastic complexity) evaluated by the expectation of $-\log p(o|\, V, X)$ for an input–output pair (X, o). For the weights estimated by the maximum likelihood method or by the Bayes posterior distribution approach, they proved that an average generalisation entropic loss of the stochastic network is

$$\overline{H}_N^{\text{A}} = H_\infty^{\text{A}} + h^* /(2N),$$

where h^* shows a complexity of the network.

For the faithful (realisable) network $h^* = h$ and for the unfaithful (unrealisable) network:

$$h^* = \text{tr}\mathbf{K}^{-1}\mathbf{G},$$

where **K** is the Hessian matrix, and **G** is the Fisher information matrix.

For a deterministic dichotomy network, Amari (1993) showed that

$$\overline{H}_N^{\text{A}} = h/\, N.$$

We will demonstrate that these general asymptotic ($N \to \infty$) results agree with the results obtained with the classical statistical framework considered in this book when the training-set size N is very large, i.e. when the expected errors are close to asymptotic ones. In finite (small) training-set cases, however, an exact statistical analysis yields a very different result.

A characteristic property of the *statistical–mechanic approach* is the so-called *thermodynamic limit*, where one examines the generalisation error as $N \to \infty$ and as the complexity $h \to \infty$ at some fixed rate. This allows us to meaningfully investigate an asymptotic generalisation error when the number of examples is half the number of parameters, twice the number of parameters, 10 times the number of parameters, and so on (Haussler *et al.*, 1994). This approach uses other mathematical methods from statistical mechanics such as the replica symmetry technique and the annealed approximation. There, the mean value of the ratio of two random variables is approximated by the ratio of the mean values of these two random variables. The validity of this approximation is still questionable. For some models the statistical–mechanic approach succeeds in obtaining the expected generalisation errors and its "phase transitions" (sudden drops in the generalisation error). For the deterministic dichotomy network, for example, a strong rigorous result was proved (Gyorgyi and Tishby, 1990; Opper and Haussler, 1991):

$$\overline{H}_N^{\text{A}} = 0.62\, h/N.$$

In certain cases, a different power law other than $1/N$ or $1/N^{1/2}$ was obtained (Haussler *et al*, 1994; Seung *et al*, 1992).

The statistical approach adopted in this book has the following positive characteristic. Provided the theoretical analysis is performed correctly, we can obtain exact expressions that are valid for a given theoretical data model. Here we do not have unknown constants or unrealistic error bounds. A negative characteristic is that we have to know the type of the probability density functions of the data. Thus, practical utilisation of the theoretical results becomes problematic. Another difficulty consists in the complexity of the exact expressions for the generalisation error and the necessity to use asymptotic expansions if the exact formulae become too complicated. Fortunately, the double asymptotics approach (when both N and h are increasing) works sufficiently well. Exact learning curves, $\overline{\varepsilon}_N^{A} = f(N)$, obtained for some theoretical models allow one to better understand theoretical questions about the small sample behaviour of distinct statistical classifiers and to find conditions such that statistical methods can be utilised successfully in small training-set situations.

3.1.6 Error Estimation

The Bayes, asymptotic, conditional and expected probabilities of misclassification are only *abstractions* which depend on unknown distributions $f_1(\boldsymbol{X})$ and $f_2(\boldsymbol{X})$. These probabilities of misclassification can be evaluated by means of special experiments. The conditional PMC of a newly-designed classifier can be estimated using an additional test data set (or the validation set) composed of pattern vectors that did not participate in the training process. We call this estimate a *test set estimate of the classification error.* To estimate the expected PMC, one needs to have a number of independent random training sets of the same size. The experimental estimation of the asymptotic and Bayes PMC is difficult.

To test a classifier we sometimes use the same pattern vectors which were used for training the classifier. Utilisation of the training-set to estimate PMC results in a *training-set error* or the resubstitution estimate. This error is often called an *empirical error* and sometimes it is called the *apparent error.* The term *apparent error* arose from the fact that in the small training-set size case, this error estimation method results in overly optimistic error estimates. That is, the classifier seems to perform better than it does in reality. We shall discuss classification error estimation methods further in Chapter 6.

3.2 The Generalisation Error of the Euclidean Distance Classifier

3.2.1 The Classification Algorithm

The discriminant function of the Euclidean distance classifier

$$h^{E}(\boldsymbol{X}) = \boldsymbol{X}^T \boldsymbol{V}^{E} + v_0 = \boldsymbol{X}^T(\hat{\boldsymbol{M}}_1 - \hat{\boldsymbol{M}}_2) - ½\ (\hat{\boldsymbol{M}}_1 + \hat{\boldsymbol{M}}_2)^T(\hat{\boldsymbol{M}}_1 - \hat{\boldsymbol{M}}_2) \tag{3.2}$$

is a function both of the random vector to be classified, $\boldsymbol{X}$, and the sample means, $\hat{\boldsymbol{M}}_1$ and $\hat{\boldsymbol{M}}_2$. If $\bar{N} \to \infty$, EDC approaches the Bayes classifier for the model of two spherically Gaussian populations sharing the common covariance matrix. In Section 2.4.2 it was demonstrated that, from the point of view of the Bayesian predictive approach, for the Gaussian priors of the vector $\Delta\boldsymbol{M} = \boldsymbol{M}_1 - \boldsymbol{M}_2$, the sample-based EDC is an ideal discriminant function to classify two spherical Gaussian populations. In the SG case, the *ideal* EDC discriminant function has a Gaussian distribution with mean

$$E[h(\boldsymbol{X}) \mid \omega_i] = [(\boldsymbol{M}_i - \tfrac{1}{2}(\boldsymbol{M}_1 + \boldsymbol{M}_2)]^T(\boldsymbol{M}_1 - \boldsymbol{M}_2),$$

and variance

$$V[h(\boldsymbol{X}) \mid \omega_i] = \sigma^2(\boldsymbol{M}_1 - \boldsymbol{M}_2)^T(\boldsymbol{M}_1 - \boldsymbol{M}_2).$$

Thus the asymptotic and Bayes probabilities of misclassification are given by

$$\varepsilon_\infty^F = P_1 Prob\,\{ h(\boldsymbol{X}) < 0 \mid \omega_1\} + P_2 Prob\,\{h(\boldsymbol{X}) \geq 0 \mid \omega_2\} = \Phi\{-\delta/2\} = \varepsilon_B,$$

where $\delta^2 = \sigma^{-2}(\boldsymbol{M}_1 - \boldsymbol{M}_2)^T(\boldsymbol{M}_1 - \boldsymbol{M}_2)$ is squared Euclidean distance scaled by σ^{-2}.

3.2.2 Double Asymptotics in the Error Analysis

In order to derive analytical expressions for the generalisation error we must find the probability that a value of the *sample discriminant function* is negative (when $\boldsymbol{X} \in \omega_1$) or positive (when $\boldsymbol{X} \in \omega_2$). The exact analytical expression for the generalisation error for the case when the true data distributions are Gaussian with a common CM (GCCM data model) requires integration of a complex analytical expression (Raudys, 1967, Raudys and Pikelis, 1980). In order to obtain a simple and easily interpreted expression, we notice that the sample-based discriminant function is the sum of n random components. Thus, one can approximate the unknown distribution of the discriminant function $h(\boldsymbol{X})$ by a Gaussian distribution. The key tool for providing this approximate distribution of $h(\boldsymbol{X})$ is the application of a central limit theorem. We assume that the number of features, n, is very large. In order to have a realistic situation we also assume that the training-set size N is large.

Thus, a simple asymptotic method for analysing distributions of complex multivariate statistics is as follows: we analyse the case when N, the training-set size, and n, the number of dimensions, are increasing simultaneously at a constant rate. This technique was first utilised by Raudys (1967), and is now widely applied in investigating the generalisation error of the statistical classification algorithms and artificial neural networks. In theoretical physics, this asymptotic approximation method is called the "thermodynamic limit" approach. In comparison with conventional asymptotic analysis, where only the sample size N

approaches infinity (see e.g. Chapter 5 in Fukunaga, 1990), this approach allows one to obtain very accurate estimates when the sample size N is comparable with the number of features n, even when N is relatively small. The *double asymptotics method* is the main technique utilised to obtain the generalisation error formulae in this chapter.

In Section 1.4, we have presented the asymptotic expression for the expected probability of misclassification for the theoretical model when the true classes covariance matrix $\bar{\Sigma}$ is proportional to the identity matrix, i.e. $\bar{\Sigma}=\sigma^2\mathbf{I}$, and $N_2=N_1$. In practice, EDC is used to classify non-spherical and even non-Gaussian pattern classes. Therefore, in this section, we do not assume that the common covariance matrix is $\bar{\Sigma}=\sigma^2\mathbf{I}$. In order to present a simple and easily understandable derivation of the generalisation error formula, we initially assume $N_2=N_1=\bar{N}$ and $P_2=P_1=½$.

In order to stress that the training vectors are considered as random vectors, one commonly denotes them by capital letters, i.e. $\boldsymbol{X}_1^{(1)}, \boldsymbol{X}_2^{(1)},\dots, \boldsymbol{X}_N^{(2)}$. For the two Gaussian pattern classes model, $N_X(\boldsymbol{M}_1, \bar{\Sigma})$, $N_X(\boldsymbol{M}_2, \bar{\Sigma})$, the sample mean vectors are Gaussian: $\hat{\boldsymbol{M}}_1 \sim N_M(\boldsymbol{M}_1, 1/\bar{N}\,\bar{\Sigma})$, $\hat{\boldsymbol{M}}_2 \sim N_M(\boldsymbol{M}_2, 1/\bar{N}\,\bar{\Sigma})$. Consequently, we need to consider the DF $h^{\mathrm{E}}(\boldsymbol{X}, \hat{\boldsymbol{M}}_1, \hat{\boldsymbol{M}}_2)$ as a random variable which depends on three independent n-dimensional random vectors $\boldsymbol{X}$, $\hat{\boldsymbol{M}}_1$ and $\hat{\boldsymbol{M}}_2$. The expected PMC can be written as the sum of two conditional probabilities:

$$\bar{\varepsilon}_N^{\mathrm{E}} = P_1\, Prob\{h^{\mathrm{E}}(\boldsymbol{X},\hat{\boldsymbol{M}}_1,\hat{\boldsymbol{M}}_2) < 0 \mid \boldsymbol{X}\in\omega_1\} + P_2\, Prob\{h^{\mathrm{E}}(\boldsymbol{X},\hat{\boldsymbol{M}}_1,\hat{\boldsymbol{M}}_2) \geq 0 \mid \boldsymbol{X}\in\omega_2\}.$$

Suppose both the dimensionality, n, and training-set size, N, are large. Then, according to the central limit theorem, the distribution of

$$h(\boldsymbol{X}, \hat{\boldsymbol{M}}_1, \hat{\boldsymbol{M}}_2) = \sum_{s=1}^{n} \left(x_s (\hat{m}_{1s} - \hat{m}_{2s}) - ½\, (\hat{m}_{1s} + \hat{m}_{2s})(\hat{m}_{1s} - \hat{m}_{2s}) \right)$$

is approximately Gaussian. In the above equation, subscript s indicates the components of random vectors $\boldsymbol{X}$, $\hat{\boldsymbol{M}}_1$, and $\hat{\boldsymbol{M}}_2$. Thus, asymptotically, when n and N are increasing, the expected probability of misclassification (the expected generalisation error) is

$$\bar{\varepsilon}_N^{\mathrm{E}} = P_1\,\Phi\{- \frac{E\left[h(\boldsymbol{X},\hat{\boldsymbol{M}}_1,\hat{\boldsymbol{M}}_2) \mid \boldsymbol{X}\in\omega_1\right]}{\sqrt{V\left[h(\boldsymbol{X},\hat{\boldsymbol{M}}_1,\hat{\boldsymbol{M}}_2) \mid \boldsymbol{X}\in\omega_1\right]}}\} + P_2\,\Phi\{\frac{E\left[h(\boldsymbol{X},\hat{\boldsymbol{M}}_1,\hat{\boldsymbol{M}}_2) \mid \boldsymbol{X}\in\omega_2\right]}{\sqrt{V\left[h(\boldsymbol{X},\hat{\boldsymbol{M}}_1,\hat{\boldsymbol{M}}_2) \mid \boldsymbol{X}\in\omega_2\right]}}\}, \tag{3.4}$$

where E and V denote the expectation and variance with respect to three independent random vectors $\boldsymbol{X}$, $\hat{\boldsymbol{M}}_1$, and $\hat{\boldsymbol{M}}_2$.

Without loss of generality, we may assume $\boldsymbol{M}_1 + \boldsymbol{M}_2 = \mathbf{0}$. For $N_2 = N_1 = \bar{N}$ the sum $\boldsymbol{Z}_1 = \hat{\boldsymbol{M}}_1 + \hat{\boldsymbol{M}}_2$ and the difference $\boldsymbol{Z}_2 = \hat{\boldsymbol{M}}_1 - \hat{\boldsymbol{M}}_2$ are independently distributed as $\boldsymbol{Z}_1 \sim N_{Z_1}(0, 4/N\, \bar{\Sigma})$, and $\boldsymbol{Z}_2 \sim N_Y(\boldsymbol{M}, 4/N\bar{\Sigma})$, where $\boldsymbol{M}_1 - \boldsymbol{M}_2 = \boldsymbol{M}$. Consequently, for $\boldsymbol{X} \in \omega_i$, we have that $\boldsymbol{Z} = \boldsymbol{X} - ½(\hat{\boldsymbol{M}}_1 + \hat{\boldsymbol{M}}_2) \sim N_Z((-1)^{i+1} ½\boldsymbol{M}, \bar{\Sigma}(1 + 1/N))$ and is independent of $\boldsymbol{Z}_2 = \hat{\boldsymbol{M}}_1 - \hat{\boldsymbol{M}}_2$. Then, $h^{\mathrm{E}}(\boldsymbol{X}, \hat{\boldsymbol{M}}_1, \hat{\boldsymbol{M}}_2) = \boldsymbol{Z}^T \boldsymbol{Z}_2$.

Recognising that $(\boldsymbol{Z}^T\boldsymbol{U})^2 = \mathrm{tr}(\boldsymbol{Z}^T\boldsymbol{U}\,\boldsymbol{Z}^T\boldsymbol{U}) = \mathrm{tr}(\boldsymbol{U}\boldsymbol{U}^T\boldsymbol{Z}\boldsymbol{Z}^T)$, one can readily find that

$$E\left[h(\boldsymbol{X}, \hat{\boldsymbol{M}}_1, \hat{\boldsymbol{M}}_2) \middle| \boldsymbol{X} \in \omega_i\right] = E\left[\boldsymbol{Z}^T\boldsymbol{Z}_2 \middle| \boldsymbol{X} \in \omega_i\right] = (-1)^{i+1} ½\, \boldsymbol{M}^T\boldsymbol{M}, \qquad (3.5a)$$

and

$$V\left[h(\boldsymbol{X}, \hat{\boldsymbol{M}}_1, \hat{\boldsymbol{M}}_2) \middle| \boldsymbol{X} \in \omega_i\right] = \boldsymbol{M}^T\bar{\Sigma}\boldsymbol{M}(1 + 2/N) + \mathrm{tr}(\bar{\Sigma}^2)4/N\,(1 + 1/N). \qquad (3.5b)$$

An expression for the expected PMC follows directly from (3.4) and (3.5 *ab*):

$$\bar{\varepsilon}_N^{\mathrm{E}} \approx \Phi\{-\frac{\boldsymbol{M}^T\boldsymbol{M}}{2\sqrt{\boldsymbol{M}^T\bar{\Sigma}\boldsymbol{M}(1+\frac{2}{N}) + \mathrm{tr}\bar{\Sigma}^2\frac{4}{N}(1+\frac{1}{N})}}\}. \qquad (3.6)$$

For large n and N, ignoring terms of order $1/N$ and n/N^2, we obtain the very simple expression

$$\bar{\varepsilon}_N^{\mathrm{E}} \approx \Phi\{-\frac{\delta^*}{2}\frac{1}{\sqrt{T_M}}\}, \qquad (3.7)$$

where $\delta^* = \dfrac{\boldsymbol{M}^T\boldsymbol{M}}{\sqrt{\boldsymbol{M}^T\bar{\Sigma}\boldsymbol{M}}}$, $T_M = 1 + \dfrac{4n^*}{\delta^{*2}N}$, $n^* = \dfrac{(\boldsymbol{M}^T\boldsymbol{M})^2(tr\,\bar{\Sigma}^2)}{(\boldsymbol{M}^T\bar{\Sigma}\boldsymbol{M})^2}$.

3.2.3 The Spherical Gaussian Case

3.2.3.1 The Case $N_2 = N_1$

Now, assume that $\bar{\Sigma} = \mathbf{I}\sigma^2$. Then $\delta^* = \delta$, and $n^* = n$, i.e., $T_M = 1 + 2n/(\delta^2\bar{N})$. We recall that n represents the number of features (dimensionality) and $N = 2\bar{N}$ represents the training-set size. Equation (3.7) shows that the increase in the expected generalisation error depends on the asymptotic error rate and is proportional to n/N, the ratio of the dimensionality to the sample size. Therefore, for fixed N and δ, the generalisation error increases as n increases.

An important characteristic while designing the classification rules is the *learning quantity* $\kappa = \bar{\varepsilon}_N^E / \varepsilon_\infty^E$ – the relative increase in the mean generalisation error. It indicates the number of times that the generalisation error can be reduced by increasing the training-set size. E.g., if $\kappa = 1.55$, then one can expect that while increasing the training-set size, one can reduce the mean generalisation error 1.55 times. Therefore, theoretical values of this characteristic can be used for a rough estimation of the training-set size. The learning quantity of the EDC, κ_{EDC}, depends mainly on the ratio N/n and depends, to a lesser extent, on the asymptotic PMC.

For data model $\Sigma = \mathbf{I}\sigma^2$ in Table 3.1 we present *exact theoretical values* for $\kappa = \bar{\varepsilon}_N^A / \varepsilon_\infty^E$ of the Euclidean distance classifier, the standard Fisher linear DF and the quadratic classifier obtained from the analytical formulae by integration (from Raudys and Pikelis, 1980). The reader can compare the asymptotic equation (3.7) with the exact values in the table and see that the asymptotic approximations are highly accurate. This evidence once more indicates that the double asymptotic analysis (when $\bar{N} \to \infty$, $n \to \infty$) is very useful tool, even in the very small training-set size case.

Table 3.1. Learning quantity, ratio $\kappa = \bar{\varepsilon}_N^A / \varepsilon_\infty^E$ of the Euclidean distance, the standard Fisher and standard quadratic classifiers versus N, the training-set size, for dimensionality n=50 and five values of distance δ and asymptotic error ε_∞ (Reprinted from Raudys and Pikelis, On dimensionality, sample size, classification error and complexity of classification algorithm in pattern recognition, *Pattern Analysis and Machine Intelligence* 2, 1980, © IEEE).

EDC	Fisher LDF	QDF	$\bar{N}$
1.82 2.34 3.09 3.66 4.22			8
1.70 2.03 2.41 2.65 2.87			12
1.54 1.70 1.84 1.92 1.99			20
1.43 1.50 1.55 1.58 1.61	2.05 3.39 8.40 19.7 52.0		30
1.30 1.32 1.33 1.34 1.35	1.62 2.15 3.61 5.95 10.6	2.21 3.25 7.87 18.3 40.6	50*
1.18 1.17 1.16 1.16 1.17	1.33 1.51 1.93 2.47 3.27	2.13 3.12 7.10 13.1 25.1	100
1.08 1.07 1.06 1.06 1.06	1.14 1.19 1.31 1.44 1.61	1.81 2.35 3.23 4.03 5.05	250
1.04 1.03 1.03 1.03 1.03	1.07 1.09 1.15 1.20 1.27	1.58 1.78 2.01 2.18 2.35	500
1.02 1.02 1.02 1.02 1.02	1.04 1.05 1.07 1.10 1.13	1.37 1.42 1.47 1.51 1.56	1000
1.01 1.01 1.01 1.01 1.01	1.01 1.02 1.03 1.04 1.05	1.18 1.16 1.18 1.18 1.20	2500
1.68 2.56 3.76 4.65 5.50	1.68 2.56 3.76 4.65 5.50	1.68 2.56 3.76 4.65 5.50	δ
0.2 0.1 0.03 0.01 .003	0.2 0.1 0.03 0.01 .003	0.2 0.1 0.03 0.01 .003	ε_∞^E

* 80 for QDF

We see that, in the spherical Gaussian case, the EDC can be trained with reasonably small training sets. Thus, in principle, the single layer perceptron can also be trained with small training sets. In Section 3.3 we show that in the non-spherical case (when $\Sigma \neq \mathbf{I}\sigma^2$) we can encounter a more complex behaviour.

3.2.3.2 The Case $N_2 \neq N_1$

An important conclusion about the *non-optimality* of the sample-based plug-in Euclidean distance classifier follows from analysis of the case when $N_2 \neq N_1$. Deev (1970, 1972) considered the discriminant function of the form

$$h^*(X) = X^T V^{(E)} + v_0 + c$$

where an additional bias term c is introduced. He showed that asymptotically as N_1, N_2 and n, the dimensionality, increase, the expected PMC tends to

$$P_1\Phi\{-\frac{1}{2}\frac{\delta^2 - n/N_1 + n/N_2 - 2c}{\sqrt{\delta^2 + n/N_1 + n/N_2}}\} +$$

$$P_2\Phi\{-\frac{1}{2}\frac{\delta^2 + n/N_1 - n/N_2 + 2c}{\sqrt{\delta^2 + n/N_1 + n/N_2}}\}. \tag{3.8}$$

When $n/N_1 << \delta^2$ and $n/N_2 << \delta^2$, the function $\Phi\{d\}$ on every side of $d = -\delta/2$ is almost linear. For $\bar{\Sigma} = \mathbf{I}\sigma^2$ ($\delta^* = \delta$, and $n^* = n$) we have no difference between (3.7) and (3.8). However, when these two conditions are not fulfilled the non-linear character of function $\Phi\{d\}$ causes an increase in the classification error. The following "unbiased" discriminant function can be recommended for case $N_2 \neq N_1$

$$h^{unbiased}(X) = X^T V^E + v_0 + bias^E(n, N_1, N_2),$$

where for the Euclidean distance classifier

$$bias^E(n, N_1, N_2) = ½\,(n/N_2 - n/N_1) = c. \tag{3.9}$$

A similar bias correcting term has to be used to improve the small sample properties of the standard Fisher linear DF. The non-optimality of the plug-in rule (when $N_2 \neq N_1$) is particularly high when the standard quadratic DF is used (Section 3.5.3).

3.3 Most Favourable and Least Favourable Distributions of the Data

One important aspect of our analysis is the investigation of cases where the statistical classifier is constructed according to one model of the multivariate density function and is applied to classify data described by another statistical model. It is a typical situation in practice. Equation (3.7) shows that, in principle, we can obtain both very small and very large increases in the generalisation error. Thus, in principle, the Euclidean distance classifier can be trained with particularly short training sets. This conclusion is very important for the preceptrons' analysis. It explains that, regardless of the formal dimensionality of the data, in some situations the single layer perceptron can also be trained with extremely short training sets.

3.3.1 The Non-Spherical Gaussian Case

From Equation (3.7) it follows that asymptotically, as the training-set size increases ($N \rightarrow \infty$), the expected generalisation error of the EDC tends to its asymptotic value $\varepsilon_\infty^E = \Phi\{-\delta^*/2\}$. In the general case when $\bar{\Sigma} \neq \mathbf{I}\sigma^2$, we note that $\delta^* \leq \delta$. Thus the asymptotic error ε_∞^E is larger than the asymptotic PMC of the standard Fisher DF $\varepsilon_\infty^F = \Phi\{-\delta/2\}$. Such a situation is illustrated in Figure 1.2.

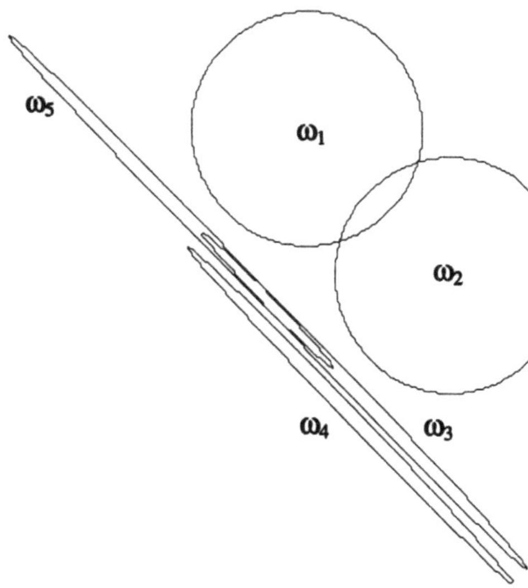

Fig. 3.2. Effect of the covariance matrix on the effective dimensionality n^*: for the classes ω_1 and ω_2, $n^* = n$; for ω_3, ω_4, $n^* >> n$; and for ω_3, ω_5, $n^* << n$ (Reprinted from *Neural Networks*, 11:297-313, Raudys, Evolution and generalization of a single neurone, 1998, with permission from Elsevier Science).

For the 20-variate Gaussian data model **C** mentioned in Section 1.5, we have that $\delta^* = 3.76$, $\delta = 4.65$, $\varepsilon_\infty^E = 0.03$ and $\varepsilon_\infty^F = 0.01$. There exists situations where the features are correlated but $\varepsilon_\infty^E = \varepsilon_\infty^F$. Two such examples are presented in Figure 3.2 (pairs of the classes ω_3, ω_4 and ω_3, ω_5). We see that the parameter δ^* controls the asymptotic PMC. Therefore, it is called the *effective Mahalanobis distance.* In the general case, $\bar{\Sigma} \neq \mathbf{I}\sigma^2$ and $1 \leq n^* \leq \infty$.

In Equation (3.7), the parameter n^* plays the role of the number of features and controls the sensitivity of the EDC to the training-set size. Therefore, it is called the *effective dimensionality.* We see that hypothetically there exist situations where the Euclidean distance classifier is either very *insensitive* to the number of training observations or, on the contrary, very *sensitive* to the training-set size.

3.3.2 The Most Favourable Distributions of the Data

When $n^*= 1$, we call the model the *most favourable distribution* of Gaussian pattern classes for the EDC. An example of densities of this type have been presented in Figure 3.2 (the pairs of the classes ω_3 and ω_5). In this example, the pattern classes are situated almost on a straight line. Here, the true (intrinsic) dimensionality of the data is close to 1.

Another example with $n^* \approx 1$ is two 100-variate Gaussian classes with common covariance matrix (GCCM): $\boldsymbol{M}_1 = -\boldsymbol{M}_2 = 1.042 \times (1, 1, ..., 1)^T$; unit variances; and the correlation between all variables $\rho = 0.3$. We call this data model **D**. In order to ensure $\delta^* = \delta = 3.76$ ($\varepsilon_\infty^E = \varepsilon_\infty^F = 0.03$), we have chosen the means, $\boldsymbol{M}_1$, $\boldsymbol{M}_2$, in a special manner. In this case, the formal dimensionality is $n = 100$, however the effective dimensionality, n^*, is $n^* \approx 1.05$, which is close to 1. Due to the low effective dimensionality for this choice of parameters, we can train the EDC with very small training sets. In a series of 10 experiments with training sets containing only *five* 100-variate vectors from each class ($N = 10$), we have obtained a very low generalisation error. The EDC yielded on average an error rate of 0.039 with the standard deviation of 0.009. In spite of the high number of variables ($n = 100$) for this very favourable distribution case, five vectors per class are sufficient to train the classifier adequately.

3.3.3 The Least Favourable Distributions of the Data

Hypothetically, there exist data models where the effective dimensionality is very large. We call such models where $n^* \rightarrow \infty$ *least favourable densities* of the pattern classes for the GCCM model. The pair classes ω_3 and ω_4 in Figure 3.2 are a perfect example of such distributions. Another example of the least favourable distribution is the following 100-variate ($n = 100$) GCCM data model:

$\boldsymbol{M}_1 = -\boldsymbol{M}_2 = 0.0018805 \times (1, 1, ...,1)^T$; unit variances; all correlations $\rho = -0.0101$.

We call this data model **E**. For the data model **E** we have that $\delta^* = \delta = 3.76$ and $\varepsilon_\infty^E = \varepsilon_\infty^F = 0.03$. However, for these GCCM classes, the effective dimensionality is $n^* \approx 10^8$! In several experiments performed with Gaussian data model **E** and different training sets chosen at random ($\overline{N}$ = 200), we always obtained the expected error for the EDC of $\hat{\varepsilon}_N^{\mathrm{E}} = 0.497$.

High sensitivity of the generalisation error of the EDC to the size of the training-set can be easily explained. In the above examples with high n^*, an insignificant deviation in the sample means $\hat{M}_1$, $\hat{M}_2$ causes a critical rotation of the decision boundary, and, thus, a crucial increase in the generalisation error.

Therefore, we can conclude that in extremely unfavourable cases, it is not expedient to utilise the EDC. For "almost singular" data, a more adequate type of the classifier should be used. For example, for the 100-variate negatively-correlated data model **E**, the more complex standard Fisher linear DF is an asymptotically optimal decision rule. Use of this classifier in the finite training-set case ($\overline{N}$ = 200), yielded a "reasonable" error of 0.058, i.e., only 1.93 times higher than the asymptotic error $\varepsilon_\infty^{\mathrm{F}} = 0.03$. This result corresponds to the theoretical Equation (1.26) for δ=3.76 and $\overline{N}$ =2n; see also Table 3.1.

3.3.4 Intrinsic Dimensionality

Consider the GCCM data model $N_X(\boldsymbol{M}_1, \overline{\Sigma})$ and $N_X(\boldsymbol{M}_2, \overline{\Sigma})$. The matrix $\overline{\Sigma}$ can be represented as $\overline{\Sigma} = \boldsymbol{\Phi\Lambda\Phi}^T$, where $\boldsymbol{\Phi}$ is an $n \times n$ orthonormal matrix of eigenvectors of $\overline{\Sigma}$ and Λ is $n \times n$ diagonal matrix of eigenvalues. Let the diagonal matrix

$$\Lambda = \begin{bmatrix} \Lambda_r & \mathbf{0} \\ \mathbf{0} & \varepsilon\mathbf{I}_{n-r} \end{bmatrix},$$

where:
Λ_r is an $r \times r$ diagonal matrix ($r < n$);
$\mathbf{I}_{p-r}$ is an $(n\text{-}r) \times (n\text{-}r)$ identity matrix;
ε is a small positive constant, such that $(n\text{-}r)\varepsilon << 1$.

Also, let $(\boldsymbol{M}_1 - \boldsymbol{M}_2)^T\boldsymbol{\Phi} = (\boldsymbol{m}^T, \boldsymbol{m}_2^T)$, where absolute values of components m_{2j} of the $(n\text{-}r)$-variate vector $\boldsymbol{m}_2$ are very small, $m_{2j} << \varepsilon$, and can be ignored. In the data described by this model, the random pattern-class vectors $\boldsymbol{X}$ lie in a subspace of dimensionality r. We say that such data has the *intrinsic dimensionality*, r. The effective dimensionality of such data is

$$n^* = \frac{(\boldsymbol{M}^T\boldsymbol{M})^2(\mathrm{tr}\,\overline{\Sigma}^2)}{(\boldsymbol{M}^T\,\overline{\Sigma}\boldsymbol{M})^2} = \frac{(\boldsymbol{M}^T\boldsymbol{\Phi\Phi}^T\boldsymbol{M})^2\,\mathrm{tr}\,(\boldsymbol{\Phi\Lambda\Phi}^T\boldsymbol{\Phi\Lambda\Phi}^T)}{(\boldsymbol{M}^T\boldsymbol{\Phi\Lambda\Phi}^T\boldsymbol{M})^2} = \frac{(\boldsymbol{m}^T\boldsymbol{m})^2\,\mathrm{tr}(\Lambda_r^2)}{(\boldsymbol{m}^T\Lambda_r\boldsymbol{m})^2}.$$

Let Λ_r be an $r \times r$ identity matrix. Then for this data model we also have that $n^*=r$. The fact that that $n^* = r$ means that the increase in the generalisation error of the EDC does not depend on the formal dimensionality n. It depends on r, the dimensionality of the subspace. The intrinsic dimensionality of the multivariate data model with $n^* \approx 1$, discussed above in this subsection, is close to 1. In real world pattern classification problems, the pattern vectors often lie in non-linear subspaces of lower dimensionality. However, the variability of the data in the other n-r dimensions is not extremely small, i.e. the condition $(n\text{-}r)\,\varepsilon \ll 1$ is not fulfilled. For this configuration we have the intermediate cases. We note also that for certain distributions of components of the diagonal matrix Λ_r and the vector $\boldsymbol{m}$, we can have high values of the effective dimensionality: $n^* \gg r$. Thus, the effective and intrinsic dimensionalities have *different interpretations*.

As a general conclusion one can say that the sensitivity of the Euclidean distance classifier to the training-set size strongly depends on the data. In principle, the sensitivity can be very low as well as extremely high. In practice, however, we seldom have distributions similar to the least favourable or to the most favourable distributions described in this section.

3.4 Generalisation Errors for Modifications of the Standard Linear Classifier

3.4.1 The Standard Fisher Linear DF

The weight vector of the standard Fisher linear DF has been defined in (1.3). When $\bar{N} \to \infty$ the Fisher LDF approaches the Bayes classifier for the model of two Gaussian classes sharing common covariance matrix (GCCM). For this model, the Bayes linear discriminant function has a Gaussian distribution with mean

$$E[h(X)\mid \omega_i] = [(\boldsymbol{M}_i - ½\,(\boldsymbol{M}_1 + \boldsymbol{M}_2)]^T \bar{\Sigma}^{-1}(\boldsymbol{M}_1 - \boldsymbol{M}_2\,),$$

and variance

$$V[h(X)\mid \omega_i] = (\boldsymbol{M}_1 - \boldsymbol{M}_2)^T \bar{\Sigma}^{-1} \bar{\Sigma}\ \bar{\Sigma}^{-1}(\boldsymbol{M}_1 - \boldsymbol{M}_2) = (\boldsymbol{M}_1 - \boldsymbol{M}_2)^T \bar{\Sigma}^{-1}(\boldsymbol{M}_1\text{-}\boldsymbol{M}_2).$$

Thus the asymptotic and the Bayes probabilities of misclassification are given by

$$\varepsilon_\infty^{\mathrm{F}} = P_1 Prob\ \{\, h^{\mathrm{F}}(X) < 0 \mid \omega_1\} + P_2 Prob\ \{h^{\mathrm{F}}(X) \geq 0 \mid \omega_2\} = \Phi\{-\delta\,/2\} = \varepsilon_B,$$

where $\delta^2 = (\boldsymbol{M}_1 - \boldsymbol{M}_2\,)^T\ \bar{\Sigma}^{-1}(\boldsymbol{M}_1 - \boldsymbol{M}_2\,)$ is a squared Mahalanobis distance.

3.4.2 The Double Asymptotics for the Expected Error

In the standard Fisher linear DF, the number of parameters to be estimated from the training-set is much larger than that for the EDC. In the two-category case, for the EDC we need to estimate $2n$ components of the mean vectors. For the Fisher linear DF we, need to estimate the additional $n(n+1)/2$ components of the covariance matrix. For the GCCM model with $N_2{=}N_1{=}\bar{N}$, the sample mean vectors are Gaussian, such that $\hat{\boldsymbol{M}}_1 \sim N(\boldsymbol{M}_1, \frac{1}{\bar{N}}\bar{\Sigma})$ and $\hat{\boldsymbol{M}}_2 \sim N(\boldsymbol{M}_2, \frac{1}{\bar{N}}\bar{\Sigma})$. The scaled covariance matrix is Wishart such that $(N\text{-}2)\hat{\Sigma} \sim \mathrm{W}(\bar{\Sigma}_n, N\text{-}2)$. Without proof, we present a final double asymptotic expression for the expected generalisation error,

$$\bar{\varepsilon}_N^{\mathrm{F}} \approx \Phi\{-\frac{\delta}{2}\frac{1}{\sqrt{T_M T_{\bar{\Sigma}}}}\}, \tag{3.10}$$

where the term $T_M = 1 + \frac{4n}{\delta^2 N}$ arises from the inexact sample estimation of the mean vectors of the classes and the term $T_{\bar{\Sigma}} = 1 + \frac{n}{N-n}$ arises from the inexact sample estimation of the covariance matrix.

Table 3.1 and the terms T_M and $T_{\bar{\Sigma}}$ allow one to evaluate the *cost for estimation* of components of the n-variate vectors $\hat{\boldsymbol{M}}_1$, $\hat{\boldsymbol{M}}_2$ and the $n \times n$ matrix $\bar{\Sigma}$ in terms of the increase in the generalisation error or in terms of the training-set size.

Example 2. Let $\delta = 5.5$ ($\varepsilon_\infty^{\mathrm{E}} = \varepsilon_\infty^{\mathrm{F}} = 0.003$) and $n = 50$. In order to have the mean generalisation error smaller than 0.005 ($\kappa \le 1.61$) to estimate the mean vectors (EDC) we need $N = 30+30$ training vectors. To estimate the covariance matrix (the Fisher classifier) we need an additional N=220+220 training vectors (Table 3.1).

3.4.3 The Conditional Probability of Misclassification

For the linear classifier, let the weights estimated from the training-set be $\boldsymbol{V}$, v_0. Then the generalisation error of the linear classifier is

$$\varepsilon_N^{\mathrm{F}} = P_1\,\Phi\{-\frac{v_0 + \boldsymbol{V}^T\boldsymbol{M}_1}{\sqrt{\boldsymbol{V}^T\bar{\Sigma}^{-1}\boldsymbol{V}}}\} + P_2\,\Phi\{\frac{v_0 + \boldsymbol{V}^T\boldsymbol{M}_2}{\sqrt{\boldsymbol{V}^T\bar{\Sigma}^{-1}\boldsymbol{V}}}\}.$$

The weights $\boldsymbol{V}$, v_0 are functions of the two sample mean vectors $\hat{\boldsymbol{M}}_1$, $\hat{\boldsymbol{M}}_2$ and the sample covariance matrix $\hat{\Sigma}$. This fact implies that the weights are random variables. Consequently the conditional PMC is also a random variable. Asymptotically, as $N \to \infty$, the increase in the conditional classification error $\Delta\varepsilon_N^{\mathrm{F}} = \varepsilon_N^{\mathrm{F}} - \varepsilon_\infty^{\mathrm{F}}$ is distributed as

$$\frac{\phi(\delta/2)}{\delta N}\left(\frac{\delta^2}{4}\chi_1^2 + (1+\frac{\delta^2}{4})\chi_{n-1}^2\right).$$

We have already used this representation to depict the distribution densities of the conditional classification error in Figure 3.1. Utilising the fact that $E(\chi_r^2) = r$, and $\mathrm{Var}(\chi_r^2) = 2r$ we obtain one more expansion for the expected classification error

$$\bar{\varepsilon}_N^{\mathrm{F}} \approx \varepsilon_\infty^{\mathrm{F}} + \frac{\phi(\delta/2)}{\delta N}\left(\frac{\delta^2}{4} + (1+\frac{\delta^2}{4})(n-1)\right). \tag{3.11}$$

3.4.4 A Standard Deviation of the Conditional Error

The representation of $\Delta\varepsilon_N^{\mathrm{F}}$ as the function of two chi-square random variables leads to a new result concerning the standard deviation of the conditional error, which is

$$\sqrt{V\varepsilon_N^{\mathrm{F}}} \approx \frac{\sqrt{2}\,\phi(\delta/2)}{\delta N}\sqrt{\frac{\delta^4}{16} + (1+\frac{\delta^2}{4})^2(n-1)}\,. \tag{3.12}$$

Formula (3.12) shows an interesting behaviour for the conditional error. When both N and n are increasing simultaneously and proportionally, the expected PMC tends to a constant value. The standard deviation, however, tends to zero! This fact suggests that, regardless of which randomly selected training-set we use in the high-dimensional case, we will obtain approximately the same conditional error. This is an important conclusion for practitioners. In the high-dimensional cases, we need to pay attention only to the expected PMC and need not be concerned about the variance of the conditional classification error.

The data in Table 3.1 can be used to verify the accuracy of expressions (3.10) and (3.11). When n is close to N, equation (3.10) is much more accurate than (3.11). Expression (3.11) shows that the increase in the expected generalisation error is proportional to ratio n/N. However, Equation (3.10) shows that this phenomenon is true only when $N >> n$. When N is close to n, the generalisation error becomes very large and then we have more complex dependence.

Equations (3.7) and (3.10) can be used to demonstrate the scissors and peaking effects discussed in Chapter 1. When the training-set size is comparatively small, instead of using the Fisher rule, one needs to use a simple decision rule – the EDC. An alternative to using a simple classifier is to use the Fisher rule and reduce the number of the features.

3.4.5 Favourable and Unfavourable Distributions

While analysing the EDC we have seen that there exist favourable and unfavourable pattern-class distributions. A similar situation is characteristic for the Fisher classifier. To design the standard Fisher classifier one must estimate the covariance matrix. In theory, one must have the training-set size at least equal to the number of the features. However, in practical cases, one needs a much larger training-set size. More precise evaluations follow from analysing the terms T_M and $T_{\bar{\Sigma}}$ in the Equation (3.10).

In principle, for non-Gaussian data models one can create special artificial data models for which the Fisher classifier can be perfectly trained using $n + 1$ training vectors. To create such an example, we leave this as an exercise for the reader. A similar conclusion is valid for the least favourable case – one can create models for which the Fisher classifier is very sensitive to the number of training vectors.

Example 3. In Figure 3.3, we have two bimodal uni-variate densities. For such data the Fisher classifier requires a tremendous number of training examples. In this case, an insignificant deviation in the sample means causes an enormous increase in the generalisation error. This data model is also unfavourable for the EDC as well as for the RDA classifier.

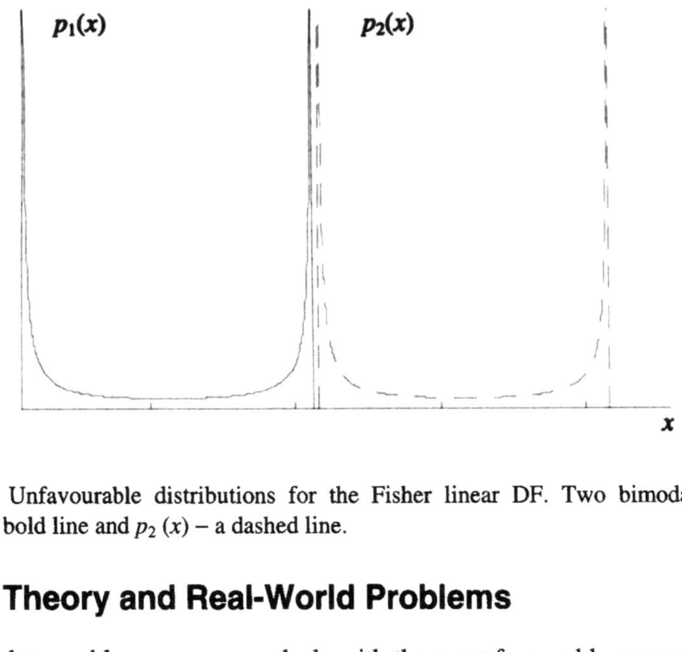

Fig. 3.3. Unfavourable distributions for the Fisher linear DF. Two bimodal densities, $p_1(x)$ – a bold line and $p_2(x)$ – a dashed line.

3.4.6 Theory and Real-World Problems

For real data problems one never deals with the most favourable case nor with the most unfavourable case. Among several dozens of real world-pattern recognition problems solved by the author of this book, no extremely bizarre cases involving unfavourable pattern-class distributions has been met. Analysis of training-set and test set error rates presented in numerous research papers in the literature also leads one to think that very unfavourable distributions are not encountered in real world problems. Most often the theoretical estimates obtained for the Gaussian model approximately characterises the learning quantity estimated experimentally. Notable exceptions are visibly multimodal data sets where the linear or quadratic classifiers should not be used. Rather, one should use nonparametric classifiers such as Parzen window, *k-NN* rule, or piecewise-linear classifiers, etc.

In Table 3.2 we present theoretical estimates (upper rows), and experimental estimates (lower rows) of the test set errors evaluated by using four real-world data sets. Each estimate is a mean value obtained from 50 repetitions of the experiment with different, randomly-chosen training sets. The theoretical estimates are calculated for a very idealised data model – multivariate spherical Gaussian distributions. Visual analysis of histograms of the data set features showed that all data sets were more or less unimodal but some features were highly asymmetrical. In spite of notable differences of the real distributions from the idealised Gaussian distributions, the theoretical estimates of κ are tolerably close to the experimental values. Therefore, the author recommends that one use the values of the learning quantity $\kappa = \bar{\varepsilon}_N^A \,/\, \varepsilon_\infty^A$ found for the spherical Gaussian model (Table 3.1, Equations (3.10) and (3.7) with $n^* = n$) as a rule of thumb.

Table 3.2. Comparison of the theoretical and empirical values of ratio $\kappa = \bar{\varepsilon}_N^A \,/\, \varepsilon_\infty^A$ (Reprinted from Raudys and Pikelis, On dimensionality, sample size, classification error and complexity of classification algorithm in pattern recognition, *Pattern Analysis and Machine Intelligence* 2, 1980, © IEEE).

	Data set 1 $n = 5$ $Nt = 500$	Data set 2 $n = 5$ $Nt = 600$	Data set 3 $n = 32$ $Nt = 300$	Data set 4 $n = 6$ $Nt = 600$
$\bar{N}$	12 20 50	12 20 50	20 50	12 20 50
E theory experiment	1.14 1.09 1.04 1.12 1.09 1.04	1.19 1.101.04 1.18 1.14 1.10	1.18 1.08 1.11 1.00	1.13 1.09 1.04 0.98 1.01 1.00
F theory experiment	1.67 1.30 1.12 1.44 1.32 1.09	1.70 1.32 1.12 2.01 1.63 1.32	4.51 2.55 13.6 6.62	1.32 1.13 1.07 1.23 1.20 1.10

3.4.7 The Linear Classifier D for the Diagonal CM

One modification of the linear Fisher DF, discussed in Section 2.3.1, is the classifier

$$\hat{h}^{D}(\boldsymbol{X}) = (\boldsymbol{X} - ½\,(\hat{\boldsymbol{M}}_1 + \hat{\boldsymbol{M}}_2))^T\, \hat{\boldsymbol{D}}^{-1}(\hat{\boldsymbol{M}}_1 - \hat{\boldsymbol{M}}_2), \tag{3.13}$$

where $\hat{\boldsymbol{D}}$ is a sample estimate of the diagonal variance matrix composed from diagonal elements of $\hat{\boldsymbol{\Sigma}}$, the pooled sample estimate of the covariance matrix.

The discriminant function (3.13) is a function of two random vectors and random diagonal matrix

$$h^{D}(\boldsymbol{X},\, \hat{\boldsymbol{M}}_1,\, \hat{\boldsymbol{M}}_2,\, \hat{\boldsymbol{D}}) = \boldsymbol{Z}^T\, \hat{\boldsymbol{D}}^{-1} \boldsymbol{Z}_2,$$

where $\boldsymbol{Z}$ and $\boldsymbol{Z}_2$ have been defined in Section 3.2.2.

Let the *true distributions* of the pattern classes be spherical Gaussian $N_X(\boldsymbol{M}_r, \mathbf{I}\sigma^2)$. We assume that the classifier designer does not know that $\bar{\Sigma} = \mathbf{I}\sigma^2$. In order to design the classifier (3.13) he utilises the variance matrix $\boldsymbol{D}$ estimated from the training-set. The matrix $\boldsymbol{D}$ is composed from n estimates $d_1, d_2, \dots, d_n$ of the variances of all n features. Let $N_2 = N_1 = \bar{N} = N/2$, and $P_2 = P_1 = ½$. Then each single element d_j of diagonal matrix $\hat{\boldsymbol{D}}$ is a scaled chi-square random variable of the form $(N-2)^{-1}\chi^2_{N-2}$.

The first two statistical moments of an inverse of a chi-square random variable are

$$E(\chi_r^2)^{-1} = \frac{1}{r-2}, \text{ and } \quad E(\chi_r^2)^{-2} = \frac{1}{(r-2)(r-4)}.$$

Thus, $E(d_j^{-1}) = \frac{N-2}{N-4}$ and $E(d_j^{-2}) = \frac{(N-2)^2}{(N-4)(N-6)}$. As in Section 3.2.2, we have that

$$E\left[h(\boldsymbol{X}, \hat{\boldsymbol{M}}_1, \hat{\boldsymbol{M}}_2, \hat{\boldsymbol{D}}) \mid \boldsymbol{X} \in \omega_i\right] = (-1)^{i+1}\frac{1}{2}\frac{N-2}{N-4}\boldsymbol{M}^T\boldsymbol{M} = (-1)^{i+1}\frac{1}{2}\frac{N-2}{N-4}\delta^2 \quad (3.14a)$$

and $V\left[h(\boldsymbol{X}, \hat{\boldsymbol{M}}_1, \hat{\boldsymbol{M}}_2, \hat{\boldsymbol{D}}) \mid \boldsymbol{X} \in \omega_i\right] =$

$$\left(\frac{N-2}{N-4}\right)^2 \sum_{j=1}^{n}\left(\frac{N-4}{N-6}\left(m_j^2 + \frac{4}{N}\right)\left(\frac{m_j^2}{4} + 1 + \frac{1}{N}\right) + \frac{m_j^4}{4}\right), \quad (3.14b)$$

where $m_1, m_2, \dots, m_n$ are the components of vector $\boldsymbol{M} = \boldsymbol{M}_1 - \boldsymbol{M}_2$, $\delta^2 = \boldsymbol{M}^T\boldsymbol{M}$, and we denote $\delta_{(4)} = \frac{1}{\delta^2}\sum_{j=1}^{n} m_j^4$.

An expression for the expected PMC follows directly from (3.4) and (3.14*ab*):

$$\bar{\varepsilon}_N^{D} \approx \Phi\left\{-\frac{\delta}{2\sqrt{\left(1+\frac{2}{N-6}\right)\left(1+\frac{2}{N}\left(1+\frac{2n}{\delta^2}\right)+\frac{4n}{\delta^2 N^2}\right)+\frac{\delta_{(4)}}{2(N-6)}}}\right\}. \quad (3.15)$$

For large n and N, ignoring the terms of order $\frac{1}{N}$, and $\frac{n}{N^2}$, we have the approximation

$$\bar{\varepsilon}_N^{\text{D}} \approx \Phi\{-\frac{\delta}{2}\frac{1}{\sqrt{T_M}}\}, \tag{3.16}$$

where the term $T_M = 1+\dfrac{2n}{\delta^2 \bar{N}}$ corresponds to the estimation of the mean vectors.

Analytical formulae for the generalisation error of EDC and the "diagonal" classifiers, (3.7) and (3.16), indicate that both expressions are asymptotically identical. Therefore estimation of n common variances asymptotically (as $N \to \infty$ and $n \to \infty$) does not affect the increase in the generalisation error! This fact suggests that the estimation of parameters that are common to both pattern classes is less important than the estimation of differing parameters. We will consider this problem more in Section 3.5.

3.4.8 The Pseudo-Fisher Classifier

In the Pseudo-Fisher classifier, instead of the conventional inverse of the sample covariance matrix $\hat{\Sigma}$ we use the pseudo-inverse (Section 2.5.1). Here instead of classifying the original vectors X we classify the new vectors $X_{new} = \Phi_1^T X$ in an r-dimensional subspace corresponding to the non-zero eigenvalues of the covariance matrix $\hat{\Sigma}$ ($r = N$-2 is the rank of the sample covariance matrix $\hat{\Sigma}$). Recall, that in the "diagonal" classifier design paradigm, one assumes that the covariance matrix of the vector to be classified is a diagonal matrix composed of the diagonal elements of the sample covariance matrix $\hat{\Sigma}$. In the new space, the Pseudo-Fisher classifier's covariance matrix is a diagonal matrix Λ composed of the variances of the vector X_{new} – the r non-zero eigenvalues $\lambda_1, \lambda_2, \ldots, \lambda_r$ of $\hat{\Sigma}$.

The generalisation error of the Pseudo-Fisher classifier can be viewed as follows. In the pseudo-inverse approach, the feature space is rotated by means of a certain (random) orthogonal transformation $X_{new} = \Phi_1^T X$ and afterwards, unlabeled data are classified by the "diagonal" classifier in the new r-variate feature space corresponding to the r non-zero eigenvalues of the sample covariance matrix $\hat{\Sigma}$. The Mahalanobis distance in the r-variate space increases with $r = N$-2, however, the accuracy of determination of the eigenvalues $\lambda_1, \lambda_2, \ldots, \lambda_r$ decreases. If both n and N are large ($N < n$), the expected error of the Pseudo-Fisher classifier is

$$\bar{\varepsilon}_N^{\text{PF}} \approx \Phi\left\{-\frac{\delta\sqrt{r/n}}{2}\frac{1}{\sqrt{(1+\gamma^2)T_M+\gamma^2\dfrac{3\delta^2}{4n}}}\right\}, \tag{3.17}$$

where $\gamma = \sqrt{V_d} / E_d$; E_d, V_d are respectively mean and variance of a random variable $1/\lambda_r$ and λ_r is a randomly chosen eigenvalue of matrix $\hat{\Sigma}$ having Wishart $W(\mathbf{I}_n, N\text{-}2)$ distribution.

Equation (3.17) is similar to (3.7). Analysis of equation (3.17) shows that the terms r/n and γ are increasing as the training-set size N increases from 1 up to n. E.g., for dimensionality n =20 we have:

$\gamma = 0.32$ when $N = 3$;
$\gamma = 1.03$ when $N=11$; and
$\gamma = 9.75$ when $N=21$.

Thus, as N increases the term r/n in the nominator of (3.17) causes a decrease in the generalisation error while the term γ in the denominator of (3.17) causes an increase the generalisation error.

The differing behaviours of the terms r/n and γ produce an interesting and unexpected behaviour of the generalisation error: with an increase in the training-set size, $N = 2\overline{N}$, from 1 to n, the generalisation error decreases at first, reaches the minimum, and afterwards begins increasing (see curve 3 in Figure 3.4).

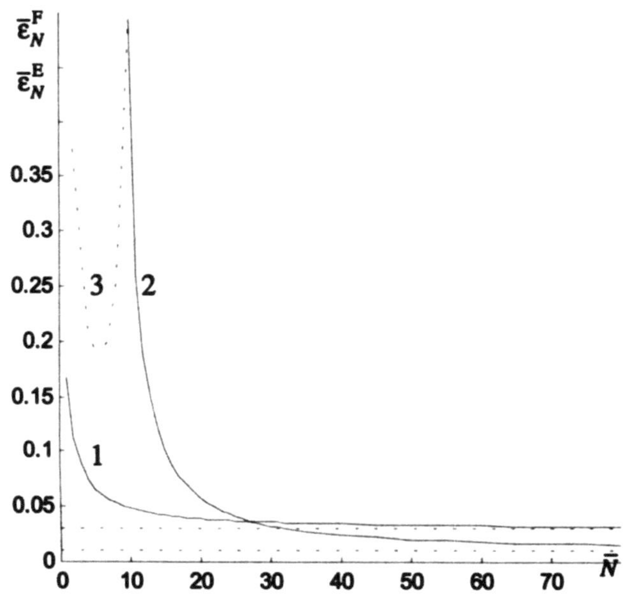

Fig. 3.4. The scissors effect: the generalisation error versus $\bar{N}$: 1 – EDC (for $n^* = 20$), 2, 3 – the Pseudo-Fisher and Fisher classifiers. For $\bar{N} < 30$ the EDC is preferred.

The minimal error is obtained for $\bar{N} = n/2$ and the maximal error is obtained for $N = n$. This complex and "strange" behaviour is a consequence of non-optimality of the plug-in Pseudo-Fisher classifier. If the training-set size is $N > n$, then we obtain the Fisher linear DF and the expected error decreases regularly as N increases. In Chapter 4 we will see that the non-linear single layer perceptron can also exhibit such peaking behaviour.

3.4.9 The Regularised Discriminant Analysis

RDA is an intermediate classifier between the EDC and the Fisher linear DF. In RDA while calculating the weights of the linear discriminant function, one uses the ridge estimate, $\hat{\Sigma}^{RDA} = \hat{\Sigma} + \lambda\mathbf{I}$, rather than the conventional pooled sample estimate $\hat{\Sigma}$. Thus, while changing the parameter λ, we obtain a sequence of classifiers ranging from the EDC (λ =0) to the Fisher linear DF ($\lambda \to \infty$). We can obtain the RDA classifier in the SLP training, too.

Positive values of λ added to each diagonal element of the sample covariance matrix help to invert the covariance matrix and act as regularisers. At the same time, the addition of $\lambda\mathbf{I}$ to the true covariance matrix distorts the weights vector and, consequently, increases the classification error. We can evaluate this effect numerically.

When the term $\lambda\mathbf{I}$ is added to the true covariance matrix Σ, we have the following discriminant function

$$h^{RDA}(X) = X^T(\hat{\Sigma} + \lambda\mathbf{I})^{-1}(M_1 - M_2) - \tfrac{1}{2}(M_1 + M_2)^T(\hat{\Sigma} + \lambda\mathbf{I})^{-1}(M_1 - M_2).$$

For the GCCM model, this linear discriminant function has a Gaussian distribution with mean

$$E[h^{RDA}(X) \mid \omega_i] = [(M_i - \tfrac{1}{2}(M_1 + M_2)]^T(\bar{\Sigma} + \lambda\mathbf{I})^{-1}(M_1 - M_2),$$

and variance

$$V[h^{RDA}(X) \mid \omega_i] = (M_1 - M_2)^T(\bar{\Sigma} + \lambda\mathbf{I})^{-1}\, \bar{\Sigma}\, (\bar{\Sigma} + \lambda\mathbf{I})^{-1}(M_1 - M_2).$$

Assuming equal prior probabilities of the classes, we have that the asymptotic probability of misclassification is

$$\varepsilon_\infty^{RDA} = \tfrac{1}{2}\,Prob\{h^{RDA}(X)) < 0 \mid \omega_1\} + \tfrac{1}{2}\,Prob\{h^{RDA}(X) \geq 0 \mid \omega_2\} = \Phi\{-\tfrac{1}{2}\,\delta_\lambda\} \geq \varepsilon_B,$$

where $\delta_\lambda^2 = \dfrac{(M^T(\bar{\Sigma} + \lambda\mathbf{I})^{-1}M)^2}{M^T(\bar{\Sigma} + \lambda\mathbf{I})^{-1}\bar{\Sigma}(\bar{\Sigma} + \lambda\mathbf{I})^{-1}M}$ is the squared modified Mahalanobis distance for the RDA classifier and $M = M_1 - M_2$.

Analysis of expression for ε_∞^{RDA} shows that growth in the regularisation parameter λ increases the asymptotic error.

Example 4. For the data model depicted in Figure 1.2 for $\lambda = 0$, we have that the asymptotic and Bayes errors are $\varepsilon_\infty^F = \varepsilon_B = 0.0401$. As $\lambda \to \infty$, this error rate gradually increases until $\varepsilon_\infty^E = 0.0912$. For the 20-variate correlated GCCM data **C**

discussed in Section 1.4, if we let $\lambda = 0$, the asymptotic and the Bayes errors are $\varepsilon_\infty^{\mathrm{RDA}} = \varepsilon_B = 0.01$. When $\lambda \to \infty$ we find that $\varepsilon_\infty^{\mathrm{RDA}} = \varepsilon_\infty^{\mathrm{E}} = 0.03$.

For very small values of λ the expected (generalisation) error can be represented by the following asymptotic formula:

$$\bar{\varepsilon}_N^{\mathrm{RDA}} \to \Phi\{-\frac{\delta_\lambda}{2}\frac{\sqrt{1+T_\lambda}}{\sqrt{T_M T_{\bar{\Sigma}}}}\}, \tag{3.18}$$

where T_λ is a certain function of $\bar{\Sigma}$, $\boldsymbol{M}$ and λ. Expression (3.18) is a very complex function of $\boldsymbol{M}$, $\bar{\Sigma}$ and is accurate only for very small λ. Therefore, we do not discuss the implications of Expression (3.18) in detail here. However, (3.18) explains that the positive term T_λ reduces the negative influence of $T_{\bar{\Sigma}}$. This term increases with λ and, to some extent, it compensates for inaccuracies ("noise") caused by the inexact estimation of the covariance matrix. When $\lambda \to 0$, the term $T_\lambda \to 0$.

When the training-set size $N \to \infty$, then $\bar{\varepsilon}_N^{\mathrm{RDA}} \to \varepsilon_\infty^{\mathrm{RDA}} = \Phi\{-\delta_\lambda/2\}$. Contrary to the asymptotic error, the learning quantity $\kappa = \bar{\varepsilon}_N^{\mathrm{RDA}} / \varepsilon_\infty^{\mathrm{RDA}}$ – the relative increase in the mean generalisation error – *decreases* with increasing λ. For the data model **C** and training set size $N = 2n = 40$ for $\lambda = 0$ (the Fisher classifier), we have $\kappa = 2.47$ When $\lambda \to \infty$ (EDC) this value decreases until $\kappa = 1.16$

Thus, we have the following dual behaviour: the growth of λ increases the asymptotic error, but improves the classifier's small sample properties (reduces the ratio $\kappa = \bar{\varepsilon}_N^{\mathrm{RDA}} / \varepsilon_\infty^{\mathrm{RDA}}$). As a result, in the finite training-set size case, as λ increases, most often the generalisation error decreases at first, arrives at the minimum and then increases again. This phenomenon is known as the *peaking effect*, similar to the peaking that arises with an increase in the number of the features (see Section 1.5).

The value of λ where the generalisation error is minimised is called the *optimal value of the regularisation parameter.* In Figure 3.5, we have three experimental graphs (1-1, 1-2, 1-3) of the generalisation error against λ, determined for the artificial 20-variate GCCM data model **C** and three randomly selected training sets of size $\bar{N} = 80$. We also present two estimates of the mean generalisation error – the average of the conditional error over 25 random training-sets of sizes $\bar{N} = 80$ (graph 2) and $\bar{N} = 16$ (graph 3). The minima of the graphs are denoted by "×".

Note that the optimal value of λ_{opt} depends on each particular data type (the dimensionality, a configuration of the data points distribution, etc.) and the training-set size. In general, λ_{opt} decreases with the increase in the training-set size. For the GCCM pattern classes we have $\lambda_{opt} \to 0$ as $N \to \infty$. However, we have noted in related experiments that λ_{opt} fluctuates with each particular training-set.

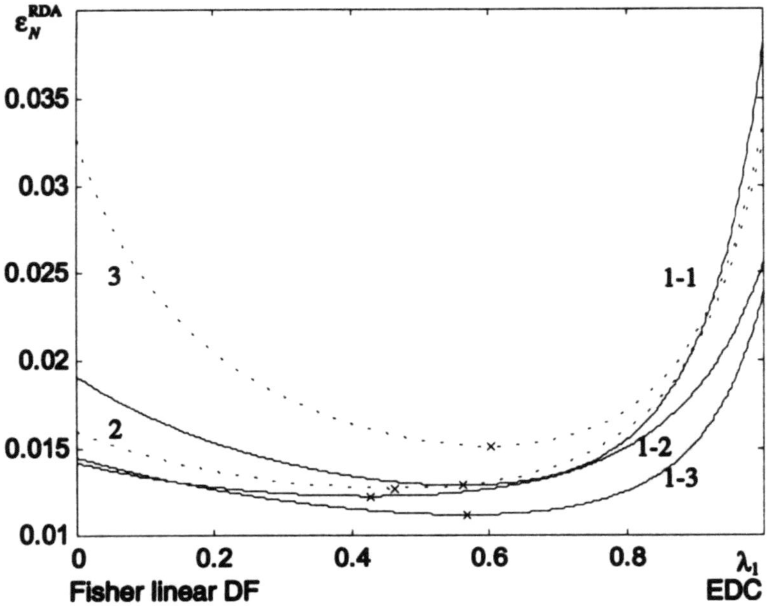

Fig. 3.5. The peaking effect: the generalisation error as a function of the regularisation parameter $\lambda_1=\lambda/(1+\lambda)$. 20-variate correlated Gaussian data: 1-1, 1-2, 1-3 give the generalisation errors for three randomly selected training-sets of size $\bar{N}$ = 80, 2 gives the generalisation error averaged over 25 random training-sets of size $\bar{N}$ = 80, 3 gives the generalisation error averaged over 25 random training-sets, $\bar{N}$ = 32.

3.5 Common Parameters in Different Competing Pattern Classes

While designing several parametric statistical classification algorithms, we note that a portion of the distribution density parameters are common to both pattern classes. For instance, in the standard Fisher linear DF, we assume that both populations share the same covariance matrix Σ. In the "diagonal classifier" D, we assume that n variances $d_1, d_2, \ldots, d_n$ are common in both populations. In both cases, we assume that the mean vectors $\boldsymbol{M}_1, \boldsymbol{M}_2$ are different. An important issue discussed in this section is the fact that for certain conditions, the parameters of the multivariate distribution density functions common for all pattern classes have little influence on the generalisation error when compared to the parameters that differ.

In the multi-layer perceptron and the radial basic function neural networks, the weights of the hidden layer are typically connected with all outputs. This relationship suggests that they are common for all pattern classes. Thus, according to this argument, the hidden layer weights should have less influence on classifier performance than the output layer weights.

3.5.1 The Generalisation Error of the Quadratic DF

The classical statistical classification method, where one assumes that the covariance matrices and means are different, is the standard quadratic DF, which is given in (2.11). The number of parameters to be estimated from the training-set is $n(n+3)/2$ per class. The double asymptotic analysis shows that in the case of GCCM classes, the expected PMC of this classifier can be asymptotically approximated as

$$\bar{\varepsilon}_N^Q \approx \Phi\{-\frac{\delta}{2}\frac{1}{\sqrt{T_{\Sigma A}T_M + T_{\Sigma B}}}\}, \tag{3.19}$$

where $T_{\Sigma A} = 1 + \frac{n}{\bar{N}-n}$ and $T_{\Sigma B} = \frac{\delta^4/2 + n(2+n/\delta^2)}{\bar{N}-n}$.

We can see differences and similarities between (3.10) and (3.19). For both discriminant functions we have the term T_M multiplied by the term T_Σ ($T_{\Sigma A}$). In the term $T_{\Sigma A}$, however, we use $\bar{N}$, the sample-size of one single class, instead of $N = 2\bar{N}$ in the term T_Σ for the linear Fisher DF. This difference is caused by the fact that to estimate the covariance matrix of each single class we use only half of the training vectors. In expression (3.19) for the quadratic discriminant function, we have *additional term*, $T_{\Sigma B}$. This term reflects the situation that the covariance matrices are *different* in both classes and thus, indicates that for small δ or large n, the increase in the generalisation error can become proportional to n^2/N. This term can be comparatively small for highly overlapping classes (when δ, the distance between the pattern classes, is small) with low dimensions. The influence of this term increases as the dimensionality n and the distance δ increase. Thus, in the high-dimensional case or when the classification error is small, the quadratic discriminant function becomes very sensitive to the training-set size. The SLP, the Anderson–Bahadur linear DF, the modified RDA (2.39) and the MLP can become good competitors to the standard quadratic discriminant function in this case.

3.5.2 The Effect of Common Parameters in Two Competing Classes

In order to design the EDC we need to estimate n components of the mean vector $\boldsymbol{M}_1$ and n components of the mean vector $\boldsymbol{M}_2$. In the "diagonal" classifier we estimate the mean vectors $\boldsymbol{M}_1$, $\boldsymbol{M}_2$, and n non-zero elements of the diagonal variance matrix $\boldsymbol{D}$. Analytical formulae for the generalisation error of both classifiers, (3.7) and (3.16), respectively, indicate that the expressions are asymptotically identical. Thus, we have the following result:

estimation of n common variances asymptotically does not affect the increase in the generalisation error.

Formula (3.16) is to some extent general and can be used for the case when we use the Fisher classifier with the constrained "the first order tree type" estimate of the covariance matrix containing $2n$-1 different components. In this covariance matrix model, $2n$-1 parameters are common for both pattern classes. Thus, asymptotically (as $N\to\infty$ and $n\to\infty$), the generalisation error for this classifier is the same as for the EDC. This formula is also valid for the number of other models with constrained covariance matrices that are discussed in Chapter 2.

A similar formula is valid for the linear statistical classifier (2.16) designed for the block-structured covariance matrix model (2.15). Here we have

$$\bar{\varepsilon}_N^{\mathrm{BD}} = P_1\Phi\left(-\frac{\sum_{j=1}^{H} \frac{N_1+N_2}{N_1+N_2-n_j}\left(\delta_j^2 - \lambda_{1j} + \lambda_{2j}\right) - 2c}{2\sqrt{\sum_{j=1}^{H}\left(\delta_j^2 + \lambda_{1j} + \lambda_{2j}\right)}} \right) +$$

$$P_2\Phi\left(-\frac{\sum_{j=1}^{H} \frac{N_1+N_2}{N_1+N_2-n_j}\left(\delta_j^2 + \lambda_{1j} - \lambda_{2j}\right) + 2c}{2\sqrt{\sum_{j=1}^{H}\left(\delta_j^2 + \lambda_{1j} + \lambda_{2j}\right)}} \right) \tag{3.20}$$

where δ_j^2 is the squared Mahalanobis distance associated with j-th n_j-dimensional block, H is a number of independent blocks, $\lambda_{ij} = n_j/N_i$, and c is a constant.

In order to better understand the above equation assume N_2=N_1= $\bar{N}$, P_2=P_1= ½, c = 0, and all blocks are of equal size, i.e. $n_1 = n_2 = , \ldots, = n_H = n/H$. Then, (3.20) can be written as

$$\bar{\varepsilon}_N^{\mathrm{BD}} \approx \Phi\{ -\frac{\delta}{2}\frac{1}{\sqrt{T_M T_{\Sigma}^{BD}}} \}, \tag{3.21}$$

where δ^2 is the squared Mahalanobis distance, the term $T_M = 1+ \dfrac{4n}{\delta^2 N}$ arises from estimation of the mean vectors of the classes and is defined in (3.10). The term

$$T_{\Sigma}^{BD} = 1 + \frac{n_H}{N - n_H} \tag{3.22}$$

is caused by the sample estimates of the separate blocks of the covariance matrix. It differs from the similar term T_{Σ} in (3.10). When we have many blocks and when n is close to N, we have an obvious gain from the block-wise structuralisation of the covariance matrix. When $n \to \infty$, $N \to \infty$, and the size of each block $n_H = n/H$ does not change, the term $T_{\Sigma}^{BD} \to 1$. We see that asymptotically, estimation of $H(n_H+1)n_H$ parameters for the common blocks does not affect the increase in the generalisation error.

Generalisation of the above results for the diagonal and block-diagonal classifiers was accomplished by Meshalkin and Serdobolskij (1978). They analysed the plug-in classification rules where the h_d characteristics of the multivariate distribution density functions are different in each of two pattern classes and that h_c characteristics are common. They showed that

> asymptotically when both the number of parameters, h_d and h_c, and the sample size N are increasing proportionally, and the distance between pattern classes does not change, the increase in the generalisation error is determined by the number of differing parameters.

This result is of fundamental significance for understanding the classification performance of the multi-layer perceptrons and radial basic function neural networks. For artificial neural networks, the weights of the hidden layer typically are connected with all outputs. Thus, they are common for all pattern classes. Therefore, one can guess that, the hidden layer weights will have less influence than the weights of the output layer.

The general asymptotic theorems, however, hide some terms that are important in the realistic case of pattern recognition problems with finite dimensions and finite training sets. For example, the term $\delta_{(4)}/(4(N-3))$ in Equation (3.15) shows that, in principle, situations can exist where the conclusion about minor influence of common parameters can be incorrect. For some non-spherical data, the term $\delta_{(4)}/(4(N-3))$ can increase as the number of the features n increases. Consequently, one can get an increase in the generalisation error. We have already discussed a similar situation in Section 3.4, where we have analysed the Pseudo-Fisher classifier in the small training-set case.

3.5.3 Unequal Sample Sizes in Plug-In Classifiers

In the plug-in approach to classifier design, we use unbiased estimates $\hat{\mathbf{Y}}_i$ of the parameter vector $\mathbf{Y}_i$ of the pattern-class densities. In spite of the fact that the estimates $\hat{\mathbf{Y}}_i$ are unbiased, the plug-in density estimates $p_i(X \mid \hat{\mathbf{Y}}_i)$ are biased. The sample plug-in discriminant function is

$$h(X) = \log p_1(X \mid \hat{\mathbf{Y}}_1, \hat{\mathbf{Y}}) - \log p_1(X \mid \hat{\mathbf{Y}}_2, \hat{\mathbf{Y}}) + \log \frac{P_1}{P_2},$$

where $\hat{\mathbf{Y}}$ is a sample estimate of the parameter vector common to both pattern classes, and $\hat{\mathbf{Y}}_1, \hat{\mathbf{Y}}_2$ are parameter vectors that are unique to each pattern class.

This discriminant function is biased, too. The bias increases as the difference between N_1 and N_2 increases, causing an unnecessary increase in the generalisation error (see e.g. Section 3.2.3.2). Therefore, the bias-correcting term (3.9) was suggested. Equation (3.20) indicates a way for obtaining a bias-correcting term c for the standard Fisher linear DF and its variant with block covariance matrix (2.16). For the linear Fisher DF the bias term is

$$bias^{F}(n, N_1, N_2) = \tfrac{1}{2}T_{\Sigma}(n/N_2 - n/N_1) = c. \tag{3.23}$$

For the quadratic DF, however, the sample covariance matrices are assumed to be *different* in both pattern classes. Therefore term $T_{\Sigma B}$ in Equation (3.19) appears. Consequently, the bias is much more significant than for the linear classification rule. For the quadratic DF, we obtain the following rather unexpected effect: an increase in the training-set size of one of the pattern classes can increase the expected classification (generalisation) error!

Example 5. For two 40-dimensional GCCM classes, δ=2.56 ($\varepsilon_{\infty}^{Q} = \varepsilon_B = 0.1$), the expected error of the standard quadratic DF is

for $N_1 = N_2 = 200$ $\quad \bar{\varepsilon}_N^{Q} \approx 0.229$,

for $N_1 = 200$, $N_2 = 2000$ $\quad \bar{\varepsilon}_N^{Q} \approx 0.265$, and

for $N_1 = 200$, $N_2 = 20000$ $\quad \bar{\varepsilon}_N^{Q} \approx 0.274$.

We see, an increase in N_2, the number of training vectors from category ω_2, notably increases the generalisation error!

Use of an unbiased estimate of the multivariate Gaussian density or the Bayes predictive approach does not help to reduce the generalisation error. This effect is due to the assumption that the prior distributions of the mean vectors and the covariance matrices are flat. In obtaining the Bayes predictive decision rule we may be averaging over an unduly dispersed prior parameter distribution.

An introduction of the bias-correcting term to the classical quadratic DF helps to obtain an unbiased quadratic DF that reduces the generalisation error. We suggest the following unbiased quadratic DF:

$$\hat{g}^{Q}_{unbiased}(X) = k_2(X - \hat{M}_2)^T \hat{\Sigma}_2^{-1}(X - \hat{M}_2) - k_1(X - \hat{M}_1)^T \hat{\Sigma}_1^{-1}(X - \hat{M}_1) +$$

$$\log|\hat{\Sigma}_2| / |\hat{\Sigma}_1| + \log P_1/P_2 + bias^{Q}(n, N_1, N_2), \tag{3.24}$$

where

$k_i = 1 - n/N_i$;

$$bias^{Q}(n, N_1, N_2) = \sum_{j=1}^{n} (\Psi((N_2 - j)/2) - \Psi((N_1 - j)/2) + n\log(N_2/N_1);$$

$\Psi(r)$ is an Euler psi function: $\Psi(r+1) = -\mathbf{C} + \sum_{s=1}^{r} 1/s$;

$\Psi(r+1/2) = -\mathbf{C} - 2\log 2 + 2\sum_{s=0}^{r-1}(1-2s)^{-1}$, and $\mathbf{C}$ is a constant.

For the new "unbiased" quadratic DF we calculate:

$$\bar{\varepsilon}_N^{\mathrm{Q}} \approx 0.229, \text{ when } N_1 = N_2 = 200;$$
$$\bar{\varepsilon}_N^{\mathrm{Q}} \approx 0.187, \text{ when } N_1 = 200, N_2 = 2000; \text{ and}$$
$$\bar{\varepsilon}_N^{\mathrm{Q}} \approx 0.183, \text{ when } N_1 = 200, N_2 = 20000.$$

For $N_2 = 20000$, the mean generalisation error diminished from $\bar{\varepsilon}_N^{\mathrm{Q}} \approx 0.274$ to 0.183. For the unequal CM case ($\Sigma_2 = 2\,\Sigma_1$) $\varepsilon_\infty^{\mathrm{Q}} = 0.34$, $n = 40$, $N_1 = 200$. An increase in N_2 from 200 to 20000 diminishes the mean generalisation error from $\bar{\varepsilon}_N^{\mathrm{Q}} \approx 0.170$ to 0.084.

These examples help one to understand the deficiency of the plug-in approach. Thus, one should diminish the bias of the quadratic DF. While training the SLP classifier we attempt to minimise the empirical probability of misclassification and do not suffer such a marked effect due to bias of the classifier. It is an advantage of the neural net approach.

3.6 Minimum Empirical Error and Maximal Margin Classifiers

There are a number of classification design algorithms that yield the minimum empirical error classifiers. While training the SLP classifier with an increase in the weights' magnitude, the SLP approaches the minimum empirical error classifier. If the number of empirical errors is zero, then in further training, the non-linear single-layer perceptron goes towards the maximal margin classifier.

In the nonparametric (structural) approach, no assumptions on the type of the multivariate distribution density are made. This is the main difference between the nonparametric (structural) minimum empirical error classifier and the parametric linear statistical classifiers. The parameters of the linear MEE classifier are searched directly from the training vectors. We avoid estimation of a great number of "unnecessary" parameters of the multivariate distribution density function. In this section, we consider consequences of this difference by analysing the generalisation error.

3.6.1 Favourable Distributions of the Pattern Classes

We have observed cardinal differences in values of the generalisation error of the Euclidean distance classifier calculated for the favourable and unfavourable distributions of the pattern classes. A similar situation arises in the analysis of the minimum empirical error classifier. We show that in the *favourable case*, one vector per class can be sufficient to train the classifier.

Example 6. Let the pattern vectors have support on a straight line in the multivariate feature space. Let the vectors from class 1 have support on the interval (A_1 A_2) on this line, and the vectors from class 2 have support on the interval (B_1 B_2). The support of each class does not overlap. We have chosen that $|A_1, A_2| < |A_2, B_1|$ and $|B_1, B_2| < |A_2, B_1|$ (Figure 3.6).

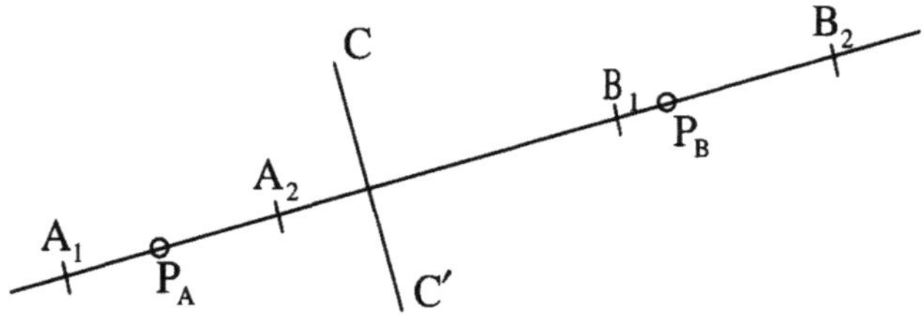

Fig. 3.6. The "most favourable" distribution of two pattern classes in two-variate feature space (Reprinted from *Neural Networks*, 11:297-313, Raudys, Evolution and generalization of a single neurone, 1998, with permission from Elsevier Science).

Suppose now, that only one observation per class is available for training – P_A and P_B. Let us design a linear classifier with maximal margin between the discriminant hyperplane and the two training vectors. Obviously, the linear decision boundary C-C', $V^T X + v_0 = 0$, crosses the interval (A_2, B_1). For this pattern class model the generalisation error will be zero. This example is one of the *most favourable* distributions of the pattern classes and is very favourable for the Euclidean distance classifier too. The pattern-class configuration is similar to the pattern-class configuration of the classes ω_3 and ω_5, depicted in Figure 3.2.

In *unfavourable* pattern-class distribution cases, in order to obtain a low generalisation error one needs many more training examples. For the linear Fisher classifier one of the unfavourable cases was presented in Figure 3.3; for the EDC it was presented in Figure 3.2 (the classes ω_3 and ω_4). The model of the pattern classes ω_3 and ω_4 can also become difficult to train for the minimum empirical error classifier.

3.6.2 VC Bounds for the Conditional Generalisation Error

The absolute and the relative increases in the generalisation error depend on the data model and its parameters **Y**. Here we have a dilemma: in order to be able to determine the increase in the generalisation error "one must know almost everything" (Vapnik, 1995). This requirement is an important deficiency of the statistical analysis approach. To overcome this difficulty Vapnik and Chervonenkis, (1974) devised a new viewpoint to analyse the classification, prediction and function approximation algorithms based on an empirical risk minimisation. Instead of characterising the *complexity of the data,* Vapnik and Chervonenkis (1968) searched for a characteristic of the *complexity of a set of classifiers.* Following the Cover's capacity concept, they succeeded in formulating a single complexity characteristic for a fraction of algorithms that minimise the empirical error that later became known as the Vapnik – Chervonenkis (VC) dimension

The VC dimension of a set F of classifiers is the maximum number of vectors h that can be divided into two classes in all 2^h possible ways using any classifier from the set F. For *linear classifiers* in an n-dimensional feature space $h = n + 1$. For multilayer perceptrons, the VCD is bounded by a number of weights. However, an exact expression does not exist yet.

For linear classifiers that minimise the empirical classification error it has been shown that the following inequality holds with probability at least 1-η (Vapnik, 1982, Equation 11.2)

$$\varepsilon_N^{\mathrm{MEE}} \le \varepsilon_{bound}^{\mathrm{MEE}} = \hat{\varepsilon}_N^{\mathrm{MEE}} + \frac{n(\ln\frac{N}{n}+1)-\log\eta}{2N}\left(1+\sqrt{1+\frac{4N\,\hat{\varepsilon}_N^{\mathrm{MEE}}}{n(\ln\frac{N}{n}+1)-\log\eta}}\right), \quad (3.25a)$$

where:

$\varepsilon_N^{\mathrm{MEE}}$ is the conditional probability of misclassification (the generalisation error) of the minimum empirical error (MEE) classifier;

$\hat{\varepsilon}_N^{\mathrm{MEE}} = N_{errors}/N$ is the empirical probability of misclassification (apparent error);

N_{errors} is the number of errors in the training-set and

$N = N_1 + N_2$ is the number of training examples.

The estimate (3.25*a*) is obtained for the worst possible type of pattern-class distributions. The last term on the right side of Expression (3.25*a*) gives an upper bound for the difference between the empirical error $\hat{\varepsilon}_N^{\mathrm{MEE}}$ and the conditional probability of misclassification $\varepsilon_N^{\mathrm{MEE}}$. Thus, for any other pattern-class distributions we should have a smaller difference between $\varepsilon_N^{\mathrm{MEE}}$ and $\hat{\varepsilon}_N^{\mathrm{MEE}}$. The bound (3.25*a*) indicates that the increase in the generalisation error is proportional to *n/N*, the dimensionality – training-set size ratio. This bound also indicates that, in theory, very "problematic" distributions of the pattern classes can occur. For such unfavourable cases, the number of training samples required to design the classifier is very large.

Example 7. For dimensionality $n = 100$, $\eta = 0.5$, and zero empirical error ($\hat{\varepsilon}_N^{\mathrm{MEE}} = 0$), the bound is

for $N = 200$ $\varepsilon_{bound}^{\mathrm{MEE}} = 0.85$; for $N = 2{,}000$ $\varepsilon_{bound}^{\mathrm{MEE}} = 0.2$;

and only for very large training-sets is the bound is comparatively reasonable: e.g.

$$\text{for } N = 20{,}000 \qquad \varepsilon_{bound}^{\text{MEE}} = \ 0.03.$$

The bound (3.25*a*) is derived for the worst-case distributions. Therefore, a number of modifications to this bound has been suggested. E.g., Cherkassky and Mullier (1998, Section 4.3.1) propose the bound

$$\varepsilon_{bound}^{\text{MEE}} = \frac{a_1 n(\log a_2 \frac{N}{n} + 1) - \ln \eta}{2N}\left(1 + \sqrt{1 + \frac{4N\hat{\varepsilon}_N^{\text{MEE}}}{\frac{N}{a_1 n(\log a_2 \frac{N}{n} + 1) - \ln \eta}}}\right), \tag{3.25b}$$

where constants a_1, a_2 must be in the range $0 < a_1 \leq 4$, $0 < a_2 \leq 2$.

Unfortunately, "for classification problems, good empirical values for a_1 and a_2 are unknown". The bounds become tighter when the training-set size N is large. Both bounds mentioned agree with conclusions from asymptotic analysis of the parametric rules: the increase in the generalisation error depends on the ratio of dimensionality to sample size, n/N. For more details concerning these error bounds the reader is directed to books by Vapnik (1982, 1995), Vidyasagar (1997), Cherkassky and Mulier (1998).

The Vapnik and Chervonenkis approach allows one to obtain a number of other error bounds for the conditional generalisation error of the classifiers within this group and to suggest a strategy for the selection of a classifier with optimal complexity. According to this strategy, called the *structural risk minimisation*,

one needs to select a rule with the minimal estimate of the error bound.

The structural risk minimisation approach is very simple to use as it does not require one to know the number of unknown characteristics of the data that are difficult or even impossible to estimate. Therefore, this approach has become very popular and has played a great role in explaining finite design set effects both in statistical pattern recognition and ANN theory. Unfortunately characterisation of the classifier's complexity by one single characteristic requires one to analyse the "worst-case functions". Then the error bounds "become too loose to be practically useful".

"These bounds become more tight (accurate) only when $N \to \infty$, an empirical risk is very close to the true risk" (Cherkassky and Mulier, 1998, Chapter 4). In comparison with the mean generalisation error values for the Euclidean distance, Fisher and zero empirical error classifiers reported above, the error bounds are incomparably large. In order to have the luxury of ignoring everything about the data except the number of dimensions, n, we have to sacrifice accuracy of the estimates. Thus, "we cannot expect this approach to provide immediate solutions to practical problem sets" (Cherkassky and Mulier, 1998).

3.6.3 Unfavourable Distributions for the Euclidean Distance and Minimum Empirical Error Classifiers

In spite of the fact that the error bounds (3.25*ab*) result in very pessimistic values, in principle, for the Euclidean distance classifier E we can obtain even higher generalisation error values. In Section 3.3, we have shown that for the EDC the effective dimensionality, n^*, is unbounded in principle. Thus, models of the pattern classes can be created where any number of the training vectors will be insufficient to design parametric classifiers, such as the Euclidean distance classifier, the Fisher linear DF, the regularised DA.

Example 8. For the unfavourable 100-variate negatively correlated data **E** (see Section 3.3.3) with $\varepsilon_{\infty}^{\mathrm{E}} = \varepsilon_{\infty}^{\mathrm{F}} = 0.03$ and $n^*=10^8$, when $N = 400$ ($\bar{N} = 200$) from (3.7) we obtain $\bar{\varepsilon}_N^{\mathrm{E}}=0.497$. In ten experiments with the EDC and ten independently chosen random training sets, we obtained the conditional PMC 0.497 (the same value, 0.497, in all 10 experiments; see subsection 3.3.3 for more details).

When $\bar{N} = 1000$ ($N = 2000$) from Equation (3.7) we have $\bar{\varepsilon}_N^{\mathrm{E}}=0.494$, and when $\bar{N} = 10000$ ($N = 20000$) then $\bar{\varepsilon}_N^{\mathrm{E}}=0.480$.

These values exceed the error bound (3.25*a*) for the least favourable case of the minimum empirical error classifier. Note for such highly correlated data models the EDC should not be used. Here the standard Fisher linear DF performs much better.

3.6.4 Generalisation Error in the Spherical Gaussian Case

In the most favourable case, one training vector per class can be sufficient to design the maximum margin classifier. From (3.25*a*) it follows that, in unfavourable cases, we need many training vectors in order to obtain the reliable classifier. In practice, we never have the most favourable nor the most unfavourable distributions for the pattern classes. In Table 3.2, we have presented experimental evaluations of the learning quantity $\kappa = \bar{\varepsilon}_N^{\mathrm{A}} / \varepsilon_{\infty}^{\mathrm{A}}$ of the Euclidean distance classifier and the standard Fisher linear DF obtained on four real-world data sets. The differences between the experimental results and the theoretical estimates obtained for the spherical Gaussian model are not large. Thus, in order to have some rule of thumb we will analyse the generalisation errors for the spherical Gaussian model.

We analyse one particular example of the minimum empirical error classifier – a *zero empirical error classifier* ($\hat{\varepsilon}_N^{\mathrm{MEE}} = 0$) – in the bench-mark model case, i.e. when the true pattern classes are spherical Gaussian $N_X(\boldsymbol{M}_1, \mathbf{I})$, $N_X(\boldsymbol{M}_2, \mathbf{I})$ and the prior probabilities of the classes are equal to ½. We will find the expected generalisation error of the zero empirical error (ZEE) linear classifier and the margin classifier trained by a hypothetical "random search" optimisation procedure.

The random search *(Monte Carlo) optimisation procedure* generates many (say, M) random discriminant hyperplanes according to a certain *prior* distribution of the weights, determined by *a priori* density $p^{prior}(\mathbf{V}, v_0)$, and selects those that classify the training sets LS^1 and LS^2, each of size $\bar{N}$, without error, as well as satisfying the following set of $N = 2\bar{N}$ conditions, S_Δ:

$$\text{for all } \bar{N} \text{ vectors } \mathbf{X}_{1j} \text{ from } LS^1, \qquad \frac{\mathbf{V}^T\mathbf{X}_{1j} + v_0}{\sqrt{\mathbf{V}^T\mathbf{V}}} > \Delta, \tag{3.26a}$$

$$\text{for all } \bar{N} \text{ vectors } \mathbf{X}_{2j} \text{ from } LS^2, \qquad \frac{\mathbf{V}^T\mathbf{X}_{2j} + v_0}{\sqrt{\mathbf{V}^T\mathbf{V}}} < -\Delta, \tag{3.26b}$$

where Δ is a bound for the margin.

The optimisation theory approach advocates that if the prior distribution $p^{prior}(\mathbf{V}, v_0)$ incorporates the optimal weight, then with an increase in the number of repetitions M of the random search, this procedure will find the minimum of the cost function with a desired accuracy. Thus, in the case that the number M tends to infinity and the training sets of opposite classes are linearly separable, then, at least theoretically, we should always succeed in finding one or more solutions that satisfy conditions (3.26*ab*). Note that the above random search training procedure will never be used in practice. The gradient training algorithms used in ANN design as well as many other algorithms mentioned in Chapter 2 allow one to estimate the weights $v_0, v_1, \dots, v_n$ much quicker and more effectively. For the random search optimisation, however, one can obtain analytical results that lead to quantitative results. The analytical expressions can serve as estimates for the expected classification errors of the linear classifiers trained by more sophisticated optimisation techniques.

We will find the *mean expected probability of misclassification* for pattern vectors that did not participate in training. This expectation is taken *both* with respect to the N random training vectors, and with respect to random character of the $(n+1)$ - variate weight vector determined by the priori density $p^{prior}(\mathbf{V}, v_0)$.

At first we consider the prior density $p^{prior}(\mathbf{V}, v_0)$ of the $(n+1)$-variate weight vector $(\mathbf{V}, v_0)^T$ to be spherical Gaussian $N_V(\mathbf{0}, \mathbf{I})$. Assume $\mathbf{M}_1 = -\mathbf{M}_2$. In this case, only vague *a priori* information on the weights $v_0, v_1, \dots, v_n$ is used to design the classification rule. To derive the formula for the expected probability of misclassification $\bar{\varepsilon}_N^{ZEE}$ we use the predictive Bayes approach discussed in Chapter 2:

$$\bar{\varepsilon}_N^{ZEE} = \int \int P(error|\mathbf{V}, v_0)\, p^{apost}(\mathbf{V}, v_0)\, d\mathbf{V}\, d v_0, \tag{3.27}$$

where:

$P(error|\mathbf{V}, v_0)$ is a conditional probability of misclassification, given $(\mathbf{V}^T, v_0)^T$;

$P(error|V, v_0) = ½\, Prob\{V^TX + v_0 < 0 \mid X \in \omega_1\} + ½\, Prob\{V^TX + v_0 \geq 0 \mid X \in \omega_2\} =$

$$½\,\Phi\{-\frac{V^TM_1 + v_0}{\sqrt{V^TV}}\} + ½\,\Phi\{\frac{V^TM_2 + v_0}{\sqrt{V^TV}}\}; \tag{3.28}$$

$p^{apost}(V, v_0)$ is *a posteriori* probability density function of $(V^T, v_0)^T$;

$$p^{apost}(V, v_0) = \frac{P(S_\Delta, V, v_0)}{P(S_\Delta)} \propto P(S_\Delta \mid V, v_0)\, p^{prior}(V, v_0); \tag{3.29}$$

and $P(S_\Delta \mid V, v_0)$ is the conditional probability of the N events S_Δ.

The conditional probability of event (3.26*a*) is $1 - \Phi\{-\frac{V^TM_1 + v_0}{\sqrt{V^TV}} + \Delta\}$. Thus, for N independent training vectors, we can write

$$P(S_\Delta \mid V, v_0) = [1 - \Phi\{-\frac{V^TM_1 + v_0}{\sqrt{V^TV}} + \Delta\}]^{\bar{N}}\, [1 - \Phi\{\frac{V^TM_2 + v_0}{\sqrt{V^TV}} + \Delta\}]^{\bar{N}}. \tag{3.30}$$

Probabilities (3.28) and (3.30) are conditioned on the vector $(V^T, v_0)^T$. Now we will show that, provided the distributions of vectors X and $(V^T, v_0)^T$ are spherical, these probabilities depend on only two independent scalar random variables. Let $\mathbf{T}$ be an $n \times n$ orthonormal matrix with the first row vector

$$t_1 = \delta^{-1} M^T,$$

where $M = M_1 - M_2$ and $\delta^2 = M^TM$ is the squared Mahalanobis distance. Then

$\mathbf{T}M = (\delta, 0, 0, \ldots, 0)^T$,

$$\frac{V^TM_1 + v_0}{\sqrt{V^TV}} = \frac{(\mathbf{T}V)^T(\mathbf{T}M\frac{1}{2} + \mathbf{T}(M_1 + M_2)\frac{1}{2}) + v_0}{\sqrt{(\mathbf{T}V)^T\mathbf{T}V}} = \frac{\vartheta_1\delta/2 + v_0}{\sqrt{\vartheta_1^2 + \sum_{i=2}^n \vartheta_i^2}},$$

$$\frac{V^TM_2 + v_0}{\sqrt{V^TV}} = -\frac{\vartheta_1\delta/2 - v_0}{\sqrt{\vartheta_1^2 + \sum_{i=2}^n \vartheta_i^2}},$$

where $V^T\mathbf{T}^T = (\vartheta_1, \ldots, \vartheta_n)$ and we used the assumption

In order to obtain a generalisation error expression suitable for numerical evaluation, we must define the prior distribution of the weights.

The spherical Gaussian prior distribution of the weights. From this assumption it follows that the Gaussian N(0,1) random variables ϑ_1, v_0 and the chi-squared random variable $\sum_{i=2}^{n} \vartheta_i^2 = \chi^2_{n-1}$ are mutually independent. Then

$$\frac{V^T M_1 + v_0}{\sqrt{V^T V}} = \frac{\vartheta_1 \delta / 2 + v_0}{\sqrt{\vartheta_1^2 + \sum_{i=2}^{n} \vartheta_i^2}} = \nu \frac{\delta}{2} + \omega ,$$

where $\nu = \frac{\vartheta_1}{\sqrt{\vartheta_1^2 + \chi^2_{n-1}}}$ and $\omega = \frac{v_0}{\sqrt{\vartheta_1^2 + \chi^2_{n-1}}}$.

By using standard statistical transformation theory one can readily show that ν and ω are mutually independent: ν is Beta and ω is Student random variables:

$$p(\nu, \omega) = \frac{n-1}{2\pi} \frac{(1-\nu^2)^{(n-3)/2}}{(1+\omega^2)^{(n+1)/2}} \equiv p^{prior}(V, v_0).$$

Consequently, the conditional probabilities (3.28) and (3.30) can be represented as functions of two independent scalar random variables:

$$P(error \mid v, \omega, \delta) = P(error \mid \nu, \omega) = ½\, \Phi\{-\nu\delta/2 + \omega\} + ½\, \Phi\{-\nu\delta/2 - \omega\}, \quad (3.31)$$

$$P(S_\Delta \mid v, \omega, \delta, \Delta) = P(S_\Delta \mid \nu, \omega) =$$

$$[1-\Phi\{-\nu\delta/2 + \omega + \Delta\}]^{\overline{N}} \; [1-\Phi\{-\nu\delta/2 - \omega + \Delta\}]^{\overline{N}} . \quad (3.32)$$

We eventually obtain a final expression for the expected generalisation error

$$\overline{\varepsilon}_N^{ZEE} = \int\int P(error \mid v, \omega, \delta)\, p^{apost}(v, \omega \mid \delta, \Delta)\, d\nu\, d\omega =$$

$$\int\int P(error \mid \{v, \omega, \delta)\, P(S_\Delta \mid v, \omega, \delta, \Delta)\, p^{prior}(\nu, \omega)\, d\nu\, d\omega. \quad (3.33)$$

Representation (3.33) can be used to calculate the mean expected error. For fixed Mahalanobis distance δ the deviation of $\overline{\varepsilon}_N^{ZEE}$ from the Bayes error ε_B depends mainly on $\overline{N}/n$, the training set size / dimensionality ratio. Here we have a similarity with parametric classification. In Table 3.3, for $n = 50$, five Mahalanobis distances, the boundary for the margin $\Delta = 0$ and different $\overline{N}$ values we present values of the learning quantity $\kappa = \overline{\varepsilon}_N^{ZEE} / \varepsilon_B$ (left columns: ZEE with random priors). For comparison we present some κ values for the standard linear Fisher classifier (from Table 3.1).

Table 3.3. Values for the ratio $\kappa = \bar{\varepsilon}_N^{ZEE} / \varepsilon_B$ for the ZEE classifier (with random and "Euclidean" prior weights) versus $\bar{N}$, the training-set size, for dimensionality n = 50 and five values of the distance δ along with the Bayes error ε_B (Reprinted from Raudys, On dimensionality, sample size, classification error of nonparametric linear classification algorithms, *Pattern Analysis and Machine Intelligence* 19, 1997, © IEEE).

ZEE with random priors					ZEE with Euclidean priors					Fisher LDF					$\bar{N}$
2.15	3.75	9.99	25.0	70.9	1.63	1.99	2.70	3.47	4.42						8
2.06	3.43	8.56	20.6	56.7	1.48	1.69	2.12	2.57	3.08						12
1.90	2.95	6.83	15.7	41.6	1.29	1.40	1.66	1.91	2.16						20
1.72	2.57	5.62	12.4	32.0	1.17	1.25	1.43	1.60	1.77	2.05	3.39	8.40	19.7	52.0	30
1.56	2.16	4.34	9.13	22.5	1.08	1.13	1.26	1.37	1.48	1.62	2.15	3.61	5.95	10.6	50
1.35	1.73	3.09	6.04	14.1	1.03	1.06	1.13	1.21	1.27	1.33	1.51	1.93	2.47	3.27	100
1.16	1.32	2.06	3.59	7.68	1.01	1.02	1.07	1.10	1.14	1.14	1.19	1.31	1.44	1.61	250
1.68	2.56	3.76	4.65	5.50	1.68	2.56	3.76	4.65	5.50	1.68	2.56	3.76	4.65	5.50	δ
0.2	0.1	0.03	0.01	.003	0.2	0.1	0.03	0.01	.003	0.2	0.1	0.03	0.01	.003	ε_B

Our main concern is to understand small training-set peculiarities that arise while training the perceptrons in a neural net classifier. The assumption of a random Gaussian prior weight vector describes an unrealistic situation for the perceptron training. This model gives *pessimistic estimates* of the expected generalisation error. To obtain *optimistic estimates* we assume that additional prior information is available in order to generate the prior weights in an alternative way.

Second choice of prior distribution. This choice is motivated by a fact already discussed in the Section 1.3: if the conditions E1 – E4 are satisfied, then the first iteration of the back propagation training of the SLP produces the weight vector of the EDC with $v_0^E = 0$ and $V^E = \eta\,(\hat{M}_1 - \hat{M}_2)$. In the EDC determination of v_0^E and V^E, we use the first statistical moments of the training sets LS^1 and LS^2, while in order to obtain the ZEE classifier we use the highest order statistical moments. Thus, we may guess that the starting (after the first iteration) and final (after the ZEE classifier is obtained) perceptron weights are correlated weakly.

Thus, it is reasonable to assume prior distribution $p^{prior}(V, v_0)$ to be determined by the weights of EDC. In addition to the authentic training sets LS^1 and LS^2, let there exist an infinite number of extra training sets $LS_1, LS_2, LS_3, \ldots$ each composed from $N=2\bar{N}$ vectors. From each set, we estimate the mean values $\hat{M}_1$, $\hat{M}_2$ and calculate the weights, V^E and v_0^E. The distribution of such vectors implies a prior distribution $p^{prior}(V, v_0)$. The additional training sets LS_1, LS_2, ... provide a considerable amount of prior information to determine the classifier's weights. One may guess that this prior weight's generation model leads to optimistically biased error estimates.

The difference between the error rates calculated for the optimistic and pessimistic prior distributions for the perceptron weights is clearly seen in Table 3.3. We emphasise that the ZEE classifier can be used even when the dimensionality n exceeds the number of training examples N. This conclusion is valid both for the optimistic and the pessimistic evaluations. In Chapter 4, we will see the generalisation error of the non-linear SLP classifier depends on the weights initialisation and generally lies between the optimistic and pessimistic estimates just considered.

3.6.5 Intrinsic Dimensionality

Consider the GCCM data model $N_X(\boldsymbol{M}_1, \bar{\Sigma})$, $N_X(\boldsymbol{M}_2, \bar{\Sigma})$ with intrinsic dimensionality $r < n$. We have already considered this data model in Section 3.3.4. For this data model

$$Prob\{ V^T X + v_0 < 0 \mid X \in \omega_1\} = \Phi\{- \frac{V^T \boldsymbol{M}_1 + v_0}{\sqrt{V^T \bar{\Sigma} V}}\} =$$

$$= \Phi\{- \frac{V^T \Phi\Phi^T \boldsymbol{M}_1 + v_0}{\sqrt{V^T \Phi\Phi^T \bar{\Sigma} \Phi\Phi^T V}}\} = \Phi\{- \frac{\boldsymbol{v}_1^T \boldsymbol{m}/2 + v_0}{\sqrt{\boldsymbol{v}_1^T \boldsymbol{v}_1}}\},$$

$$Prob\{ V^T X + v_0 \geq 0 \mid X \in \omega_2\} = \Phi\{- \frac{\boldsymbol{v}_1^T \boldsymbol{m}/2 - v_0}{\sqrt{\boldsymbol{v}_1^T \boldsymbol{v}_1}}\}, \tag{3.34}$$

where $\boldsymbol{v}_1 = \phi_1 V$ is r-variate subvector, a part of vector $\Phi^T V = \begin{bmatrix} \boldsymbol{v}_1 \\ \boldsymbol{v}_2 \end{bmatrix}$, and $\Phi^T = \begin{bmatrix} \phi_1 \\ \phi_2 \end{bmatrix}$.

The above representations indicate that for this almost singular data model with intrinsic dimensionality equal to r, the small training-set properties of the zero empirical error classifier can be analysed in an r-variate space. In this space, the r-variate vector $X_r = \phi_1 X$ is Gaussian with distribution $N_X(\boldsymbol{m}/2, \mathrm{I}_r)$, or $N_X(-\boldsymbol{m}/2, \mathrm{I}_r)$. Thus, we can use the formulae derived for the multivariate spherical Gaussian data model, as well as Table 3.3.

3.6.6 The Influence of the Margin

We have the margin classifier in the random search (Monte Carlo) optimisation procedure (3.26*ab*), when the bound for the margin $\Delta > 0$. The representations (3.32), (3.33) in (3.28) and (3.30) can be used to calculate the mean expected generalisation error for each particular Δ value. Numerical calculations indicate that an increase in Δ, on average diminishes the mean expected generalisation error $\bar{\varepsilon}_N^{ZEE\,\&\Delta}$. In practice we observe overtraining. This fact suggests that the classification performance is conditioned by the particular training-set. The training sets that lead to larger margins, on average, result in a smaller generalisation error.

This conclusion agrees with an error bound derived by Vapnik (1976). In cases where there is an empty zone between the training sets ($\hat{\varepsilon}_N^{\text{MEE}} = 0$), for the maximal margin classifier (MMC) instead of bound (3.25*a*) one can use a tighter bound obtained for a schema of the empirical risk minimisation calculated for an unlabeled validation set vectors of size N

$$\varepsilon_N^{\text{MC}} \leq \frac{d(\ln \frac{2N}{d} + 1) - \log \eta}{N},$$

where d is the smaller value of two quantities, n and $\dfrac{H^2}{\rho^2} + 1$,

H is a diameter of labeled training and unlabeled validation sets,
ρ is a minimal distance between vectors of opposite classes in training and validation sets.

The minimal distance ρ matches up with the margin width and indicates that the bound for the generalization error diminishes as the margin Δ increases. While contemplating the values of $\bar{\varepsilon}_N^{\text{ZEE}\,\&\Delta}$, analytically calculated for different Δ, one needs to remember the following fact. According to the random search "training" conditions (3.26*ab*), the mean generalisation error $\bar{\varepsilon}_N^{\text{ZEE}\,\&\Delta}$ is an average value calculated for the training sets of the same size and for a number of weight vectors weights generated according to density $p^{prior}(V, v_0)$. Thus, this analytical approach does not allow one to investigate the influence of the margin's width on the generalisation performance for one particular training-set and one particular training session. This approach allows analysis only of the *average behaviour* defined by $p^{prior}(V, v_0)$. Analogous conclusion is valid for the bound $\varepsilon_N^{\text{MM}}$.

Example 9. The SLP was used to demonstrate the influence of the margin width on the conditional PMC. In this example, we had one particular linearly separable training-set. Spherical Gaussian data was used. In Figure 3.7 we have three graphs that are typical for the Gaussian patterns: the conditional classification error $\varepsilon_N^{\text{SLP}}$ versus the margin width M for three different initialisations. In all three training experiments, we translated the data centre $\hat{\boldsymbol{M}} = ½\,(\hat{\boldsymbol{M}}_1 + \hat{\boldsymbol{M}}_2)$ into the zero point. We used the sigmoid activation function and trained the perceptron in batch mode with the standard back-propagation algorithm using the targets 1 and 0. In order to obtain a large margin quickly we increased the learning step η progressively with each iteration number t, η=0.0005*1.1^t. The progressive increase of the learning step prevents the gradient of the SLP cost function from converging to zero and allows one to obtain the full range of statistical classifiers during the perceptron training process (we will have more details in Chapter 4).

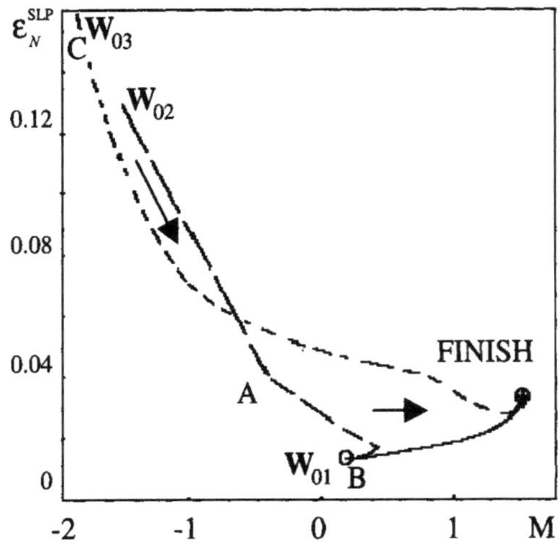

Fig. 3.7. The generalisation error ε_N^{SLP} versus margin M: $\mathbf{W}_{01}\rightarrow$ FINISH – zero initialisation; $\mathbf{W}_{03}\rightarrow$ C $\rightarrow$ FINISH – random N(0, 0.4) initialisation; $\mathbf{W}_{02}\rightarrow$ A $\rightarrow$ B $\rightarrow$ FINISH – an intermediate case (Copy from Raudys, On dimensionality, sample size, classification error of nonparametric linear classification algorithms, *Pattern Analysis and Machine Intelligence* 19, 1997, © IEEE).

When $V_{(t=0)} = \mathbf{0}$ and $N_2 = N_1$, the first training iteration yields the EDC, a rule which is an optimal sample-based classifier for the spherical Gaussian pattern vectors (see Section 2.4.2). Therefore, further training can only increase the generalisation error (curve $\mathbf{W}_{01}\rightarrow$ FINISH in Figure 3.7). When the initial weights vary widely, the SLP uses either no or vague prior information. In this case, the training process gradually reduces the generalisation error; see learning curve $\mathbf{W}_{03}\rightarrow$ C $\rightarrow$ FINISH which corresponds to the initial weight vector generated according to $N_V(\mathbf{0},\ \sigma_{in}^2\mathbf{I}_{n+1})$ with $\sigma_{in}^2 = 0.4$. The curve $\mathbf{W}_{03}\rightarrow$ C $\rightarrow$ FINISH in Figure 3.7 shows only 81 to 850 iterations. The information in the figure indicates that in the case of unsuccessful initialisation, an increase in the margin width decreases the generalisation error. We will return to the initialisation problem in Section 4.5.2.

The behaviour of SLP in the spherically Gaussian case agrees with the theoretical conclusion: the maximal margin classifier is different from the EDC. Therefore, the MMC is not the best classifier for the spherical Gaussian data model. On average, for such data any non-EDC decision rule will perform worse.

3.6.7 Characteristics of the Learning Curves

The universal learning curves (the decrease in the generalisation error $\bar{\varepsilon}_N^A$ with an increase in the training-set size N) advocate that in the case when the classes (general populations, the densities $p_1(X)$ and $p_2(X)$) overlap, the increase in the generalisation error $\bar{\varepsilon}_N^A$ - ε_∞^A diminishes as $1/N$ with N. Unfortunately, the universal curves are obtained in the traditional asymptotic method only where N is increasing. Therefore, the universal curves say nothing about the behaviour of the generalisation error when N is comparatively small and the generalisation error $\bar{\varepsilon}_N^A$ notably exceeds its asymptotic value ε_∞^A. In fact, the latter situation is the most interesting one for practitioners. Exact and asymptotic generalisation error values of the ZEE, standard Fisher linear, quadratic, and the EDC classifiers confirm the universal behaviour of the learning curves when N is very large. The characteristics of the learning curves, however, are different in the case of small training sets.

In Table 3.4, we have the relative increase in the generalisation error $\kappa = \bar{\varepsilon}_N^{ZEE} / \varepsilon_\infty^{ZEE}$ as a function of $\bar{N}/n$, the ratio of the training-set size to dimensionality, calculated for 50-variate spherically Gaussian data model with $\delta = 3.76$ ($\varepsilon_B = 0.03$). In addition, for each three subsequent κ values, we calculated the order coefficient τ in an approximation $\kappa = 1 + \alpha_\tau \bar{N}^{-\tau}$.

Table 3.4. The relative increase in the generalisation error $\kappa = \bar{\varepsilon}_N^{ZEE} / \varepsilon_\infty^{ZEE}$ and the order parameter r versus $\bar{N}/n$, the ratio of training-set size to dimensionality.

N/n	.16	.24	0.4	0.6	1	2	5	10	20	50	100	200	500	1000
κ	10	8.58	6.77	5.58	4.34	3.09	2.06	1.59	1.34	1.15	1.077	1.039	1.016	1.008
τ		.05	0.3	0.4	0.5	0.6	0.6	0.7	0.7	0.8	0.9	1	1	

Table 3.4 indicates that for very small training-set sizes, the generalisation error $\bar{\varepsilon}_N^{ZEE}$ decreases at a very small rate: $\tau = 0.1$. With an increase in the training-set size τ, the rate coefficient, increases until $\tau = ½$, and gradually approaches the asymptotic value $\tau = 1$ which follows from the traditional (only the sample size is increasing) asymptotics, VC bounds, computational learning theory, statistical mechanics and information–theoretic approaches.

Contrary to the results for the ZEE classifier, for very small training-set sizes the generalisation error of the Fisher classifier $\bar{\varepsilon}_N^F$ decreases quickly: $\tau = 2 \div 3$ (Table 3.5). In the upper part of this table, we have κ and τ values for $\delta = 2.56$ ($\varepsilon_B = 0.1$); in the lower part, $\delta = 3.76$ ($\varepsilon_B = 0.03$).

Table 3.5. The relative increase in the generalisation error $\kappa = \bar{\varepsilon}_N^F / \varepsilon_\infty^F$ and the order parameter τ, versus the ratio of training-set size to dimensionality, n/N.

N/n	0.6	0.8	1	2	5	10	20	50	100	200	500	1000
κ	3.34	2.52	2.14	1.51	1.19	1.092	1.046	1.018	1.0091	1.0045	1.0018	1.0009
τ		2	1.4	1.2	1.1	1	1	1	1	1	1	
κ	8.15	4.80	3.55	1.93	1.31	1.145	1.074	1.028	1.014	1.0069	1.0027	1.0014
τ		3	2	1.6	1.3	1.2	1.1	1	1	1	1	

With an increase in N the rate coefficient τ diminishes and gradually approaches the "universal" value $\tau = 1$. We note that the characteristics of the learning curves also depend on the distance between the pattern classes δ. For the simple parametric classifier EDC and the ZEE classifier with the Euclidean initialisation, the expected error probability decreases at the rate n/N.

For fixed N/n, the ratio $\kappa = \bar{\varepsilon}_N^A / \varepsilon_\infty^A$ for both the parametric and nonparametric classifiers depend on the asymptotic error rate ε_∞^A : κ increases as ε_∞^A decreases. In contrast, the difference $\Delta_{error} = \bar{\varepsilon}_N^A - \varepsilon_\infty^A$ increases with ε_∞^A. For Gaussian patterns, the ZEE classifier is preferable to the Fisher classifier when the dimensionality n is close to the training-set size N. The use of prior information about the weights makes the ZEE classifier preferable in almost all situations. Thus, we see that while training the SLP classifier in the proper way (when the conditions E1 – E4 are satisfied and we obtain EDC just after the first iteration), we may reasonably hope to obtain good small training-set properties for the perceptron.

3.7 Parzen Window Classifier

The well known Radial basis-functions (RBF) network has much in common with the Parzen window spherical-kernel based classifier. In this section, we define an intrinsic dimensionality concept. We also advocate that the intrinsic dimensionality, not a formal number of inputs n, plays the main role in determining the small training-set size properties of the PW and RBF classification rules.

3.7.1 The Decision Boundary of the PW Classifier with Spherical Kernels

When the training-set sizes N_1 and N_2 are increasing without bound and the smoothing parameter of the PW classifier (2.49) λ tends to zero, the decision boundary of the Parzen window classifier approaches that of the optimal Bayes classifier. It is a very favourable property of the Parzen window classifier. In order to profit from this property we need to collect and to store a very large training-set. Moreover, the computer time required to perform necessary multiplications and summations is also very large. In practice, we deal with training sets of finite length and, therefore, we can rarely utilise this favourable property of the Parzen window classifier.

The complexity of the Parzen window classifier depends on the value of the smoothing parameter λ. When $\lambda \to \infty$ the PW classifier (2.49) with $\boldsymbol{D} = \mathbf{I}$ produces the linear decision boundary, the hyperplane. This hyperplane is parallel to the discriminant hyperplane of the simplest statistical classifier – the Euclidean distance classifier. Equation (2.51) in Section 2.6.3 indicates that the distance between these two hyperplanes depends on tr($\hat{\Sigma}_2 - \hat{\Sigma}_1$), the trace of a difference of two sample CM, $\hat{\Sigma}_2 - \hat{\Sigma}_1$. We see that when the sample covariance matrices are different we will not obtain EDC. In the finite training-set case, the distance mentioned will fluctuate with $\hat{\Sigma}_1$ and $\hat{\Sigma}_2$. When $\lambda \to 0$, the PW classifier with Gaussian kernel approaches the *k-NN* rule with $k=1$.

In Section 3.2, it was shown that the increase in the generalisation error of the EDC depends on sample size/dimensionality ratio (Equation (3.7), Table 3.1). Thus, one can expect that for spherical Gaussian pattern classes the PW classifier with large λ can be relatively insensitive to the training-set size. However, for pattern classes with high effective dimensionality n^* one can expect that the PW classifier with large λ will be sensitive to the training-set size.

Example 10. In Figure 3.8, we present a scatter diagram of 100 bi-variate Gaussian vectors from two pattern classes with highly correlated features. The means and the covariance matrix of this data:

$$\boldsymbol{M}_1 = -\boldsymbol{M}_2 = (0.1, 0.1)^T,\ \bar{\Sigma} = \begin{bmatrix} 1 & -0.99 \\ -0.99 & 1 \end{bmatrix}.$$

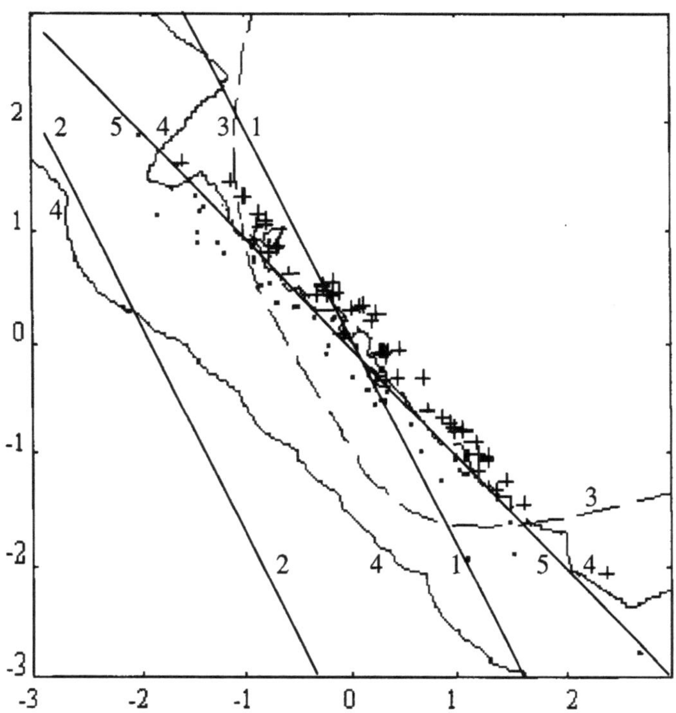

Fig. 3.8. An influence of the effective dimensionality and the smoothing parameter λ^2 on complexity of the Parzen window classifier: 1 – the decision boundary of the EDC, 2 – the PW classifier, λ= 1000, 3 – λ = 2, 4 – λ = 0.001, 5 – the Fisher linear DF.

For this data model the EDC is asymptotically optimal: the asymptotic error of the EDC and the Fisher classifier $\varepsilon_\infty^F = \varepsilon_\infty^E = 0.0786 = \varepsilon_B$ (the Mahalanobis distance δ=2.8284). The training-set size/dimensionality ratio is high: N/n =100/2 = 50. Therefore, the Fisher linear classifier results in a rather exact decision boundary (line 5 in Figure 3.8). Contrary, for EDC the effective dimensionality $n^* = 39602$. Therefore, ratio N/n^* is very low: $N/n^* = 100/39602 = 0.0025$. Thus, the decision boundary of the EDC (line 1) is far from the optimal one. For large λ the PW classifier results in the linear discriminant boundary (straight line 2). It is parallel to that of EDC. Due to the random character of $\hat{\Sigma}_1$ and $\hat{\Sigma}_2$ (see Equation (2.51)), with each new randomly chosen training-set this linear decision boundary fluctuates to side of boundary 1. For small λ we obtain a much better boundary (two meandering curves, 4).

3.7.2 The Generalisation Error

In this subsection, we analyse the generalisation error of the PW classifier with the Gaussian kernel function (Equation (2.49) with $\boldsymbol{D} = \mathbf{I}$) in the limit case, when the smoothing parameter λ tends to zero. Then the PW classifier approaches the *k-NN* rule with $k = 1$. Again we use one of our bench-mark models – the multivariate Gaussian with common covariance matrix. We used this data model already while analysing the small sample properties of the parametric statistical classifiers.

At the fixed point $\boldsymbol{x}$ of the multivariate feature space, Ω, a value of the Parzen window distribution density estimate

$$\hat{p}_i(\boldsymbol{x}) = \frac{1}{N_i} \sum_{j=1}^{N_i} N_{\boldsymbol{x}}(\boldsymbol{X}_j^{(i)}, \mathbf{I}\lambda). \tag{3.35}$$

depends on N_i vectors of the training-set $\boldsymbol{X}_1^{(i)}, \boldsymbol{X}_2^{(i)}, \ldots, \boldsymbol{X}_{N_i}^{(i)}$ considered here as random ones. Therefore, the density (3.35) can be analysed as a random variable. We are making the classification errors in a case where the multivariate vector $\boldsymbol{x}$ belongs to ω_i and $\hat{p}_i(\boldsymbol{x}) < \hat{p}_{3-i}(\boldsymbol{x})$. Therefore, the probability of misclassification conditioned on the particular vector $\boldsymbol{x}$ is determined by

$$P(\textit{misclassification} \mid \boldsymbol{x}, \boldsymbol{x} \in \omega_i) = P(\hat{p}_i(\boldsymbol{x}) < \hat{p}_{3-i}(\boldsymbol{x})), \; (i = 1, 2). \tag{3.36}$$

According to the central limit theorem when $N_i \to \infty$, the distribution of the sum (3.35) of random terms $N_{\boldsymbol{x}}(\boldsymbol{X}_j^{(i)}, \mathbf{I}\lambda)$ tends to the Gaussian one. Thus, the mean generalisation error is determined conditionally by means E and variances V of the estimates $\hat{p}_1(\boldsymbol{x})$ and $\hat{p}_2(\boldsymbol{x})$ at one particular point $\boldsymbol{x}$

$$P(\textit{misclassification} \mid \boldsymbol{x}, \boldsymbol{x} \in \omega_i) \approx \Phi\{\frac{E\hat{p}_1(\boldsymbol{x}) - E\hat{p}_2(\boldsymbol{x})}{\sqrt{V\hat{p}_1(\boldsymbol{x}) + V\hat{p}_1(\boldsymbol{x})})} (-1)^i\}. \tag{3.37}$$

The conditional mean of the nonparametric density estimate (conditioned at fixed point $\boldsymbol{x}$) with respect to all possible training sets consisting of N_i observations, is

$$E\,\hat{p}_i(\boldsymbol{x}) = \frac{1}{N_i} \sum_{j=1}^{N_i} \int N_{\boldsymbol{x}}(\boldsymbol{X}_j^{(i)}, \mathbf{I}\lambda) N_{\boldsymbol{x}}(\boldsymbol{M}_i, \Sigma)\, d\boldsymbol{X}_j^{(i)} = N_{\boldsymbol{x}}(\boldsymbol{M}_i, \Sigma + \mathbf{I}\lambda). \tag{3.38}$$

From (3.38) we see that the nonparametric Parzen window density is a biased estimator. Its expectation is $N_x(\boldsymbol{M}_i, \bar{\Sigma} + \mathbf{I}\lambda)$ which is not equal to the true density value $N_x(\boldsymbol{M}_i, \bar{\Sigma})$ at the point $\boldsymbol{X}$. The bias, which is the difference $\Delta(\boldsymbol{X}) = N_x(\boldsymbol{M}_i, \bar{\Sigma} + \mathbf{I}\lambda) - N_x(\boldsymbol{M}_i, \bar{\Sigma})$, changes its sign depending on the distance $(\boldsymbol{X} - \boldsymbol{M}_i)^T \bar{\Sigma}^{-1}(\boldsymbol{X} - \boldsymbol{M}_i)$. In general, the bias increases as the smoothing parameter λ increases. However, for very small λ, we have a minor bias. Note that the bias does not depend on the number of the training examples N_i. For the above data model at the fixed point $\boldsymbol{x}$, the variance of the PW density estimator is

$$V\ \hat{p}_i(\boldsymbol{x}) = \frac{1}{N_i}\left[\frac{|2\bar{\Sigma} + \mathbf{I}\lambda|^{1/2}}{\lambda^{n/2}}(N_x(\boldsymbol{M}_i, 2\bar{\Sigma} + \mathbf{I}\lambda))^2 - (E\ \hat{p}_i(\boldsymbol{x}))^2\right]. \tag{3.39}$$

Consider the following data model. Let $\boldsymbol{\Phi}$ be an $n \times n$ orthonormal matrix such that $\bar{\Sigma} = \boldsymbol{\Phi}\Lambda\boldsymbol{\Phi}^T$ (Λ is a diagonal matrix of the eigenvalues with elements $\lambda_1, \lambda_2, \ldots, \lambda_n$). This model has been discussed in Section 3.3.4. Then

$$V\ \hat{p}_i(\boldsymbol{x}) = \frac{1}{N_i}\left[\prod_{j=1}^{n}\sqrt{1+\frac{2\lambda_j}{\lambda}}\,(N_x(\boldsymbol{M}_i, 2\bar{\Sigma} + \mathbf{I}\lambda))^2 - (E\ \hat{p}_i(\boldsymbol{x}))^2\right]. \tag{3.40}$$

For very small λ, the variance of the PW estimator is controlled mainly by the term

$$\frac{1}{N_i}\prod_{j=1}^{n}\sqrt{1+\frac{2\lambda_j}{\lambda}}\,. \tag{3.41}$$

This term diminishes as λ, the smoothing parameter, and N_i, the training-set size, are increasing. Let the eigenvalues of the CM $\boldsymbol{\Sigma}$ be equal: $\lambda_1 = \lambda_2 \ldots = \lambda_n = d$ and let the number of features n be increased. Then for small λ we can conclude that in order to keep the variance (3.40) constant, the number of training vectors N_i should increase exponentially as a function of the dimensionality n at the rate:

$$N_i \equiv \left(1+\frac{2d}{\lambda}\right)^{n/2}. \tag{3.42}$$

3.7.3 Intrinsic Dimensionality

Let n-r eigenvalues of the covariance matrix $\bar{\Sigma}$ be very small:

$$\lambda_1 = \lambda_2 \ldots = \lambda_r = d, \qquad \lambda_{r+1} = \lambda_{r+2} = \ldots = \lambda_n = \varepsilon \to 0.$$

We call r the *intrinsic dimensionality* of the data. For the above data model we have

$$N_i \equiv \left(1+\frac{2d}{\lambda}\right)^{r/2}. \tag{3.43}$$

This result means that the small sample size properties of the nonparametric Parzen window density estimator with the spherical kernel (3.35) are not determined by the formal dimensionality of the data, n, but by the true *intrinsic dimensionality*, r. Therefore, the number of training vectors required to design this classifier should increase exponentially with the intrinsic dimensionality.

3.7.4 Optimal Value of the Smoothing Parameter

Three remarks follow from the above theoretical analysis:

1. The conclusion about the intrinsic dimensionality is valid only for the PW estimator classification rule using *spherical kernels* and a *common* smoothing parameter λ for all n variables.

2. In real-world problems, the intrinsic dimensionality of the data can be different in various parts of the multivariate feature space Ω. Therefore, the sensitivity of the PW classifier to the finiteness of the number of the training examples can also be different in various parts of the feature space Ω.

3. It is important to know that for small λ the estimator (3.35) has a large positive asymmetry. Consequently, for small λ, one will have difficulty in deriving exact analytical formulae that relate the generalisation error, the asymptotic error, the dimensionality, the smoothing parameter and the training-set size.

In Table 3.6 we depict values of learning quantity $\kappa = \bar{\varepsilon}_N^{\mathrm{PW}}(\lambda\ ,\ N)/\varepsilon_\infty^{\mathrm{PW}}(\lambda)$ obtained by simulation for the spherical Gaussian pattern classes with Mahalanobis distances $\delta = 2.56$ and $\delta = 4.65$. The data in Table 3.6 indicates that a characteristic of the dependence of the expected error rate on the number of training examples essentially relies on the value of smoothing parameter λ.

As predicted by Equation (3.42) the ratio (sample-size/dimensionality) found from Table 3.6 has the following approximate structure: $N = \alpha \times \beta^n$ where α and β are two positive scalars. In Section 3.6.7 we have that for the parametric classifiers EDC, Fisher DF, and quadratic DF the relative increase in the expected PMC $\kappa = \bar{\varepsilon}_N^{\mathrm{A}} / \varepsilon_\infty^{\mathrm{A}}$ is proportional to $\kappa = 1 + \alpha_\tau N^{-\tau}$. For small N the degree τ exceeds 1 and τ approaches 1 as the training-set size increases. For the PW classifier this dependency is confirmed only for large values of λ. For large values of λ, the PW classifier is similar in behaviour to the Euclidean distance classifier and τ is close to 1. However, for small λ, $\tau = \frac{1}{2}$ or even $\tau = \frac{1}{3}$. Thus, the PW classifier behaves similarly to the structural nonparametric ZEE classifier.

Table 3.6. Values of the learning quantity – the ratio $\kappa = \bar{\varepsilon}_N^{PW}(\lambda, N) / \varepsilon_\infty^{PW}(\lambda)$ – of the Parzen window classifier as a function of number of training examples N and dimensionality n for two values of the smoothing parameter λ.

$\gamma = \bar{N}/n$	$n=3$	$n=5$	$n=8$	$n=3$	$n=5$	$n=8$
λ=0.01		$\delta = 2.56$			$\delta = 4.65$	
0.6	1.97	2.15	2.28	3.53	3.55	4.29
1.0	1.90	1.98	2.13	2.92	3.24	3.48
2.0	1.78	1.87	1.95	2.61	3.07	3.18
5.0	1.64	1.71	1.91	2.32	2.56	2.72
10.0	1.50	1.66	1.84	2.15	2.16	2.28
50.0	1.39	1.62	1.81	1.53	1.86	2.14
λ=0.64		$\delta = 2.56$			$\delta = 4.65$	
0.6	1.96	2.12	2.26	3.51	3.53	4.21
1.0	1.80	1.94	2.05	2.86	3.15	3.41
2.0	1.68	1.80	2.90	2.51	2.87	3.08
5.0	1.46	1.58	1.76	2.18	2.38	2.46
10.0	1.23	1.44	1.65	1.71	1.90	2.10
50.0	1.06	1.12	1.29	1.20	1.27	1.54

The classification of unlabeled data into two spherical multivariate Gaussian populations with equal identity covariance matrices is not a representative data model of real-world problems. In real-world classification problems, we prefer to use the PW classifier to classify populations with complex multimodal distribution density functions. The bias of the Parzen window estimator (see Equation (3.38)) and its asymptotic PMC both increase as the smoothing parameter λ increases. However, the learning quantity κ of the PW classifier usually decreases with increasing λ. Thus, typically the function $\bar{\varepsilon}_N^{PW} = f(\lambda)$ has a minimum. For complex distributions of the pattern classes and complex decision boundaries it can have more than one minimum.

Example 11. The peaking phenomenon is illustrated by Figure 3.9 where we have three graphs of the dependence of the generalisation error ε_N^{PW} on the smoothing parameter λ. The results are for artificial bi-variate data with a complex shaped distribution (see the scatter diagrams in Figures 2.6 and 2.12). The graphs correspond to three randomly chosen training sets of different sizes. For this data model all three graphs exhibit two minima.

We see a sophisticated behaviour for the generalisation error as a function of the smoothing parameter. We call the value of λ where $\varepsilon_N^{PW} = f(\lambda)$ has a minimum, an *optimal smoothing value* and denote it by λ_{opt}^{PW}. Configurations of curves $\varepsilon_N^{PW} = f(\lambda)$ essentially depend on the number of training pattern vectors and the true pattern-class distributions.

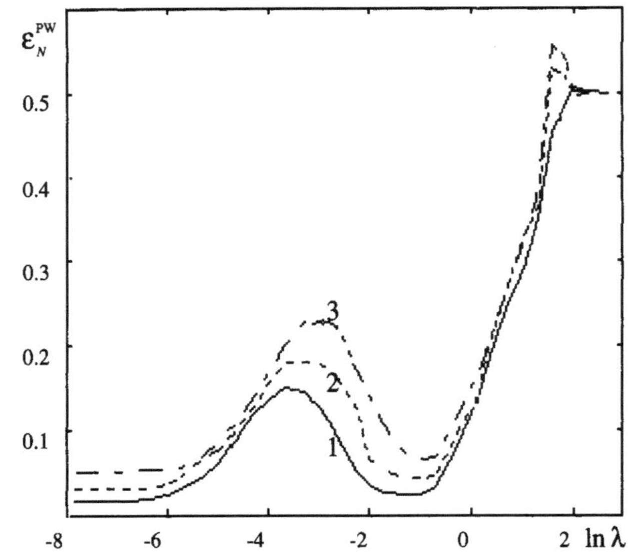

Fig. 3.9. Dependence of the generalisation error on the smoothing parameter λ. For three randomly chosen training sets: 1 – N = 2000, 2 – N = 500, 3 – N = 200.

When we use the PW classifier with a single value for the smoothing parameter for all n features, e.g., estimators (3.35), we recommend that one "normalise" the data in advance by transforming it so that the variances of all n features are equal to 1. The bias of the PW estimates depends on the value of the smoothing parameter λ. Therefore, in order to avoid the discriminant function's bias we recommend using the same λ value for all pattern classes.

Determination of λ_{opt}^{PW}, the optimal value of the smoothing parameter, is very important for solving real-world pattern recognition tasks. However, in evaluating λ_{opt}, theoretical estimates are practically useless because we use the PW classifier to solve complex non-linear real-world problems where multivariate densities are unknown. For that reason, the appropriate decision boundary will almost certainly be non-linear. In order to find λ_{opt}^{PW} for a particular pattern recognition problem, we recommend that one evaluate the classifiers' performance for several values of λ, then choose the value that provides the best generalisation performance.

Recommendations. We make the following suggestions for applying the Parzen window classifier to real-world pattern classification problems:

1. We advise that one normalise the data in order to have the variances of all n features equal to 1. Then the optimal value $\lambda_{optimal}^{PW}$ will usually fall in the interval (0.0001, 100). For most practical problems the "valley" (an interval where the minimum can be found) of the curve $\varepsilon_N^{PW} = f(\lambda)$ is rather flat. Thus, a set of ten

values: 10^{-8}, 10^{-6}, 10^{-4}, 10^{-2}, 10^{-1}, 1, 10 10^2, 10^3, 10^4 is often sufficient to evaluate the curve $\varepsilon_N^{PW} = f(\lambda)$ and to determine $\lambda_{optimal}^{PW}$.

2. In high-dimensional feature space, evaluation of the classification errors of the Parzen window classifiers for ten different values of $\lambda_{optimal}^{PW}$ becomes computationally demanding. Most of the computation time is spent on calculating the distances $H(X, X_j^{(i)})$ between the validation set pattern X and $X_j^{(i)}$, the jth training pattern from i^{th} class:

$$H(X, X_j^{(i)}) = (X - X_j^{(i)})^T(X - X_j^{(i)}) = \sum_{s=1}^{n} (x_s - x_{js}^{(i)})^2.$$

To conserve computer processing time, we recommend that the error rates for all values of λ be estimated *simultaneously*. For each single training vector $X_j^{(i)}$ we recommend that one find the distance $H(X, X_j^{(i)})$ and calculate ten terms $h_m^{ij} = \frac{H(X, X_j^{(i)})}{\lambda_m}$, $m = 1, \ldots, 10$ corresponding to ten values of λ_m. We use an $N \times 10$ table of estimates h_m^{ij} to evaluate the multivariate densities ten times, and classify each single unknown vector X ten times for each value of λ_m. In the high-dimensional case, the computer time required to obtain ten simultaneous estimates of error rates is considerably smaller than the time for ten independent experiments.

3. In most practical problems, the shape of the kernel function $\kappa\{H(X, X_j^{(i)})\}$ does not essentially affect the generalisation error. The value of the smoothing parameter λ is much more important. However, in some problems, hyper-rectangular windows perform worse than smooth "bell-shaped" windows (Skurichina, 1991). The reason for such behaviour is not completely clear.

3.7.5 The *k-NN* rule

In this rule, the class membership of the input pattern vector X is chosen to be the class of a majority of its k nearest neighbours. Frequently the Euclidean distance is used for distance calculations in the original or the "normalised" n-variate feature space. However, the Mahalanobis metric can sometimes lead to better performance.

The *k-NN* and the Parzen window classifiers have many similar characteristics. They both have a varying width of spherical hard-limiting hyper-rectangular window function in the n-dimensional feature space Ω. Both classifiers allow us to obtain complex non-linear decision boundaries. The curvature of the decision boundary depends on the values of the smoothing parameters, k and λ. When $k = 1$ or $\lambda \to 0$, the curvature is maximal and diminishes with an increase in k or λ.

In the finite training-set case, the performance of the *k-NN* classifier essentially depends on *k*, the number of nearest neighbours. Therefore, the optimal number of neighbours should be selected in accordance with the number of training pattern vectors and a configuration of the optimal decision boundary. In practice, the configuration is unknown. For that reason, we recommend estimating the classification error for several values of *k* simultaneously to determine the optimal number of neighbours, *k*.

The *k-NN* classifier is faster than the Parzen window classifier. Numerous studies with large scale real-world data have shown that the *k-NN* classifier often outperforms the MLP-based classification rules.

3.8 Multinomial Classifier

The multinomial classifier M is a nonparametric algorithm for classifying the objects described by categorical variables. This classifier has much in common with decision tree classifiers. In designing co-operative neural networks, one uses the class numbers of decisions of the partner networks (local experts). Thus, one deals with the categorical variables in order to make a final decision. This model is useful in designing co-operative neural networks and analysing decision tree classifiers and genetic learning algorithms. In this section, we consider small sample properties of the multinomial classifier in the two category case.

The multinomial classifier M uses the probabilities of the cells $P_j^{(i)}$ ($i = 1, 2$; $j = 1, 2, \ldots, m$) to allocate the multivariate vector $\boldsymbol{X}$ with discrete components to one of the pattern classes. The asymptotic and the Bayes probabilities of misclassification of the multinomial classifier are equal to

$$\varepsilon_\infty^{\mathrm{M}} = \varepsilon_B = \sum_{j=1}^{m} min\{ P_1 P_j^{(1)}, P_2 P_j^{(2)} \}. \tag{3.44}$$

The sample based multinomial classifier M uses the frequencies estimated from the training set: $\hat{P}_j^{(i)} = N_j^{(i)} / N_i$. Here, $\hat{P}_j^{(i)}$ is a sample estimate of the true probability $P_j^{(i)}$ and $N_j^{(i)}$ is the number of observations chosen from N_i observations in the training-set sampled from the i-th class with state s_j (Section 2.9). The generalisation error of the sample based decision rule exceeds $\varepsilon_\infty^{\mathrm{M}} = \varepsilon_B$. A classification error occurs if the multivariate vector $\boldsymbol{X}$ having state s_j actually belongs to ω_i, but $P_i \hat{P}_j^{(i)} < P_{3-i} \hat{P}_j^{(3-i)}$. Therefore, the expected PMC can be written as

$$\bar{\varepsilon}_N^{\mathrm{M}} = \sum_{j=1}^{m} P\{ P_1 \hat{P}_j^{(1)} < P_2 \hat{P}_j^{(2)} \} P_1 P_j^{(1)} + \sum_{j=1}^{m} P\{ P_1 \hat{P}_j^{(1)} > P_2 \hat{P}_j^{(2)} \} P_2 P_j^{(2)} +$$

$$\sum_{j=1}^{m} P\{ P_1 \hat{P}_j^{(1)} = P_2 \hat{P}_j^{(2)} \}(P_1 P_j^{(1)} + P_2 P_j^{(2)})/2. \quad (3.45)$$

For the case $P_2 = P_1 = ½$ and $N_2 = N_1 = \bar{N}$, we use simple combinatorial results to obtain

$$\bar{\varepsilon}_N^{\mathrm{M}} =$$

$$\frac{1}{2}\sum_{j=1}^{m}\Big[\sum_{t=r+1}^{\bar{N}}\sum_{r=0}^{\bar{N}-1}\frac{\bar{N}!}{r!(\bar{N}-r)!}(P_j^{(1)})^r(1-P_j^{(1)})^{\bar{N}-r}\frac{\bar{N}!}{t!(\bar{N}-t)!}(P_j^{(2)})^t(1-P_j^{(2)})^{\bar{N}-t}P_j^{(1)} +$$

$$\sum_{t=r-1}^{\bar{N}-1}\sum_{r=1}^{\bar{N}}\frac{\bar{N}!}{r!(\bar{N}-r)!}(P_j^{(1)})^r(1-P_j^{(1)})^{\bar{N}-r}\frac{\bar{N}!}{t!(\bar{N}-t)!}(P_j^{(2)})^t(1-P_j^{(2)})^{\bar{N}-t}P_j^{(2)} +$$

$$\sum_{r=0}^{\bar{N}}\frac{\bar{N}!}{r!(\bar{N}-r)!}(P_j^{(1)})^r(1-P_j^{(1)})^{\bar{N}-r}\frac{\bar{N}!}{r!(\bar{N}-r)!}(P_j^{(2)})^r(1-P_j^{(2)})^{\bar{N}-r}(P_j^{(1)}+P_j^{(2)})/2\Big]. \quad (3.46)$$

Equation (3.46) is a function of all $2m$ probabilities $P_j^{(i)}$. To estimate these $2m$ probabilities is a difficult task. There are three approaches one can use to analyse the small sample characteristics of the multinomial classifier theoretically.

In the first approach, one assumes a prior distribution for $2m$ probabilities $P_1^{(1)}, P_2^{(1)}, \dots, P_m^{(2)}$) and averages the error rate (3.46) over this prior distribution. The result, the *mean expected probability of misclassification,*

$$\bar{\bar{\varepsilon}}_N^{\mathrm{M}} = \int \bar{\varepsilon}_N^{\mathrm{M}} f^{prior}(P_1^{(1)}, P_2^{(1)}, \dots, P_m^{(2)})\, d P_1^{(1)}\, d P_2^{(1)} \dots d P_m^{(2)},$$

characterises all possible classification problems defined by the prior distribution

$$f^{prior}(P_1^{(1)}, P_2^{(1)}, \dots, P_m^{(2)}).$$

In this case, one does not need to estimate values of unknown parameters. Unfortunately, the mean expected probability of misclassification is averaged over a variety of theoretically possible problems and yields little information about a particular problem. For the uniform prior distribution this approach results in very pessimistic estimates of the classifier performance.

In the second approach, one analyses the classifier for the best and the worst cases. The results yield lower and upper error bounds. First, let

$$P_3^{(1)} = P_4^{(1)} = \dots = P_m^{(1)} = P_3^{(2)} = P_4^{(2)} = \dots = P_m^{(2)} = \varepsilon,$$

where ε is an extremely small positive constant such that

$$P_3^{(1)} + P_4^{(1)} + .. + P_m^{(1)} = (m\text{-}2)\varepsilon,$$

which is practically zero.

Then only two states, s_1 and s_2, actually influence the increase in the classification error. The contributions of other m-2 cells is zero. In this case, we virtually have a classification problem with two states, i.e. m = 2. We refer to this data model as a *most favourable* case. Note that one can suggest a more favourable but unrealistic model with three non-empty cells having cell probabilities $P_1^{(1)} = P_3^{(2)} = 1 - \varepsilon_B$, $P_2^{(1)} = P_2^{(2)} = \varepsilon_B$, $P_3^{(1)} = P_1^{(2)} = 0$. Here only a few observation vectors are sufficient to train the classifier in order to get an ideal classification rule where $\bar{\varepsilon}_N^{\mathrm{M}} = \varepsilon_B$. In the extreme case, when $\varepsilon_B = 0$, only one vector per class is sufficient to obtain perfect generalisation.

Now, let $m = 2r$ (r is an integer) and let us consider a data model in which

$$P_1^{(1)} = P_2^{(1)} = \ldots = P_r^{(1)} = 2\,\varepsilon_B/m, \qquad P_{r+1}^{(1)} = P_{r+2}^{(1)} = \ldots = P_m^{(1)} = 2(1-\varepsilon_B)/m,$$

$$P_1^{(2)} = P_2^{(2)} = \ldots = P_r^{(2)} = 2(1-\varepsilon_B)/m, \quad P_{r+1}^{(2)} = P_{r+2}^{(2)} = \ldots = P_m^{(2)} = 2\varepsilon_B/m. \tag{3.47}$$

In this *very unfavourable* situation, one needs to estimate the conditional probabilities $P_j^{(i)}$ of *all* cells. Therefore, the increase in the expected probability of misclassification due to the finite number of training examples is large. In Table 3.7 we have the expected probabilities of misclassification for the very unfavourable model of the data computed by using formula (3.46).

Table 3.7. The expected probabilities of misclassification of the multinomial classifier for the least favourable case of distributions of the pattern classes.

$\bar{N}$	$\varepsilon_\infty^{(M)} \backslash m$	10	20	30	40	50	100	200	500	1000
10	0.10	.191	.286	.339	.371	.392	.441	.469	.487	0.493
	0.01	.068	.186	.260	.307	.339	.412	.454	.481	0.490
20	0.10	.128	.198	.251	.290	.318	.393	.441	.475	0.487
	0.01	.017	.075	.140	.191	.231	.340	.412	.463	0.481
30	0.10	.110	.155	.200	.237	.267	.353	.416	.463	0.481
	0.01	.011	.034	.077	.120	.160	.281	.374	.445	0.472
40	0.10	.103	.132	.168	.201	.229	.319	.393	.452	0.475
	0.01	.010	.019	.045	.078	.111	.233	.340	.428	0.463
50	0.10	.101	.119	.147	.175	.201	.291	.372	.441	0.469
	0.01	.010	.013	.029	.052	.079	.193	.310	.412	0.454
100	0.10	.100	.102	.103	.121	.134	.202	.292	.393	0.441
	0.01	.010	.010	.011	.014	.020	.080	.194	.341	0.412
200	0.10	.100	.100	.100	.101	.105	.134	.203	.321	0.393
	0.01	.010	.010	.010	.010	.010	.020	.081	.235	0.341
500	0.10	.100	.100	.100	.100	.100	.102	.121	.203	0.292
	0.01	.010	.010	.010	.010	.010	.010	.014	.081	0.195
1000	0.10	.100	0.10	.100	.100	.100	.100	.102	.135	0.203
	0.01	.010	0.01	.010	.010	.010	.010	.010	.021	0.081

We can use the generalisation error values calculated for the very unfavourable case as upper bounds for the expected PMC. Also, we can use the generalisation errors calculated for the most favourable case (m=2) as lower bounds of the expected PMC. Thus, the data in Table 3.7 can help us to evaluate a possible increase in the generalisation error due to the inaccurate estimation of the probabilities $P_j^{(i)}$.

In the third approach, we need to know all $2m$ probabilities and calculate the expected error according formula (3.46). In many practical situations, a significant portion of the probabilities $P_z^{(1)} + P_z^{(2)} = P_z$ are very close to zero. Then the states s_z with very small $P_z = (P_z^{(1)} + P_z^{(2)})/2$ play a very insignificant role in determining the small sample properties of the multinomial classification rule. This is an intermediate approach between the favourable and unfavourable cases.

Example 12. Consider a multi-modular ANN composed of six independent "expert" neural networks. Each expert performs the classification into three pattern classes. For this particular pattern classification problem the multinomial classifier is used as a "boss" classifier to make a final decision based on six decisions of individual experts. After designing six expert networks, we used an independent validation set (1000 vectors from each class) to estimate $2m = 2 \times 729$ probabilities $P_z^{(1)}$, $P_z^{(2)}$ (z = 1, 2, … , 729). In Figure 3.10 we have a scatter diagram of distribution of $m = 3^6 = 729$ estimates of the bi-variate vector ($P_z^{(1)}$, $P_z^{(2)}$). The distribution of ($P_z^{(1)}$, $P_z^{(2)}$) is depictured in two scales. In order to better display the number of cells with identical values of vector ($P_z^{(1)}$, $P_z^{(2)}$) a small amount of noise (uniform in an interval (-0.00035, 0.00035)) was added to each $P_z^{(i)}$ value.

From the total number of 729 cells, 297 cells have zero conditional probabilities, i.e. 40% of cells are empty. Thus, instead of 729 cells, the formal complexity of the problem is $m < 430$. Taking into account that in 146 cells, the conditional probability of one of the classes is zero and in another one, only 0.001, we may conclude that the actual complexity of the problem is still lower. The asymptotic and Bayes errors are $\varepsilon_B = 0.059$. The expected generalisation error rate calculated for m = 430 cells, according formula (3.46), is $\bar{\varepsilon}_N^{\mathrm{M}} = 0.34$ for $\bar{N} = 25$, $\bar{\varepsilon}_N^{\mathrm{M}} = 0.29$ for $\bar{N} = 50$, and $\bar{\varepsilon}_N^{\mathrm{M}} = 0.24$ for $\bar{N} = 100$.

An example with a high percentage of almost empty cells is *typical* for real-world problems with categorical variables. Usually, in practical problems, there is a high number of empty cells and the increase in the classification error is significantly smaller than that predicted by the least favourable case. One recommendation for the practical evaluation of the generalisation error is to estimate the number of non zero cells from the training data set and then use this number (say $m_{effective}$) in calculations according to Equations (3.46) and (3.47). In this approach, we analyse the least favourable model for $m_{effective}$ non empty cells. Hence, one must remember that this error estimate remains pessimistically biased.

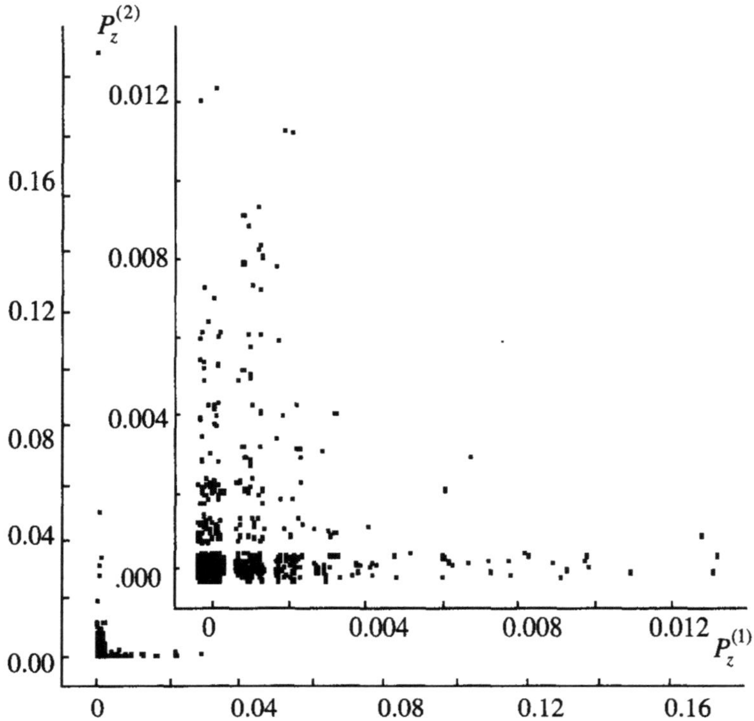

Fig. 3.10. The distribution of 729 values of probabilities $P_z^{(1)}$, $P_z^{(2)}$, which were obtained in decision making on the basis of six expert networks in the multi-modular ANN.

The high percentage of almost empty cells also explains the advantage of the application of the decision-tree classifiers. Here, in order to make classifications, many empty cells are merged with the non-empty ones. Thus, for most practical pattern recognition problems, the number of cells for which the designer needs to estimate probabilities $P_z^{(1)}$, $P_z^{(2)}$ is dramatically reduced. Then one can obtain a very simple classification rule.

3.9 Bibliographical and Historical Remarks

The performance of the adaptive linear classifier known as adaline was first studied by Widrow and Hoff (1960). They concluded that N, the training-set size required to achieve a particular learning quality, should be proportional to n, the number of variables. Cover (1965) introduced the concept of the capacity, a measure of the complexity, and showed that the generalisation error decreases in proportion to n/N, the ratio of the dimensionality to the training-set size.

A number of different approaches have been proposed to study the generalisation error in the finite training-set size situations. In Sections 3.1.5, 3.6.2 and 3.6.7 we reviewed the Vapnik and Chervonenkis, the information–theoretic, and the statistical–mechanic approaches. Unfortunately, the results are valid only when the training-set sizes are very large and the expected classification errors very close to the asymptotic error. However, for practitioners, the most interesting cases are where the number of training vectors is small and we have a significant difference between the asymptotic and generalisation errors.

Among other approaches not considered in this book, the most popular is the *probable almost correct* (PAC) framework (Valiant, 1984). The *combining statistical physics with VC-bounds* methodology allows one to incorporate some problem-specific information (see Kowalczyk, 1996, and references therein). In a stream of papers concerning this approach, researchers demonstrated that the introduction of limited information on the distribution of error patterns to the classical VC formalism permits much tighter bounds on learning curves. The phase transitions, as well as significant drops in learning errors, can be modelled for low training-set sizes, for which the classical VC-bounds are void. The *probably almost Bayes* (PAB) *decisions* framework (Anoulova *et al*, 1992) allows one to obtain upper bounds for the training-set size for classifying feature vectors with Boolean or real entries. Gaussian distributions with unknown means and unknown, diagonal and known covariance matrices were considered, however, the conclusions obtained are qualitatively different from those reported in this book.

A great deal of research has been done on the analysis of the small sample behaviour of statistical classifiers. As the statistical–mechanic approach, classical statistical analysis also requires knowledge of the input signal distribution $p_i(X)$. This is the weak point of both approaches. However, assumptions on the probabilistic structure of the pattern classes and on the parameters allows one to obtain narrower error bounds. In some cases, exact results can be obtained and only one question remains – how to use these results in practice, where the true pattern-class distributions are unknown.

Rao (1949) was the first to emphasise the problems that arise in cases where the number of training examples is approximately the number of dimensions. The first estimate of the difference between the generalisation and the asymptotic errors was obtained by numerical simulation at the Institute for Numerical Analysis of the University of California in Los Angeles (see references in Solomon, 1956). Sitgreaves (1961) derived the first exact formula for the expected classification error of the standard Fisher linear discriminant function (DF) in a form of a five times infinite sum of products of certain hypergeometric functions. Estes (1965) succeeded in calculating this sum and Pikelis improved the calculation accuracy and presented a table (Pikelis, 1974, see also Raudys and Pikelis, 1980, and references therein). The first asymptotic expansion for the expected classification error of the Fisher linear DF belongs to Okamoto (1963). It is obtained asymptotically, where $N \rightarrow \infty$, and yields inaccurate values when the dimensionality n is large and sample size N is small. John (1961) represented the linear discriminant function with known covariance matrix as a difference of two independent chi-square variables and expressed the expected error in a form of infinite sum. Raudys (1967) used this result and derived the first simple asymptotic formula for the expected probability of misclassification (PMC) of the Euclidean distance classifier (3.7). Faithful and unfaithful cases were first analysed here, as well as the double asymptotics approach (the thermodynamic limit) where both $N \to \infty$ and $n \to \infty$.

Deev, working in A. N. Kolmogorov's Laboratory of Statistical Methods at Moscow State University, formalised the double asymptotics approach in a strictly mathematical way. He formally required $N_1 \to \infty$, $N_2 \to \infty$, $n \to \infty$, $n/N \to const.$ and Mahalanobis distance $\delta = const.$ Under this approach, several subsequent asymptotic expansions were obtained for Gaussian and non-Gaussian models. Two simple formulae for the expected error of the standard Fisher linear DF were obtained by Deev (1970, 1972) and Raudys (1972). The representation of the increase in the conditional PMC as a sum of two chi-square random variables and subsequent expressions for its mean (3.11) and the variance (3.12) is from Efron (1975). Further analysis (Pikelis, 1976; Wyman *et al.*, 1990; Takeshita and Toriwaki, 1995) has shown that the double asymptotic expansions give very accurate estimates and better accuracy than the asymptotic expansions where only $N_1 \to \infty$, $N_2 \to \infty$, such as asymptotic expansions by Okamoto, Efron, Kharin, Fukunaga and several others. The double asymptotic approach was used to obtain the generalisation error for the quadratic DF, linear and non linear classifiers for independent Gaussian variables (Raudys, 1972), classifiers assuming block and tree type dependencies between the Gaussian variables (Deev, 1974; Zarudskij, 1979), and a classifier for independent categorical variables (Meshalkin, 1976). The bias term (3.9) to make the discriminant function unbiased was independently proposed by Deev (1970, 1972) and Chandrasekaran and Jain (1979). Barsov (1982) and Serdobolskij (1983*a*) derived asymptotic expected errors for two modifications of regularised DA. Formula (3.18) is from Raudys and Skurichina (1994), Raudys *et al.* (1995) and expression (3.17) is from Raudys and Duin (1998). Meshalkin and Serdobolskij (1978) and Serdobolskij (1979) proved the fundamental limit theorem for the generalisation error for arbitrary non-Gaussian classes. Table 3.2 is from Raudys and Pikelis, 1980, however, in Raudys, Pikelis and Juskevicius (1975) the reader can find more extensive tables.

The *curse of dimensionality* was first described by Allais (1966), Hughes (1965) and Lbov (1966), and the *scissors effect* was noticed in Raudys (1970) and Kanal and Chandrasekaran (1971). In small training-set cases, simple structured classification rules are more efficient than complex classification rules. In large training-set cases, complex classifiers are more efficient. Use of a random search optimisation procedure to analyse the generalisation error of the ZEE and maximal margin classifiers in the multivariate Gaussian case was suggested in Raudys (1993), along with the concept of intrinsic dimensionality. Table 3.3 is from Raudys (1997) and Table 3.6 for the Parzen window classifier is from Raudys (1991). The analytical expression for the generalisation error of the multinomial classifier was presented in Griskevicius and Raudys (1979).

4. Neural Network Classifiers

In this chapter we will utilise the methods from multivariate statistical analysis to investigate the pattern classification algorithms that can be obtained while training artificial neural networks. Our attention will be primarily focused on the similarities and differences between the statistical and neural approaches. For an introduction and a detailed acquaintance with artificial neural networks, the reader is referred to the textbooks of Hertz, Krogh and Palmer (1991), Bishop (1995), Haykin (1999) and others.

In our analysis, particular emphasis will be given to complexity and generalisation. It will be shown that, during training, the perceptron's weights increase along with its complexity. During training of the perceptron, the training is stopped for a moment to allow us to analyse its generalisation and complexity relationships from the statistical point of view. We advocate that the number of parameters of the SLP and MLP classifiers is insufficient to characterise their complexity. We will consider factors that influence the perceptron training process and analyse tools which can be utilised to control its complexity. It will be shown that proper initial values of the perceptron can contain a substantial amount of useful information. In order to save this information one needs to stop training optimally. At the end, we suggest how to use statistical classification algorithms for categorical variables and regularisation techniques to design a "boss" rule (also known as a "combining" or "gating" rule) of the cooperative neural networks.

4.1 Training Dynamics of the Single Layer Perceptron

4.1.1 The SLP and its Training Rule

The non-linear single layer perceptron (SLP) is a greatly simplified mathematical model of an elementary information processing cell in living organisms – a neurone. Following Rumelhart *et al.* (1986), the SLP has been defined as having a number of inputs, $x_1, x_2, \dots, x_n$, and one output o which is calculated according to Equation (4.1)

$$o = f(V^T X + v_0), \tag{4.1}$$

where v_0, $V^T = (v_1, v_2, \ldots, v_n)$ are weights of the discriminant function to be learned, and $f(net)$ is a non-linear activation function, such as functions (1.6) or (1.8) already considered in Section 1.2.

The output of SLP can be used to perform classification of the vector X. The decision boundary is linear. When the activation function (1.8) is used, one needs to compare the output o with zero threshold. To find the weights, a certain cost function is minimised. In the feedforward ANN design, the most popular cost function used is the sum of squares, defined in Section 1.2. Instead of the quadratic loss one can use the Kulback – Leibler distance (see e.g. Haykin, 1999). We concentrate here on the quadratic loss. In this chapter, we consider a more general form of the training-set cost with an additional regularisation term

$$cost_t = \frac{1}{N_1 + N_2} \sum_{i=1}^{2} \sum_{j=1}^{N_i} \left(t_j^{(i)} - f(V^T X_j^{(i)} + v_0) \right)^2 + \lambda (V^T V - c^2)^2, \quad (4.2)$$

where: $t_j^{(i)}$ is a desired output (a target) for $X_j^{(i)}$, the j-th training set observation from ω_i, λ and c^2 are parameters of the penalty (regularisation) term. An alternative to this term is the standard "weight decay" term $+\lambda V^T V$.

In artificial neural network training, the gradient iterative procedure is the most popular method for minimising the cost function and finding the weights. At iteration t, the weight vector is updated according to the equation

$$V_{(t+1)} = V_{(t)} - \eta \frac{\partial cost_t}{\partial V}, \quad v_0(t+1) = v_0(t) - \eta \frac{\partial cost_t}{\partial v_0}, \quad (4.3)$$

where $\frac{\partial cost_t}{\partial V}$ is a gradient of the cost function, and η is a learning-step.

4.1.2 The SLP as Statistical Classifier

4.1.2.1 The Euclidean Distance Classifier

Let us use the tanh activation function (1.8) and let the targets $t_j^{(1)} > 0$, $t_j^{(2)} < 0$. Temporarily, we relax the requirement $N_2 = N_1$. Denote

$$k_1 = \frac{N_1}{N_1 + N_2}, \quad k_2 = \frac{N_2}{N_1 + N_2},$$

and let $\hat{M} = \frac{1}{N_1 + N_2} \sum_{i=1}^{2} \sum_{j=1}^{N_i} X_j^{(i)} = k_1 \hat{M}_1 + k_2 \hat{M}_2$ be the centre of the training vectors. Suppose that the following conditions are fulfilled:

E1) the centre $\hat{\boldsymbol{M}}$ is moved to the zero point;
E2) training begins from zero weights;
E3) the target $t_2 = - t_1 N_1 / N_2$;
E4) the total gradient training (batch mode) is used.

The gradient of the cost function (4.2) without the regularisation term (λ=0) is

$$\frac{\partial cost_l}{\partial v_0}\Big|_{v_0=v_{0(t)}} = 2(-(t_1 k_1 + t_2 k_2) + v_{0(t)} + (k_1 \hat{\boldsymbol{M}}_1 + k_2 \hat{\boldsymbol{M}}_2)^T \boldsymbol{V}_{(t)}), \tag{4.4}$$

$$\frac{\partial cost_l}{\partial \boldsymbol{V}}\Big|_{\boldsymbol{V}=\boldsymbol{V}_{(t)}} = 2(-(t_1 k_1 \hat{\boldsymbol{M}}_1 + t_2 k_2 \hat{\boldsymbol{M}}_2) + (k_1 \hat{\boldsymbol{M}}_1 + k_2 \hat{\boldsymbol{M}}_2)\, v_{0(t)} + \mathbf{K}\boldsymbol{V}_{(t)}), \tag{4.5}$$

where $$\mathbf{K} = \frac{1}{N_1 + N_2} \sum_{i=1}^{2} \sum_{j=1}^{N_i} \boldsymbol{X}_j^{(i)} (\boldsymbol{X}_j^{(i)})^T. \tag{4.6}$$

It was assumed that $v_{0(0)} = 0$, $\boldsymbol{V}_{(0)} = \mathbf{0}$ (assumption E2). Therefore, after the first iteration, one has

$$v_{0(1)} = 2\eta(t_1 k_1 + t_2 k_2), \text{ and } \boldsymbol{V}_{(1)} = \boldsymbol{V}_{(0)} - 2\eta \frac{\partial\ cost_t}{\partial \boldsymbol{V}}\Big|_{\boldsymbol{V}=\boldsymbol{V}_{(0)}} =$$

$$2\eta(t_1 k_1 \hat{\boldsymbol{M}}_1 + t_2 k_2 \hat{\boldsymbol{M}}_2).$$

The targets satisfy condition $t_2 N_2 = -t_1 N_1$ (assumption E3). Therefore

$$\boldsymbol{V}_{(1)} = 2\eta\, t_1\, k_1\, \Delta\hat{\boldsymbol{M}},\ v_{0(1)} = 0, \tag{4.7}$$

where $\Delta\hat{\boldsymbol{M}} = \hat{\boldsymbol{M}}_1 - \hat{\boldsymbol{M}}_2$.

Vector (4.7) is proportional to the weight vector of the Euclidean Distance Classifier designed for centred data, i.e., $\hat{\boldsymbol{M}} = \mathbf{0}$ (assumption E1). The classification according to the numerical sign of the linear discriminant function with weights (4.7) is asymptotically (as $N \to \infty$) optimal when the classes are spherical Gaussian $N_X(X, \boldsymbol{M}_i, \mathbf{I}\sigma^2)$, but also in many other situations. The single-layer perceptron has the useful property of being able to become a comparatively good statistical classifier after just the first training iteration. To achieve this, one has to satisfy conditions E1–E4 enumerated above.

If the number of training vectors from the pattern classes are different ($N_2 \neq N_1$), in order to obtain EDC after the first iteration we have to use *asymmetrical targets*, i.e. for the tanh activation function $t_2 = -t_1 N_1 / N_2$.

4.1.2.2 The Regularised Discriminant Analysis

Now we are able to analyse the dynamics of the weight vector after the second and following iterations. Let us use the activation function (1.8), targets $t_j^{(1)} = 1$, $t_j^{(2)} = -1$. Let $N_2 = N_1 = \bar{N} > n/2 + 1$, i.e. the sample covariance matrix $\hat{\Sigma}$ is not singular. Assume that the learning step η is small and after t iterations the weights remain small. Then the weighted sums $|V^T X_j^{(i)} + v_0|$ are also small. In such a case, the non-linear activation function (1.8) acts as a linear function, i. e.

$$f(V^T X_j^{(i)} + v_0) \approx V^T X_j^{(i)} + v_0.$$

After the second iteration, utilisation of the total gradient adaptation rule (4.3) with the gradients (4.4) and (4.5) results in:

$$v_{0(2)} = 0, \qquad V_{(2)} = V_{(1)} - \eta \frac{\partial\, cost_t}{\partial V}\Big|_{V=V_{(1)}} =$$

$$\eta\, \Delta\hat{M} - \eta(-\Delta\hat{M} + 2\mathbf{K}\, V_{(1)}) = (\mathbf{I} - (\mathbf{I} - \eta\,\mathbf{K})^2)\,\mathbf{K}^{-1}\,\Delta\hat{M}\,.$$

In further iterations,

$$v_{0(t)} = 0, \qquad V_{(t)} = (\mathbf{I} - (\mathbf{I} - \eta\,\mathbf{K})^t)\,\mathbf{K}^{-1}\,\Delta\hat{M}\,, \tag{4.8}$$

where $\mathbf{K} = \frac{1}{2\bar{N}} \sum_{i=1}^{2} \sum_{j=1}^{\bar{N}} X_j^{(i)} ((X_j^{(i)})^T = \frac{\bar{N}-1}{\bar{N}} \hat{\Sigma} + \frac{1}{4}\, \Delta\hat{M}\, \Delta\hat{M}^T.$

To derive (4.8), the matrix $\mathbf{K}$ is assumed to be non-singular. Employing the first terms of expansions

$$(\mathbf{I} - \eta\,\mathbf{K})^t = \mathbf{I} - t\,\eta\,\mathbf{K} + \tfrac{1}{2}\, t(t-1)\eta^2\,\mathbf{K}^2 - \ldots \quad \text{and} \quad (\mathbf{I} - \beta\,\mathbf{K})^{-1} = \mathbf{I} + \beta\,\mathbf{K} + \ \ldots$$

for small η and t, one can obtain

$$V_{(t)} \approx (t\,\eta\mathbf{K} - \tfrac{1}{2}t(t-1)\eta^2\mathbf{K}^2))\,\mathbf{K}^{-1}\Delta\hat{M} = t\,\eta(\,\mathbf{I} - \tfrac{1}{2}(t-1)\,\eta\,\mathbf{K})\,\Delta\hat{M} \approx$$

$$t\,\eta(\mathbf{I} + \tfrac{1}{2}(t-1)\,\eta\,\mathbf{K})^{-1}\Delta\hat{M} = \frac{2t}{(t-1)}(\mathbf{I}\frac{2}{(t-1)\eta} + \mathbf{K})^{-1}\Delta\hat{M} =$$

$$\frac{2t}{(t-1)}(\mathbf{I}\,\frac{2}{(t-1)\eta} + (\frac{\bar{N}-1}{\bar{N}}\,\hat{\Sigma} + \frac{1}{4}\,\Delta\hat{M}\,\Delta\hat{M}^T)^{-1})\,\Delta\hat{M}\,.$$

Sample CM $\hat{\Sigma}$ is assumed to be not singular. Then after some matrix algebra the following is obtained

$$V_{(t)} = \left(\mathrm{I}\frac{2}{(t-1)\eta}\,\frac{\bar{N}}{\bar{N}-1} + \hat{\Sigma}\ \right)^{-1} \Delta \hat{\boldsymbol{M}}\ k_{\mathrm{R}}, \quad v_{0(t)} = 0, \qquad (4.9)$$

where k_{R} is a scalar coefficient.

When classifying according to the sign of the discriminant function, the coefficient k_{R} is irrelevant. Therefore, the weight vector $V_{(t)}$ is equivalent to that of the regularised discriminant analysis (2.38*a*) with the regularisation parameter

$$\lambda = \frac{2}{(t-1)\eta}\,\frac{\bar{N}}{\bar{N}-1}.$$

4.1.2.3 The Standard Linear Fisher Classifier

The above expressions indicate that when the number of the training iterations increases, $(\mathrm{I}\frac{2}{(t-1)\eta}\,\frac{\bar{N}}{\bar{N}-1} + \hat{\Sigma}\ ) \rightarrow \hat{\Sigma}$ and the resulting classifier approaches *the standard Fisher linear DF*. The Fisher classifier can be obtained also when we utilise the linear perceptron (here, $f(net) = net$) and equate the derivatives (4.4) and (4.5) to zero and solve the resulting equations with respect to v_0 and $\boldsymbol{V}$. Then for the centred data one has $\hat{v}_0 = 0$, and $\hat{\boldsymbol{V}} = \mathbf{K}^{-1}(\hat{\boldsymbol{M}}_1 - \hat{\boldsymbol{M}}_2)$ (see Section 1.3).

4.1.2.4 The Pseudo-Fisher Classifier

While deriving the weight vector (4.9), it was assumed that the sample covariance matrix is not singular. If the number of training samples $N < n + 2$, the matrix $\hat{\Sigma}$ is singular. Now one can show that with an increase in the number of iterations, the resulting classifier approaches the Fisher linear DF with the pseudo-inversion of the sample covariance matrix. We assume the weights are small, the training data is centred, $t_1 = -t_2 = 1$, and $N_2 = N_1 = \bar{N}$. The weight vector (4.8) can be written in a way that does not require the matrix $\mathbf{K}$ to be non-singular

$$V_{(t)} = \sum_{s=1}^{t} C_t^s\,(-\eta)^s\,\mathbf{K}^{s-1}\,\Delta\hat{\boldsymbol{M}}\ .$$

Let the orthogonal $n \times n$ matrix $\boldsymbol{\Phi}$ satisfy representation $\boldsymbol{\Phi}^T\mathbf{K}\,\boldsymbol{\Phi} = \begin{bmatrix}\lambda & 0\\ 0 & 0\end{bmatrix}$. Then

$$V_{(t)} = \sum_{s=1}^{t} C_t^s(-\eta)^s\boldsymbol{\Phi}(\boldsymbol{\Phi}^T\mathbf{K}\,\boldsymbol{\Phi})^{s-1}\boldsymbol{\Phi}^T\Delta\hat{\boldsymbol{M}} = \sum_{s=1}^{t} C_t^s(-\eta)^s\boldsymbol{\Phi}\begin{bmatrix}\lambda & 0\\ 0 & 0\end{bmatrix}^{s-1}\boldsymbol{\Phi}^T\Delta\hat{\boldsymbol{M}} =$$

$$\boldsymbol{\Phi}\left(\sum_{s=1}^{t} C_t^s(-\eta)^s\begin{bmatrix}\lambda & 0\\ 0 & 0\end{bmatrix}^s\right)\begin{bmatrix}\lambda^{-1} & 0\\ 0 & 0\end{bmatrix}\boldsymbol{\Phi}^T\,\Delta\hat{\boldsymbol{M}} =$$

$$\Phi\,(\,\mathbf{I} - (\,\mathbf{I}\text{-}\,\eta \begin{bmatrix} \lambda & 0 \\ 0 & 0 \end{bmatrix})^t\,)\,\Phi^T \Phi \begin{bmatrix} \lambda^{-1} & 0 \\ 0 & 0 \end{bmatrix} \Phi^T \Delta \hat{M} =$$

$$\Phi\,(\,\mathbf{I} - (\,\mathbf{I}\text{-}\,\eta \begin{bmatrix} \lambda & 0 \\ 0 & 0 \end{bmatrix})^t\,)\,\Phi^T V^{\mathrm{PF}}, \qquad (4.10)$$

where $V^{\mathrm{PF}} = \Phi \begin{bmatrix} \lambda^{-1} & 0 \\ 0 & 0 \end{bmatrix} \Phi^T \Delta \hat{M} = \mathbf{K}^{+} \Delta \hat{M}$, and the pseudo-inverse $\mathbf{K}^{+}$ is defined by Equation (2.35).

For small values of η with an increase in t

$$(\,\mathbf{I} - (\,\mathbf{I}\text{-}\,\eta \begin{bmatrix} \lambda & 0 \\ 0 & 0 \end{bmatrix})^t\,) \rightarrow \mathbf{I}.$$

Then $V_{(t)} \rightarrow V^{\mathrm{Fpseudo}}$ (the weight vector of the *Fisher linear DF with pseudo-inversion*). This conclusion is correct while the inputs $net = V^T X + v_0$ to the activation function $o(net)$ vary in the linear part of the function $o(net)$.

4.1.2.5 Dynamics of the Magnitudes of the Weights

In the ANN literature, it is recommended that one starts training the perceptron with small initial weights. Above we have presented the arguments that in the SLP perceptron training, it is beneficial to begin from zero-valued initial weights. Initially, in both cases, the weights of the perceptron are small. While training, the magnitudes of the weights increase. We can illustrate this phenomenon theoretically.

First, we rewrite the cost function (4.2) without the regularisation term in following way

$$cost_t = \frac{1}{N_1 + N_2} \sum_{i=1}^{2} \sum_{j=1}^{N_i} (\,t_j^{(i)} - f(G_{ij}))^2,$$

where $G_{ij} = c(V^T X_j^{(i)} + v_0)$, the weights v_0, V are determined by the weights of the Fisher DF (Equation (1.3)), and a constant c controls a magnitude of the weights.

In the high-dimensional case, we can assume a set of the values G_{11}, G_{12}, ..., G_{2N} have the Gaussian distribution. To find an optimal value of c we note that the mean values E_1, E_2 and a common standard deviation, sd, of G_{ij} for both classes are:

$$E_i = (-1)^{i+1}\,½\,c\,\hat{\delta}^2, \text{ and } sd = c\,\hat{\delta},$$

where $\hat{\delta}^2 = (\hat{M}_1 - \hat{M}_2)^T \hat{\Sigma}^{-1} (\hat{M}_1 - \hat{M}_2)$ is the sample squared Mahalanobis distance.

The search for a minimum of $cost_t$ with linear and non-linear activation functions for limiting target values results in the optimal value: $c_{opt} = 1$. Therefore, the mean values and standard deviations of the weighted sums $V^T X_j^{(i)} + v_0$ are

$$\text{for } \hat{\delta} = 1, \quad |E_i| = 0.5, \quad sd = 1,$$
$$\text{for } \hat{\delta} = 2, \quad |E_i| = 2, \quad sd = 2,$$
$$\text{for } \hat{\delta} = 8, \quad |E_i| = 32, \quad sd = 8.$$

The above considerations show that in the training process, the weights can increase up to certain values. These values depend on the separability of the training sets of opposite pattern classes, δ: for close classes, we should obtain small weights and, for distant classes, large ones. If $\hat{\delta}$ is infinitely large, then the magnitude of the weights is unbounded.

At the beginning of training, the weights are small, and all weighted sums G_{ij} are small too. Later, the weights and the weighted sums G_{ij} are increasing. At the very end of the training process, we approach a minimum of the cost function. Then for very distant pattern classes (large $\hat{\delta}$) the outputs of SLP for almost all training vectors $X_j^{(i)}$ should become very close to the boundary values of the activation function.

4.1.2.6 The Robust Discriminant Analysis

With an increase in the number of iterations, the magnitudes of the weights should grow. Consequently, a major part of the weighted sums $|V^T X_j^{(i)} + v_0|$ becomes large. The outputs of the tanh activation function are bounded by -1 and 1, i.e. $-1 \leq f\,(V^T X_j^{(i)} + v_0) \leq 1$. As a result, for large weighted sums $|V^T X_j^{(i)} + v_0|$ the activation function begins to act as the non-linear function. For large weights, the non-linearity of the activation function reduces the influence of distant atypical training vectors (outliers) and we obtain a robust linear classification rule.

Note, in the finite iteration case, we have a *robust and regularised discriminant function.* This is a new way to design the classification rule, which has no analogue in statistical pattern recognition. The robust discriminant function can be obtained also for the case where the target values differ from the limit ones (e.g. $t_1 = 0.8$ and $t_2 = -0.8$ for tanh activation function (1.8)).

4.1.2.7 The Minimum Empirical Error Classifier

When the targets values are +1 and -1 and the empirical classification error is small the weights may become very large. Then outputs of SLP, $o = f(V^T X_j^{(i)} + v_0)$ become very close to either -1 or +1. Consequently, while minimising the cost

(4.2), roughly, we are minimising the empirical classification error as well (theoretically, we minimise the empirical classification error only in situations where the weights and the weighted sums $|V^T X_j^{(i)} + v_0|$ are extraordinarily large).

In situations where the number of empirical errors is high, the weights cannot become too large. In order to minimise the number of training-set errors one ought to increase the weights purposefully. To do this one may fix certain values of the parameters λ and c^2 in the cost function (4.2) and obtain an "anti-regularisation" effect (Section 4.6.3).

4.1.2.8 The Maximum Margin (Support Vector) Classifier

When the number of training vectors, N, is small in comparison with the number of inputs n then after a certain amount of training, the number of empirical (training-set) errors can become equal to zero. In such a situation, we obtain the zero empirical error classifier. Suppose we incorporate certain requirements in the cost function in order to prevent an excessive growth of the weights' magnitudes (e.g., we add a term $\lambda(V^T V - c^2)^2$ with sufficiently large c^2 to the cost function). Then in order to diminish the cost, the training algorithm should maximise distances from the training vectors to a separating hyperplane, $X^T V_{(t)} + v_{0(t)} = 0$.

Training vectors which are closest to the hyperplane, $X^T V_{(t)} + v_{0(t)} = 0$, have maximal contribution to the cost (4.2). Due to the exponential character of the activation function (1.8), their contribution can be orders of magnitude larger than contributions of more distant vectors. Therefore, the training algorithm reacts to the closest training vectors. Thus, it maximises the margin between the hyperplane $X^T V_{(t)} + v_{0(t)} = 0$ and the closest training vectors. This is the maximal margin classifier. In cases when, instead of working in the original feature space, we map the input vectors X into a high-dimensional feature space Ω_{new} through some non-linear mapping, chosen *a priori*, we have the SV classifier.

4.1.3 Training Dynamics and Generalisation

It has been shown that while satisfying conditions E1 – E4, one can obtain seven statistical classifiers of differing complexity. These are beneficial characteristics of the single layer perceptrons. In Chapter 5, we will utilise these properties to integrate the statistical and neural approaches in designing linear classifiers. In this subsection, we illustrate these properties by describing several characteristic simulation experiments with bi-variate data sets. In these experiments, we demonstrate the influences of the data, and the parameters of the training algorithm on the type of classifier obtained.

Example 1. In Figure 4.1, we have the distribution of two bi-variate Gaussian classes **A** (already depicted in Figure 1.3): two GCCM "signal" classes contaminated with 10% additional Gaussian noise. The noise patterns are indicated by "*" and "+", the signal classes by two small ellipses.

In all training experiments reported in this section, we use the centred training data and the starting weight vector $v_{(0)} = 0, \mathbf{V}_{(0)} = \mathbf{0}$. We train the single layer perceptron with the sigmoid activation function and targets t_1=1 and t_2=0. We train for $t_{max} = 1000$ iterations by standard back-propagation in batch mode, with the learning step $\eta = 5$. The training-set size is $N_1 = N_2 = \bar{N} = 250$. After the first iteration (boundary 1 in Figure 4.1), we obtain the EDC (boundary 2) yielding an error rate of 22%. After 250 iterations, the resulting classifier (boundary 3) becomes very close to the Fisher linear discriminant (boundary 4) and yields an error rate of 12%.

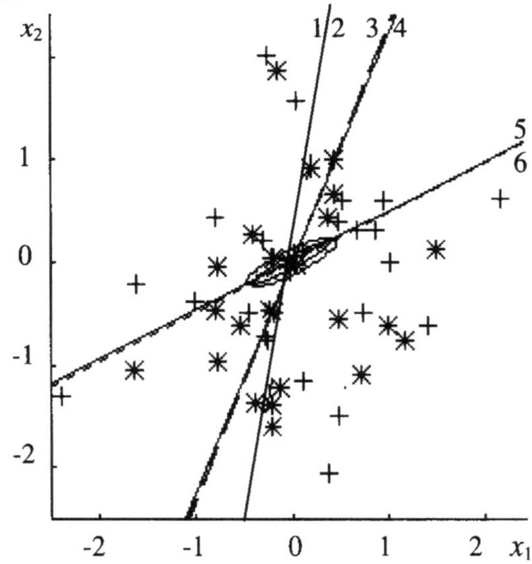

Fig. 4.1. Dynamics of the SLP training process: the distribution of two Gaussian pattern classes contaminated by noise and the positions of the discriminant lines: 1 – SLP after the first iteration, 2 – Euclidean distance classifier, 3 – SLP after 250 iterations. 4 – the Fisher linear DF, 5 – the MEE classifier, 6 – SLP at the end of the training process (Reprinted from *Neural Networks*, 11:283-296, Raudys, Evolution and generalization of a single neurone, 1998, with permission from Elsevier Science).

After 750 more iterations with the learning step η=5, the decision boundary of SLP actually comes extremely close to the boundary of the Fisher linear discriminant (boundary 4). A significant increase in the learning step (up to η=100) helps to move the decision boundary of SLP (boundary 5, after 1000 iterations) to boundary 6 of the minimum empirical error classifier (error rate of 5.5%).

Example 2. More details on designing the maximal margin classifier can be perceived from Figure 4.2. In this bi-variate data model, each class consists of a mixture of two Gaussian densities. Each subclass is distributed on its own straight "data line" in the bi-variate space. All four data lines are parallel. Conventional training of the SLP allows us to obtain the zero empirical error classifier, however, it does not allow us to maximise the margin between the training vectors and the discriminant boundary $v_0 + v_1x_1 + v_2x_2 = 0$. The reason is simple: after a certain amount of training, the weights become rather large and diminish the gradient of the cost function. Thus, the training process essentially stops.

In order to obtain the maximal margin, one needs to have large weights. One way to do this is to increase the learning step. Constant values of the learning step guarantee the learning process only at the very beginning of iteration, while the weights are small, and the activation function $o(g)$ is unsaturated.

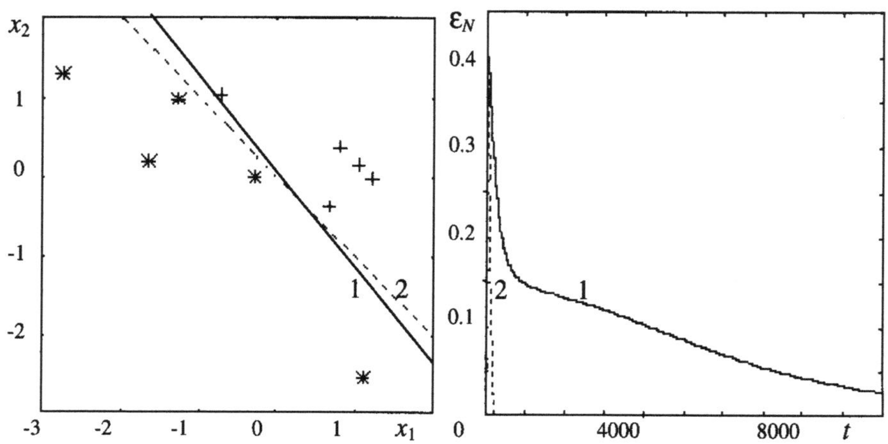

Fig. 4.2. SLP as the maximum margin classifier. *a* shows the training data, a mixture of Gaussian subclasses: 1 – discriminant line after training with $\eta = 0.5$, 2 – discriminant line after training with varying η ($\eta=0.5\times1.05^t$). Only four vectors contribute to the determination of the exact position of the boundary. *b* shows the generalisation error versus *t*, the number of iterations: 1 – $\eta = 0.5$, 2 – $\eta=0.5\times1.05^t$ (Reprinted from *Neural Networks*, 11:283-296, Raudys, Evolution and generalization of a single neurone, 1998, with permission from Elsevier Science).

After training with the exponentially increasing learning step ($\eta=0.5\times1.05^t$), the decision boundary is placed approximately halfway between the closest vectors of opposite pattern classes. This is the maximum margin classifier. The remaining vectors from the other two subclasses do not affect the position of the decision boundary.

Example 3. Details concerning the exponentially increasing learning step technique are presented in Figure 4.3. We present the change in the magnitude of the weights of SLP during 800 iterations for 100-dimensional Gaussian $N(\boldsymbol{M}_i, \Sigma)$ data. The parameters of the data model are $\boldsymbol{M}_2 = -\boldsymbol{M}_1 = \boldsymbol{M} = (m_1, m_2, \ldots, m_{100})^T$. Randomly χ_1^2 distributed components m_i^2 were normalised ($\boldsymbol{M}^T\boldsymbol{M} = 4$). The variances of all features were set to unity, $\sigma_{ii} = 1$, and the covariances were set to $\sigma_{ij} = 0.3$. The training set size is set at $\bar{N} = 100$.

In this high-dimensional example, we have two well-separated pattern-classes and a comparatively small number of training vectors. Therefore, the training data is linearly separable. After achieving the zero empirical error, we obtain a certain margin between the decision boundary and the training vectors. In this experiment, we compare two strategies to control the learning step η. In the first three experiments, the parameter η is kept constant, in the fourth experiment, the parameter η is exponentially increasing with the iteration number t, $\eta = \eta_o \times \gamma^t$. In practice, we need fix a bound for a maximal value η_{max}. We see the value of the learning step η and its behaviour with an increase in the number of iterations affects the magnitude of the weights and indirectly influences the outcome of the training process. Thus, the learning step is one of main factors which influence the statistical properties of the classification rule and its generalisation error.

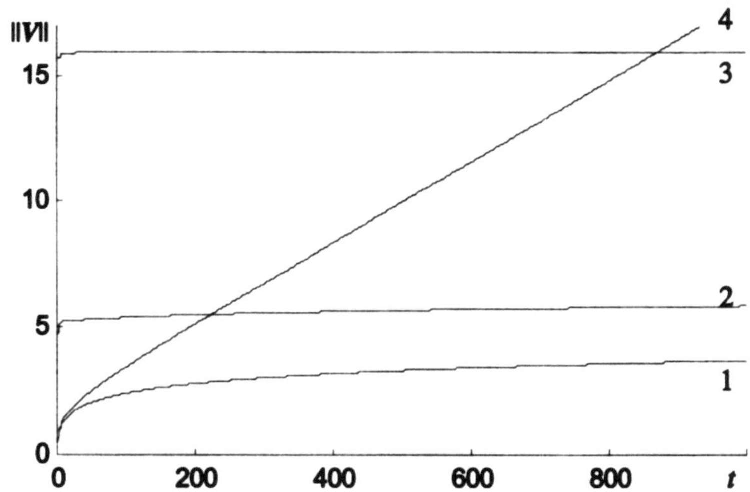

Fig. 4.3. An increase in the magnitude ||V|| of the weights versus t, the number of iterations: 1 – η= 0.01, 2 – η =0. 1, 2 – η = 0. 3333, 4 – η = 0.01×1.05^t.

4.2 Non-Linear Decision Boundaries

In the previous section, we demonstrated that in its dynamic evolution, SLP can realise seven linear classification algorithms of different complexity. In order to obtain non-linear boundaries, we have either to utilise more complicated algorithms or prior to training, perform non-linear feature transformations.

4.2.1 The SLP in Transformed Feature Space

A standard approach to obtaining non-linear decision boundaries by means of simple algorithms is to map the input vectors X into a high-dimensional feature space through some non-linear mapping, chosen *a priori*

$$y_\beta = f(X, \mathbf{Y}_\beta), \qquad \beta = 1, 2, \dots, m,$$

where m is the dimensionality of the new space, and $\mathbf{Y}_1, \mathbf{Y}_1, \dots, \mathbf{Y}_m$ is a set of known vector parameters.

In this m-variate space, one constructs a linear classifier which, in the original low-dimensional space, forms the non-linear decision boundary. Two classical examples are the polynomial classifiers of Schuermann (1977) and the support vector (SV) machines of Vapnik (1995). Below, an example using the SLP is presented.

Example 4. In Figure 4.4 we have a distribution of two unimodal bi-variate populations (100 points from each pattern class) with slightly asymmetrical distribution densities of the features. To discriminate the pattern classes we used the standard quadratic DF at first (decision boundary Q).

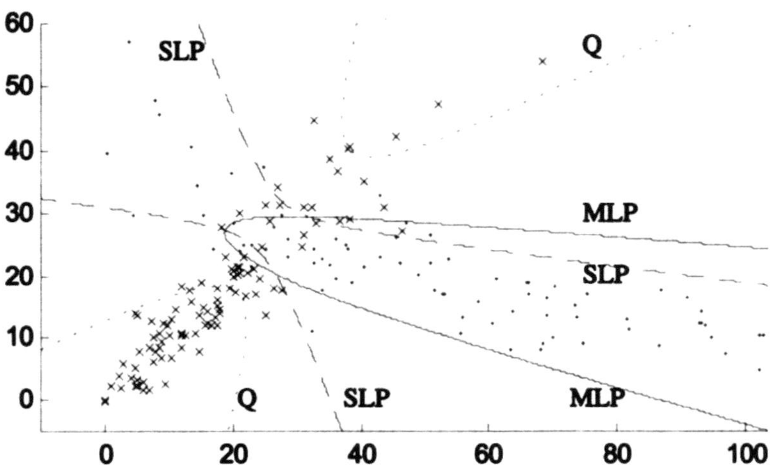

Fig. 4.4. The non-linear decision boundaries from the standard quadratic discriminant function Q (six weights, 19.5% of errors), the multilayer perceptron MLP with two hidden units (nine weights, 11.5% of errors), and the SLP in the transformed five-variate polynomial feature space (six weights, 9.5% of errors).

In order to obtain the better decision boundary, we used MLP (decision boundary MLP). In addition, we mapped the data into five-variate polynomial feature space: $y_1 = x_1$, $y_2 = x_2$, $y_3 = x_1^2$, $y_4 = x_2^2$, $y_5 = x_1 x_2$ and trained the SLP in order to obtain the minimal number of errors while classifying 200 training vectors. We obtained the same type of quadratic decision boundary as in the first case. The weights, however, were different and resulted in a different decision boundary with half the number of classification errors.

In the high-dimensional feature space, the new features were highly correlated. Therefore, to assure convergence, we had to whiten the data (see Section 5.5.1 for details) and to use the antiregularisation technique (see Section 4.6.3 for details).

The polynomial feature transformation is the first and most popular choice for forming "the high-dimensional feature space through some non-linear mapping, chosen *a priori*". Another popular class of functions is radial basis functions:

$$y_\beta = \kappa(\boldsymbol{X}, \boldsymbol{C}_\beta). \tag{4.11}$$

As a simple example, consider the spherical Gaussian density

$$\kappa(\boldsymbol{X}, \boldsymbol{C}_\beta) = N_X(X, \boldsymbol{M}_i, \mathbf{I}\sigma_\beta^2) = \prod_{j=1}^{n} (2\pi)^{-1/2} \sigma_\beta^{-1} e^{-1/2 (x_j - c_{\beta j})^2 / \sigma_\beta^2}, \quad (4.12)$$

where σ_β is a radius of βth radial function and $\boldsymbol{C}_\beta = (c_{\beta 1}, c_{\beta 1}, \ldots, c_{\beta n})^T$ is its centre vector.

In principle, more complicated radial basis functions can be chosen. One more class of mapping functions is non-linear transformations of the weighted sums

$$y_\beta = f(\boldsymbol{X}^T \boldsymbol{V}_\beta + v_{0\beta}), \quad (4.13)$$

where $f(net)$ is a non-linear function, e.g. $f(net) = \tanh(net)$, $v_{0\beta}$, and

$\boldsymbol{V}_\beta^T = (v_{\beta 1}, v_{\beta 2}, \ldots, v_{\beta n})$ are coefficients of the βth mapping function.

In this approach, to design the non-linear classifiers, the parameters σ_β (the radius), $c_{\beta 1}, c_{\beta 1}, \ldots, c_{\beta n}$ (coordinates of the centre vector), and $v_{0\beta}, v_{\beta 1}, v_{\beta 2}, \ldots, v_{\beta n}$ (the coefficients of the mapping function) are chosen *a priori*. In training the classifier, one needs to find weights $w_0, w_1, \ldots, w_m,$ of the final linear classifier

$$output = \sum_{\beta=1}^{m} w_\beta y_\beta + w_0. \quad (4.14)$$

Instead of using the SLP to find the weights in the new high-dimensional feature space, one can utilise any of a number of known linear classifiers. Schuermann utilised the standard Fisher classifier with the pseudo-inversion of the covariance matrix. Vapnik used the linear maximal margin classifier. The SLP is advantageous in the sense that, while training the perceptron in an adaptive way, we can obtain both linear classifiers just mentioned and five others (Section 4.1). In the new high-dimensional feature space, we face a serious additional difficulty: the new features are highly-correlated and the SLP classifier's training can become very slow. In chapter 5 we will discuss peculiarities of training SLP in the high-dimensional highly-correlated feature space.

4.2.2 The MLP Classifier

The MLP classifier is characterised by a large number of hidden layers and output layer weights. Theory shows that the standard MLP with one hidden layer and smooth non-linear activation functions can realise an arbitrary non-linear decision boundary. For this we need to have a sufficient number of hidden units. The information processing scheme of the MLP classifier with one hidden layer is similar to (4.14) with the non-linear transformations of the weighted sums (4.13). A main difference is that in MLP the coefficients of the mapping functions ($v_{0\beta}, v_{\beta 1}, v_{\beta 2}, \ldots, v_{\beta n}$, $\beta = 1, 2, \ldots, h$) should be found from the training data. Previously, in this book, we have presented three examples of non-linear decision boundaries obtained by utilising MLP (Figures 1.5, 2.1 and 4.4).

A standard method of finding the weights is to use the gradient descent optimisation (a back propagation method) where we calculate derivatives of the cost function and find the weights in an iterative way. To perform the optimisation task we need to fix starting values for the weight vector. This stage of the training process is called "the weights initialisation". In Section 4.5.2 we will show that the weights initialisation is very important in determining the performance of the neural network. In this book, we focus on the complexity and generalisation problems. Therefore, for standard details concerning back propagation and other training procedures the reader is referred to the excellent textbooks of Hertz, Krogh and Palmer (1991), Bishop (1995) and Haykin (1999).

4.2.3 Radial Basis Function Networks

The information processing scheme of the Radial Basis Functions (RBF) network is similar to (4.14) with the non-linear transformations of the weighted sums (4.11) and (4.12). A main difference consists in that, in RBF, the coefficients of the mapping functions should be found from the training data. The discriminant function used to make the decision is similar to that discussed for the statistical classifier (2.44) derived for the mixtures of Gaussian or non-Gaussian spherical densities (Section 2.6.1). In the statistical approach, in order to find the unknown coefficients of the decision rule we use statistical parameter estimation methods. Typically, these parameters are different for each pattern class. In the neural network approach, we have to choose the cost function and minimise it. Here, in determining the parameters of the network, training vectors of all pattern classes are used simultaneously. This is one of the advantages of the RBF networks over the statistical classifiers. Equation (4.15) is an example of the cost function for the two category case

$$cost_t = \frac{1}{N_1 + N_2} \sum_{i=1}^{2} \sum_{j=1}^{N_i} \psi\Big(t_j^{(i)} - \sum_{\beta=1}^{m} v_{i\beta}\, \kappa(X_j^{(i)}, C_{i\beta}, \sigma_{i\beta})\Big). \tag{4.15}$$

where $\psi(c)$ is a loss function (e.g. quadratic, robust, etc.).

In the RBF approach, an important problem is to choose the targets, $t_j^{(i)}$. One possibility is to use zeros and ones that indicate the class membership of each training vector $X_j^{(i)}$. As the starting values of the unknown coefficients $v_{i\beta}$, $\sigma_{i\beta}$ and $c_{i\beta 1}, c_{i\beta 2}, \ldots, c_{i\beta n}$ the standard statistical mixture decomposition or cluster analysis method can be used (for cluster analysis, see Fukunaga, 1990, Duda *et al.*, 2000).

In a modification of RBF, as the output of the network one can use the ratio

$$P_s(X) = \frac{\sum_{\beta=1}^{m} v_{s\beta}\, \kappa(X, C_{s\beta}, \sigma_{s\beta})}{\sum_{i=1}^{2} \sum_{\beta=1}^{m} v_{i\beta}\, \kappa(X, C_{i\beta}, \sigma_{i\beta})}. \tag{4.16}$$

If one supposes that expression $\sum_{\beta=1}^{m} v_{s\beta}\ \kappa(X,\ C_{s\beta},\ \sigma_{s\beta}))$ approximates the class conditional density $f_s(X)$, then following the statistical pattern recognition theory, one can conclude that expression (4.16) will represent the *a posteriori* probability of s-th class. Use of (4.16) in the cost function (4.15) results in a differentiable function with an easy-to-find gradient. This approach can be used for formally introducing a rejection option into the algorithm. Some authors call such modifications of the RBF networks *probabilistic neural networks*.

4.2.4 Learning Vector Quantisation Networks

A simplification of the numerical calculation process in the RBF networks during the recognition phase follows if, instead of the sum $\sum_{\beta=1}^{m} v_{s\beta}\kappa(X, C_{s\beta},\ \sigma_{s\beta}))$, one analyses each of the m components separately as an independent new subclass. Then a piecewise-linear discriminant function similar to (2.46) can be constructed. Such types of decision-making is called the learning vector quantisation network. This scheme is very similar to the *piecewise-linear classifiers* discussed in Section 2.6.2. A decision-making procedure which performs these calculations has been depicted in Figure 2.4. To estimate the unknown centres, $C_{s\beta}$, and radiuses, $\sigma_{s\beta}$, one has to minimise a chosen cost function. As the starting values of the unknown coefficients, one can utilise the coefficients of the piecewise-linear discriminant function discussed in Section 2.6.2. Various approaches, including old ones traditionally used to design the statistical pattern classifiers, can be used to find the centres $C_{s\beta}$. These methods include the cluster analysis methods, mixture decomposition methods and the great variety of decision tree design methods (Section 2.8.3). In the neural net approach, however, to find the coefficients, training vectors of all pattern classes take part simultaneously.

4.3 Training Peculiarities of the Perceptrons

The essential property of the cost functions utilised in ANN training is the non-linearity of the activation function. The non-linearity helps to obtain non-linear smooth decision boundaries. However, at the same time it burdens the iterative training process. One more training difficulty arises in cases where the training data are almost singular, i.e. we have an immense difference between the smallest and largest eigenvalues of the data covariance matrix.

4.3.1 Cost Function Surfaces of the SLP Classifier

The non-linear SLP classifier realises a hyperplane in the n-dimensional feature space, Ω. The position of this hyperplane is determined by n independent parameters. The SLP classifier, however, has n+1 weights that are determined in the training process. Consequently, one weight is excessive. Therefore, in a multivariate weight space, the cost function has a deep and long trench.

Example 5. In Figure 4.5*a*, we present two sections of the sum of squares cost function surface. We consider SLP which determines a discriminant function $g(x_1) = v_1x_1+v_0 = w_{m1}(x_1+ w_{m0})$ utilised to classify uni-variate observations into two populations. The graphs are presented as the $cost_t$ versus w_{m0} for two values of a coefficient w_{m1} (a solid graph for $w_{m1} = 100$, here we have almost the hard-limiting activation function, and a dotted graph for $w_{m1} = 20$, here we have the smoother soft-limiting activation function).

Apparently, for the hard-limiting activation function ($w_{m1} = 100$) each training observation contributes a separate step into the cost function surface. We have stated earlier that the relative slope of the cost function depends on the magnitude of the weights. Therefore, near the origin ($w_{m1} = 20$, the small weights) the activation function acts almost as a linear one and the cost function is smooth. With an increase in the magnitude of the weights, the activation function acts almost as a hard-limiting function. Then the steps exhibit themselves more clearly. It becomes quite obvious from 2D and 3D plots of the cost function (Figure 4.5*bc*).

In this figure, we see four clear minima – four ditches in the landscape of the cost function. In spite of simplicity of the classification problem, the effect of multi-extremality of the cost function is obvious: the cost function is composed of numerous ditches and long hills spread along, like the rays from the origin of the co-ordinate axis.

4.3.2 Cost Function Surfaces of the MLP Classifier

In comparison with the SLP, the multilayer perceptrons with n inputs and h hidden neurones have more weights to be adjusted. Therefore, the analysis and understanding of the MLP cost function surfaces in an $(n+1)h+(h+1)$-variate weight space Θ_{MLP} are much more complicated. If the empirical error is zero, then, as a rule, the global minimum of the cost function surface is expressed more clearly.

Example 6. We consider the classification problem with two bi-variate pattern classes, where the vectors of the first pattern class are inside another one: vectors of bi-variate spherical Gaussian distribution N(0, **I**) are inside a circle ($x_1^2 + x_2^2 = 1.1$) and vectors of the second class are outside a larger circle ($x_1^2 + x_2^2 = 1.45$). It is data **SF2**. The number of training vectors is $N_1 = N_2 = 50$. The weights were initialised randomly in an interval (-3, 3) and MLP with three sigmoid neurones in the hidden layer was trained 5000 cycles by the stochastic back propagation method with targets 0.9 and 0.1 and learning step $\eta = 0.2$.

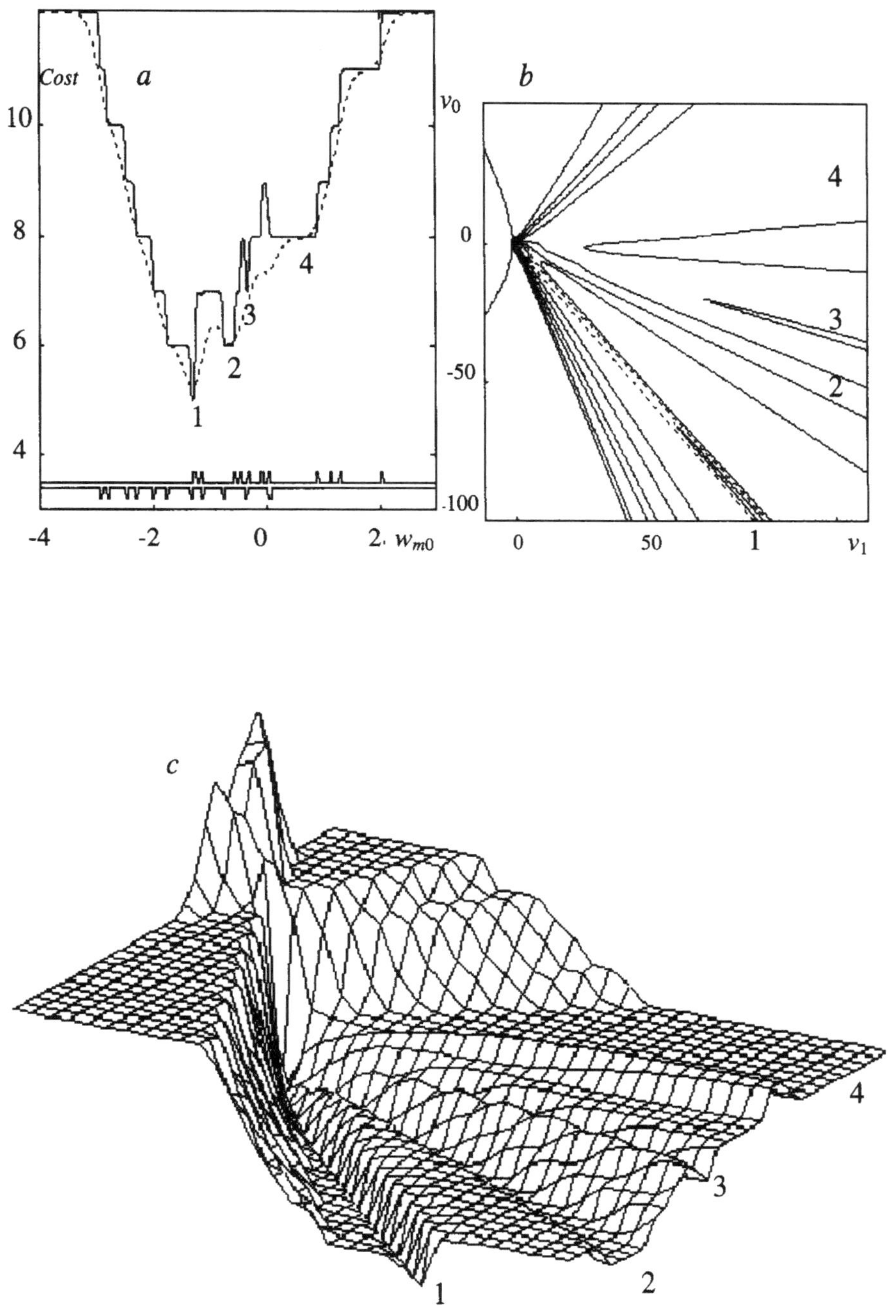

Fig. 4.5. *a* – two sections of the cost function of the sum squares versus w_{m0}, the threshold coefficient of DF, for the hard-limiting activation function (solid line) and for the soft-limiting activation function (dotted line); twelve uni-variate Gaussian N(0,1) and N(1.68,1) training observations from each class are depicted by positive and negative impulses; *b* – 2D plot of the cost function; *c* – 3D plot of the cost function: long trenches (the minima) are marked by numbers 1 (the global minimum), 2, 3, and 4 (the local minima).

In the back propagation stochastic gradient training, the weights wandered for a while around an origin of the co-ordinate axis until zero empirical error was achieved (≈250 cycles). Afterwards, the weights began increasing steadily until they reached some "local trench" and moved further along this trench. We see changes in nine hidden layer weights and the output layer weights during the training in five weight trajectory plots, presented in Figure 4.6.

In Figure 4.6, the weights values are plotted on the axes x and y, however, they are different for each of the 5 plots:

- plots 1, 2, and 3 represent the weight pairs - v_{j1} versus v_{j2} of three hidden layer neurones (j = 1, 2, 3);
- plots 4 and 5 represent the weight pairs w_1 versus w_3 and w_2 versus w_3 of the output-layer neurone.

The most distant points of each of the five weight trajectory plots correspond to the weights obtained after 2000 additional training cycles, when the targets 1.0 and 0.0 were used.

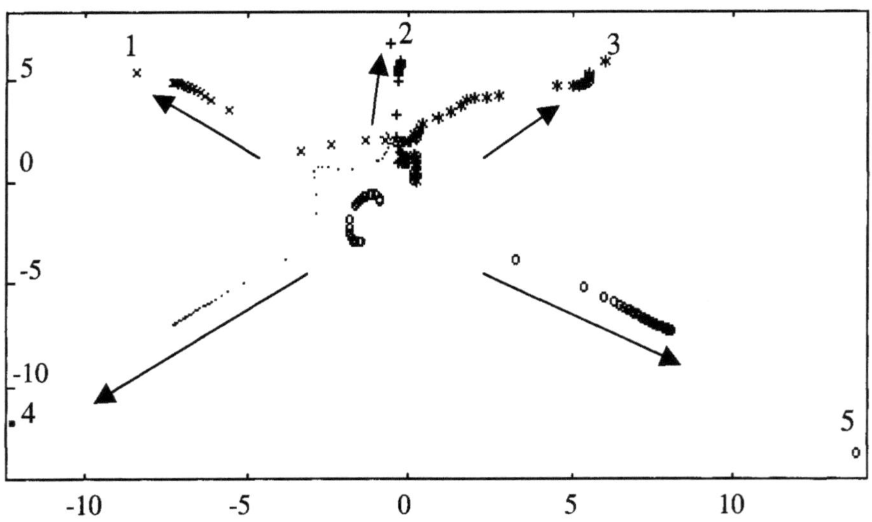

Fig. 4.6. "Explosion of universe" in MLP training: 1, 2 and 3 show the hidden layer weights; 4, 5 show the output layer weights (for each "weight history" the co-ordinates are different).

This example demonstrates that the local minima positions depend on the target values. A linear proportional increase in the values of the weights indicates that approximately correct positions of the individual hyperplanes have already been found during the preceding training iterations. In subsequent iterations, the network increases the magnitudes of the weights without changing the positions of discriminating hyperplanes notably. An increase in the magnitudes of the weights of the hidden layer neurones sharpens the curvatures of the decision boundary.

Thus, the control of the magnitudes of the weights permits us to obtain optimal curvatures of the decision boundary near the intersection of two or more of the discriminating hyperplanes. We have presented an illustration in Section 1.2 (Figure 1.5).

When the empirical error is zero, the output-layer neurone performs decisions in a linearly separable space. Therefore, we do not have the "curvature" problems there. Consequently, the output-layer weights have a tendency to increase without bound. We can notice that after 2000 additional training cycles with the targets 1.0 and 0.0, points 4 and 5 of the output neurone move much farther than the points 1, 2, and 3, corresponding to the hidden neurones.

As in the SLP classifier, each hidden neurone is characterised by $n+1$ weights, however the position of the hyperplane corresponding to this neurone is determined by n independent parameters. Thus, one parameter in each neurone is excessive in determining the position of the hyperplane. In such a way, at the end of the training process, the cost function surface of MLP has a multidimensional flat area. For the single layer perceptron, we had the one-dimensional "long narrow ditch". In that case, the BP training is extremely slow.

Example 7. In Figure 4.7, we have 2D and 3D plots of the cost function surface of an *insufficiently trained* MLP with eight hidden units. The weights are still small. In the two-dimensional space of two hidden unit weights, there exists only one, global, minimum point and there are no local minima. However, the error surface consists of a great number of flat plane surfaces, steep slopes and wide or narrow ditches, and, in fact, it is very difficult to find the global minimum point.

We have depicted only the two-dimensional section of the cost function surface. The number of weights is much larger actually and the situation is much more complex. It is not easy to find the right direction in which to move in this perplexity of ditches and plateaux. In the BP training with a constant learning step, the training algorithm gradually stops at one flat local minimum. Numerous simulation studies with data artificially generated by a teacher MLP indicate that despite the fact that, in principle, the MLP can separate the training data without error, often the back propagation training fails to do this.

One more specific peculiarity of the MLP classifiers is that there exist a number of different combinations of the network weights that result in approximately the same classification accuracy. The amount of satisfactory solutions is usually significantly larger when the number of neurones in the hidden layer is high, e.g. interchange of two hidden neurones and corresponding output layer weights does not change the decision boundary.

When the training vectors of the opposite pattern classes overlap, larger numbers of local ditches can be found. The situation is similar to that of the single-layer perceptron already discussed at the beginning of this section. One more characteristic difficulty in the MLP training arises when several hidden neurones become very similar. Each new initialisation and subsequent training of MLP can lead to a new configuration of the hyperplanes produced by the hidden neurones. Therefore, one should train the perceptron many times, each time starting from different initial weights.

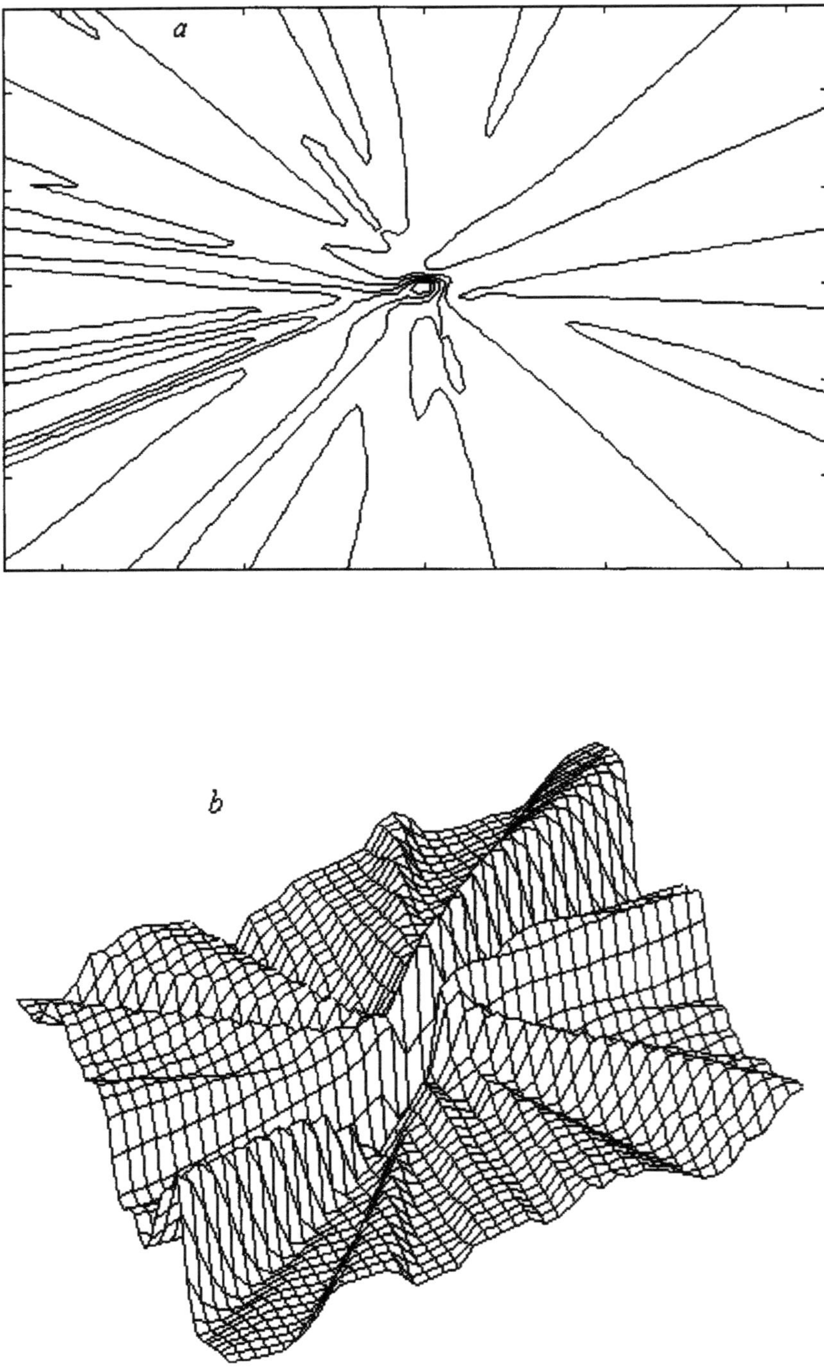

Fig. 4.7. 2D and 3D cost function plots of an undertrained MLP (with small weights) with eight hidden units.

4.3.3 The Gradient Minimisation of the Cost Function

The gradient minimisation of the cost function is favourable in the sense that, in SLP training, it is possible to obtain regularised discriminant analysis (RDA). In principle, to speed up the optimisation procedure one can utilise more sophisticated second order methods (e.g., a Newton method or its modifications), however, in this case, we bypass RDA. In this section we consider an unfavourable property associated with the eigenvalues of the training data when we employ the traditional gradient (back-propagation) training procedure.

Such a situation arises when the training-set size N is small in comparison with n, the number of inputs, when the original features are highly correlated and when we map the input vectors into a high-dimensional space. Then the new features become highly correlated and the sample covariance matrix becomes singular or almost singular. A number of eigenvalues of this matrix can be small or equal to zero.

As in the previous sections, consider the linear SLP and the traditional sum of squares cost function and the total gradient descent optimisation procedure. Using simple matrix algebra, we can rewrite the sum of squares cost function in the following way

$$cost_t(V) = \frac{1}{N_1 + N_2} \sum_{i=1}^{2} \sum_{j=1}^{N_i} (t_j^{(i)} - (V^T X_j^{(i)} + v_0))^2 = cost_{min} + (V - \hat{V})^T \mathbf{K} (V - \hat{V})$$

$$= cost_{min} + (V - \hat{V})^T \mathbf{\Phi\Phi}^T \mathbf{K} \mathbf{\Phi\Phi}^T (V - \hat{V}) = cost_{min} + U^T \Lambda U = cost_t(U), \quad (4.17)$$

where $\hat{V} = \mathbf{K}^{-1}(\hat{M}_1 - \hat{M}_2)$, $\mathbf{\Phi}$ is an orthogonal eigenvectors matrix of the matrix

$$\mathbf{K} = \frac{1}{N_1 + N_2} \sum_{i=1}^{2} \sum_{j=1}^{N_i} X_j^{(i)} X_j^{(i)T}, \quad \text{such that} \quad \mathbf{K} = \mathbf{\Phi \Lambda \Phi}^T,$$

$$\Lambda = \begin{bmatrix} \lambda_1 & 0 & \dots & 0 \\ 0 & \lambda_2 & \dots & 0 \\ \dots & \dots & \dots & \dots \\ 0 & 0 & \dots & \lambda_n \end{bmatrix}$$ is an eigenvalues matrix of $\mathbf{K}$, and $U = \mathbf{\Phi}^T(V - \hat{V})$. Note,

the term $cost_{min} = \frac{1}{N_1 + N_2} \sum_{i=1}^{2} \sum_{j=1}^{N_i} (t_j^{(i)} - (\hat{V}^T X_j^{(i)} + \hat{v}_0))^2$ does not depend on U.

Representation (4.17) allows us to express the gradient in a very simple form

$$\frac{\partial\, cost_t}{\partial U}\bigg|_{U=U_{(t)}} = 2\,\Lambda\, U_{(t)}.$$

Then the gradient training rule of the transformed weight vector $U = \Phi^T(V\text{-}\hat{V})$ is

$$U_{(t+1)} = U_{(t)} - \eta\, \frac{\partial cost_t}{\partial U} = U_{(t)} - \eta 2\,\Lambda\, U_{(t)} = (\mathbf{I} - 2\,\eta\,\Lambda)\, U_{(t)}. \tag{4.18}$$

In order to ensure convergence to zero, the following conditions should be satisfied

$$|\, 1 - 2\eta\lambda_i \,| < 1 \qquad \text{for } i = 1, 2, \dots, n. \tag{4.19}$$

Let λ_{max} be the maximal eigenvalue of **K**. Then condition (4.19) can be formulated as

$$0 < \eta < 1/\lambda_{max}. \tag{4.20}$$

The convergence time depends on all spectra of eigenvalues of the matrix **K**. In order to obtain the fastest convergence it is suggested that one should use

$$\eta_{opt} = \frac{1}{\lambda_{min} + \lambda_{max}} \quad \text{or} \quad \eta_{opt} = \mu \frac{1}{2\lambda_{max}}, \text{ where } 0 < \mu < 1. \tag{4.21}$$

We see that in situations where the training data is almost singular, i.e. we have an immense difference between the smallest and largest eigenvalues of the data covariance matrix, it is difficult, if not impossible, to ensure fast BP convergence of the training algorithm.

4.4 Generalisation of the Perceptrons

4.4.1 Single Layer Perceptron

4.4.1.1 Theoretical Background

If the training conditions E1 – E4 are satisfied, then in back-propagation, one can obtain seven statistical classifiers with different generalisation error – training-set size properties. At first we have EDC with generalisation error (3.7), then RDA with (3.18), and the Fisher classifier with (3.10). If the training-set is very small, then we approach the Fisher classifier with the pseudo inversion of the covariance matrix (Equation (3.17)). Later, with an increase in the magnitudes of the weights, we approach the minimum empirical error classifier discussed in Section 3.6.4. Consequently, the generalisation error of the SLP classifier dramatically depends on the method utilised to train SLP. In the case of a very good initialisation (conditions E1 – E4 and spherically Gaussian data), the generalisation error of SLP can be determined by that of EDC. Suppose the weights are initialised randomly in a wide interval. Then the generalisation error of SLP is much higher. In the zero empirical error case, it can be determined by the left columns of Table 3.3.

An important aspect of the SLP classifier training is that the generalisation errors of some classifiers (EDC and ZEE) depend on a hidden (intrinsic, effective) dimensionality of the data. Unfortunately, the definition of the "intrinsic dimensionalities" for each classifier is different. The type and statistical properties of the SLP classifier obtained in the back propagation training, depend on the number of iterations, initialisation, learning step and peculiarities of the data. Therefore, most often we do not know which particular type of statistical classifier we have at each moment. Hence, the numerical values of the generalisation error and estimates of the necessary training-set size discussed in Chapter 3 are difficult to use practically. Whereas the learning quantity $\kappa = \bar{\varepsilon}_N^{\mathrm{SLP}} / \varepsilon_\infty^{\mathrm{SLP}}$, the ratio between the generalisation and the asymptotic errors, depends on the training conditions, it is impossible to express the generalisation error of SLP by a single formula. Thus, in order to guide oneself in the SLP training process, the researcher needs to take into account that in each particular stage of the training process, *different generalisation error equations* are applicable.

4.4.1.2 The Experiment Design

In order to illustrate the effect of the training conditions on the type of classification rule and its generalisation error, we present several experimental results. In the simulations, we used the GCCM and SG data, the batch-mode BP training algorithm and the sum of squares cost function with the *sigmoid* activation function (1.6). In the experiments, if not stated otherwise, the conditions E1 – E4 were fulfilled. Most often we used the target values $t_1 = 1$ and $t_2 = 0$. Close targets, e.g. $t_1 = 0.55$ and $t_2 = 0.45$, force the sigmoid activation function to act as the linear function. Thus, for $t_1 = 0.55$ and $t_2 = 0.45$, after minimising the cost function we should obtain the Fisher DF. To consider a more realistic situation, in some of our experiments, we analysed the proximal targets $t_1 = 0.9$, $t_2 = 0.1$, the values recommended by Rumelhart *et al.* (1986).

At different moments, the training process was stopped for an instant and the generalisation error calculated. In this particular analysis, we know that the true distribution of the data is Gaussian. Therefore, to find the generalisation error ε_N we do not need an independent test set – we can calculate ε_N analytically.

Let the sample estimates of weights of the linear discriminant function (DF) be $\hat{v}_0$ and $\hat{V}$, the true means be M_1, and M_2, and the CM, $\bar{\Sigma}$. Then simple matrix algebra allows us to calculate the conditional means $\hat{V}^T M_i + \hat{v}_0$ $(i=1,2)$, and the variance $\hat{V}^T \bar{\Sigma} \hat{V}$ of the discriminant function $g(X) = net = \hat{V}^T X + \hat{v}_0$. The linear discriminant function is a Gaussian random variable. Therefore, the conditional generalisation error (conditioned on $\hat{v}_0$ and $\hat{V}$) is

$$\varepsilon_N^{\mathrm{SLP}} = \frac{1}{2}\Phi\{-\frac{\hat{v}_0 + \hat{V}^T M_1}{\sqrt{\hat{V}^T \Sigma \hat{V}}}\} + \frac{1}{2}\Phi\{\frac{\hat{v}_0 + \hat{V}^T M_2}{\sqrt{\hat{V}^T \Sigma \hat{V}}}\}. \tag{4.22}$$

This expression allows us to calculate the generalisation error analytically.

4.4.1.3 The SLP and Parametric Classifiers

If the empirical classification error is small, the target value has a significant influence on the magnitudes of the weights and on the result obtained. Thus, the target values can guide SLP both to the parametric and to nonparametric (structural) classification rules. The generalisation error graphs in Figure 1.10 are a nice illustration. The graphs differ in the target values used. Recall that for Figure 1.10 the 20-variate GCCM data **C** was used and the training-set size was $\bar{N}$ = 14 vectors from each class. In order to make the training process faster, a slightly increasing learning step (η=10 $\times 1.0005^t$) was utilised. In both cases, after the first iteration we have EDC with $\varepsilon_N^{\mathrm{SLP}}$ = 0.058. At the beginning of training, the generalisation error decreases: there we have the linear regularised discriminant analysis. The different target values, however, lead to different classification rules later. With targets 0.9 & 0.1 (graph 1) we are approaching the standard Fisher DF with $\varepsilon_N^{\mathrm{SLP}}$=0.093. With targets 1 & 0 (graph 2) we move towards the minimal empirical error and the maximal margin classifiers. We see that for an extremely small training-set size (n=20, N=28) and good initialisation (after the first iteration we have EDC whose weight vector serves as a very successful initialisation) case, the targets 1 & 0 result in significantly smaller generalisation error. Thus, the targets 0.9 & 0.1 can help to obtain parametric statistical classifiers.

Figure 4.8 demonstrates experimental learning curves: the expected generalisation error versus training-set size. Each curve is an average value obtained from 50 randomly selected training sets (the 20-variate GCCM data **C**). The SLP was trained with the targets 0.9 & 0.1 and compared with the learning curves of EDC, the Fisher linear classifier and the regularised DA (with the optimal value of λ). In Section 3.4.8 (Figure 3.4), we demonstrated that the learning curve of the Pseudo-Fisher classifier exhibits *peaking behaviour* in the interval ($1 < N < n$). In the experiment with data **C**, the Fisher classifier also shows a minimum close to $n/2$=10. The experiment (Figure 4.8*b*, curves 2 and 3) confirms theoretical findings. The learning curve of the non-linear SLP with targets 0.9 & 0.1 (2*a* in Figure 4.8*a*) also exhibits a clear *peaking behaviour* in the interval ($1 < N < n$). The shape of this curve resembles experimental (curves 3 and 2 in Figure 4.8*b*) and theoretical (Figure 3.4) curves for the standard Fisher DF and the Pseudo-Fisher DF. The learning curve of SLP after the first iteration, (curve 1 in Figure 4.8*a*), coincides with that of the EDC, (curve 1 in Figure 4.8*b*). Both experimental curves are very close to the theoretical one. Both RDA with optimal regularisation parameter λ_{opt}, (curve 4 in Figure 4.8*b*) and SLP with optimal number of iterations t_{opt} (curve 4 in Figure 4.8*a*), result in the lowest classification errors. Note, λ_{opt} and t_{opt} were determined individually for each training-set.

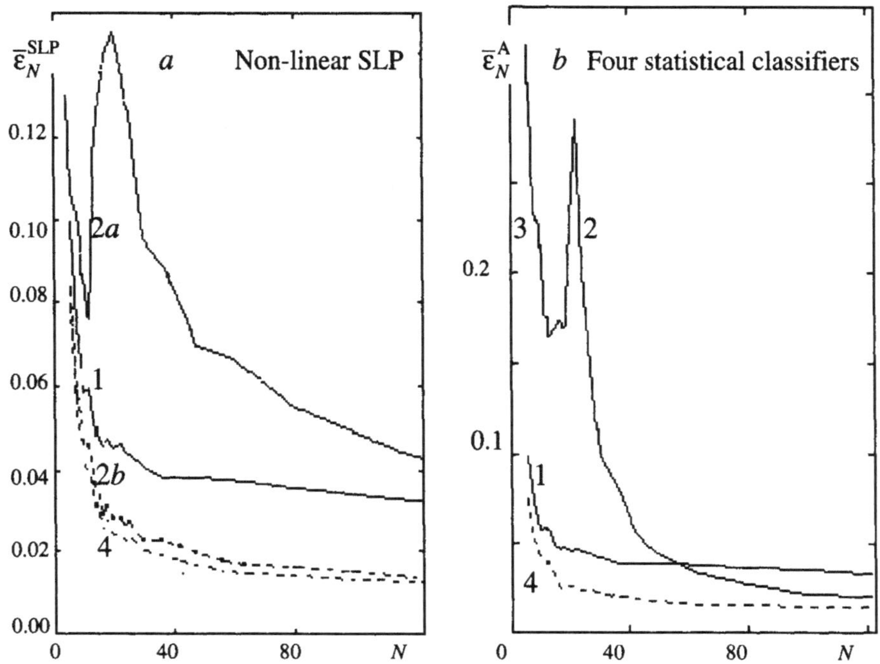

Fig. 4.8. Scissors effect in practice: the generalisation error versus the training set size N. (a) the non-linear SLP: 1 – after the first iteration, $2a$ – after 500 iterations (targets 0.9 & 0.1), $2b$ – after 100 iterations (targets 1 & 0), 4 – after the optimal number of iterations; (b) the statistical classifiers: 1 – EDC, 2 – Fisher DF, 3 – Pseudo-Fisher DF, 4 –regularised DA for optimal λ (Reprinted from *Neural Networks*, 11:297–313, Raudys, Evolution and generalization of a single neurone, 1998, with permission from Elsevier Science).

For $N > 1.5\,n$, the experimental learning curve 2 in Figure 4.8b becomes very close to the theoretical curve 2 for the Fisher DF in Figure 3.4. The same can be said about the experimental learning curve 4 in Figure 4.8a of SLP after the optimal number of iterations t_{opt} (targets 1 & 0), and curve 4 in Figure 4.8b for the regularised DA with the optimal value of the regularisation parameter λ_{opt}. The curve $2b$ in Figure 4.8a corresponds to targets 1 & 0. In this case, the target values force the activation function to act as the non-linear function. For this type of data, the targets 1 & 0 allow us to obtain essentially smaller generalisation errors, and confirms that the *target values are very important*.

Figure 4.8b demonstrates an obvious scissors effect: for small training sets (up to $N \approx 60$) it is preferable to use the simple structured EDC instead of the complex Fisher linear DF, and vice versa. That is, in large training-set cases, the Fisher linear DF can be used more efficiently. In principle, similar conclusions can be made for the SLP:

- in the small training-set case, it is preferable to train the SLP for a small number of iterations,
- in the large training-set case, one needs to use more iterations.

Other regularisation factors, such as target and learning step values, affect the training process simultaneously and the problem of finding optimal values for all of these parameters is not easy. Theoretical considerations concerning the effective dimensionality n^* of EDC indicate situations where SLP can be perfectly trained by using particularly small training sets. In Section 3.3 we have analysed an exceptional case: the 100-variate GCCM data model **D** with effective dimensionality n^* close to 1: $n^* \approx 1.05$, and asymptotic error $\varepsilon_\infty^E = 0.03$. Theoretical calculation gives the generalisation error of EDC $\bar{\varepsilon}_N^E = 0.0318$. This theoretical estimate advocates that for this data, the SLP classifier also can be trained with an exceptionally small training-set. In a series of 10 experiments with training sets containing five 100-variate vectors from each class, a very small generalisation error was obtained: the EDC yielded, on average, 0.039 error with the standard deviation 0.009. The same result was obtained for the SLP after the first iteration.

Similar theoretical considerations concerning the effective dimensionality n^* indicate situations where it is difficult to train the SLP classifier. The 100-variate GCCM data model **E** with $n^* \approx 10^{10}$ is an excellent example. Theoretical calculation gives the generalisation error of EDC $\bar{\varepsilon}_N^E = 0.4997$. In a series of 10 experiments with training sets of size $\bar{N} = 200$, a very high generalisation error was obtained - EDC yielded, on average, 0.4997. After the first iteration, SLP gave the same result. The Fisher DF, however, yielded a "reasonable" error 0.058, i.e., only 1.93 times higher than the asymptotic error $\varepsilon_\infty^E = 0.03$.

Thus, "almost singular" data is a very difficult problem for the BP training (see Section 4.3.3). In such a situation, a "decorrelating" transformation $\boldsymbol{Y}=\mathbf{T}\boldsymbol{X}$ is very helpful. An $n \times n$ transformation matrix can be obtained from $\hat{\Sigma}$, an estimate of the covariance matrix: $\mathbf{T} = \Lambda^{-1/2}\boldsymbol{\Phi}^T$, where $\boldsymbol{\Phi}$ is an orthonormal $n \times n$ matrix such that $\boldsymbol{\Phi}^T \hat{\Sigma} \boldsymbol{\Phi} = \Lambda$ (diagonal matrix of the eigenvalues). Then, in a new space Ω_Y, again we obtain the EDC after the first iteration, however, this classification rule is equivalent to Fisher's rule in the original Ω_X space. We will present more details in Chapter 5.

4.4.1.4 The SLP and Structural (Nonparametric) Classifiers

In non-linear SLP training, the weights can become very large. In such cases, SLP can become similar to the minimum empirical error and the maximum margin classifiers. In the random search optimisation (the Gibbs algorithm) training, the generalisation error of the zero empirical error classifier depends on the prior distribution of the weight vector (Section 3.6.4). We hypothesise that in the non-random (gradient descent) training, the starting position $v_{0(0)}$, $\boldsymbol{V}_{(0)}$ of the weight vector can affect the generalisation error too. Simulation experiments confirm this hypothesis.

Let the pattern classes be spherically Gaussian $N_X(\boldsymbol{M}_1, \mathbf{I})$, $N_X(\boldsymbol{M}_2, \mathbf{I})$. Then the optimal Bayes decision rule is the Euclidean distance classifier with weight vector $\boldsymbol{V}^E = \Delta\boldsymbol{M} = \boldsymbol{M}_1 - \boldsymbol{M}_2$, $v_0 = -\frac{1}{2}(\boldsymbol{M}_1 + \boldsymbol{M}_2)^T \boldsymbol{V}^E$. The predictive Bayes approach to designing the classification rules (Section 2.4.2) says that the sample based EDC is the optimal decision rule when the prior distribution of the vector $\Delta \boldsymbol{M}$ is spherically Gaussian. Therefore, one can expect that the sample based vector $(\hat{\boldsymbol{V}}^{\mathrm{E}},\ \hat{v}_0)$ can become a good starting position in the adaptive training of the SLP classifier. If the training conditions E1 – E4 are fulfilled, then just after the first iteration we have EDC. In other words, just after the first iteration we can obtain the best classifier, and do not need to train the perceptron any more. If we start training from random weights or if the pattern classes differ from the spherical Gaussian model, we will not have the best classifier after the first iteration.

Two learning curves, depicted in Figure 1.9, are typical examples of experimental results obtained with the spherical Gaussian data. When starting from zero initial weights, just after the first iteration we have the best weight vector – the sample EDC. Hence, we have a constant increase in the generalisation error later (curve 2). After starting from a randomly generated, inexact initial weight vector, the training process "corrects" the initial weight vector. Therefore, the generalisation error reduces at first. Later on, however, the training procedure leads to the maximal margin classifier. The maximal margin (support vector) classifier is far from being the best one for the spherical Gaussian patterns. Therefore, after reaching the minimum, we obtain an increase in the generalisation error, and gradually we approach the learning curve, which is obtained in the zero weight initialisation case (curve 1, in dots, iterations 26 – 150 only).

The minimum of curve 1 with random initialisation is notably higher than the minimum of the generalisation error with the zero weight initialisation. This experiment witnesses once more that random initialisation and the search for the *maximal* margin is not always the best strategy in classifier design. The correct initialisation can reduce the generalisation error. Thus, almost correct perceptron weights can store a large amount of useful information. In Section 4.5.2 we will consider this important problem in more detail.

Simulation experiments indicate that with an increase in the width of the weights initialisation interval, the generalisation error of the SLP classifier increases and approaches the theoretical value of the mean generalisation error of the ZEE classifier calculated for the random Gaussian priors (Section 3.6.4). If the initialisation interval becomes too wide, then just before the first iteration we can have very large weights and the saturation of the activation function. Then the perceptron does not learn or learns very slowly. In such situations, we can have a very high classification error.

We see that the number of weights is far from being a *sufficient parameter* to determine the small sample properties of the single layer perceptron. The parameters of the perceptron and the training conditions are very important too.

4.4.2 Multilayer Perceptron

The non-linearity of the activation function, the continuous evolution of the output layer SLP and the expansion of the hidden layer weights make a precise analysis of the generalisation error of the MLP classifiers almost impossible. The theoretical considerations, however, can explain only the generalisation behaviour of the SLP in the output layer. An accurate investigation of the generalisation error of the MLP can be performed by means of simulation. In this section, we present theoretical and experimental evidence that advocates that, while determining the generalisation error of the MLP classifier, the number of network weights is a deficient parameter of the complexity.

4.4.2.1 Weights of the Hidden Layer Neurones are Common for all Outputs

In Chapter 3, it was demonstrated for the parametric statistical classification rules that the parameters of the class distribution density functions that are common for both pattern classes asymptotically (when the number of training samples and the dimensionality are increasing) do not affect the expected probability of misclassification. In fully connected feedforward multilayer perceptrons, the output of each hidden neurone is transferred to all output layer neurones. Any deviation, $\Delta v_{\beta\alpha}$, of each single hidden layer neurone weight, $v_{\beta\alpha}$, affects all outputs of the network. Consequently, it can be said that the weights of the hidden layer neurones of MLP are common to all pattern classes.

An analogy with statistical pattern classification hints that the theoretical results concerning parametric statistical classifiers possibly may be extended to the multilayer perceptrons. Unfortunately, there are no such theoretical results for the multilayer perceptrons so far. Simulation experiments, however, advocate that in certain situations, this guess is correct.

The simple data. In Figure 4.9*a* we have two graphs which show the mean generalisation error versus the number of dimensions, n, obtained for very simple structured data – two spherical Gaussian classes. The lower graph corresponds to the multilayer perceptron with five units ($h = 5$) in the hidden layer trained by the stochastic gradient BP algorithm, sigmoid activation function, targets $t_1 = 0.9$ and $t_2 = 0.1$. The upper graph corresponds to the standard Fisher linear DF. The same training data sets were used to train both classification algorithms. Apparently, for this kind of the data the MLP classifier with $(n+1)h+(h+1)$ weights is less sensitive to the dimensionality of the input vector than is the standard Fisher DF with only $n+1$ weights. It agrees with the above guess, based on the analogy with the statistical classifiers. Thus, one may speculate that the accuracy of the weights that are common for all outputs are less important than the accuracy of the weights of the final (output) layer.

In addition to formal statistical analysis, there is an intuitive explanation. For very simple distributions of the pattern classes, the neurones of the hidden layer are similar. Therefore, a minor inaccuracy in determination of one weight of the hidden-layer neurone can be reduced by effects of other similar hidden units, and, most importantly, by subsequent tuning of the weights of the output layer. In the above example, we have only six weights to be adjusted in the output layer neurone and this number does not change with an increase in the number of inputs. Thus, for simple distributions of the pattern classes, the MLP classifier adapts to the simplicity of the problem and can perform satisfactorily even in a case where the number of weights is significantly larger than the number of training vectors.

Note that in the example described above, there were no clear local minima effects.

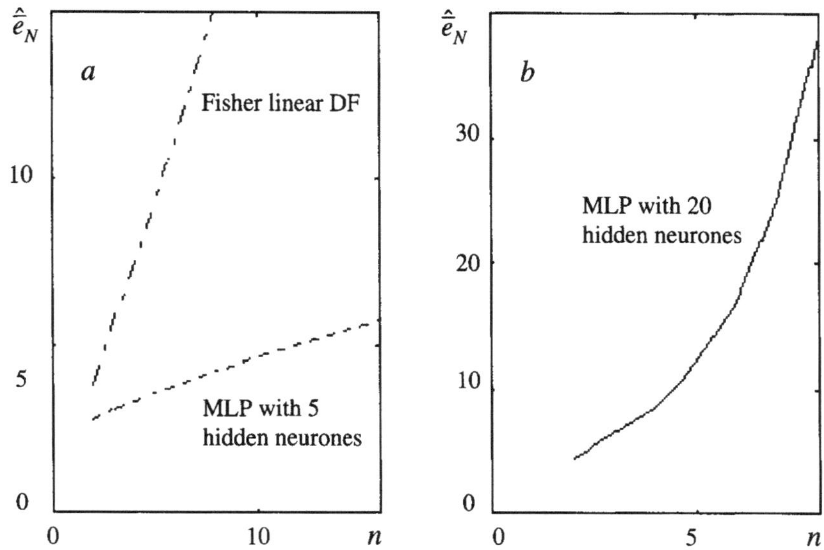

Fig. 4.9. Generalisation error (in percentage) versus dimensionality, *n*, in: *a*) an easy duty and *b*) heavy duty cases.

The complex data. In a case of classification with pattern classes having complex-shaped distributions, the hyperplanes that correspond to different hidden layer neurones are different. Thus, a small alteration of the hidden unit weight can have opposite effects on different outputs of the network and cannot be compensated by tuning the weights of the output layer. Contrary to the case of simply-shaped pattern classes, in this situation, the network can become more sensitive to inaccuracies in the hidden layer weights.

The heavy-duty spherical non Gaussian classes **SF2** considered earlier can serve as an example of such a situation. Here, vectors of the first class are inside the second one: vectors from a bi-variate spherical Gaussian distribution $N_X(0, \mathbf{I})$ inside the circle, $(x_1^2 + x_2^2 = 1.1)$, were chosen for class ω_1, and vectors outside the larger circle, $(x_1^2 + x_2^2 = 1.45)$, were chosen for class ω_2. To make the training task more difficult, in this simulation experiment, we added six Gaussian $N_X(0, \mathbf{I})$ zero mean uninformative features. The Bayes probability of incorrect classification is zero, however, the pattern classes are non-linearly separable. We will use this eight-variate data once more (in Section 4.6.8) and will call it **SF8**. The training sets were composed of $\bar{N} = 70$ vectors from each pattern class, and the test set contained $Nt = 1000 = 500 + 500$ vectors. The graph in Figure 4.9*b* shows that in this heavy-duty case, the generalisation error of MLP increases exponentially with an increase in the number of the features. Its small sample behaviour is more similar to the behaviour of the nonparametric local classifiers (*k-NN*, Parzen window and multinomial classifiers).

Evidently, MLP can adapt to the complexity of the pattern classification problem. In the "easy-duty" case, the multilayer perceptron recognises the simplicity of the problem and exhibits even better small training-set behaviour as the statistical classifiers do. Therefore, *the behaviour of MLP is dual: it depends on the data to be classified.* The MLP classifier can behave similarly to the parametric or the nonparametric local classifier.

4.4.2.2 Intrinsic Dimensionality Problems

Many researchers claim that the "real dimensionality" of real world data is usually much smaller than the number of features. This hypothesis is based on an assumption that in real life, only a few unknown independent factors influence the variability of a large number of the features measured. This unknown, but intuitively supposed, dimensionality of the data is called *the intrinsic dimensionality*. In Chapter 3, it was demonstrated that the small sample properties of EDC, the Parzen window classifier, and the zero empirical error classifier depend on the intrinsic (effective, hidden) dimensionality of the data. There exist theoretical and experimental arguments that it is also true for the non-linear SLP classifier. Unfortunately, there is no unique definition of the "intrinsic dimensionality". For EDC, it was the parameter n^* (Equation (3.7)), for the PW and zero empirical error classifiers it was r, the number of non-zero eigenvalues of the GCCM model. In the GCCM data model case, the Fisher classifier, however, is sensitive to all features. Consequently, the dimensionality, r, of the subspace where the data points are situated is not a sufficient definition of the intrinsic dimensionality. A rigorous definition depends both on a true distribution of the pattern classes and on the type of the classifier used.

Example 8. In Table 4.1 we have average values (upper rows) and standard deviations (lower rows) of the generalisation errors of the MLP classifiers for three pairs of 100-variate GCCM data models with Mahalanobis distance $\delta = \delta^* = 3.76$ (asymptotic error is 0.03). The three data models have different effective dimensionality parameters (n^* = 1.05, 100 or 10000). The number of hidden neurones was either h = 10 or 100 (1021 or 10201 the perceptron's weights), and the target values were: t = 0.7 and 0.3; t = 0.9 and 0.1; or t = 1.0 and 0.0 (the standard sigmoid activation function was used). A standard gradient descent (back-propagation) MLP training algorithm from a Matlab neural networks toolbox was used to train the networks. The generalisation errors were evaluated in 10 experiments with 10 randomly chosen training sets containing $\overline{N} = 10$ multivariate vectors from each of two pattern classes. Note, $N \ll n$=100. To estimate the generalisation error, 500+500 independent test set vectors were used. For each set of experimental conditions in Table 4.1, we present two generalisation error values:

- an optimally stopped perceptron (on the left of "/"), and
- at the end of the training process – after 2,000 iterations (on the right, after "/").

Table 4.1. Mean values (upper rows) and standard deviations (lower rows) of the generalisation errors of the MLP classifiers for three pairs of Gaussian pattern classes sharing a common covariance matrix. Dimensionality $n = 100$, training-set size $N = 10 + 10$.

n^*	$h = 10$ *target* = 0.7	$h = 10$ *target* = 0.9	$h = 10$ *target* = 1.0	$h = 100$ *target* = 0.7	$h = 100$ *target* = 0.9	$h = 100$ *target* = 1.0
1.05	.173/.214	.061/.070	.046/.050	.062/.091	.049/.077	.046/.069
	.059/.070	.020/.024	.014/.016	.021.035	.015/.027	.013/.020
100	.379/.435	.377/.433	.374/.435	.397/.411	.316/.323	.249/.308
	.065/.053	.062/.049	.058/.045	.053/.049	.047/.044	.036/.037
10000	.476/.486	.462/.471	.455/.463	.463/.481	.463/.481	.463/.487
	.015/.022	.025/.028	.025/.026	.028/.033	.023/.026	.022/.023

Table 4.1 confirms that the data type (the effective dimensionality n^*) and the training conditions (the target values and stopping moment) are very important. The simulation results obtained for the spherical data ($n^* = n = 100$) can be explained by the theoretical results presented in Table 3.1. For the spherical data any hidden neurone does not have any preference over other ones. Thus, one may make an assumption that after training, the weights of the hidden layer neurones become random. Assume the weights of the hidden layer are independent zero-mean random variables and the activation functions of the hidden layer neurones behave as linear functions. For simplicity, suppose the distribution of the weights is Gaussian. Then for n-variate spherically Gaussian data, it is possible to calculate the Mahalanobis distance of the populations at outputs of the hidden layer with h neurones $\delta_{\text{hidden}} \approx \delta\sqrt{h/(n+h-1)}$.

For 10 hidden units we have $\delta_{\text{hidden}} \approx 1.14$ with asymptotic error $\varepsilon_\infty \approx 0.29$, and for 100 hidden units we have $\delta_{\text{hidden}} \approx 2.666$ with $\varepsilon_\infty \approx 0.091$. Under the random weights assumption, for $\delta_{\text{hidden}} \approx 1.14$ and n=10 (h = 10) Equation (3.7) for EDC gives the expected error $\bar{\varepsilon}_N^{\text{E}} = \approx 0.36$. For $n = 100$ (h = 100) and $\delta_{\text{hidden}} \approx 2.666$ we calculate $\bar{\varepsilon}_N^{\text{E}} \approx 0.25$. Note, in this analysis, the number of hidden units, h, plays role of dimensionality in the output layer SLP. These $\bar{\varepsilon}_N^{\text{E}}$ values are fairly close to the average experimental values of the optimally stopped MLP obtained for h = 10 and h = 100 and the target values 1 & 0 ($\hat{\bar{\varepsilon}}_N^{\text{SLP}} = 0.\ 374$ and 0.249).

The experimental values at the end of the training process are closer to the pessimistic theoretical generalisation error estimates of the ZEE classifier. Calculation according equations presented in Section 3.6.4 for ZEE classifier with random Gaussian priors for h=10 and $\delta_{\text{hidden}} \approx 1.14$ gives $\bar{\varepsilon}_N^{\text{ZEE}} = 0.47$. For h=100 and $\delta_{\text{hidden}} \approx 2.666$ we calculate $\bar{\varepsilon}_N^{\text{ZEE}} = 0.41$. For n^* = 100 Table 4.1 shows only slightly smaller error values at the end of training: $\hat{\bar{\varepsilon}}_N^{\text{SLP}} = 0.435$ and 0.308.

For target values 0.7 & 0.3, the weights of the output-layer neurone are small. Consequently, the activation function of this neurone actually behaves like a linear function. Therefore, in this case, we obtain a classifier which is similar to the standard Fisher (when $h < N$) or the Pseudo-Fisher classifier (when $h > N$). In Section 3.4.8, we have shown that if dimensionality exceeds the training-set size, then the generalisation error of the Pseudo-Fisher classifier is notably smaller than 0.5). In the experiment we obtain similar values.

For data with small n^* (n^*=1.05), EDC gives a small generalisation error. The same can be said about the MLP classifier. We also notice a parallelism between the performances of EDC and SLP classifiers for data with high intrinsic dimensionality (n^* = 10,000): both classifiers result high generalisation errors.

The above results indicate that one cannot reject a possibility that in certain pattern classification tasks, the weights of the hidden layer neurones of the MLP classifier to some extent are determined in a random manner. In cases where this is true, the number of weights in the hidden layer does not serve as a characteristic of the complexity of the network. Moreover, the hidden layer weights are common to all outputs. In this situation, the number of weights in the output neurone is the more important characteristic. On the other hand, owing to a constant evolution of the output neurone during the iterative training process, the number of weights in the output layer of the network also becomes an insufficient characteristic to determine a real effective complexity of the network.

4.4.2.3 An Effective Capacity of the Network

In Section 4.3.2, it was demonstrated that the local minima and flat areas of the cost function often make difficult the task of designing complex-shaped decision boundaries. Often, known optimisation methods do not allow one to realise a large number of dichotomies as predicted by VC dimension. In the output layer of the MLP, we have the single layer perceptrons. The complexity of the SLP classifier depends on the number of training iterations, the data model, peculiarities of the cost function, the training algorithm and its parameters. Therefore, the number of weights to be adjusted in the training process is a very rough and *insufficient characteristic of the network complexity.*

Kraaijeveld and Duin (1994) experimentally investigated a number of dichotomies that can be realised by MLP and back propagation training. They found that a practical, effective VC dimension is much smaller than that theoretically predicted by using the upper and even lower bound. We present below data from Kraaijeveld and Duin which show the dependence of the "effective capacity" – the average number of dichotomies obtained in the simulation study – versus h, the number of hidden units of MLP and n, the number of features.

Table 4.2. The estimated effective capacity d^* of MLP as a function of h, the number of hidden units. Dimensionality n = 2.

h	1	2	5	10	20	50	100
# of free parameters	5	9	21	41	81	201	401
effective capacity d^*	3	5	6	7	7	6	5

Table 4.3. The estimated effective capacity d^* as a function of n; $h = 100$.

n	1	2	5	10	20
# of free parameters	301	401	701	1201	2201
effective capacity d^*	4	5	7	11	15

We see that "the estimated effective capacity" may be orders of magnitude smaller than the theoretical capacity of the network. This proves once more that "the searching capabilities of the back propagation algorithm are very limited" (Kraaijeveld and Duin, 1994). In SLP training, we move from the simplest EDC to the regularised DA, up to the most complex maximal margin classifier. Undoubtedly, a similar complexity change effect exists in MLP training.

4.5 Overtraining and Initialisation

A characteristic phenomenon in ANN training is overtraining (overfitting). With an increase in the number of iterations, the generalisation error decreases at first, reaches a minimum and then begins to increase. We come across such network behaviour in Figures 1.9 and 1.10. The overtraining effect can be explained by the fact that in a finite training-set case, the network adapts to the training data too much. In this section, this important ANN training peculiarity is considered more thoroughly. We advocate that, this effect depends on:

- adaptation to the training data,
- the initial weight values of the perceptron and on
- the constant changing of the cost function in the BP training process.

4.5.1 Overtraining

One rational explanation of the overtraining effect of the single layer classifier is based on the fact discussed in Section 4.1: during the iterative training process, we obtain several classification rules of increasing complexity. In the finite training-set case, one of the classifiers results in the smallest generalisation error and appears to be the best. Thus, we need to choose a classifier of proper complexity. In Section 4.4.1.1, we hypothesised that in the small training-set case, it is preferable to train the SLP for a short time and, in the large training-set case, one needs to use more iterations. Therefore, with very large training-set sizes, one may train SLP until the minimum empirical error is obtained. When the data are spherically Gaussian (SG), however, it is reasonable to satisfy conditions E1 – E4 and train the perceptron for only one iteration. We have already seen such an example in Figure 1.9 where further training of SLP increases the generalisation error more than two times.

Theoretical considerations presented in Chapter 3 and in Section 4.1 can give conditions where the overtraining effect is very noticeable. For example, Table 3.1 indicates that for 50-variate spherical Gaussian data with Mahalanobis distance

$\delta = 4.56$ (the Bayes and the asymptotic errors are 0.01) and training-set size $\bar{N} = 30$, one can expect after the first iteration to obtain the generalisation error 0.016 (EDC). If one uses the targets 0.9 and 0.1, then in further training, SLP will approach the Fisher classifier with more than 10 times the generalisation error (0.197). If one uses targets 1 and 0, then in further training one will get the zero empirical error classifier with a slightly smaller generalisation error – 0.124 (Table 3.3). In both cases we obtain tremendous overtraining.

The overtraining effect can be explained also by the fact that there exist two different cost functions in the training process:

- $cost_t$, to be minimised during the training process, is based on the *training pattern vectors* and
- $cost_{gen}$ of the classification error measured on the *general population* (in practice, it is measured on a separate test or validation set); we had named this the conditional classification error or the generalisation error.

Each cost function has its own landscape in the multivariate weight space, and minimisation of the first function does not imply the minimisation of the second one.

Example 9. In Figure 4.10 in two-variate weight space, we have depicted a final weight vector $\hat{V}_1$ that corresponds to a minimum of the sample-based cost function $cost_t$ and a true minimum V^* that corresponds to the true (asymptotic) classification error. Suppose, the classification error depends only on the distance of the weight vector from the ideal value V^*. Let us start training from initial weight V_0^1 and move to the sample-based minimum $\hat{V}_1$ along a straight line. Then a minimum classification error will be obtained at $\hat{V}^1_{opt}$, the closest point to V^*. Thus, in a segment $\hat{V}^1_{opt}$ - $\hat{V}_1$ we have overtraining.

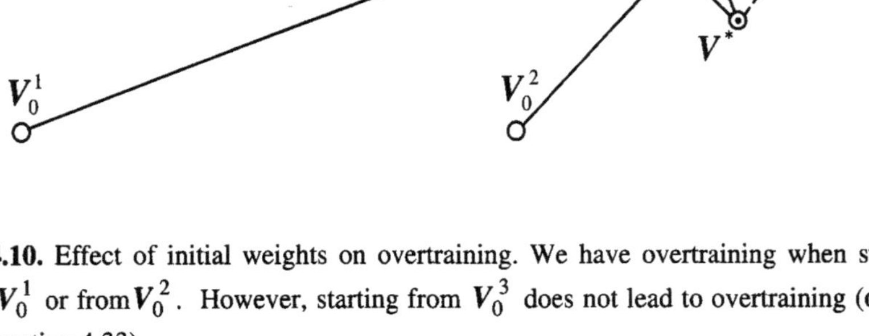

Fig. 4.10. Effect of initial weights on overtraining. We have overtraining when starting from V_0^1 or from V_0^2. However, starting from V_0^3 does not lead to overtraining (α_{opt}>1, see Equation 4.33).

It is a consequence that instead of minimising the true cost, $cost_{gen}$, with the minimum in V^*, we minimise the sample-based cost, $cost_t$, with the minimum in another place ($\hat{V}_1$). If we start with V_0^2 and move straight to $\hat{V}_1$, we need to stop at $\hat{V}_{opt}^2$. In comparison with $\hat{V}_{opt}^1$, vector $\hat{V}_{opt}^2$ results in a smaller generalisation error. If we start with V_0^3 and move straight to $\hat{V}_1$, we need to train until the end (the minimum of the cost function). In this case, we have no overtraining.

This graphical example advocates that the overtraining effect depends on the initial values. In the next subsection, we will perform more complete analytical investigation.

4.5.2 Effect of Initial Values

Figure 4.10 demonstrates that overtraining appears only in a part of training experiments and that it depends on the configuration of the starting, V_0, final, $\hat{V}_1$, and ideal, V^*, weight vectors. In this section, we will show that in high-dimensional cases, the *overtraining almost always occurs.* To simplify analysis, consider an elementary linear model

$$y = X^T V^* + \xi = t, \tag{4.23}$$

where y is the output, V is the weight vector, X is n-dimensional input vector, $X \sim N_X(\mathbf{0}, \mathbf{I})$, ξ is Gaussian $N(0, \sigma^2)$ independent noise and t stands for the target value.

Let us have the training set $(X_1, y_1), (X_2, y_2), \ldots, (X_N, y_N)$ and let us utilise the standard sum of squares cost function in order to evaluate an unknown weight vector. Minimisation of the sum of squares cost results in

$$\hat{V}_1 = \left(\frac{1}{N}\sum_{j=1}^{N} X_j X_j^T\right)^{-1} \frac{1}{N}\sum_{i=1}^{N} X_i y_i = \left(\frac{1}{N}\sum_{j=1}^{N} X_j X_j^T\right)^{-1} \frac{1}{N}\sum_{j=1}^{N} (X_j X_j^T V^* + X_j\xi_j),$$

where we have used $y_j = X_j^T V^* + \xi_j$. According to definition, $E\xi_j = 0$.

Consequently,

$E\hat{V}_1 = V^*$, $\hat{V}_1 - V^* = \hat{V}_{1*} = \left(\frac{1}{N}\sum_{j=1}^{N} X_j X_j^T\right)^{-1} \frac{1}{N}\sum_{i=1}^{N} X_i y_i$ and the covariance matrix of the weight vector $\hat{V}_1$

$$\Sigma_{V_1} = E\hat{V}_{1*}\hat{V}_{1*}^T = E\left(\frac{1}{N}\sum_{j=1}^{N} X_j X_j^T\right)^{-1} \frac{1}{N}\sum_{i=1}^{N} X_i y_i \, \frac{1}{N}\sum_{i=1}^{N} y_i X_i^T \left(\frac{1}{N}\sum_{j=1}^{N} X_j X_j^T\right)^{-1} =$$

$$E\left(\frac{1}{N}\sum_{j=1}^{N} X_j X_j^T\right)^{-1} \frac{\sigma^2}{N^2}\sum_{i=1}^{N} X_i X_i^T \left(\frac{1}{N}\sum_{j=1}^{N} X_j X_j^T\right)^{-1} = \frac{\sigma^2}{N} E\left(\frac{1}{N}\sum_{j=1}^{N} X_j X_j^T\right)^{-1}.$$

The standard multivariate statistical analysis gives

$$E\left(\frac{1}{N}\sum_{j=1}^{N}X_jX_j^T\right)^{-1} = \frac{N}{N-n-1}\mathbf{I}. \tag{4.24}$$

Thus, the asymptotic (when $N \to \infty$) distribution of the final weight vector

$$\hat{V}_1 \sim N_{V_1}(V^*, \Sigma_{V_1}) \text{ with } \Sigma_{V_1} = \frac{\sigma^2}{N-n-1}\mathbf{I}. \tag{4.25}$$

Let $(\hat{V}_1 - V^*)^T(\hat{V}_1 - V^*) = d_1^2$, which is a squared error – a characteristic of the accuracy of determination of the final weight vector $\hat{V}_1$. For randomly generated training data $(X_1, y_1), (X_2, y_2), \ldots, (X_N, y_N)$ one can consider $\hat{V}_1$ as a random vector. The mean squared error of $\hat{V}_1$ is

$$mse(\hat{V}_1) = E(\hat{V}_1 - V^*)^T(\hat{V}_1 - V^*) = \text{tr}\,\Sigma_{V_1} = \frac{\sigma^2 n}{N-n-1}. \tag{4.26}$$

Let us start training with the initial weight vector V_0. The covariance matrix Σ_{V_1} is proportional to the identity matrix (Equation (4.25)). Therefore, without loss of generality we can assume that only the first component of the starting vector differs from the ideal vector V^*, i.e. $V_0 - V^* = (D, 0, \ldots, 0)^T$. In order to analyse the accuracy of the linear move from V_0 to $\hat{V}_1$, let us introduce a *weighted estimate*

$$\hat{V}_{new} = \alpha\,\hat{V}_1 + (1-\alpha)\,V_0, \tag{4.27}$$

where α is a weighting factor ($0 \le \alpha \le 1$).

Then the squared error of the new estimate, $\hat{V}_{new}$, is

$$(\hat{V}_{new} - V^*)^T(\hat{V}_{new} - V^*) = (\alpha\,\hat{V}_1 + (1-\alpha)\,V_0 - V^*)^T(\alpha\,\hat{V}_1 + (1-\alpha)\,V_0 - V^*) =$$

$$(\alpha\,\hat{V}_{1*} + (1-\alpha)(V_0 - V^*))^T(\alpha\,\hat{V}_{1*} + (1-\alpha)(V_0 - V^*)) =$$

$$(\alpha\,\zeta_1 + (1-\alpha)\,D)^2 + a^2\sum_{j=2}^{n}\zeta_j^2 = (D + \alpha(\zeta_1 - D))^2 + a^2\Theta, \tag{4.28}$$

where $\zeta_1, \ldots, \zeta_n$ are components of the vector $\hat{V}_{1*} = \hat{V}_1 - V^*$, and $\Theta = \sum_{j=2}^{n}\zeta_j^2$.

In order to find the optimal weighting factor, α_{opt} we equate a derivative of (4.28) to zero:

$$2(D + \alpha(\zeta_1 - D))(\zeta_1 - D) + 2\alpha\Theta = 0,$$

and obtain

$$\alpha_{opt} = \frac{D(D-\zeta_1)}{(D-\zeta_1)^2 + \Theta}. \tag{4.29}$$

By scaling the variables ζ_1 and Θ by the factor $\frac{N-n-1}{\sigma^2}$ we can represent α_{opt} as a function of two independent, Gaussian (ξ) and chi-square (χ^2_{n-1}), random variables

$$\alpha_{opt} \sim \frac{D(D-\xi\sigma/\sqrt{N-n-1})}{(D-\xi\sigma/\sqrt{N-n-1})^2 + \sigma^2/(N-n-1)\chi^2_{n-1}} \tag{4.30}$$

Thus, the optimal weighting factor α_{opt} depends on two random variables ξ and χ^2_{n-1}. Consequently, α_{opt} can be analysed as a random variable. Representation (4.30) allows us to derive the distribution density of α_{opt} and to calculate the mean and variance of α_{opt}. An expression for the mean is rather simple

$$E\alpha_{opt} = \frac{1}{1 + \dfrac{\sigma^2 n}{(N-n-1)D^2}}. \tag{4.31}$$

Equation (4.31) shows that, in inaccurate initial weights case (large D), the final weight vector, $\hat{V}_1$, ought to play more important role ($E\alpha_{opt}$ is close to 1). In SLP training it means: we need to train the perceptron almost until the end.

In order to compare the accuracy of the initial V_0 and final $\hat{V}_1$ weights, it would be desirable to utilise the same units. In (4.26), the accuracy of the weight vector $\hat{V}_1$ was determined in terms of the training-set size. One can use (4.26) and express the accuracy of V_0 in terms of an *imaginary training-set* size, N_0, that should give a certain squared error of V_0:

$$(V_0 - V^*)^T(V_0 - V^*) = D^2 = \frac{\sigma^2 n}{N_0 - n - 1}. \tag{4.32}$$

Use of (4.32) in (4.31) results in

$$E\alpha_{opt} = \frac{N-n-1}{N_0 + N - 2n - 2}. \tag{4.33}$$

From Equation (4.33), it is seen that with an increase in the accuracy of the determination of the initial weight vector (in this representation, with an increase in the imaginary sample size N_0), we need to scale the final $\hat{V}_1$ weight with the smaller coefficient, α. In perceptron training, this means we have to stop training earlier. For $N = 30$ and $N_0 = 22, 26, 30, 40$ we have following mean values of the weighting factor: $\alpha_{opt} = 0.90, 0.65, 0.50, 0.32$.

Now we will evaluate the gain that can be obtained from optimal weighting the initial and final vectors. Inserting the mean value of the weighting factor (4.33) into the expression for the generalisation error of the weighted estimate (4.28), we obtain the mean generalisation error

$$mse(\hat{V}_{new\&opt})=\frac{\sigma^2 n}{N_0+N-2n-1}. \tag{4.34}$$

Suppose for a moment that all N_0 vectors from the imaginary training-set can be utilised for training the perceptron. Then from Equation (4.26), we conclude that the generalisation error would be

$$mse(\hat{V}_{opt})=\frac{\sigma^2 n}{N_0+N-n-1}. \tag{4.35}$$

Comparison of (4.34) with (4.35) indicates that if instead of all N_0 training vectors we use only the weight vector V_0, we are losing just n training vectors. If N_0 and N are large, ratio n/N_0 is small. Thus, the initial weight vector V_0 can carry almost all information contained in the N_0 vectors of the imaginary training-set. To save this information we need to stop training in time.

Up to now, we considered only mean values. Figure 4.10 demonstrated that the overtraining phenomenon appears only in some of training experiments. Analysis of variances of optimal weighting factor α_{opt} (Equation 4.30) leads to the conclusion that in high-dimensional cases, overtraining almost always occurs. In Figure 4.11, we have four distribution density functions of α_{opt} found from the representation (4.30) by numerical methods for distinct n, N, and four initial weights of differing accuracy (N_0 = 22, 26, 40 and 212). From Figure 4.11, we see that for n = 20, N_0 = 22, and N = 30, the weighting factor $\alpha_{opt} > 1$ in 7.5% cases. This means that in 7.5% of cases, the overtraining will not be observed. A variance of the distribution of α_{opt} diminishes with simultaneous increase in the number of features, n, and the training-set size (N_0 and N_1). E.g. for n = 200, N_0 = 212 and N =300, we obtain the same value of $E\alpha_{opt}$ (0.90). In the latter case, however, we have a smaller variance and the overtraining effect will always be observed.

Large variances of the distribution of α_{opt} indicate that in small dimensional cases, in order to utilise all information contained in V_0, we need to stop individually for each pair of V_0 and $\hat{V}_1$. In principle, in some cases, the individually optimal stopping allows us to obtain a generalisation error smaller than (4.35).

In order to stop training optimally, however, we ought to utilise certain *additional information*. The possibility of making use of the information contained in the initial weight vector is a peculiarity both of the prediction and the classification problems. In Chapter 3 it was demonstrated that, in the classification task, the analytical expressions for the generalisation error are much more complicated than Equation (4.26). Consequently, analytical expressions for α_{opt} should be even more complex than (4.31).

As a conclusion we claim that the initial weights can contain useful information. This information can be utilised in improving the generalisation performance of the network. To save this information we need to stop training in time.

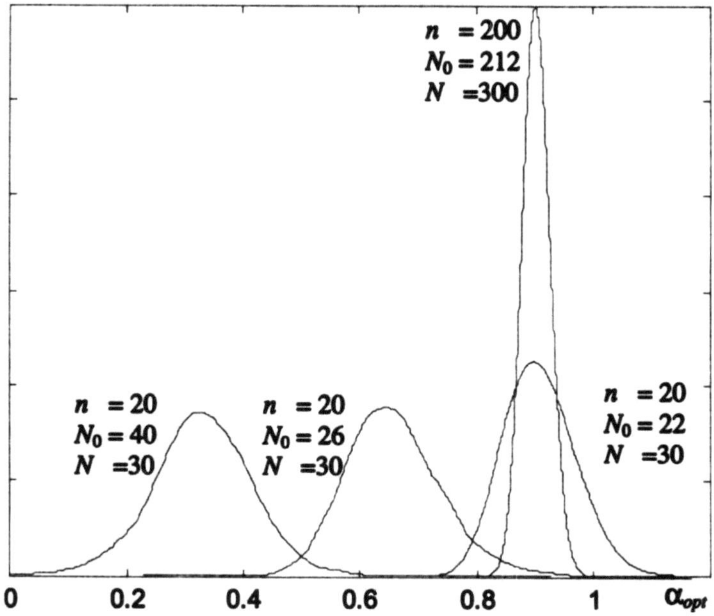

Fig. 4.11. Effect of the accuracy of the weights initialisation (the imaginary training-set size N_0) and dimensionality, n, on the distribution density function of the optimal weighting factor α_{opt}.

This peculiarity of the adaptive network training is one of the key items that help to integrate the statistical and neural net approaches.

4.6 Tools to Control Complexity

In SLP and MLP training, one can obtain many different classification rules. The overtraining and scissors effects advocate that in the finite training-set size situation, it is important to choose a classifier of proper complexity. In this book, we already have met several factors that affect the network's training result. The objective of this section is to enumerate and explain all factors that influence the training result and can be used for an intelligent control of the classifier's complexity. We categorise the factors associated with: (1) the cost function and (2) the optimisation technique used to find the minimum of the cost function.

The most popular cost function used in feedforward ANN design is the sum of squares defined in Section 4.1. Instead of the quadratic loss, one can use the

Kulback–Leibler distance (see e.g. Haykin, 1999). We concentrate here on the quadratic loss (4.2) only. The parameters that determine the cost (4.2) are:

- the character of the activation function $f(net)$;
- the target values $t_j^{(i)}$;
- the weights $\boldsymbol{V}$ themselves (most important are their magnitudes);
- the input patterns $\boldsymbol{X}_j^{(i)}$.

We consider the effects of each of these factors on peculiarities of the cost function and on the type of the classification rule obtained. Note, all these factors influence each other and their optimal values are mutually dependent.

The character of the activation function (a linear function, soft-limiting, the threshold function) introduces new possibilities into SLP training. In dependence on the target values and the magnitude of the weights, we have different types of association between the weighted sums $G_j^{(i)} = \boldsymbol{V}^T\boldsymbol{X}_j^{(i)} + v_0$ and the contribution terms $(t_j^{(i)} - f(G_j^{(i)}))^2$ in the sum $cost_t$. Small weights make the activation function linear, large weights together with the boundary values of the targets (+1 and -1 for tanh(G) activation function) affect the term $(t_j^{(i)} - f(G_j^{(i)}))^2$, moving it towards the threshold function and allowing it to minimise the empirical probability of misclassification.

4.6.1 The Number of Iterations

In non-linear SLP training, with an increase in the number of iterations one can obtain seven statistical classifiers of differing complexity (EDC, RDA, standard Fisher LDF, Pseudo-Fisher LDF, robust DA, minimum empirical error classifier, and the maximum margin (support vector) classifier). Without doubt, the number of iterations is the most important factor which determines the type of classification rule obtained in MLP training.

4.6.2 The Weight Decay Term

The addition of the "weight decay" term, $\lambda\boldsymbol{V}^T\boldsymbol{V}$, to the standard cost function reduces the magnitudes of the weights. Nowadays, it is the most popular technique utilised to control the complexity of the network. For very small weights, the activation function acts as a linear one. Thus, for the linear and non-linear SLP, addition of the regularisation term is equivalent to using a "ridge" estimate of a covariance matrix in a linear regularised discriminant analysis. Suppose we add the "weight decay" term $\lambda\boldsymbol{V}^T\boldsymbol{V}$, use the targets $t_1 = 1$ and $t_2 = -1$, and instead of the tanh activation function, use the linear one, i.e. $f(net) = net$. Then, equating the derivatives (4.4) and (4.5) to zero and solving the equations, we can show that, for the centred data ($\hat{\boldsymbol{M}} = 0$), $\boldsymbol{V} = (\mathrm{I}\lambda + \hat{\Sigma})^{-1}\Delta\hat{\boldsymbol{M}}\, k_{\mathrm{WD}}$ and $v_{0(t)} = 0$ (k_{WD} is a scalar which does not depend on $\boldsymbol{X}$, the vector to be classified). Thus, the "weight decay" term leads to regularised discriminant analysis.

An alternative to the weight decay term is the term $+\lambda(V^TV - c^2)^2$. Here, a positive parameter c^2 controls the magnitude of the weights and acts as the traditional regulariser.

4.6.3 The Antiregularisation Technique

After starting from small or even zero values, the weights of the perceptron increase gradually. The non-linear character of the activation function assists in obtaining the complex classifiers (the robust DA, the robust regularized DA, the minimum empirical error and the maximum margin classifiers). The magnitudes of the weights, however, depend on the separability of the training sets (the empirical classification error). If the training sets of opposite pattern classes overlap, the weights cannot be increased very much. Consequently, small weights can prevent us from obtaining one of the complex classifiers.

When the pattern classes are highly intersecting, in order to be able to control the type of classifier obtained at the end, we can utilise the complementary term added to the traditional cost function. We can subtract the weight decay term instead of adding it. Then we obtain large weights and begin to minimise the empirical classification error. This technique is called *antiregularisation.* It was demonstrated that for non-Gaussian pattern classes characterised by a number of outliers, the antiregularisation can reduce the generalisation error radically. Often the traditional weight decay term destabilises the training process. Therefore, the term $+\lambda(V^TV - c^2)^2$, used to control the magnitudes of the output layer weights is preferred. In a modification of this technique, c^2 increases with t, the number of iterations.

Example 10. In Section 4.2.1 we used the antiregularisation term in order to obtain a non-linear decision boundary in the five-variate polynomial feature space (Figure 4.4). In Figure 4.12, we illustrate this technique with a two-variate example where we have Gaussian N($\boldsymbol{M}_i$, Σ) data with highly correlated features. The data is contaminated by 10% noise N(**0**, **N**):

$$\boldsymbol{M}_1 = -\boldsymbol{M}_2 = \begin{bmatrix} +0.030 \\ -0.023 \end{bmatrix}, \quad \Sigma = \begin{bmatrix} 0.040 & 0.0196 \\ 0.0196 & 0.01 \end{bmatrix}, \quad \mathbf{N} = \begin{bmatrix} 1.0 & -0.7 \\ -0.7 & 1.0 \end{bmatrix}.$$

For training, 100 bi-variate vectors from each class were used (Figure 4.12*a*). For testing, we used 1000+1000 vectors. We'd like to draw attention to the fact that, in bi-variate data **A2**, we have a comparatively large number of training vectors ($N_1 = N_2 = 100$), and the signal and noise components have opposite correlations. The variance of noise is much larger than that of the signal. In traditional training (conditions E1 – E4, $\eta = 0.5$), we did not have any success (decision boundary 1 in Figure 4.12*a* and learning curve 1 in Figure 4.12*b*). Adding the antiregularisation term $0.02 \times (V^TV - 25)^2$ to the cost function does not influence the learning curve at the beginning but, later on, when the weights increase substantially, the decision boundary begins approaching the optimal boundary (2 in Figure 4.12*a*) with 12% generalisation error (see curve 2 in Figure 4.12*b*).

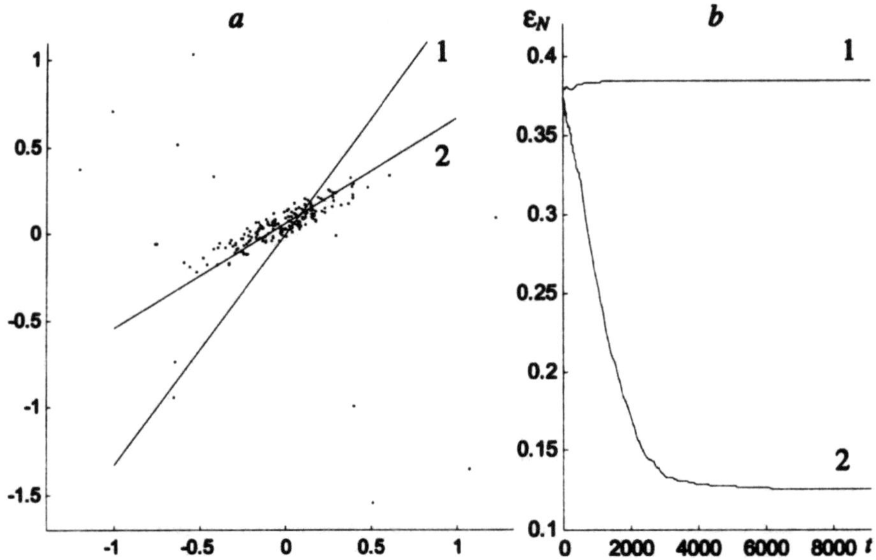

Fig. 4.12. Effect of the antiregularisation technique in SLP training: 1 – standard BP training, 2 – with antiregularisation.

4.6.4 Noise Injection

Another popular method for stabilising solutions while training artificial neural net classifiers is noise injection. Noise can be added to inputs of the network, to outputs, to the targets and to the weights of the network.

4.6.4.1 Noise Injection to Inputs

In this approach, we add a zero mean and small covariance noise vectors $\mathbf{n}_\alpha$ to the training vector $X_j^{(i)}$ at each training iteration:

$$X_{j\beta}^{(i)} = X_j^{(i)} + \mathbf{n}_{j\beta}^{(i)}, \quad (\beta = 1, 2, ..., t_{max}), \tag{4.36}$$

where t_{max} is the number of training sweeps (presentations of all vectors in the training-set).

This technique is also called jittering of the data. While injecting noise $m = t_{max}$ times to each training vector we artificially increase the number of training observations m times.

For the linear classification, we can find a link between noise injection and regularised disriminant analysis. Let the mean of noise vector $\mathbf{n}_{j\beta}^{(i)}$ be zero and the covariance matrix be $\lambda \times \mathbf{I}$. Then the covariance matrix of random vectors $\boldsymbol{X}_{j\beta}^{(i)}$ (β =1, 2, ..., m) with noise added will be $\Sigma_i + \lambda \times \mathbf{I}$, where Σ_i is the true covariance matrix of $\boldsymbol{X}_j^{(i)}$. Consider now the sample covariance matrix of the jittered training-set composed of mN_i vectors $\boldsymbol{X}_{j\beta}^{(i)}$ (j=1, 2, ..., N_i β = 1, 2, ..., m). When $m \to \infty$, the new sample estimate of the covariance matrix tends to

$$\hat{\Sigma}_N^{(i)} = \frac{1}{N_i - 1} \sum_{j=1}^{N_i} (\boldsymbol{X}_j^{(i)} - \hat{\boldsymbol{M}}_j^{(i)})(\boldsymbol{X}_j^{(i)} - \hat{\boldsymbol{M}}_j^{(i)})^T + \lambda \times \mathbf{I}. \tag{4.37}$$

The covariance matrix (4.37) coincides with the ridge (regularised) estimate (2.37) used in regularised discriminant analysis. In Section 4.1, it was shown that the two-class linear classifier derived by the mean squared error criterion (4.2) and the weight decay regularisation term using an equal number of sample patterns from each class ($N_2 = N_1$) is equivalent to RDA. Therefore when $m \to \infty$, the noise injection technique also approximates the regularisation approach using the weight decay.

In the limit when $m \to \infty$, jittering the training data (4.36) with spherical Gaussian noise is similar to the nonparametric Parzen window probability density estimate (2.48) with $\boldsymbol{D}$=$\mathbf{I}$.

Example 11. In Figure 4.13*a* we present a histogram obtained from seven one-dimensional randomly-selected data points, where to each of the seven observations we added m = 80 independent Gaussian N(0, 0.05) random numbers. 100 bins were used to draw the histogram. In Figure 4.13*b* we present the histogram where we added m = 20,000 random numbers. The histogram with m = 20,000 is similar to the Parzen window density estimate obtained with the Gaussian kernel and a smoothing parameter λ = 0.05 (Figure 4.13*c*).

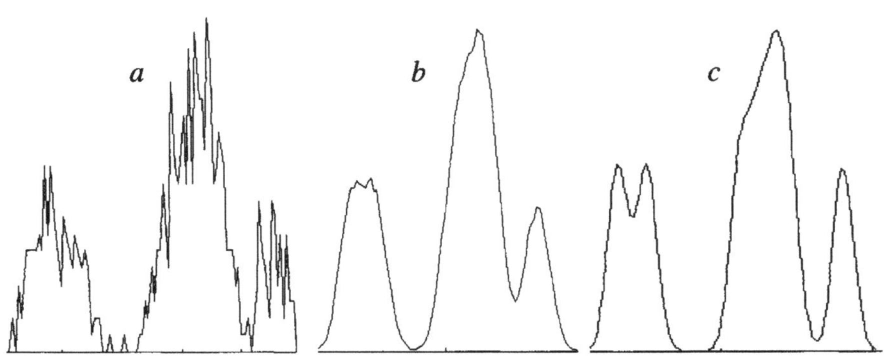

Fig. 4.13. Histograms obtained where, to each of seven one-dimensional observations, *a* m = 80 or *b* m = 20000 independent Gaussian N(0, 0.05) random numbers have been added; *c* the Parzen window density estimate.

One needs a great number of noise injections, m, in order to approach the Parzen window density estimate. In the multivariate case, the number of noise injections has to be much higher. Therefore, in very high-dimensional cases, the spherical noise injection can become ineffective.

> Adding a noise essentially amounts to introducing new information which states that the space between the training vectors is not empty.

It is very important in MLP design, since the network (more precisely the cost function to be minimised) does not know that the pattern space between the training observation vectors is not empty. A noise injected to inputs introduces this information. In practice, it is important to choose the correct value of λ, the noise variance. Similarly to regularised discriminant analysis and smoothing in the Parzen window classifiers, an optimal value of λ (the regularisation parameter or the noise variance) depends upon the number of training vectors and the complexity of the problem.

4.6.4.2 Noise Injection into the Weights and into the Outputs of the Network

Adding noise to the weights is a common practice to tackle local extrema problems in optimisation. In addition to fighting the local minima problems, noise injection into the weights increases the overlap of the training sets. Consequently, noise injection reduces the magnitudes of the weights and acts as a tool to control the complexity of the classification rule. In the MLP classifier design, noise injection into the weights of the hidden layer acts as noise injection into the inputs of the following layer and acts as the regulariser of the output layer neurons.

During the training process, noise can be also added to the outputs of the networks (or the targets). Such noise injection also reduces the magnitudes of the weights and influences the complexity of the classification rule. In all cases, an optimal value of a noise variance should be selected. Typically in situations with unknown data, the variance is determined by the cross validation technique.

A drawback of training with noise injection is that it usually requires one to use a small learning rate constant and many sample presentations, m, over the noise. In high-dimensional space, this problem is particularly visible.

4.6.4.3 "Coloured" Noise Injection into Inputs

As a rule, one injects into network inputs a "white" noise – spherical uniform or Gaussian N(0, $\mathbf{I}\lambda$) random vectors. In high-dimensional, real-world pattern classification problems, data is situated in non-linear subspaces of much lower dimensionality than the formal number of the features. This means that for large λ spherical noise injection can distort data configuration. In *k-NN* directed noise injection, *k-NN* clustering should be used to determine the local intrinsic data dimension; and the added noise should be limited to this intrinsic dimension. Then we have minor data distortion and, in comparison with spherical noise injection, we obtain a gain. One can add noise to the training vector $\boldsymbol{X}_j^{(i)}$ in the directions of k of its nearest neighbours.

An alternative way is to use k nearest neighbours to calculate a singular sample covariance matrix, $\hat{\Sigma}_{ij}^{k}$, around $X_j^{(i)}$, and then to add Gaussian $N(\mathbf{0}, \lambda \hat{\Sigma}_{ij}^{k})$ noise. Thus, instead of white noise we are adding "coloured" noise. The optimal number of nearest neighbours k, as well as a scale parameter, λ, should be determined in an experimental way.

4.6.5 Control of Target Values

One more factor which always affects the magnitudes of the weights is the *target values*. Let us analyse the classification problem with two pattern classes using SLP trained by the sum of squares cost function (4.2) and tanh activation function (1.8).

Suppose targets t_1 and t_2 are close to each other, e.g. $t_1 = 0.5$ and $t_2 = -0.5$. Then *after* minimisation of the cost function, we obtain small values of the sums $G_{ij} = \sum_{\alpha=1}^{n} v_\alpha x_{\alpha j}^{(i)} + v_0$ and, consequently, small weights. Thus, the weighted sum G_{ij} varies in a small interval around zero. Essentially, the activation function, $o(G)$, is acting as a linear function. Hence, with proximal targets we will not obtain the robust classification rule, the minimum empirical error and maximal margin classifiers.

When $t_1 \to 1$ and $t_2 \to -1$, the weights will increase. Then the trained SLP classifier will begin to ignore training vectors distant from the decision hyper-plane $\sum_{\alpha=1}^{n} v_\alpha x_{\alpha j}^{(i)} + v_0 = 0$. Thus, the target values can be utilised as a tool to control the "robustness" of the classification rule. To obtain the minimum empirical error and the maximal margin classifier, we need to use target values that are very close to the boundary activation function values (1 and -1 for activation function (1.8)). *Values outside the interval* (-1, 1) assist in fast growth of the magnitudes of the weights and speed up the training process. However, they also increase the probability of being trapped at a local minimum (the local trench).

4.6.6 The Learning Step

The learning step, η, affects the speed of the iterative training process. A small learning step slows down the training and forces the weights to remain small for a long time. Thus, while training the non-linear SLP, a small learning step assists in obtaining a more complete sequence of the regularised classifiers and the standard linear discriminant function with the conventional or with the pseudo-inverse covariance matrix.

A large learning step speeds up the growth of the weights. However, too large learning step can stop the training process after just the first iteration. When we use a very large learning step, then after the first iteration we can obtain enormous weights. Consequently, the gradient of the cost function can become very small and the training algorithm can stop. If we fulfil the conditions E1 – E4, enumerated in Section 4.1, we get EDC after the first iteration and do not move further towards other classification rules (see e.g. curve 3 in Figure 4.3). Large and intermediate learning step values can stop the training process soon after RDA is obtained and do not allow one to obtain RDA with a small regularisation parameter. A large learning step leads immediately to large weights. Thus, it increases the possibility of being trapped at local minimum.

Furthermore, if a constant learning step is utilised, then with an increase in the magnitude of the weights, the training process slows down and stops. One can say that the *effective value* of η decreases. In this case, the fixed value of the learning step can prevent the algorithm from getting to the minimum empirical error or the maximum margin classifier. One solution to overcome this difficulty is to use a *variable learning step* η, where after a certain number of iterations η is either increased or reduced. In back propagation training, in order to obtain the maximal margin classifier, it was suggested that the learning step η should increase exponentially, e.g. $\eta = \eta_0\ (1+\varepsilon)^t$, where t is the iteration number, and ε is a small positive constant chosen by trial and error. Typically, one can use larger ε values when one has small or even no error while classifying the training-set. A larger learning step can prevent us from obtaining the standard statistical linear classifiers. It can allow us to obtain the robust regularised discriminant function. The degree of regularisation and the robustness can be controlled by the learning step value. Therefore, one should choose ε value carefully.

Example 12. In Figure 4.14, we present four pairs of learning curves: the generalisation error as function of the number of iterations for four η values.

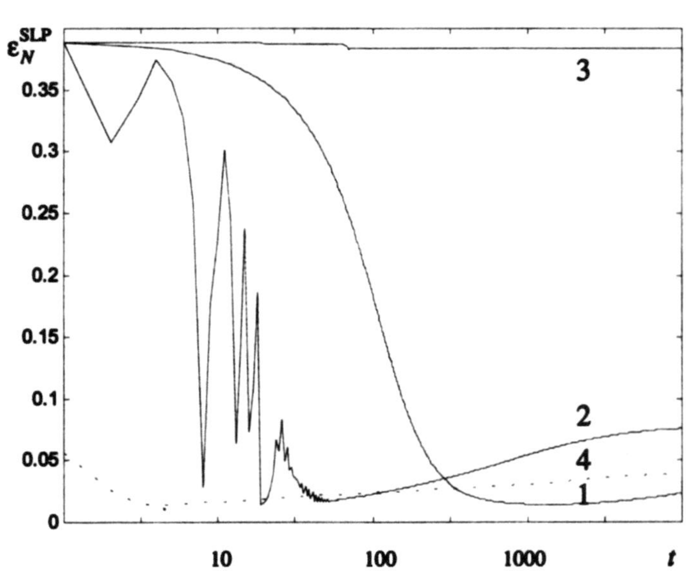

Fig. 4.14. Generalisation error as a function of the number of iterations t for different values of the learning step η: $1 - \eta = 0.001$, $2 - \eta = 0.1$, $3 - \eta = 10$ (targets 0.9 & 0.1) ; $4 - \eta = 1.0 \times 1.005^t$ (after whitening data transformation; targets 1 & 0).

Here we used two 20-variate GCCM pattern classes with correlated features ($\rho = 0.9$), the Mahalanobis distance $\delta = 4.65$ (the Bayes error $\varepsilon_B = 0.01$), targets $t_1 = 0.9$, $t_2 = 0.1$, (for graphs 1, 2, 3) and one training-set composed of 30 + 30 vectors. The straight line 3 shows that for $\eta = 10$, the adaptation process after the first few iterations practically stops. We have very slow (at the beginning) training when the learning step is too small (curve 1 for $\eta = 0.001$). A whitening data transformation (see Section 5.4.3) together with the exponential increase in the learning step $\eta = 1.005^t$, results in a fast training and the smallest generalisation error, the generalisation error 1.4% (curve 4).

Thus, the value of the learning step is an extremely important factor that affects the result of the training process: the minimal generalisation error and the optimal number of iterations.

4.6.7 Optimal Values of the Training Parameters

In linear single layer perceptron training, the regularisation techniques based on weight decay, spherical noise injection, and early stopping can be equivalent to classical linear regularised discriminant analysis. In all four complexity control methods, we need to choose optimal values of λ or the optimal number of iterations. It was shown theoretically that in RDA, the optimal value of the regularisation parameter λ depends on N, the training-set size: λ_{opt} decreases when N increases (see Section 3.4.9). Bellow we present an illustration of equivalence of these complexity control techniques.

Example 13. In Figure 4.15, we present the generalisation error versus λ, the conventional regularisation parameter in RDA (*a*), the regularisation parameter in the weight decay procedure (*b*), and the noise variance in the noise injection regularisation (*c*). In this experiment, we used artificial eight-variate GCCM data with strongly dependent features. It is important to note that the optimal values of the complexity control parameters under discussion significantly depend on the particular randomly chosen training-set. Therefore, the experiments were repeated 20 times with different randomly chosen training sets. In Figure 4.15, we have averaged the values.

For each value of N, the number of training examples, all three families of the graphs approximately exhibit the same generalisation error at minima points and explain, by example, the equivalence of all three regularisation techniques. This experiment confirms the theoretical conclusion: the optimal values of the regularisation parameters decrease when the number of training examples increase.

In SLP training, the number of iterations, the learning step, the targets, the noise, the weight decay term, and the non-linearity of the activation function are all acting together. The influence of one regularisation factor is diminished by the other ones. This circumstance causes additional difficulties in determining the optimal values of the complexity control parameters.

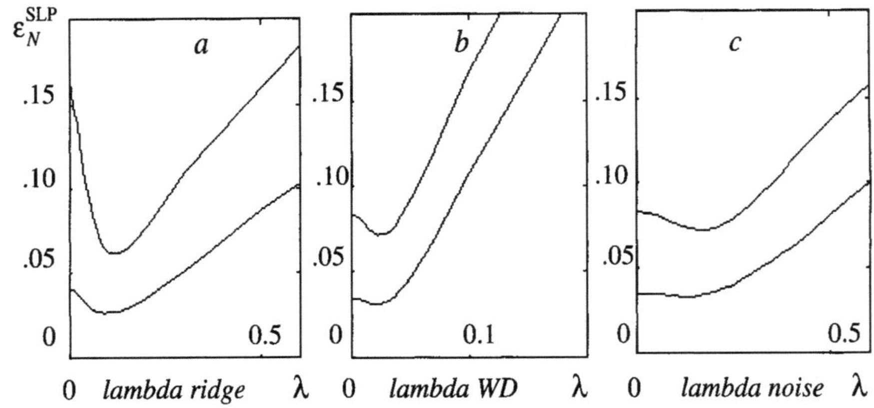

Fig. 4.15. Three types of regularisation of the SLP classifiers for two sizes of the learning sets ($N_1 = N_2 = 5$ and 10): *a* – the regularised discriminant analysis with the ridge estimate of the covariance matrix, *b* - weight decay, *c* – noise injection to inputs.

The targets, the learning step (to some extent even the number of iterations) do not act in a clearly visible way. Thus, they can be considered as *automatic regularisers*. In neural network training, however, their effects cannot be ignored.

Considerations presented in this section are valid for the gradient type search techniques used to find the weights of the perceptrons. Utilisation of more sophisticated optimisation techniques such as a second order Newton method or its modifications can speed up the training process. However, at the same time it introduces definite shortcomings. For example, in the case of the linear pereceptron, the second order (Newton) method, in principle, allows us to minimise the cost function in just one step, however, it prevents us from obtaining the regularised discriminant analysis. In this sense, the back propagation algorithm is more desirable. Nevertheless, this shortcoming of the Newton method can be diminished by introducing the regularisation term.

4.6.8 Learning Step in the Hidden Layer of MLP

In comparison with SLP, in MLP training several additional aspects arise. The learning step is the first important *secret factor* that affects the complexity. In the gradient descent optimisation procedure, a fixed value of the learning step η causes a random fluctuation of the parameters to be optimised (in our case, the components of the weight vector). Asymptotically, for fixed η, and large t, the number of iterations, the weight vector $V_{(t)}$ oscillates around $\hat{V}_N$, an optimal weight vector for this particular training-set. In his classic paper, Amari (1967) has shown that, asymptotically, for large t, the weight $V_{(t)}$ is random Gaussian $N(\hat{V}_N, \eta\Sigma_{V_t})$, where Σ_{V_t} is a covariance matrix that depends on the data, a configuration of the network and peculiarities of the cost function near the optimum. In optimisation, in order to find the minimum exactly, the parameter η should converge to zero with a certain speed.

Random fluctuation of the hidden units' weight vector $V_{(t)}$ suggests that the outputs of the hidden layer neurones are random variables too. Thus, we have a *chaos* (a process noise) inside the feedforward neural network. Random outputs serve as random inputs to the single-layer perceptrons of the output layer. Consequently, in the output layer, we have a type of data jittering. The noise variance depends on the value of the learning step η_h used to adapt the hidden units. Note, a noise injected into the inputs of the output layer is coloured.

Hence, in MLP training, the learning step η_h in the hidden layer, a traditional noise injection, the weight decay term, as well as the number of iterations are producing similar effects. At the same time, we need to remember that if the hidden units' weights become large, the non-linear character of the activation function flattens the minima of the cost function, reduces the gradient and diminishes the variance of the noise injected to the output layer. Hence, we have an automatic reduction of the process noise variance.

Example 14. The effect of regularisation of the multilayer perceptron performed by three different, but at the same time similar, techniques: weight decay, jittering of the training data by a spherical Gaussian noise and jittering the inputs of the output layer controlled by η_h, the learning step of the hidden neurones (*eta hidden*), is illustrated in Figure 4.16. The MLP with eight inputs, eight hidden neurones and one output was used. In this experiment we used the artificial non-Gaussian data, **SF8**, already discussed in Section 4.4.2.1. The training-set size was N = 140 (70 observation vectors from each class) and the test set Nt = 1000 = 500 + 500. Average values of the generalisation error estimated from seven independent randomly generated training sets are presented in the figure.

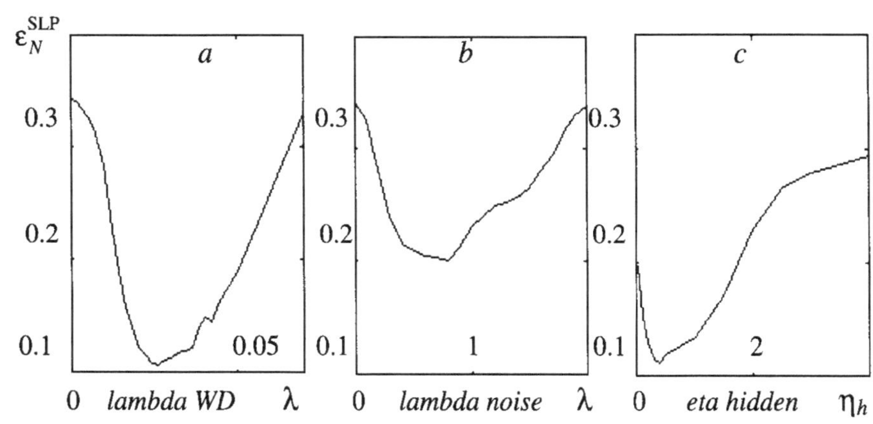

Fig. 4.16. Three types of regularisation of the multilayer perceptron: *a* – weight decay, *b* – uniform noise injection into the inputs, *c* – learning step of the hidden layer neurones.

This experiment confirms the theoretical conclusion that the learning step η_h used to train the hidden layer neurones has a similar effect to that of the weight decay and noise injection. Thus, the parameter η_h can be used to control the classifier's complexity. At the same time, the learning step is an obligatory parameter in BP training. Hence, the learning step η_h acts in an inexplicit way and affects value of other regularisation tools like the weight decay parameter, the variance of noise, the target values, etc.

4.6.9 Sigmoid Scaling

The SLP classifier performs classification of an unknown vector, $\boldsymbol{X}$, according to a sign of the discriminant function $g(\boldsymbol{X}) = v_1 x_1, v_2 x_2, \ldots, v_n x_n + v_0$. Multiplication of all weights, $v_1, v_2, \ldots, v_n, v_0$, by a positive scalar α does not change the decision boundary. In MLP classifiers, however, the effect of the multiplication of the hidden layer weights has more important consequences.

A proportional increase in the magnitude of the hidden units' weights creates sharp angles in the edges of the decision boundary. A proportional decrease in the magnitudes of all hidden layer weights smoothes the sharp angles of the decision boundary and changes the complexity of the MLP classifier. Thus, the control of the magnitudes of the hidden layer weights is one of the possible techniques that could be utilised to determine the classifier's complexity. We have illustrated this phenomenon by the example already discussed in Section 1.2 (Figure 1.5).

Example 15. In Figure 4.17*a* we have 15 + 15 bi-variate training vectors from two artificially generated pattern classes where vectors from the first class are inside the second one, and there is a ring-shaped margin between the pattern classes.

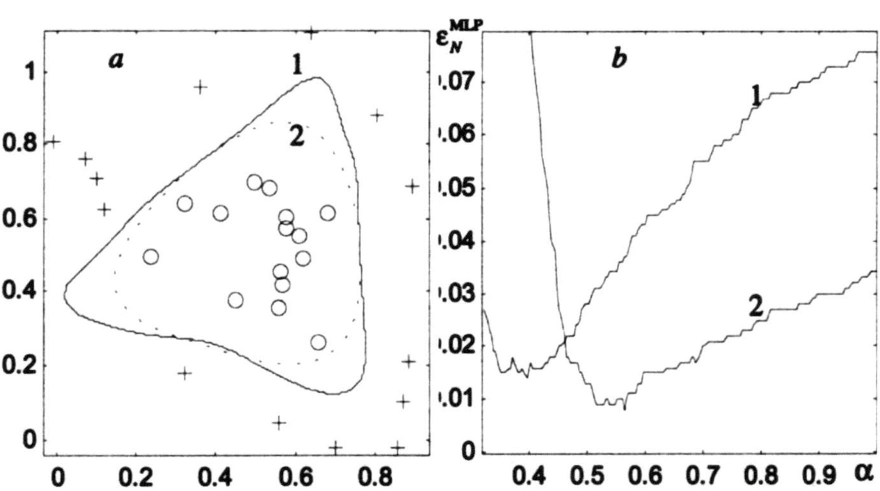

Fig. 4.17. *a* The training vectors from two pattern classes and the decision boundaries: 1– decision boundary of overtrained MLP (after 10,000 training sweeps), 2 – the smoothed decision boundary of the optimally stopped MLP; *b* The generalisation error as a function of the scaling parameter α: 1 – scaling of the weights of the overtrained perceptron), 2 – scaling of the optimally stopped perceptron.

After training MLP with 10 hidden units for 10,000 iterations in batch-mode, we obtained the non-linear decision boundary 1 with generalisation error, 7.6% (for estimation, we used 500 + 500 test vectors). In back-propagation training, we observed a significant overtraining: optimal early stopping resulted in a generalisation error two times smaller (3.4%).

The proportional reduction of all hidden layer weights by a factor $\alpha = 0.35$ smoothed the decision boundary and reduced the generalisation error to 1.5% (see curve 1 in Figure 4.17*b*). In this experiment, a notably better smooth decision boundary (curve 2 in Figure 4.17*a*) was obtained after smoothing the decision boundary of the optimally stopped MLP – the generalisation error was reduced from 3.4% to 0.09% (curve 2 in Figure 4.17*b* with a minimum at $\alpha_{opt} = 0.53$). Thus, in order to reduce the generalisation error we had to optimise both the number of iterations and the weights scaling parameter α.

As a possible generalisation of the scaling method, the magnitudes of the weights can be controlled individually for each hidden unit. An alternative to the scaling of the hidden layer weights by the factor α is to add the regularisation term, $\lambda(V_{hidden}^T V_{hidden} - h^2)^2$, to the cost function. Here, the parameter h controls the magnitudes of the hidden layer weights V_{hidden}. A success of the sigmoid scaling technique is caused of the fact that, in MLP training, the large weights of the output layer reduce magnitudes of the error transferred back to adapt the hidden units' weights.

4.7 The Co-Operation of the Neural Networks

One of the principal methods to control the complexity of the ANN is to choose a proper architecture of the network. The architecture and the complexity of the network should be chosen in accordance with the training-set size: for short learning sequences, one should use simple structured networks and for long sequences, one can utilise complex ones.

There are three ways to change the network architecture. One is to *prune* the network, i.e. sequential rejection of the features, the weights or the separate neurones of the network. Another possibility is *incremental learning* where one designs a simple network at first and then gradually adds new neurones, one after the another. The third way is *evolutionary training*, where the features, weights or neurones are added and removed sequentially. These three approaches represent the backward, forward and mixed feature selection procedures to be discussed in Chapter 6.

One more popular approach to selecting the architecture is to design several simple networks ("local experts") and then to join their individual solutions. To achieve this decision-making strategy, one has to design a final, "boss" (also known as "combining" or "gating" rule) decision-making algorithm.

4.7.1 The Boss Decision Rule

For complex data configurations, it often happens that in spite of a large number of perceptron training experiments with various architectures, initialisations and training algorithm parameters, the researcher does not succeed in minimising the cost function satisfactorily and thus does not obtain sufficiently good classification performance. Typically, in spite of the fact that each time the training procedures stop at different points of the multivariate weights space, the minimal cost function values are close to each other. The weights obtained in different initialisations of the network, however, are different.

Often, it becomes visible that one preceptron performs well in one *region of the multivariate feature space*, while another one is a good expert in another region. Some researchers suppose that the local minima and the flat multidimensional areas of the ANN cost function are "windmills" that are impossible to fight, and suggest, instead, designing a complex well-tuned cooperative network in the high-dimensional feature space. Thus, in spite of fighting the "windmills" one can try to make use of them.

An alternative to the direct building of complex networks is to make several "small" networks and then to join their solutions. The small networks are called local experts, local classifiers, or local neural networks, and the approach of synthesising the complex ANN from simple ones is called a co-operation of neural networks, ensemble of local experts, modular neural networks, etc. We show that the statistical methods described in this book can help to solve the network synthesis problem in a reasonable way.

A starting point of the co-operation approach is an assumption that different members of the co-operative network – the local experts – perform well in different regions. Then the boss – the output network – should be created and use solutions of all the local experts. On the basis of this information, the boss ought to perform the final decision.

Voting. It is the simplest technique used to make the decision. The voting can perform well if the decisions of the experts are statistically independent and all experts are equally qualified. More often, separate experts make very similar or identical decisions. Therefore, their decisions are statistically dependent and one needs more sophisticated methods to make the final classification. Moreover, different experts have diverse qualifications. Then, instead of the ordinary voting, a *weighted voting* can be utilised. The number of methods for designing the linear classifier can be put to use in determining the weights for each expert.

Nonparametric classification methods. In more complex situations, we can apply the local decision rules discussed in Chapter 2. Suppose we have r local experts, and let the j-th expert perform classification of an unknown vector $\boldsymbol{X}$ into one of m_j classes. We suppose various experts can be authorities in classifying into the different number of classes. This is a generalisation of a standard situation where $m_j = L$, the number of the classes. The total number of possible solutions (bins, cells) made by the r experts is $m = \prod_{j=1}^{r} m_j$. Denote a decision made by the j-th expert as o_j and that made by a set of experts by the vector $\boldsymbol{O} = (o_1, o_2, ..., o_r)^T$. Each vector $\boldsymbol{O}$ can assume only one bin, b_s, from the m bins: $b_1, b_2, ..., b_{m-1}, b_m$.

To design the final, boss classifier, we assume $\boldsymbol{O} = (o_1, o_2, \dots, o_r)^T$ to be discrete valued random vector. Then the conditional distribution of the i–th class vector $\boldsymbol{O}$ taking one bin from m is characterised by m probabilities

$$P_1^{(i)}, P_2^{(i)}, \dots, P_{m-1}^{(i)}, P_m^{(i)}, \quad \text{with} \qquad \sum_{j=1}^{m} P_j^{(i)} = 1, \quad (i=1, 2, \dots, L).$$

Let P_i be the prior probability of the pattern class ω_i. Then the optimal Bayes rule should make the final classification according to decisions of r local experts:

to allocate vector $\boldsymbol{O}$, falling into the s-th bin, according to the maximum of products

$$P_1 P_s^{(1)}, \quad P_2 P_s^{(2)}, \dots, \quad P_L P_s^{(L)}.$$

This is the *multinomial classifier* for categorical data discussed in Section 2.9.1. To design this classifier, we have to know the probabilities $P_1^{(1)}, P_2^{(1)}, \dots, P_m^{(L)}$. The maximum likelihood and Bayes approaches to estimate these probabilities from the training data can be used. E.g. in the maximum likelihood approach, we use $\hat{P}_j^{(i)} = n_{ij} / N_i$, where n_{ij} are a number of training examples from the i-th class with j-th bin.

Example 16. We demonstrate the statistical decision functions approach to designing the boss rule by considering a problem of classifying the lung-sounds data by three local experts. Each local expert uses a different part of the data (early expiration, middle expiration or late expiration) and performs classification into one of three pattern classes. Thus, $m_j = 3$, and $m = 3\times3\times3 = 27$. To make the decision, each local expert (MLP with six inputs, seven hidden units and three outputs) used six cepstral coefficients calculated from a certain segment of the acoustic lung signal. In the first class, we have 180 vectors, in the second class 190 vectors and in the third one 200 vectors.

The decision-making scheme of the boss classifier is illustrated by Table 4.4. In rows 2, 3, and 4, we have all possible answers of the three experts. In rows 5, 6, and 7 (# of ω_1, # of ω_2, and # of ω_3), we present n_{ij}, the numbers of training examples from each of three classes within each of 27 bins.

In row 8 (Multinom), we have decisions of the Bayes (the multinomial classifier) that performs judgements according to the maximum of n_{1j}, n_{2j}, and n_{3j}. In the row 9, we present the decisions of the voting algorithm. In dubious cases, we give preference to the decision of the first expert (or the second one). Decisions made by voting and by the multinomial classifier differ in 11 bins (printed in bold) out of the 27. For this data set, the empirical error rates, nevertheless, are similar: 25.6% for the multinomial classifier and 30.5% for the voting rule.

Table 4.4. Classification by three local experts.

N.of bin	1	2	3	4	5	6	7	8	9	10	11	12	13	14	15	16	17	18	19	20	21	22	23	24	25	26	27
Expert1	1	1	1	1	1	1	1	1	1	2	2	2	2	2	2	2	2	2	3	3	3	3	3	3	3	3	3
Expert2	1	1	1	2	2	2	3	3	3	1	1	1	2	2	2	3	3	3	1	1	1	2	2	2	3	3	3
Expert3	1	2	3	1	2	3	1	2	3	1	2	3	1	2	3	1	2	3	1	2	3	1	2	3	1	2	3
# of ω_1	76	5	8	14	3	0	3	2	3	7	1	0	7	8	3	1	0	2	7	3	1	5	3	2	5	2	9
# of ω_2	9	7	5	7	16	1	2	1	2	3	3	3	10	66	9	2	1	3	1	1	5	4	13	7	1	4	4
# of ω_3	4	4	0	5	1	1	8	7	11	7	1	0	2	0	1	3	3	15	0	1	1	0	2	6	8	9	100
Multinom	1	2	1	1	2	2	3	3	3	1	2	2	2	2	3	3	3	3	1	1	2	1	2	2	3	3	3
Voting	1	**1**	1	1	2	**1**	**1**	**1**	3	**2**	2	2	2	2	2	**2**	**2**	3	1	**3**	**3**	**3**	2	**3**	3	3	3

4.7.2 Small Sample Problems and Regularisation

When the number of the local experts and the number of the classes are large, the number of bins m becomes enormous. Hence, utilisation of the multinomial classifier becomes impractical. In such cases, one ought to simplify the decision rule. For this purpose, the decision-tree, the nonparametric Parzen window, or the *k-NN* classifiers discussed in Chapter 2 can be put to use. Recall that in the small training-set case, simpler classification rules can perform better than the complex ones. Consequently, one needs to select the complexity of the boss rule properly. This entails selecting the optimal smoothing parameters of the PW classifier, the optimal number of neighbours, the appropriate structure and the complexity of the decision tree.

Strictly speaking, the training data used to design separate experts cannot be used to estimate the unknown parameters of the boss decision rule. Usage of the training-set to estimate parameters of the boss rule leads to biased estimates of these parameters and worsens the decision-making algorithm (in such cases, each expert network boasts itself and deceives the boss). In principle, a *separate independent validation data* set should be used. Often it is difficult to have an independent validation set. However, in spite of this warning, researchers often ignore the bias problem and decide to use the training-set data once more.

In order to reduce the bias, one can perform regularisation of the boss decision making algorithm. One of possible ways to regularise the boss classifier is through *noise injection*. In the above medical diagnosis problem with the lung data, we have jittered the six cepstral coefficients by adding zero-mean and variance λ noise. In this way we increased the number of vectors 20 times. Later we classified this semi-artificial validation set by means of three local experts and estimated the probabilities $P_1^{(1)}, P_2^{(1)}, \ldots, P_m^{(L)}$. Note, the jittered signal was not used to train the expert networks. It was used only to estimate the probabilities $P_1^{(1)}, P_2^{(1)}, \ldots, P_m^{(L)}$. This way of injecting noise has led to coloured noise injection into the outputs of the local experts. In the previous Section, we advocated that jittering of the data carries supplementary information that while recording the data, the measurements were performed with some error.

The noise variance, λ, plays the role of the regularisation parameter. As in other regularisation problems, the curve generalisation error versus the regularisation parameter λ has a minimum. It is important to choose the proper value of λ. This value should be selected in accordance with the training-set size. In the experiment considered, after proper selection of the noise variance, we have succeeded in reducing the generalisation error substantially.

If as the boss rule, we use the decision tree or the Parzen window with special kernels, the complexity of the decision rules should be controlled by the number of the decision tree's final leaves or the smoothing parameter of the PW classifier. Techniques to select the classifier of optimal complexity will be discussed in Chapter 6.

4.8 Bibliographical and Historical Remarks

The mathematical model of the neurone was first described in McCulloch and Pitts (1943) and the supervised learning algorithm of the perceptron was suggested in Rosenblat (1958). Widrow and Hoff (1960) introduced the least mean square cost function, the training algorithm and the linear adaptive element called an adaline. Cybenko (1989) and Hornik et al. (1989) demonstrated that the multiplayer perceptrons are universal approximators. Koford and Groner (1966) were first to show that minimisation of the sum of squares cost in the linear SLP leads to the standard linear Fisher DF. Raudys (1995*ab*, 1996, 1998*b*) demonstrated that in BP training, six other statistical classifiers can be obtained. Broomhead and Lowe (1988) first introduced the RBF concept into ANN design and the idea of learning vector quantisation belongs to Kohonen (1986). The analysis of the effect of eigenvalues on training speed discussed in the Section 4.3.3 belongs to Le Cun (1987).

Section 4.4 on relations between the training-set size and generalisation of SLP is from Raudys (1998*c*) and Raudys (1995*a*). Comparison of the standard adaline training algorithm with two other modifications (relaxation and the fixed increment algorithms) was carried out by Smith (1972). He concluded that these two algorithms are more sensitive to the training-set size. The overtraining effect was noticed and described by a number of authors (see e.g. Hertz, Krogh and Palmer (1991) and Bishop (1995) and references therein). Its explanation by extra two factors is new: 1) the initial weight values of the perceptron and 2) the constant changing of the cost function in the BP training process. Equation (4.33) for α_{opt} was derived in Raudys and Amari (1998). In the analysis of the initialisation accuracy, a more general result than (4.27) with α_{opt} determined by (4.33) is known. Let $\hat{V}_0$ and $\hat{V}_1$ be estimators derived from these two sets. Then

$$\hat{V}_{opt} = \mathbf{G}^{-1} (N_0 \, \mathbf{G}_0 \hat{V}_0 + N_1 \, \mathbf{G}_1 \hat{V}_1), \tag{4.38}$$

where $\mathbf{G}_0 = \mathbf{G}(\hat{V}_0)$, $\mathbf{G}_1 = \mathbf{G}(\hat{V}_1)$ and $\mathbf{G} = N_0\mathbf{G}_0 + N_1\mathbf{G}_1$.

For large training-set sizes N_0, N_1, and fixed dimensionality n, we may put the matrix $\mathbf{G}_0 = \mathbf{G}$, and we have (4.33). This is the first-order asymptotic theory, and we can show the second-order result by using the ancillary statistics (Amari, 1987).

Tools to control the perceptron complexity are reviewed according to Raudys (2000*d*). It has been known for a long time that a weight decay and noise injection can improve generalisation (Plaut *et al.* 1986; Hinton, 1989). However, antiregularisation technique has been proposed only recently (Raudys, 1995*b*, 1998*b*). The coloured noise injection has been suggested by Duin (1993) and considered later by Skurichina, Raudys and Duin (2000). More details and bibliographical references on the means to control complexity can be found in Reed (1993), Reed *et al.* (1995), Bishop (1995), An (1996), Mao and Jain (1993), Jain, Mao and Mohiuddin (1996). Effective capacity study by simulation reported in Section 4.4.2.3 belongs to Kraaijeveld and Duin (1994) and remarks on a different effect of accuracy of the hidden and output layer weights to an increase in generalisation error to Raudys (1994, 1995*a*). Considerations on co-operation of neural networks as well as suggestion to regularise it in small sample situations are from Güler *et al.* (1996). More information about the co-operation of neural networks, multi-modular ANN, mixture of local experts and committee machines can be found in Mazurov (1971), Rastrigin and Erenstein (1981), Fogelman-Soulie, Vinnet and Lamy (1993), Chapter 7 of Haykin (1999) and Tax *et al.* (2000) and references therein.

5. Integration of Statistical and Neural Approaches

The sheer number of statistical and neural network-based classification methods induces the important and practical question: "Which classification method or methods are superior?" In this chapter we address the similarities and differences between statistical pattern classification methods and nonparametric (structural) neural network classification methods. Rather than focusing on the confrontation between these two classification paradigms, we focus on integrating them in order to utilise their particular strengths and properties and to diminish their shortcomings.

5.1 Statistical Methods or Neural Nets?

For a number of years a scientific discussion concerning the preference of parametric or nonparametric classification rules has been ongoing. A number of empirical comparisons have been made (for comments and additional references see e.g. Raudys *et al.*, 1975; Michie *et al.*, 1994; Duin, 1996; Cherkassky and Mulier, 1998; Sohn, 1999; Lim *et al.*, 2000 and Ho and Basu, 2000). Advocates of statistical pattern recognition have insisted that a vector X is a random vector and its properties can be described by a multivariate distribution density. In the parametric classification approach, advocates assume that the density function of vector X is known. *Assumptions concerning the type of pattern-class density function* is prior information that is infused into the classifier design process. There are only a few examples of potentially useful prior information that can help improve a classification rule in the finite training-set size case: the assumption that the data is Gaussian with common covariance matrix, the assumption that 70% of the eigenvalues of the covariance matrix are equal to zero, the assumption that the features are independent, and the assumption that components of the input vector constitute a stationary time series described by the 4-th order auto-regression process. When additional (prior) information is at least approximately correct, one can use this information to reduce the classification error.

Some scientists advocate that making assumptions about the type of pattern-class multivariate distribution densities and their parameters in order to construct a classifier is unwise. They stress the fact that in real-world pattern classification and prediction problems, theoretical assumptions about the distribution density functions are frequently violated. Instead of making assumptions about the distribution density functions of the feature vector X, these scientists recommend that one make *assumptions about the structure of the classification rule.* For example, one could assume a linear discriminant function in the space of original or transformed features and then estimate the unknown coefficients (weights) of the decision rule directly from the training data. For this classification paradigm, one could choose to minimise the empirical error (empirical risk). This is a typical approach to the classifier formulation problem utilised in the artificial neural network approach. Using this approach, we do not parameterise the distribution densities. Therefore, this methodology for designing linear classifiers is often viewed as a nonparametric classifier design approach. In order to distinguish this methodology from the nonparametric density function estimation method used in statistics, we refer to this methodology as a structural approach.

In spite of the very useful features associated with including prior information in the design of a statistical parametric classifier, followers of the structural (neural net) approach continually emphasise their main argument concerning the inconsistency of prior assumptions in real-world problems. They continue to criticise statistical classifier design and the application of parametric-based classification algorithms. Following Vapnik (1995,) they "stress that for estimation with finite samples it is always better to solve a specific estimation problem (i.e., classification, regression) rather than attempt a general joint (input, output) density estimation". According to several authors "this point while obvious, has not been clearly stated in the classical texts on statistical estimation and pattern recognition" (Cherkassky and Mulier, 1998; page 55). We diametrically oppose the statement that "this point is obvious" and seek configuration and training sample size conditions where the structural classifier design approach is not flawless.

Advocates of statistical theory maintain that, when solving real-world problems, one needs to take into account the problem complexity and the training-set size. A number of case studies have been published that compares the structural and statistical approaches. The discussion between followers of these different classifier design paradigms is ongoing.

5.2 Positive and Negative Attributes of Statistical Pattern Recognition

In the statistical classifier design approach, we make assumptions about the distribution density functions of the pattern classes and we choose the performance criterion. We then utilise the training data to design an optimal decision rule.

Positive attributes of the statistical approach are:

SP1. The possibility of obtaining strictly optimal algorithms.

SP2. The possibility of using the information contained in the statistical hypothesis about type of pattern-class distribution density functions. In the case of correct strong assumptions, the training-set size can be very small.

SP3. The performance – complexity – the training-set size relationships for certain popular statistical classification algorithms is known.

Negative attributes of the statistical approach are:

SN1. In many practical cases, we do not know the correct statistical pattern-class model. The model selected can be far from reality and lead to a significant increase in the classification error.

SN2. The plug-in technique to derive sample based classification rules is not optimal in the unequal training-set size case.

SN3. The Bayes predictive technique for deriving sample based classification rules requires one to know the prior distribution densities of unknown parameters. Utilisation of "wide", almost flat prior distributions leads to classification rules that are optimal for a variety of potentially possible (realisable) pattern classification problems. These rules, however, are not optimal for any particular problem.

SN4. In many multivariate data models, both the analytical expressions for the decision rule and for the performance – complexity – the training-set size relationships are very complex and cannot be practically applied.

SN5. Complex statistical classification algorithms require one to estimate a large number of parameters from the training data and, therefore, suffer from the curse of dimensionality.

SN6. For each particular pattern-recognition problem we need to choose the best algorithm from a large number of possible candidates.

5.3 Positive and Negative Attributes of Artificial Neural Networks

In the neural network classifier design approach, we make assumptions about the type of the decision boundary and utilise the training data directly in order to determine the unknown coefficients (the weights) of the classification rule.

Positive attributes of the neural network approach are:

NP1. We do not need to make assumptions about the distribution densities and can utilise the training-set data directly in order to determine unknown coefficients (weights) of the decision rule.

NP2. The neural networks are universal approximators.

NP3. While training the SLP classifier, we can obtain several statistical classifiers of differing complexity.

NP4. In some cases, SLP, MLP and RBF based classifiers can have very good small training-set size properties.

NP5. The information contained in almost correct initial weights of the SLP classifier can be saved if we optimally stop the training process.

Negative attributes of the neural network approach are:

NN1. We must choose the architecture of the network and fix the training parameters.

NN2. We need to somehow stop training optimally.

NN3. Except for some cases associated with different stages of the SLP training and for the unrealistic error bounds, the performance – complexity – the training-set size relationships are unknown.

NN4. The training process is affected by the singularity of the data, the weights initialisation, local minima and the plateau phenomenon. Often the training process is very slow and some authors are almost correct in saying that "training the neural network is not a science, it's an art".

5. 4 Merging Statistical Classifiers and Neural Networks

5.4.1 Three Key Points in the Solution

Both the statistical approach and artificial neural networks have their positive and negative attributes. Rather than bickering about the attributes of each classifier design approach, one would be wise to exploit the positive aspects of each of them in order to create an integrated approach.

Understanding the dependence of the neural network's performance on the initial conditions is the first key to solving this problem. We can design a linear classifier and use its weights $\hat{V}_0$, $\hat{v}_0$ as a starting point for training of the single layer perceptron. Then in further SLP training, we can obtain several classification rules of differing complexity. The second key to solving the problem is understanding of this fact and that some of the classifiers obtained in the non-linear SLP training are insensitive to the traditional normality assumptions practised in parametric statistical classification.

To design the linear statistical classifier

$$g(X) = (X - \tfrac{1}{2}(\hat{M}_1 + \hat{M}_2))^T \hat{\Sigma}_e^{-1} (\hat{M}_1 - \hat{M}_2). \tag{5.1}$$

we use the inverse of a certain sample CM estimator, say $\hat{\Sigma}_e$. In the simplest case, we assume $\hat{\Sigma}_e$ is the identity matrix and the resulting classifier is the EDC. In another instance, we use the traditional maximum likelihood estimate and obtain the standard Fisher classifier. Many other choices have been considered in Chapter 2 such as structured covariance matrix based classifiers and regularised discriminant analysis and its modifications.

Instead of using $\hat{\Sigma}_e$ to design the linear statistical classifier (5.1), we can use the matrix $\hat{\Sigma}_e$ to transform the data. After the first iteration in the new feature space one can obtain EDC, which in the original feature space corresponds to classifier (5.1). The third key is understanding that this classifier serves as good initialisation weights for further SLP training. We present more details below.

5.4.2 Data Transformation or Statistical Classifier?

Let Φ be an $n \times n$ eigenvectors matrix of $\hat{\Sigma}_e$, let Λ be its $n \times n$ diagonal eigenvector matrix, i.e. $\hat{\Sigma}_e = \Phi\Lambda\Phi^T$, and let us perform the linear data transformation

$$Y = \mathbf{F}\, X, \tag{5.2}$$

where $\mathbf{F} = \Lambda^{-1/2}\Phi^T$, and train the SLP afterwards satisfying the conditions E1 – E4 presented in Section 4.1. We repeat these conditions once more:

E1) the centre of the data $\hat{M}$ is moved to the zero point,
E2) we start training from zero weights,
E3) the target is $t_2 = - t_1N_1/N_2$ (for tanh activation function),
E4) we use total gradient training (batch mode).

Then after the first iteration we obtain the Euclidean distance classifier in the new transformed feature space

$$g^{(t=1)}(Y) = (Y - ½(\hat{M}_{y1} + \hat{M}_{y2}))^T(\hat{M}_{y1} - \hat{M}_{y2}))\, k_E, \tag{5.3}$$

where $\hat{M}_{yi} = \mathbf{F}\hat{M}_i$ $(i = 1, 2)$ are the sample mean vectors in the transformed space and k_E is a constant.

Utilisation of $\hat{\Sigma}_e^{-1} = \Phi\Lambda^{-1}\Phi^T$, $\hat{M}_{yi} = \Lambda^{-1/2}\Phi^T\hat{M}_i$ and $Y = \Lambda^{-1/2}\Phi^T X$ allows one to represent the discriminant function (5.3) as

$$g^{(t=1)}(Y) = (X - ½(\hat{M}_1 + \hat{M}_2))^T\Phi\Lambda^{-1/2}\Lambda^{-1/2}\Phi^T(\hat{M}_1 - \hat{M}_2)\, k_E =$$

$$(X - ½(\hat{M}_1 + \hat{M}_2))^T\hat{\Sigma}_e^{-1}(\hat{M}_1 - \hat{M}_2)\, k_E. \tag{5.4}$$

The above representation shows that after the first iteration we obtain the classifier that in the original feature space, $\boldsymbol{X}$, is equivalent to the standard linear Fisher classifier with the CM estimator $\hat{\Sigma}_e$ (Equation (5.1)). Thus, after the data transformation and after the first iteration performed such that conditions E1 – E4 are satisfied, we obtain a good "natural" initial weight vector.

5.4.3 The Training Speed and Data Whitening Transformation

Let to determine the transformation matrix $\mathbf{F} = \Lambda^{-1/2}\boldsymbol{\Phi}^T$ we use the true population covariance matrix $\boldsymbol{\Sigma}$. The covariance matrix of the vector Y is

$$\Sigma_Y = E\, YY^T = \Lambda^{-1/2}\boldsymbol{\Phi}^T E\, XX^T\, \boldsymbol{\Phi}\, \Lambda^{-1/2}$$

$$= \Lambda^{-1/2}\boldsymbol{\Phi}^T \boldsymbol{\Sigma\Phi}\, \Lambda^{-1/2} = \Lambda^{-1/2}\boldsymbol{\Phi}^T \boldsymbol{\Phi}\lambda\boldsymbol{\Phi}^T \boldsymbol{\Phi}\, \Lambda^{-1/2} = \mathbf{I},$$

where, in this case, $\boldsymbol{\Phi}$ and Λ are determined by the representation $\boldsymbol{\Sigma} = \boldsymbol{\Phi}\Lambda\, \boldsymbol{\Phi}^T$.

This transformation is known as a *data whitening transformation.*

Let to determine the transformation matrix $\mathbf{F}$ we use the sample population covariance matrix, $\hat{\Sigma}$, and we note that $\Sigma_Y \neq \mathbf{I}$. In this case $\hat{\Sigma}_Y$, the sample covariance matrix of Y, becomes the identity matrix. Consequently, all n eigenvalues of the matrix $\hat{\Sigma}_Y$ are equal to 1. In Section 4.3.3 we have demonstrated that in situations where the data and the sample covariance matrix are almost singular, i.e. when we have an immense difference between smallest and largest eigenvalues of the covariance matrix, it is difficult, if not impossible, to ensure fast BP convergence of the training algorithm. Therefore, training the perceptron in the transformed feature space helps one to overcome the singularity problem and to speed up the convergence rate.

Suppose now that to determine the transformation matrix $\mathbf{F}$ we use a certain *sample estimator,* $\hat{\Sigma}_e$, of the true population covariance matrix $\boldsymbol{\Sigma}$. Thus, both Σ_Y, the pattern-class covariance matrix and $\hat{\Sigma}_Y$, the estimated covariance matrix of Y, will differ from the identity matrix. If the matrix $\hat{\Sigma}_e$ is similar to $\hat{\Sigma}$, then $\hat{\Sigma}_Y$ is similar to the identity matrix. Thus, after the data transformation, the components of the new vectors Y will be almost uncorrelated and all new features will have approximately the same variances. Thus, the training rate of the SLP should be fast if training is performed in the new transformed feature space.

If, however, $\hat{\Sigma}_e$ is an inaccurate estimator, then the following *negative consequence* can occur: we can obtain a large dispersion of the eigenvalues of $\hat{\Sigma}_Y$. In such case, the training process can become slow.

5.4.4. Dynamics of the Classifier after the Data Whitening Transformation

Analysis of the SLP similar to that performed in Section 4.1.2.2 but done in the transformed feature space, $Y = \Lambda^{-1/2}\Phi^T X$, indicates that after t iterations we have the classifier

$$g^{(t)}(Y) = (X - ½(\hat{M}_1 + \hat{M}_2))^T(\hat{\Sigma}_e \frac{2}{(t-1)\eta} \frac{\overline{N}}{\overline{N}-1} + \hat{\Sigma})^{-1}(\hat{M}_1 - \hat{M}_2))k_t. \quad (5.5)$$

Equation (5.5) shows that as the number of training iterations t increases, the covariance matrix's structurisation or regularisation effects vanish.

Thus, as t increases, the resulting decision rule approaches the standard Fisher linear discriminant function. This conclusion is precisely correct at the beginning of the training process while the perceptron's weights are small and the activation function behaves as a linear function. The fact that we are approaching the Fisher classifier means that further training of SLP can diminish negative effects of wrong assumptions used to obtain $\hat{\Sigma}_e$. At the same time, it means that further increase in t diminishes the positive effects of the correct assumptions. It creates a need to stop training optimally.

In perceptron training, as the weights are increasing, the activation function begins to act as a non-linear function. Then we have both a robust and regularised classification rule. This rule pays less attention to outliers, e.g. atypical training patterns. The classifier progression to the robust classifier algorithms depends both on the learning step η and on the number of iterations t. Thus, in order to find the best balance between saving the information contained in the covariance matrix structure assumptions and diminishing outlier effects, we need to control both the learning step and the number of iterations.

Further training can realise a significant increase in the magnitude of the weights. Then we obtain a classification rule that minimises the empirical error. In the case that all training patterns are classified correctly, we can obtain the maximal margin (support vector) classifier in the space of transformed variables, Y. In the case of non-Gaussian training data, when the SLP training is stopped optimally, the last three linear decision rules can outperform standard parametric statistical classifiers.

A very favourable attribute of the integrated approach is that we can approach the maximal margin classifier from a good standpoint. Information from correct statistical guesses about the data structure (type of the distribution density function, etc.) can be utilised. It is a result of successful initialisation.

5.5 Data Transformations for the Integrated Approach

5.5.1 Linear Transformations

In the data whitening transformation, we perform the linear transformation

$$Y = \mathbf{F}(X - \hat{M}), \tag{5.6}$$

where $\hat{M} = ½ \, (\hat{M}_1 + \hat{M}_2))$, $\mathbf{F} = \Lambda^{-1/2}\Phi^T$, and Λ, Φ^T are eigenvalues and eigenvectors of the sample CM estimator $\hat{\Sigma}_e$.

In Chapter 2, we reviewed several constrained CM models: the diagonal, the block diagonal, the Toeplitz model and its modifications, the first order tree dependence model, etc. In addition to the utilisation of structured matrices, one can exploit different regularised CM estimators such as:

a) "classical" ridge estimators: $\hat{\Sigma}_{\mathrm{RDA}}{}^{(1)} = \hat{\Sigma} + \lambda\mathbf{I}$, $\hat{\Sigma}_{\mathrm{RDA}}{}^{(2)} = \hat{\Sigma} + \lambda \, \mathrm{diag}(\hat{\Sigma})$;

b) the scaled rotation CM estimator: $\hat{\Sigma}_{\mathrm{SR}} = \Phi^{\alpha} \, (\Lambda + \lambda\mathbf{I}) \, \Phi^{\alpha T}$; and

c) the Friedman's CM estimator for the two populations case:

$$\hat{\Sigma}_{\mathrm{FRIEDMAN}}{}^{(1)} = \lambda_1 \hat{\Sigma}_1 + \lambda_2 \hat{\Sigma}_2 + (1-\lambda_1-\lambda_2)\mathbf{I}, \text{ or its modification}$$

$$\hat{\Sigma}_{\mathrm{FRIEDMAN}}{}^{(\mathrm{MOD})} = \Phi \, (\lambda_1 \Lambda_1 + \lambda_2 \Lambda_2 + (1-\lambda_1-\lambda_2)\mathbf{I}) \, \Phi^T,$$

where Λ_1, Λ_2 are eigenvalue matrices of the covariance matrices $\hat{\Sigma}_1, \hat{\Sigma}_2$. In the last model, the eigenvectors matrix Φ is assumed to be common to both populations.

The number of models proposed in the multivariate statistical analysis and pattern recognition literatures is much larger. The reader can combine known models and invent new ones quite easily. Unfortunately, many good models have not been applied to practical real-world problems. One of the reasons for this is the negative attribute SN1 in Section 5.2: the model can be very inaccurate and can, therefore, lead to a significant increase in the classification error. The integrated approach, however, has the potential to reduce the effect of this shortcoming and to "rescue" these theoretical models.

After training the SLP in the transformed feature space, $Y = \mathbf{F}(X - \hat{M})$, we obtain the linear discriminant function

$$g(Y) = \hat{W}^T Y + \hat{w}_0, \tag{5.7}$$

where $\hat{w}_0$, $\hat{W}$ are the perceptron's weights, $\hat{M}$ is a vector and $\mathbf{F}$ is an $r \times n$ matrix.

To classify the unlabeled vector $\boldsymbol{x}^*$ we have two possibilities:

a) we perform the linear transformation $\boldsymbol{y}^* = \mathbf{F}(\boldsymbol{x}^* - \hat{\boldsymbol{M}})$, and use the discriminant function (5.7) to classify $\boldsymbol{y}^*$ afterwards;

b) we return the discriminant function into the original feature space and use the modified discriminant function

$$g(\boldsymbol{X}) = \hat{\boldsymbol{V}}^T \boldsymbol{X} + \hat{v}_0, \tag{5.8}$$

where $\hat{\boldsymbol{V}} = \mathbf{F}^T \hat{\boldsymbol{W}}$, and $\hat{v}_0 = \hat{w}_0 - \hat{\boldsymbol{W}}^T \mathbf{F} \hat{\boldsymbol{M}}$.

This expression for the classifier weights follows from the representation

$$g(\boldsymbol{Y}) = \hat{\boldsymbol{W}}^T \mathbf{F}(\boldsymbol{X} - \hat{\boldsymbol{M}}) + \hat{w}_0 = (\mathbf{F}^T \hat{\boldsymbol{W}})^T \boldsymbol{X} + (\hat{w}_0 - \hat{\boldsymbol{W}}^T \mathbf{F} \hat{\boldsymbol{M}}).$$

5.5.2 Non-Linear Transformations

The idea of transforming the data in order to obtain the best sample based classifier immediately following the first iteration can be extended to non-Gaussian data models. In the theory of statistics, it is well known that the non-linear transformation $x = \Psi^{-1}(F(y))$ can convert a distribution $F(y)$ of any non-Gaussian univariate random variable y into the Gaussian random variable.

The notation $\Psi^{-1}(c)$ indicates the inverse distribution function of the standard Gaussian $N(0,1)$ variable. $F(y)$ is a cumulative distribution function of y. We can use this idea to transform multivariate non-Gaussian data with independent components. We can also try to exploit the above ideas in order to transform non-Gaussian asymmetrical multivariate data with dependent components into the spherical Gaussian. We present two examples of the transformation of bi-variate non-Gausian data into the spherical Gaussian data.

Example 1. In Figure 5.1*a* we depict 500 bi-variate data points after rotation and the subsequent transformation with the non-linear transformation $y_i = \exp(x_i)$ of correlated Gaussian vectors. This is "the original non-Gaussian data" that we need to normalise and to decorrelate.

We perform this task by means of an iterative application of the non-linear transformation $x_i = \Psi_i^{-1}(\hat{F}_i(y_i))$ to each component y_i of the vector $\mathbf{y} = (y_1, y_2)^T$ and subsequent linear transformation $\boldsymbol{Y} = \mathbf{T}\boldsymbol{X}$. $\hat{F}_i(y_i)$ is the sample estimate of the cumulative distribution function of the component y_i. $\mathbf{T}$ is a 2×2 orthonormal matrix composed from two bi-variate eigenvectors of the sample covariance matrix for the vector $\boldsymbol{X}$ after each step of the transformation $x_i = \Psi_i^{-1}(\hat{F}_i(y_i))$. Typically, after several cycles of the application of both transformations, we obtain distributions very similar to the spherical Gaussian distribution. Figure 5.1*b* shows the 500 data points after the first iteration of the above two-stage procedure and *c* shows them after the fourth iteration.

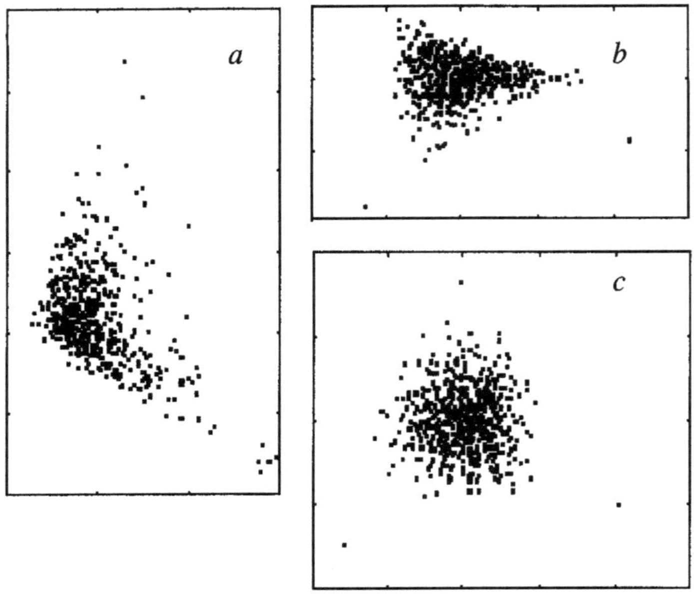

Fig. 5.1. Distributions of 500 bi-variate vectors: *a* – original data, *b* – after the first iteration consisting of non-linear "normalising" transformation and subsequent linear decorrelation, *c* – after the fourth iteration.

Example 2. We illustrate the non-linear feature transformations to solve the classification task. In Figure 5.2 we have 50 + 50 bi-variate training vectors from two pattern classes. This artificial non-Gaussian bi-variate data is obtained after application of the non-linear $x_i = \exp(\xi_i)$ transformation of two GCCM classes (i =1, 2). After an ideal (known *a priori*) normalising transformation, $y_i = \ln(x_i)$ the generalisation error is 8.5%. This is the Bayes error rate. The generalisation error of the standard linear Fisher DF is 16% and that of the non-linear SLP is 15%. In this experiment, we forget the data generation method and test two approaches to transforming the data in order to improve the classification performance.

In the first approach, we attempt to find some non-linear transformation $\boldsymbol{Y} = \Psi(\mathbf{T}\boldsymbol{X})$ that normalises and decorrelates the vector $\boldsymbol{X}$. For this we apply the iterative two-stage procedure described above. This procedure makes use of the non-linear transformation $y_i = \Psi^{-1}(\hat{\boldsymbol{F}}(z_i))$ of each single component z_i of vector $\mathbf{Z}$ obtained after the linear decorrelation transformation of vector $\boldsymbol{X}$: $\mathbf{Z} = \mathbf{T}\boldsymbol{X}$. In the two-category case, we applied this sequence of transformations only to the vectors of one pattern class. After converting vectors of the first class into approximately spherically Gaussian data, we have learned the new transformation, $\boldsymbol{Y} = \Psi^{-1}(\mathbf{T}\boldsymbol{X})$, by the MLP composed from two inputs, 12 hidden *non-linear* neurones and two *linear* neurones in the outputs. The training-set composed from the first pattern-class vectors was used to learn the non-linear feature transformation operation.

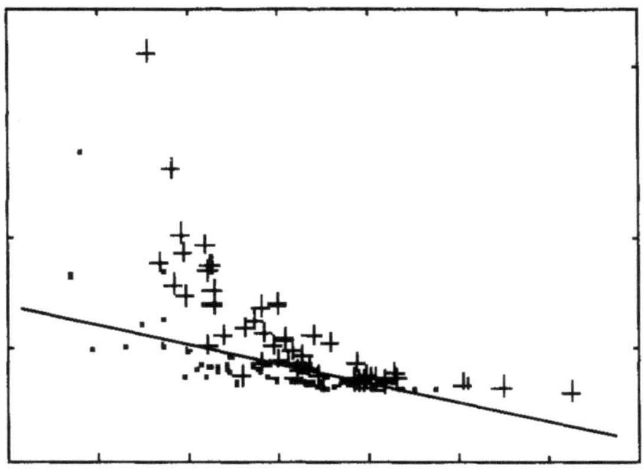

Fig. 5.2. Distribution of two highly asymmetrical bi-variate pattern classes and the decision boundary of the non-linear SLP classifier.

Later, we applied this non-linear data transformation both to the training and to the test sets. After training the SLP in the transformed (***Y***) space, we obtained only 3% errors while classifying the training-set (the resubstitution error) and 10% errors while classifying the test set. This is only slightly higher than the Bayes error (8.5% errors) and notably smaller than 15%, the generalisation error of the SLP classifier in the original (***X***) space.

The two-stage decision-making scheme just discussed consists of an MLP used for the feature transformation and of the non-linear SLP used for the classification. In classifying new vectors, the two-stage solution can be simplified. In order to bring together both stages we remark that the MLP feature transformer's outputs are *linear*. Therefore the output SLP classifier can use the 12 outputs of the hidden layer neurones of the feature transformation MLP directly as its inputs. As a result, we can devise a new simpler, single layer MLP classifier with two inputs, 12 hidden neurones, and one non-linear output. An interesting perspective arises when ones uses weights of this MLP classifier as the starting weights for further training.

The second data transformation method consists of introducing new derivative features, x_1^2, x_1x_2, and x_1^2, in addition to the original features, x_1 and x_2. We have already described this technique in Section 4.2.1. We applied the SLP to solve the above pattern classification problem in the new five-variate space and obtained the test-set error of 10%. This is the same accuracy as that found in applying the previous two-stage technique composed of the SLP and the MLP.

We have tested the "derivative features" approach on a number of other non-linear pattern classification problems and have found that in the finite training-set case, this approach often outperforms the conventional back propagation MLP classifier and the standard quadratic discriminant function.

The theoretical and experimental demonstrations presented above confirm that the linear and non-linear data transformation techniques can become powerful tools in designing simple neural classifiers with good generalisation properties. As in the feature extraction approach, we shift the most difficult portion of the pattern recognition problem into the feature definition stage.

5.5.3 Performance of the Integrated Classifiers in Solving Real-World Problems

We have attempted to evaluate the efficacy of the integration of the statistical and neural net approaches for solving real world pattern classification problems.

Example 3. In Figure 5.3 we present a characteristic example with real-world data: the vowel classification problem, with two pattern classes, 20 speakers, 28 spectral features, and the training set sizes $N_1 = N_2 = 20$. To estimate the generalisation error we used $Nt = 800$ vectors. We trained the SLP classifier in the original feature space (FS), curve 1, and in the transformed FS, curve 2. We used the standard linear transformation $Y = \mathbf{F}(X - \hat{M})$, where $\mathbf{F}$ was obtained from the regularised sample covariance matrix. In both experiments, we shifted the training-set mean vector to the centre of the co-ordinates, used the standard sum of squares cost function with the sigmoid activation function with targets of either 1 or 0. For training we applied the total gradient descent training procedure with the zero initial weight vector. In order to obtain the maximal margin quickly, we gradually increased the learning step η according to the rule $\eta = 0.001 \times 1.03^t$, where t is the current iteration number. On the right of Figure 5.3, we have the generalisation error $\hat{\varepsilon}_N^{SLP}$ versus the number of iterations and on the left we have $\hat{\varepsilon}_N^{SLP}$ versus the margin.

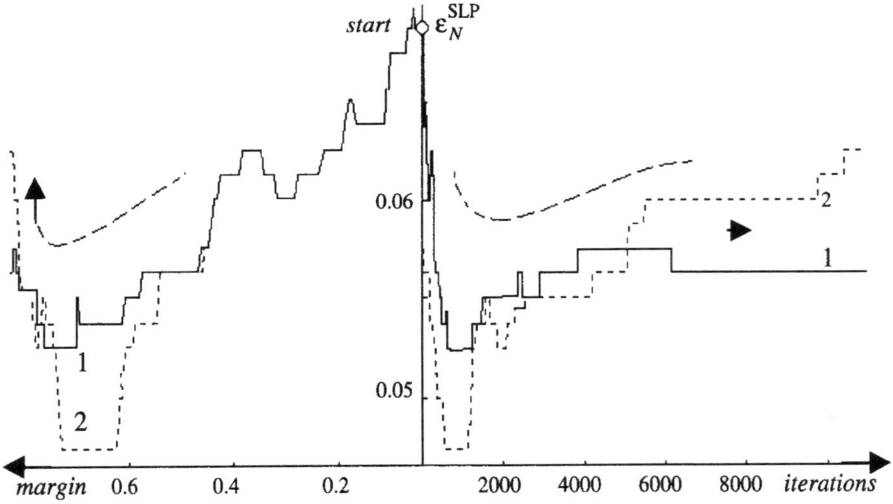

Fig. 5.3. Utilisation of the SLP to classify the vowel data: the generalisation error $\hat{\varepsilon}_N^{SLP}$ versus the number of iterations and versus the margin in the original (curves 1) and in the transformed (curves 2) feature spaces (Reprinted from *Neural Networks*, 13: 9–11, Raudys, How good are support vector machines? 2000, with permission from Elsevier Science).

The graphs show that after the first iteration in the original FS, the EDC gives 7% generalisation errors. The regularised discriminant analysis (SLP after the first iteration in the transformed FS) gives 5.7% errors and the maximal margin classifier (SLP in the transformed FS after 110,000 iterations) gives 6.2% errors. The optimally stopped SLP in the original FS yields an even better result: 5.3% errors. The best result, however, was obtained by an optimally stopped SLP trained in the transformed FS, which gives a classification error of 4.7%.

This experiment supports the previous chapter's conclusions that excessive growth in the margin width increases the generalisation errors. The minimal generalisation error (4.7%) is obtained much earlier before we encounter the SV classifier (6.2%). Thus, for this classification problem, the integrated approach merging the statistical and neural net classifier design methods was useful.

While analysing the effectiveness of the integrated approach we performed several thousand training experiments with a dozen 18 - to 166-variate real-world data sets. We used various data rotation and scaling methods, two dozen covariance matrix structurisation methods and different, randomly-chosen large and small training sets. In most of the experiments, we found the integrated approach yielded excellent results. In majority of the experiments, conventional structurisation of the covariance matrices was inferior to regularised discriminant analysis. Typically, the well-trained SLP classifier outperformed the RDA classifier. I

In complicated cases with high dimensional data sets and small training sets, however, we have almost singular estimated CM with several extremely small or even zero eigenvalues. Then the SLP trains very slowly and is inferior to RDA.

Example 4. As a summarising example, we present results with 24 different data structures performed on ten real-world data sets. In Figure 5.4, we have a histogram of distributions of the relative efficacy of different classifiers (211 sequences of experiments with the 24 CM structures; each sequence of the experiments was performed 25 times with different randomly-chosen training sets). The efficacy was measured as a ratio – the generalisation error of the optimised standard RDA (a benchmark method) divided by the generalisation error of the classifier under consideration: $\gamma = \varepsilon_N^{\text{RDA}} / \varepsilon_N^{\text{classifier}}$. We see the black histogram (SLP after the data transformations) is shifted noticeably to the right.

Utilisation of statistical methods to whiten the data and subsequent intelligent training (the conditions E1 – E4) very often improves the classification performance. Exceptions constitute cases where an extremely small size of the training-set was insufficient to perform a useful data transformation. It was noticed that in cases where the training sets were extremely small, it was difficult to discover and to utilise the CM structure properly. The experiments show that typically, a gain in classification performance is obtained in situations where the statistical methods without any data transformation perform poorly.

Thus, the SLP classifier training improves when *approximately correct statistical assumptions* are utilised. In order to obtain the best results a number of different CM structurisation or CM regularisation methods for each particular data type should be examined.

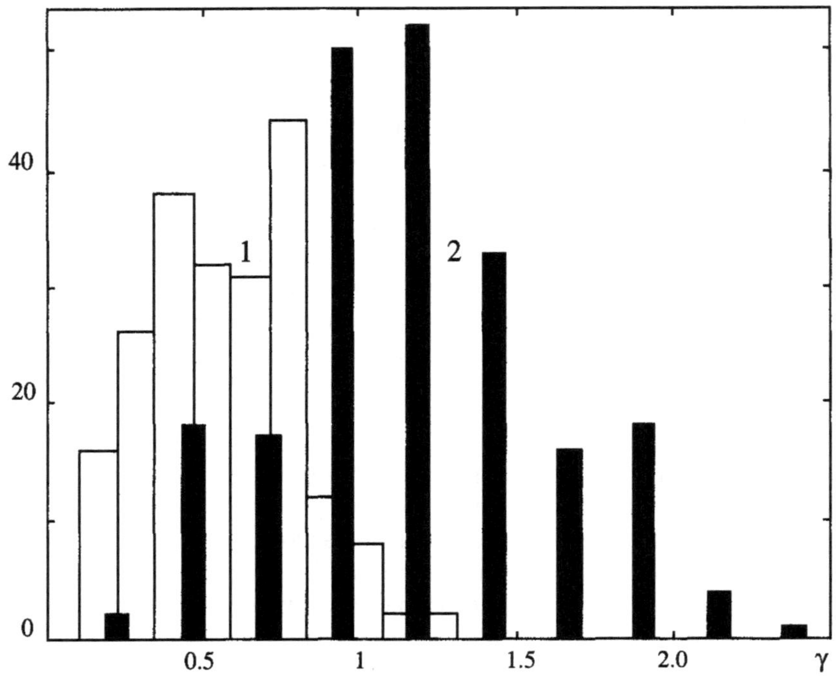

Fig. 5.4. The efficacy of structurisation in 211 series of the experiments with the stuctured CM used to design the statistical classifiers: 1 – a histogram of the gain γ for the linear discriminant analysis with differently structured sample CM, 2 – a histogram for optimally trained SLP after the linear data transformation obtained from structured sample CM (each series consists of 25 independent experiments).

5.6 The Statistical Approach in Multilayer Feedforward Networks

In SLP classifier training, the data whitening transformation plays a doubly beneficial role:

- it gives a good start and reduces the generalisation error,
- it improves the convergence rate.

No doubt the data whitening transformation is useful for the multilayer feedforward networks training. In this case, however, we cannot begin training from zero initial weights and obtain a good start: in order to become different hidden units, one has to start training from different initial weight vectors. Nevertheless, a number of ways may be suggested to utilise statistical methods. While training feedforward neural networks, one can use the statistical methods to choose good starting weights. Three options can be suggested:

1. Use weights of the statistical classifier directly to determine the starting multilayer network's weights. In MLP design one can use the weights of a statistically designed piecewise-linear classifier to determine the weights of the hidden layer neurones (Raudys and Skurichina, 1992), use prototypes and other statistical techniques (Denoeux and Langelle, 1993). To fix the initial weights of the output layer neurone one should carefully train them for a while by the standard methods. In RBF and LVQ neural networks, a standard approach is to determine the initial weights by cluster analysis techniques. The decision tree classifiers can be used, too (Kubat, 1998).

2. Use a well-trained good statistical classifier in order to edit the training-set and exclude incorrectly classified training vectors. In a modification of this approach, one can "increase" the training-set by injecting noise and then edit the new larger training-set before training the perceptron. It was noticed that the edited training-set improves the training speed and assists in reducing the possibility of being trapped into bad local minima. In this technique, the edited training-set is utilised for MLP weights initialisation.

3. Map the original design set vectors into a low-dimensional space where it is easier to avoid trapping local minima. As an extreme case, the two-dimensional mapping can be applied. Here an operator can inspect solutions (decision boundaries) and interfere in the training process interactively (A. Raudys, 2000). After training in the low-dimensional space, remaining directions (transformed features) are added sequentially in order to return to a higher-dimensional space.

A certain additional improvement can be obtained when after training the feedforward network, we train the output layer neurones using the integrated approach. Clearly, more techniques to integrating the statistical methods into complex feedforward network design can be and should be developed to improve classification performance.

5.7 Concluding and Bibliographical Remarks

In the integrated approach to classifier design, we employ all positive attributes of the neural network approach (NP1 – NP5) as well as the positive attributes SP1 and SP2 of the statistical approach. Moreover, we diminish the harmful influence of the negative attributes SN1, SN2, NN1 and NN4.

The dependence of the generalisation error of the perceptron on the initial conditions, earlier referred as a negative attribute, now becomes an extremely positive property that plays a central role in the integrated classifier approach. In the case that one starts with almost correct initial conditions, the perceptron weights will, at some point, closely approximate the weight vector where the true minimum of the generalisation error occurs. Then optimal stopping can be very effective. In statistical classification and prediction algorithm design, the designer utilises all his skill and knowledge (prior information and the training-set vectors) to design the best possible rule. In the integrated classifier design approach, the designer should utilise this skill and knowledge in order to transform the data. Then the classifier designer obtains the best statistical rule after the first iteration.

There are five basic reasons for the success of the integrated approach:

1. Statistical methods can be utilised to select good initial weights. The good start can help obtain a smaller generalisation error.

2. The employment of prior guesses about probability density functions allows one to improve the small sample properties of statistical classification and prediction algorithms. E.g., the common covariance matrix characterised by a small number of parameters does not affect the generalisation error if both the dimensionality and the training-set size are large.

3. The use of the SLP allows one to obtain robust, minimum empirical error and maximal margin classifiers and to classify non-Gaussian patterns well.

4. For many theoretical data models the SLP can have very good small sample properties.

5. In order to obtain a full range of statistical classification and prediction algorithms, one needs to satisfy conditions E1 – E4 and apply the gradient descent training that performs better in the transformed feature space.

Many facets concerning the integration of statistical and neural network classification paradigms remain unresolved. As an example we mention the necessity of developing a wider scale of statistical models to characterise the covariance matrix by a few parameters, analysis of situations where the pattern classes have different covariance matrices, developing methods for the case when training-set sizes in each pattern class are different, designing simple and reliable CM estimation algorithms, fast, reliable and simple non-linear data transformation methods, finding ways to utilise the integrated approach in the many pattern-classes case, designing MLP and RBF classifiers, and obtaining better model choice algorithms.

The first hints that one should decorrelate the inputs were from visual cortex investigators in biological systems. In an analysis of retinal ganglion cells, Atick and Redlich (1990) proposed that the purpose of retinal processing is to improve the efficiency of visual representation by recording the input into a spatially-decorrelated form. A bit later, the decorrelation dynamics of lateral interaction between orientation selective cells in the early visual cortex was shown to yield quantitative predictions about orientation contrast, adaptation, and the development of orientation selectivity that are in agreement with experiments (Dong, 1993, 1994). Similar explanation was suggested in Buchsbaum and Gottshalk (1983) in analysis of the colour perception.

Le Cun (1987) and Le Cun, Kanter, and Solla (1991) have shown that convergence properties of the perceptron training process depend on the ratio of the largest and smallest eigenvalues of the training data covariance matrix. In order to improve convergence properties of the gradient descent algorithm, researchers have suggested that one transform the input data by removing the mean and decreasing correlations across input variables (Halkaaer and Winter, 1996).

There are a number of contributed papers, survey papers and books that review and analyse artificial neural networks from the statistical perspective. Many of them have been mentioned in previous chapters. Three additional sources of interest are survey papers by Cheng and Titterington (1994), Ripley (1994) and Jain, Duin and Mao (2000).

The first two keys to successfully consolidating the statistical and neural net approaches and using both techniques simultaneously are understanding the effect of initial values (Raudys and Amari, 1998) and understanding the dynamic theory of progressive development of the SLP during its training (Raudys, 1998*b*). First, the integrated approach of utilising the positive qualities of statistical pattern recognition in the adaptive neural classifier design was applied to save the useful information obtained in the scaled rotation regularisation (Section 2.5.3). Then the integrated approach was used to improve the efficacy of the stucturisation of the covariance matrices. The first publications on the integrated approach appeared in 1998 (Raudys 1998*ab*). Large-scale experimental investigations with dozens of artificial and real world data sets were published in Saudargiene (1999), Raudys (2000*c*), and Raudys and Saudargiene (1998, 2001).

6. Model Selection

In the previous chapters, it was shown that the number of algorithms for designing the linear and non-linear classification rules is very large and there exist a great variety of strategies for developing the classification algorithm from the design set. There are a number of parametric statistical algorithms suggested for the standard, Gaussian or exponential families of multivariate distribution densities. A great variety of algorithms arise from differing assumptions about the covariance matrices and their estimation methods. Apart from the mixture models, there exist nonparametric density estimation methods that lead to different modifications of the Parzen window and *k-NN* classification rules. Piecewise-linear and MLP-based models increase the number of potentially applicable algorithms further. The fact that many algorithms depend on continuous parameters such as smoothing, regularisation constants and the number of iterations, increases the field of potential possibilities. The abundance of algorithms can be increased many times by feature selection, feature extraction and ANN architecture selection techniques. The integrated approach to designing the classification rule also increases the number of possible alternatives.

Therefore, a natural problem arises: the selection of the algorithm that best fits a given pattern-recognition problem. One of the most popular criteria is to select an algorithm similar to that which was utilised successfully in previous analogical applications. In fact, it is the unformalised, rough Bayes approach. For this purpose a number of empirical comparisons have been performed (see e.g. Raudys *et al.*, 1975; Michie *et al.*, 1994; Duin, 1996; Cherkassky and Mulier, 1998; Sohn, 1999; Lim *et al.*, 2000 and Ho and Basu, 2000). Another approach is to estimate performances of each competing model precisely and select the best algorithm.

In many applications, one of the principal characteristics in designing the pattern-recognition system is the classification error. Therefore, the model selection should be based on this parameter. Unfortunately, in real situations, we often have to compare a tremendous number of competing models and the error estimation becomes too expensive a task. As a result, a great number of approximate and easy to calculate performance measures have appeared in the literature. Utilisation of approximate measures, however, leads to error in the model selection. The validation set begins to serve as an additional training-set. As a result, a model selection bias arises.

A few remarks concerning the terminology should be restated. The validation set is a part of the design set and is used to evaluate the performance of the competing variants of the pattern-recognition system. In fact, the validation set is also used for training, however, in a different way. So, an important problem is to split the design set into the training and validation sets. The answer depends on the data, the classifier used, on the number of variants compared and on the performance estimation method. Unfortunately, the problem of optimal splitting has not yet been solved. The test set is used to evaluate the performance of the final variant and should be used only once. The performance evaluation techniques applied to the validation set and to the test set are the same.

6.1 Classification Errors and their Estimation Methods

6.1.1 Types of Classification Error

In the previous chapters, we have met the Bayes, asymptotic, conditional and expected classification errors.

The *optimal* or *Bayes PMC*, denoted by ε_B, is the probability of misclassification when one has a complete knowledge of the prior probabilities $P_1, P_2, \dots, P_L$ of L classes, the class-conditional density functions $p_i(X)$. The optimal or Bayes PMC is given in (3.1) by

$$\varepsilon_B = \int_{\Omega} min\{P_1 p_1(X), \dots, P_L p_L(X)\} dX.$$

The *conditional PMC* (the *generalisation error*), denoted by $\varepsilon_N^{\mathsf{A}}$, is the probability of misclassification that is obtained when one uses a fixed training-set and a fixed classifier design method, say A. The value of the conditional PMC depends directly upon the classifier design method A, the training-set size, the statistical characteristics of the data and the particular training-set.

The *expected PMC* (the *mean generalisation error*), denoted by $\bar{\varepsilon}_N^{\mathsf{A}}$, is the expectation of the conditional PMC, $\varepsilon_N^{\mathsf{A}}$, over all theoretically possible training sets of the given size ($N_1, N_2, \dots, N_L$ vectors from each pattern class), $\bar{\varepsilon}_N^{\mathsf{A}} = E\,\varepsilon_N^{\mathsf{A}}$.

The *asymptotic PMC*, denoted by $\varepsilon_\infty^{\mathsf{A}}$, is a limit, i.e. the probability of misclassification of the classifier design method A when one has a complete knowledge of the class conditional density functions $p_i(X)$. The asymptotic PMC may be expressed as

$$\varepsilon_\infty^{\mathsf{A}} = \lim_{N_1 \to \infty \;\dots\; N_L \to \infty} \bar{\varepsilon}_N^{\mathsf{A}}.$$

These four probabilities of misclassification have different interpretations and different applications. For instance, if we wish to evaluate the classification performance of a particular pattern-recognition system that we have just designed, then the conditional PMC, $\hat{\varepsilon}_N$, (the conditional generalisation error) is an appropriate measure of classification accuracy. If we wish to evaluate a dissimilarity of several pattern classes, then the Bayes, PMC, ε_B, is a suitable performance measure. One may be interested in evaluating the classification performance of some pattern-recognition system to be designed in the future by using some unknown training-set composed of N_1, N_2, ..., N_L, vectors from each class. Then, the expected error rate (the expected generalisation error), $\bar{\hat{\varepsilon}}_N$, can be fitted best to evaluate the algorithm's performance and select the best model.

In the previous chapters, the training-set error (empirical or apparent error) has also been discussed. It is the frequency of classification errors obtained while classifying the training-set vectors. Sometimes this estimate is used to solve the model selection problem and it will be discussed in subsequent sections. While solving the model selection task, one uses sample-based approximate performance estimates. Therefore, three new error estimates arise: an apparent error in the selection, an ideal error and a true error in the model selection (Section 6.5). These errors should not be confused with other classification error types.

6.1.2 Taxonomy of Error Rate Estimation Methods

A large number of the error rate estimation methods proposed in the pattern recognition literature can be categorised into two types:

- parametric based estimators and
- nonparametric based estimators.

Furthermore, each of these two groups can be partitioned according to following two properties:

- the way in which the multivariate observations are used to train and to test (validate) the classifiers.
- the type of pattern error function which determines the contribution of each observation of the test (validation) set to the estimate of the appropriate PMC.

We consider several widely utilised error rate estimation methods in each of the two major groups: parametric based and nonparametric based error rate estimators.

6.1.2.1 Methods for Splitting the Design Set into Training and Validation Sets

1. The hold-out method (HM) is the simplest and, possibly, the most often used approach to estimating the classification error rate. In this method, the design set observation vectors are split into two separate sets: the training set (*TS*) and the validation set (*VS*).

If the validation set is used only once, then it can be called the test set. If the same validation set is used many times, a separate independent test set should be provided.

The classification rule is trained by using the observations belonging to the training-set. The performance of the classification rule is estimated as a proportion of misclassified observations from *VS*. For the two category case, it is

$$\hat{\varepsilon}_{HM} = \frac{K_{HO}}{N_{v1} + N_{v2}}, \tag{6.1}$$

where: N_{vi} is a number of the test set's (or the validation set's) vectors from the i-th pattern class;

$$K_{HO} = \sum_{j=1}^{N_{v1}} K_1(g(X_{1j})) + \sum_{j=1}^{N_{v2}} K_2(g(X_{2j})) \tag{6.2}$$

$K_i\,(g)$ is an indicator (a pattern error) function.

In an *error counting estimate*, function $K_i(g)$ expresses the classification errors:

$K_1(g(X_{1j})) = 1$ if $g(X_{1j}) < 0$, and X_{1j} belongs to ω_1; $K_1(g(X_{1j})) = 0$ otherwise,

$K_2(g(X_{2j})) = 1$ if $g(X_{2j}) > 0$, and X_{2j} belongs to ω_2; $K_0(g(X_{2j})) = 0$ otherwise;

$g(X)$ is the discriminant function score. In an error counting estimate, the sum K_{HO} expresses a number of misclassifications. In Section 6.1.2.3, we will introduce more pattern error functions.

In the hold-out method, we split the training observations of the design set into two mutually exclusive sets. A shortcoming of this approach is that neither the training-set nor the validation set can utilise all information contained in the design set. Suppose we have a large design set, which is sufficient for training the classifier and for obtaining an accurate estimate of its error. Then the major problems in error rate estimation are the amount of available computer memory and the time required to perform the necessary computations. However, in the small design set case, many problems can occur. One problem is to find an optimal partition of the design set into the training-set and the validation set. This method is sometimes called a cross-validation or one-fold cross-validation.

2. The resubstitution method uses all design set observations as a training-set and then reuses the complete design set as a test (or the validation set). This is the *empirical error,* $\hat{\varepsilon}_{RM}$. Some people call it an *apparent error.* For the two category case, it is

$$\hat{\varepsilon}_{RM} = \frac{K_R}{N_{t1} + N_{t2}}, \tag{6.3}$$

where N_{ti} is a number of vectors from the i-th class in the design (training) set, and

$K_R = \sum_{j=1}^{N_{t1}} K_1(g(X_{1j})) + \sum_{j=1}^{N_{t2}} K_2(g(X_{2j}))$ is a sum of the pattern error functions calculated for all design (training) set vectors.

3. The leaving-one-out method (LOOM) also utilizes all the design set vectors for training. In this method, we split the design set, consisting of $N_d = N_{d2} + N_{d2}$ observation vectors, into the training-set, consisting of N_d - 1 observations, and a test (validation) set consisting of a single observation. The procedure of training the classifiers and testing their performance on the single test vector is repeated N_d times with different observation vectors behaving as the test set at each new iteration. The LOO estimate is a proportion of misclassified observations over all N_d splits

$$\hat{\varepsilon}_{LOOM} = \frac{K_{LOO}}{N_{d1} + N_{d2}}, \tag{6.4}$$

where K_{LOO} is a sum of the pattern error functions.

There are many other modifications of the LOO method where more than one observation vector comprises the test sample. For instance, a Π (rotation) method is a compromise between the LOO and the hold-out estimation methods. This method consists of partitioning the total design set into k separate sets of size N_k. The training of the classifier is performed on a set consisting of $(k-1)N_k$ vectors and tested on the remaining N_k vectors. This procedure is repeated k times and the resulting error rate is an average of the hold-out error rates for the k separate sets. Frequently this method is called the *k-fold cross-validation.*

4. The bootstrap method (BM) uses the bootstrap sampling concept popularised by Efron (1982). In this method, the original design set, *DS,* is treated as the population of interest and a bootstrap training set, *BS,* is formed by sampling with replacement from the initial design (training) set. A brief description of the bootstrap error-rate estimation method is as follows.

A bootstrap training set, *BS,* is selected randomly (with replacement) from the original training observations, *DS*, and the classification rule is trained using the bootstrap set. Then, the resubstitution classification error estimate $\hat{\varepsilon}_{RM}^{(B)}$ is found using the bootstrap set, *BS*. Afterwards, an estimate $\hat{\varepsilon}_{N}^{(B)}$ of the conditional error rate is found by calculating the estimated error rate using the vectors of the data set *DS* which were not selected into *BS*. These bootstrap calculations are repeated r times in order to evaluate the bias of the resubstitution estimator $\hat{\varepsilon}_{RM}$. The bias is evaluated as

$$Bias(\hat{\varepsilon}_{RM}) = \overline{\hat{\varepsilon}_{N}^{(B)} - \hat{\varepsilon}_{RM}^{(B)}},$$

where the upper bar means that the average is calculated from r randomly chosen boostrap sets.

Then the bootstrap estimator of the error rate is

$$\hat{\varepsilon}_{BM} = \hat{\varepsilon}_{RM}^{(B)} + Bias(\hat{\varepsilon}_{RM}). \tag{6.5}$$

The bootstrap method results in the almost unbiased estimates of the conditional PMC. The estimated bias term $Bias(\hat{\varepsilon}_{RM})$ is a double random variable. It is influenced by the random character of the design set vectors, *DS*. In addition, it is affected by the r randomly-formed bootstrap sets. With an increase in r, the effect of the second factor decreases. How large must r be? As a rule of thumb, we recommend $r \geq 20$. This suggestion is derived from a requirement: a variance initiated by the limited number of r constitutes 5% of a total variance of the bootstrap estimate. It means an increase in r can reduce the variance by only 5%.

6.1.2.2 Practical Aspects of Using of the Leave-One-Out Method

The LOO estimator is computationally intensive. Therefore, for the parametric linear and quadratic classifiers, special recursive formulae have been derived to diminish the computational effort. In this approach, we need to invert the covariance matrices only once. The amount of calculation can be reduced by employing the Bartlett equality, often used in multivariate statistical and neural net analysis:

$$(\mathbf{A} + \mathbf{U}\mathbf{V}^T)^{-1} = \mathbf{A}^{-1} - \mathbf{A}^{-1}\mathbf{U}(1 + \mathbf{V}^T\mathbf{A}^{-1}\mathbf{U})^{-1}\mathbf{V}^T\mathbf{A}^{-1}, \tag{6.6}$$

where $\mathbf{A}$ is the $n \times n$ positive defined matrix and $\mathbf{U}$ and $\mathbf{V}$ are n-variate vectors.

In the L pattern class case, let $D_S(\boldsymbol{X}_j^{(i)}) = (\boldsymbol{X}_j^{(i)} - \hat{\boldsymbol{M}}_i)^T \hat{\Sigma}^{-1}(\boldsymbol{X}_j^{(i)} - \hat{\boldsymbol{M}}_i)$ be the standard linear DF corresponding to the s-th pattern class (here we perform the classification according to a minimum of $\{D_1(\boldsymbol{X}), D_2(\boldsymbol{X}), \ldots, D_L(\boldsymbol{X})\}$). Then the linear DF trained by *DS*, with the exception of the test observation, $\boldsymbol{X}_j^{(i)}$, is

$$g_S(\boldsymbol{X}_j^{(i)}) = -k_{1i}\{D_S(\boldsymbol{X}_j^{(i)}) + \frac{[D_s(\boldsymbol{X}_j^{(i)})]^2}{k_{2i} - D_s(\boldsymbol{X}_j^{(i)})}\}, \tag{6.7}$$

where $k_{1i} = \begin{cases} 1 & \text{if } i \neq s, \\ (\frac{N_i}{N_i - 1})^2 & \text{if } i = s, \end{cases}$, $k_{2i} = (N_i - 1)(\sum_{j=1}^{L} N_j - L)/N_i$, and

N_i is a number of vectors from the i-th class in the design (training) set.

For the quadratic discriminant we have $D_s(\boldsymbol{X}_j^{(i)}) = (\boldsymbol{X}_j^{(i)} - \hat{\boldsymbol{M}}_i)^T \hat{\Sigma}_s^{-1} (\boldsymbol{X}_j^{(i)} - \hat{\boldsymbol{M}}_i)$,

$$g_s(\boldsymbol{X}_j^{(i)}) = -k_{3i}\{D_s(\boldsymbol{X}_j^{(i)}) + \frac{[D_s(\boldsymbol{X}_j^{(s)})]^2}{k_{4s} - D_s(\boldsymbol{X}_j^{(s)})}\} - \ln|\hat{\Sigma}_i| - \ln[1 - \frac{D_s(\boldsymbol{X}_j^{(i)})}{k_{4i}}] - k_{5i}, \text{ if } i = s,$$

$$g_s(\boldsymbol{X}_j^{(i)}) = -D_s(\boldsymbol{X}_j^{(i)}) - \ln|\hat{\Sigma}_s|, \qquad \text{if } i \neq s, \qquad (6.8)$$

where $k_{3i} = N_i^2 (N_i-2)/(N_i-1)^3$, $k_{4i} = (N_i-1)^2 / N_i$, $k_{5i} = n \ln((N_i-1)/(N_i-2))$.

For the nonparametric k-nearest neighbour and the Parzen window classifiers, the leaving-one-out method does not require additional computational effort. In the maximum margin (support vector) classifier (for details see Chapter 2), the linear discriminant boundary is defined as the maximal distance from the training-set vectors. The vectors on the boundary are called the supporting patterns. They determine the position of the discriminant boundary and can be straightforwardly utilised to speed up the leaving-one-out estimate of the classification error.

6.1.2.3 Pattern Error Functions

1. Error counting. The simplest way to estimate the classification error is to find the frequency of incorrectly classified observations (Equation (6.2)) and use it as the error estimate $\hat{\varepsilon}_{EC}$. In this method, only the number of misclassifications is counted. All misclassified pattern vectors have the same contribution to the classification error estimate. A contribution of the vector $\boldsymbol{X}_j$ to the error estimate does not depend on the distance of the vector $\boldsymbol{X}_j$ from the decision boundary. This method is called error counting and can be used with all four design set splitting methods discussed in Section 6.1.2.1.

2. The smoothed error rate estimator is similar to the error counting error rate estimator. In the sum (6.2), instead of a threshold function, one uses a more general pattern error function $K(g(\boldsymbol{X}_j))$. A small perturbation in the value of the discriminant $g(\boldsymbol{X}_j)$ corresponds to a small change in contribution to the error estimate. In general, it is required that (we consider a case, where $\boldsymbol{X}_j$ belongs to ω_1).

$$K(g(\boldsymbol{X}_j)) \to 1 \text{ as } g(\boldsymbol{X}_j) \to -\infty \text{ and } K(g(\boldsymbol{X}_j)) \to 0 \text{ as } g(\boldsymbol{X}_j) \to \infty.$$

The logistic sigmoid function $K(g(\boldsymbol{X}_j)) = 1 - 1/(1+e^{-g(\boldsymbol{X}_j)})$ can serve as an example of the kernel (curve 1 in Figure 6.1). Another choice of the kernel function is the Gaussian cumulative function with variance λ^2. The kernel function can be piecewise-linear, like line 2 in Figure 6.1. Change of λ or the slope of the piecewise-linear function controls a contribution of each correctly and incorrectly classified pattern vector to the estimate of the classification error rate. With the increase in λ or in the slope, more pattern vectors contribute to sum (6.2). An extreme case arises when we use the threshold function as the kernel, i.e.

$K(g(X_j)) = 0$ if $g(X_j) > 0$, and $K(g(X_j)) = 1$ otherwise (piecewise-linear line3 in Figure 6.1). Then we have the error counting estimate.

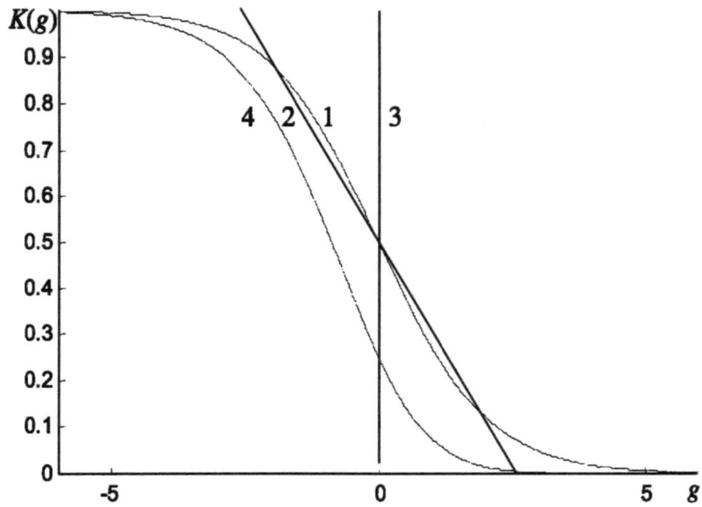

Fig. 6.1. The pattern error functions: 1 – logistic function $K(g)=1-1/(1+ e^{-g})$, 2 – piecewise-linear function, 3 – threshold function, 4 – pattern error function of the sum of squares (4.2).

The cost function of the squares (1.7) can be utilised to estimate the classification error. For the targets $t_1 = 1$ and sigmoid activation function, $K(g) = (1+ e^{g})^{-2}$. In Figure 6.1 (curve 4), we depict this function. In Chapter 4, we have seen that the cost function begins to calculate the classification error as the weights of the single layer perceptron increase. Hence, in estimation the classification error, the cost function of the sum of squares with large weights can be sufficiently exact.

While estimating the classification error rates, the smoothed error rate estimators can invoke a bias. However, a variance of the estimator $\hat{\varepsilon}_{SM}$ is smaller than that of the error counting estimate $\hat{\varepsilon}_{EC}$. Both the bias and the variance, depend on smoothing. The bias increases with λ, whereas the variance decreases with λ. One problem with formulating the estimator $\hat{\varepsilon}_{SM}$ is the choice of the best smoothing parameter λ.

3. Parametric estimators for Gaussian patterns. In Section 3.4.1, for the two pattern class case, we had the following formula for the asymptotic probability of misclassification of the standard Fisher linear discriminant function:

$$\varepsilon_{\infty}^{F} = \Phi\{-\delta/2\}, \tag{6.9}$$

where δ^2 is the squared Mahalanobis distance.

This formula gives the exact values of the asymptotic error for the GCCM data model when the mean vectors M_1, M_2 and the common matrix $\overline{\Sigma}$ are known. When these parameters are unknown, they can be replaced by their sample estimates $\hat{M}_1$, $\hat{M}_2$ and $\hat{\Sigma}$. Then the sample squared Mahalanobis distance is

$$\hat{\delta}^2 = (\hat{M}_1 - \hat{M}_2)^T \hat{\Sigma}^{-1} (\hat{M}_1 - \hat{M}_2), \tag{6.10}$$

and the following simple parametric estimate (called *D* estimate) of the classification error has been suggested in the literature

$$\hat{\varepsilon}_D = \Phi\{-\hat{\delta}/2\}. \tag{6.11}$$

The estimate (6.11) depends on two random vectors, $\hat{M}_1$ and $\hat{M}_2$ and random matrix $\hat{\Sigma}$. Therefore it is a random variable too. By means of the standard orthogonal transformations traditionally used in multivariate statistical analysis, it can be shown that $\hat{\delta}^2$ is distributed as a scaled ratio of the non-central and central chi-square random variables (the scaled non-central *F* random variable):

$$\hat{\delta}^2 \sim \frac{(N_1+N_2)(N_1+N_2-2)}{N_1 N_2} \frac{\chi^2_{\frac{N_1N_2}{N_1+N_2}\delta^2,\, n}}{\chi^2_{N_1+N_2-n-1}}. \tag{6.12}$$

Its expectation is:

$$E\,\hat{\delta}^2 = \frac{(N_1+N_2)(N_1+N_2-2)(\frac{N_1N_2}{N_1+N_2}\delta^2+n)}{N_1N_2(N_1+N_2-n-3)} > \delta^2. \tag{6.13}$$

We see that $\hat{\delta}^2$ is a biased estimate of the Mahalanobis distance δ^2. The use of (6.10) in estimator (6.9) results in an optimistically biased estimate of the Bayes classification error. An unbiased estimator of the distance δ^2 is given by

$$\hat{\delta}^2_{DS} = \frac{(N_1+N_2-n-3)}{N_1+N_2-2}\hat{\delta}^2 - \frac{N_1+N_2}{N_1N_2}n, \tag{6.14}$$

An expected value $E\,\hat{\delta}^2_{DS} = \delta^2$. The estimator (6.14) can be used in (6.9) in order to reduce the bias of the asymptotic classification error estimate:

$$\hat{\varepsilon}_{DS} = \Phi\{-\delta^2_{DS}/2\}. \tag{6.15}$$

In spite of the fact that (6.14) is unbiased, the estimator *DS* (6.15) is a slightly biased estimator of the asymptotic error $\hat{\varepsilon}_\infty^{(F)}$. This bias is caused by the non-linear characteristic of the Laplace function $\Phi(c)$.

The unbiased estimate (6.14) also is a random variable. Therefore, in the small training sample size N case, the estimator (6.14) may sometimes be negative. In order to avoid negative values, it is proposed that one skip the last negative term in (6.14). The parametric error estimates $\hat{\varepsilon}_D$ and $\hat{\varepsilon}_{DS}$ are appropriate for evaluating the classification performance if the data can be described by the GCCM data model. The parametric estimates, however, do not work well if the pattern classes differ from this Gaussian model.

4. A pseudo-parametric error rate estimator has been suggested as a compromise between the parametric and non-parametric approaches. It combines the LOO method with an assumption that the discriminant function scores $g(X_j^{(i)})$ $(i = 1, 2;\ j = 1, 2, \ldots, N_i)$ are conditionally Gaussian distributed. This assumption is based on a central limit theorem: each value of the discriminant $g(X_j^{(i)})$ is a sum of a large number of weakly dependent random components. Consequently, it is approximately Gaussian distributed. This assumption is especially appropriate when the discriminant function is linear, i.e. $g(X_j^{(i)}) = v_0 + \sum_{s=1}^{n} v_s x_{js}$, the number of features and the sizes of the training sets are large. Letting $\hat{E}[g_1(X)]$ and $\hat{E}[g_2(X)]$ represent the group means of the discriminant scores corresponding to both pattern classes and letting $\hat{V}[g_1(X)]$ and $\hat{V}[g_2(X)]$ be the sample variances of the respective discriminant scores, the pseudo-parametric error rate estimator can be written as

$$\hat{\varepsilon}_{PP} = \Phi\{-\hat{\delta}_{PP}/2\}. \tag{6.16}$$

where $\hat{\delta}^2_{PP} = \dfrac{[\hat{E}[g_1(X)] - \hat{E}[g_2(X)]]^2}{(N_1\hat{V}[g_1(X)] + N_2\hat{V}[g_2(X)])/(N_1 + N_2)}$.

The error counting and smoothed pattern error functions; as well as the pseudo-parametric error rate estimators, can be used with any of the four methods of splitting the design set into the training-set and test (validation) set (the hold-out, resubstitution, leaving-one-out and the bootstrap sample splitting methods). In principle, one can acquire a great number of different classification error estimation methods.

6.2 Simplified Performance Measures

A large number of competing pattern classification models arise in the feature definition phase. Here the designer needs to select a small number of most informative features from a pool of candidates. In other cases, the designer performs a linear or non-linear transformation of the input measurement vectors in order to extract a small number of informative features. To extract the new features, one introduces a certain performance measure and optimises it. A characteristic requirement for feature extraction measures is that these criteria should be differentiable in order to apply simple optimisation algorithms.

Feature selection and feature extraction are computationally intensive procedures. In real situations, we have to compare an immense number of competing models and the error estimations become computationally very expensive. Similar problems arise in ANN architecture selection. Therefore, simple and fast feature evaluation criteria are necessary. As a result, numerous approximate and easy to calculate performance measures have appeared in the literature. Almost every performance measure from that listed below can be used to solve all tasks: feature selection, feature extraction, and ANN architecture adjustment.

6.2.1 Performance Criteria for Feature Extraction

6.2.1.1 Unsupervised Feature Extraction

A standard and most popular linear mapping technique, used in both multivariate data analysis and pattern recognition, is the *principal component* method often known as a discrete Karhunen-Loev expansion. The feature mapping criterion to be minimised is

$$Cost_{PC} = \frac{1}{N}\sum_{i=1}^{N} (\boldsymbol{X}_i - \boldsymbol{X}^*_i)^T(\boldsymbol{X}_i - \boldsymbol{X}^*_i) = \frac{1}{N}\sum_{i=1}^{N} (\boldsymbol{X}_i - \mathbf{B}^T\boldsymbol{Y}_i)^T(\boldsymbol{X}_i - \mathbf{B}^T\boldsymbol{Y}_i), \quad (6.17)$$

where

$\boldsymbol{X}_i$, $(i = 1, 2, ..., N)$ are the n-variate vectors of the design (training) set,

$\boldsymbol{Y}_i = \mathbf{B}\boldsymbol{X}_i$, $(i = 1,2, ..., N)$ are new vectors in the r-variate new feature space Ω_r,

$\boldsymbol{X}^*_i = \mathbf{B}^T\boldsymbol{Y}_i$, is an inverse transformation of vector $\boldsymbol{Y}_i$ into the n-variate space,

$\mathbf{B} = \begin{bmatrix} \mathbf{C}_1 \\ \mathbf{C}_2 \\ \dots \\ \mathbf{C}_r \end{bmatrix}$ is an $r \times n$ transformation matrix,

$\mathbf{C}_1, \mathbf{C}_2, ..., \mathbf{C}_r$ are $1 \times n$ orthonormal vectors, eigenvectors of the sample covariance matrix $\hat{\boldsymbol{\Sigma}} = \frac{1}{N}\sum_{i=1}^{N} (\boldsymbol{X}_i - \hat{\boldsymbol{M}})(\boldsymbol{X}_i - \hat{\boldsymbol{M}})^T$, $\hat{\boldsymbol{M}} = \frac{1}{N}\sum_{i=1}^{N} \boldsymbol{X}_i$.

The distance $(\boldsymbol{X}_i - \mathbf{B}^T\boldsymbol{Y}_i)^T(\boldsymbol{X}_i - \mathbf{B}^T\boldsymbol{Y}_i)$ characterises the mapping error for one observation vector. The principal component method does not use any information about the class membership of the vectors $X_1, ..., X_N$. Therefore, in spite of a large number of advantageous features that are characteristic of the principal component method (maximal accuracy of the representation of the pattern vectors and the covariance matrix, maximal entropy function if the pattern vectors are Gaussian; see, e.g., Young and Calvert, 1974, Chapter 6), the application of this method to pattern classification tasks at times destroys the separability between the pattern classes.

An *inter-distances method* uses a criterion

$$Cost_{ID} = \frac{1}{N(N-1)} \sum_{j=i+1}^{N} \sum_{i=1}^{N} (H_{ij}^{o} - H_{ij}^{tr})^2, \tag{6.18}$$

where $H_{ij}^{o} = (X_i - X_j)^T (X_i - X_j)$ is a distance between the pattern vectors X_i and X_j in the original n-dimensional space Ω_n and $H_{ij}^{tr} = (Y_i - Y_j)^T (Y_i - Y_j)$ is a distance between the pattern vectors Y_i and Y_j in the transformed r-dimensional space Ω_r.

An unknown $r \times n$ data transformation matrix $\mathbf{B}$ is found by the iterative search technique. At instant t, the matrix $\mathbf{B}_t$ is updated according to the following formula

$$\mathbf{B}_{t+1} = \mathbf{B}_t \mathbf{T}_{\mathbf{B}_t} \mathbf{R}^{-1},$$

where $\mathbf{R} = \frac{1}{N(N-1)} \sum_{j=i+1}^{N} \sum_{i=1}^{N} (X_i - X_j)(X_i - X_j)^T$ and

$$\mathbf{T}_{\mathbf{B}_t} = \frac{1}{N(N-1)} \sum_{j=i+1}^{N} \sum_{i=1}^{N} \frac{(X_i - X_j)^T (X_i - X_j)}{(X_i - X_j)^T \mathbf{B}_t^T \mathbf{B}_t (X_i - X_j)} (X_i - X_j)(X_i - X_j)^T.$$

A start matrix $\mathbf{B}_0$ is obtained by the principal component method: $\mathbf{B}_0 = \mathbf{B}_{PC}$. The principal component method preserves a *global structure* of the data. The inter-distances method tries to preserve *local structures* of the data.

There are several methods for a *non-linear mapping* into the low-dimensional feature space. In the non-linear mapping, one searches for $r \times N$ coordinates of r-variate vectors $Y_1, Y_2, ..., Y_N$ directly. Here we cannot use such a criterion function as in Equation (6.18). One has to introduce a normalisation of the distances. One of the first non-linear mapping algorithms proposed in the literature (Sammon, 1969; Niemann, 1980) were procedures based on the following criteria

$$Cost_S = \frac{1}{\sum_{i<j} H_{ij}^{o}} \sum_{j=i+1}^{N} \sum_{i=1}^{N} \frac{(H_{ij}^{o} - H_{ij}^{tr})^2}{H_{ij}^{o}}, \text{ and} \tag{6.19}$$

$$Cost_N = \frac{1}{\sum_{i<j} (H_{ij}^O)^2} \sum_{j=i+1}^{N} \sum_{i=1}^{N} (H_{ij}^O - H_{ij}^{tr})^2 \; . \tag{6.20}$$

Minimisation of the above criteria may be interpreted as the non-linear transformation of vectors from the n-dimensional space Ω_n into the r-dimensional space Ω_r such that all inter-distances between the vectors are preserved as much as possible. Both cost functions are multi-extremal. The minimisation is performed by means of iterative procedures.

The non-linear mapping procedures preserve the local structures of a complex pattern space, however, they do not provide an explicit algorithm to process the forthcoming pattern vectors. One of the possibilities for obtaining the explicit mapping algorithm is to approximate the function $Y = f(X)$ by MLP with n inputs and r outputs. In MLP training, we utilise the n-dimensional vectors $X_1, X_2, \ldots, X_N$ as inputs and the n-dimensional vectors $Y_1, Y_2, \ldots, Y_N$ obtained by the non-linear mapping, as desired outputs of the network. We already utilised this technique in Section 5.5.2.

6.2.1.2 Supervised Feature Extraction

In *pattern classification*, however, one is interested in a transformation such that the *class separability* is maximally preserved. One of such criteria used for the two-class problem is Fisher's criterion

$$Cost_F \; (V_1) = \frac{V_1^T \hat{\Sigma}_B V_1}{V_1^T \hat{\hat{\Sigma}} \, V_1} , \tag{6.21}$$

where V_1 is the n-variate transformation $y_1 = V_1^T X$ vector to be determined during the minimisation process, $\hat{\Sigma}_B$ is the "between the classes covariance matrix": $\hat{\hat{\Sigma}}_B = (\hat{M}_1 - \hat{M}_2)(\hat{M}_1 - \hat{M}_2)^T$ and $\hat{\hat{\Sigma}}$ is the sample covariance matrix pooled over two pattern classes $\hat{\hat{\Sigma}} = ½\,(\hat{\Sigma}_1 + \hat{\Sigma}_2)$.

Minimisation of (6.21) results in a new feature $y_1 = V_1^T X$ with the maximal discriminative power. At the second step, we may maximise $Cost_F\,(V_2)$ under the constraint that V_2 is orthogonal to the weight vector V_1 determined in the first step, i.e. $V_1^T V_2 = 0$. The vectors V_1 and V_2 determine the optimal discriminant plane. This concept may be expanded to yield the "optimal discriminant set of vectors".

In a generalisation of this approach, one can use any of the discriminant function techniques to obtain the new features. The new features may be postulated to be orthogonal to the previously determined vectors; they may also be determined on the condition of obtaining the best discrimination only from some part of the training vectors.

There are a couple of methods which minimise the classification error directly. The first of them minimises a decrease in the probability of misclassification in the classification problem of the L multivariate normal populations (Tubbs, Coberley and Young, 1982) In the linear feature reduction procedure $Y = \mathbf{B}X$, the $r \times n$ transformation matrix $\mathbf{B}$ is expressed as

$$\mathbf{B} = \mathbf{A}\mathbf{U}_1,$$

where $\mathbf{A}$ is an arbitrary $r \times r$ non-singular matrix, $\mathbf{U}_1$ is an $r \times n$ partition of the $n \times n$ matrix $\mathbf{U}$ that consists of the orthonormalised eigenvectors of $n \times n$ matrix $\hat{\mathbf{C}}\hat{\mathbf{C}}^T$ and $\hat{\mathbf{C}} = [\hat{M}_2, ..., \hat{M}_L, \hat{\Sigma}_2 - \mathbf{I}, ..., \hat{\Sigma}_L - \mathbf{I}]$ is an $n \times ((n+1)(L-1))$ matrix composed of sample estimates of the means $\hat{M}_i$ and covariance matrices $\hat{\Sigma}_i$ under the standard linear transformation such that $\hat{M}_1 = \mathbf{0}$ and $\hat{\Sigma}_1 = \mathbf{I}$ (the identity matrix).

Unfortunately, this method can become useless if the data is multimodal or asymmetric. To extract the linear features for more complex non-linearly separable data, the MLP with one hidden layer can be utilised (A. Raudys and Long, 2000). In this approach, a number of hidden units h in the first hidden layer is equal to the number of new features. Thus, the number h determines a degree of "non-linear separablility of the data". The weighted sums $y_i = X^T V_i + v_{i0}$ (before submitting them to the activation function) are calculated in h hidden units and serve as the new features. The technique is based on the fact that with an increase in the magnitude of the weights, the cost function of the non-linear single layer perceptron (in the output layer) begins to minimise the empirical classification error (see section 4.1.2.7). A complexity of a non-linear decision boundary utilised to evaluate the separability of the pattern classes in the new feature space depends on h, the number of new features.

6.2.2 Performance Criteria for Feature Selection

The simplest performance measure is the *Mahalanobis distance*. It is a perfect separability measure for the GCCM classes. When the covariance matrices are different, this measure can result in errors in the feature selection and extraction.

Another widely used separability measure is a *divergence*. The divergence between the classes ω_i and ω_j is given by

$$Div(i,j) = \int (p_i(X) - p_j(X)) \ln(p_i(X) / p_j(X)) dX.$$

For the Gaussian classes the divergence can be written as

$$Div(i, j) = ½ \operatorname{tr} [(\hat{\Sigma}_i - \hat{\Sigma}_j)(\hat{\Sigma}_i^{-1} - \hat{\Sigma}_j^{-1})] + ½ \operatorname{tr} [(\hat{\Sigma}_i^{-1} + \hat{\Sigma}_j^{-1})(M_i - M_j)(M_i - M_j)^T],$$

where M_i is the mean, and Σ_i is the covariance matrix of the i-th class.

In the L category case, an average interclass divergence is presented as

$$Div = \sum_{i=1}^{L}\sum_{j=1}^{L} Div(i,j). \qquad (6.23)$$

Many quality measures are based on the *information theory*. Examples are the Shannon information and entropy, the conditional entropy, and Vajda's average conditional quadratic entropy. There are more distance measures that enable one to obtain simplified estimates of the quality of the feature subsets. Devijver's Bayesian distance, Minkovski measures of nonuniformity, Bhattacharyya bound, Chernoff bound, Kolmogorov variational distance, Devijver's and Lissack and Fu's generalisation of variational distance, Ito's approximating functions, Jeffreys–Matusita distance are examples of separability measures.

There are a number of criteria for **choosing the ANN architecture**. Weights sensitivity calculation methods are used to evaluate the usefulness of the single features and hidden nodes. One of the popular measures is an *equivocation* called the *entropic loss*, log loss or stochastic complexity – the expectation of the logarithm of *the predictive (a posteriori) probability*

$$e = -\sum_{i=1}^{L} P_i \int p_i(\boldsymbol{X}) \log P(\omega_i | \boldsymbol{X})\, d\boldsymbol{X}. \qquad (6.24)$$

This measure does not contain a threshold function and leads to comparatively simple formulae in analytical investigations.

A *saliency* is one more popular measure in the feature and weights selection (pruning) in the ANN design. The saliency characterises an importance of the weight. It is defined by the second derivatives $H_{ij} = \dfrac{\partial^2 cost(\boldsymbol{X})}{\partial v_{ij}^2}$ of the cost function. If one uses the cost function of the sum of squares and approximates matrix $((H_{ij}))$ by a diagonal matrix composed from diagonal elements of $((H_{ij}))$, the saliency of the ij-th connection weight v_{ij} is approximated around a minimum v_{ij}^*, by:

$$s_{ij} = \frac{\partial^2 cost(\boldsymbol{X})}{\partial v_{ij}^2}\, v_{ij}^2. \qquad (6.25)$$

In the feature selection, one uses sums of the saliencies corresponding to each single feature. A simple and reliable measure to determine the partial contribution of the ij-th weight is

$$\pi_{ij} = \frac{|v_{ij}|}{\sum_k |v_{ik}|}, \qquad (6.26)$$

where the summation over all weights of the i-th neurone should be performed.

6.2.3 Feature Selection Strategies

The feature selection methods are specified by:

- a procedure (strategy) used to select a subset of r features out of a list of n total features and
- a criterion used to evaluate the quality of each subset.

Each of the criteria discussed in Section 6.2.2 can be used with different feature selection algorithms. Suppose one wishes to select the subset of r features from a list of n original features. An entire number of subsets of the size r is given by

$$C_n^r = \frac{n!}{(n-r)!r!}.$$

It is clear, that the number of subsets C_n^r to be evaluated can become very large even for moderate feature selection problems. For example, to select the best subset of 10 features out of a possible 30, one requires 30,045,015 subset evaluations. In order to reduce the number of subsets evaluated, one should use *suboptimal search procedures.*

The simplest technique ranks variables according to an estimate of the performance when the features are used separately. Such ranking of individual performance measures of the single features is based on an assumption that separate features are statistically independent. Justification for this strategy lies in the fact that the feature with a low error rate when used alone should be a valuable member of the subset of the features. For correlated features, this strategy can sometimes reject very good features. Two examples are presented in Figure 6.2. Here, the combinations of two individually almost uninformative features can discriminate two pattern classes perfectly.

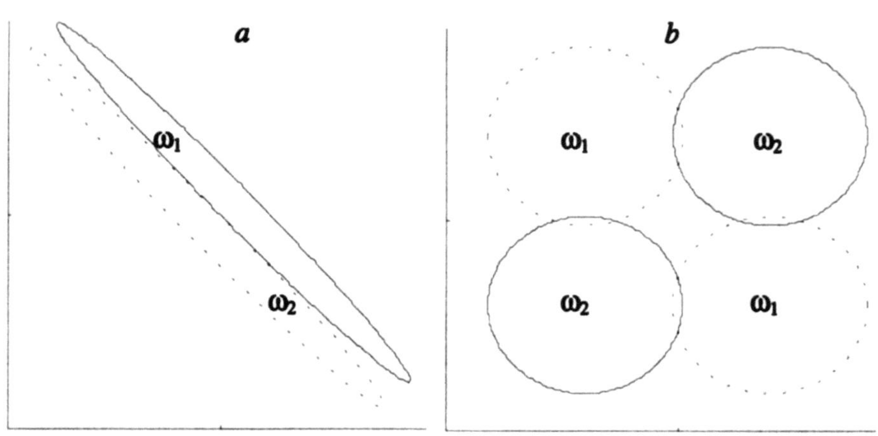

Fig. 6.2. Examples of two bi-variate distributions when a pair of individually uninformative features can discriminate two classes, ω_1 and ω_2, well.

In the *successive addition* procedure AD, the first step is to select the best single feature x_b. Then the second step is to select the best pair $x_b\, x_s$, which contains the best single feature x_b obtained in the previous step. This process continues by selecting a single feature that appears to be the best when combined with the previously selected subset of features. Often this procedure is called a *forward selection* and has much in common with successive augmentation of the ANN architecture. The number of subsets investigated in order to find the subset of r features from n possible features is given by

$$\sum_{i=1}^{n}(n-i+1) = r(n-r-1)/2).$$

To select 10 features out of 30 we need to evaluate 255 subsets.

It is an annoying fact that individually the top variable or the best subset of 2, 3, 4, etc. variables sometimes can not participate in the best subset selection of higher dimensionality. Thus, in some forward selection procedures, one begins from the best subset of variables determined by a full exploration of all C_n^k possible combinations of k variables ($k << r$).

In the *successive elimination* (*backward selection*) procedure EL, at first we determine the worst single variable x_w, which provides the smallest decrease in the classification accuracy. In certain cases, the rejection of the worst features causes an increase instead of a decrease in the performance. In the second step, variable x_w is eliminated and the worst single variable x_{ws} is again omitted from the remaining n - 1 variables. We eliminate the variable x_{ws} in the second step, etc. The variables are eliminated iteratively until optimal classification performance subsets are obtained. The number of subsets investigated in order to find the subset of r features from n possible ones is much smaller than C_n^r.

A *combined procedure*, named ADEL, consists of successive applications of two previous procedures, the AD and EL procedures. Let us, at the t-th step of the algorithm, have k variables included into the feature set. We successively add one from the remaining n - k variables and estimate the quality of the obtained feature subset. We repeat this procedure n - k times. The best subset composed from k + 1 variables is selected. In the next step, we use the successive elimination procedure to delete one of the variables. After two such substeps (addition and subsequent elimination) we return to k-variate space. If we succeed in obtaining a better subset of k features, then we continue the procedure of successive addition and elimination with the new subset composed of k variables. Otherwise, we continue the procedure with the subset composed of k + 1 variables.

This procedure may operate in reverse. At first, two variables are deleted as in the backward selection EL, then one feature is added successively from the remaining ones, etc. This procedure is called ELAD. Both procedures are primary variants of a training technology, nowadays called *evolutionary computation*.

In the *random search* feature selection, a number, say m^*, of subsets is generated: each subset consists of r variables selected from n original ones in a random way. Then performances of all m^* subsets are estimated and the best one is selected. In spite of the simplicity, the effectiveness of this procedure is similar to that of the other methods.

In a *random search with adaptation* procedure (Lbov, 1965) several random subsets, say m^*, are generated in a random way. Each subset consists of r variables. At the beginning, the probability of occurrence of all variables are equal: $q_1 = q_2 = ... = q_n$. Afterwards the performance criterion is estimated for all m^* subsets of the variables and the prior probabilities $q_1, q_2, ..., q_n$ are changed. Variables, which are often included in worthy subsets, are prompted by increasing their prior probabilities. Variables which often fall into unworthy subsets are suppressed by decreasing their prior probabilities. Several repetitions of the procedure allow one to obtain a subset near to the optimal one.

In the *synthesis* method, all C_n^k possible combinations consisting of r variables are explored (k = 2, 3, 4 or 5). Then, the best r variables that most often fall into the worthy subsets are selected.

There are many more heuristic feature selection procedures proposed in the literature. Branch and bound methods, heuristic search algorithms, dynamic programming methods, genetic algorithms and simulated annealing algorithms are suggested for this purpose. In Section 6.5 we will present arguments, that if one uses inexact performance measures in the feature selections, there is no need to utilise complex, expensive feature selection strategies.

In many pattern recognition problems, there are an excessively large number of variables. Even the procedures of the simplest variable selection, such as forward or backward selection, become troublesome. As a side note, the features are often known to be redundant. To overcome the difficulty arising in the feature selection problem with an excessively large number of initial variables, Jain and Dubes (1978) proposed a strategy for *feature definition.* The strategy involves two phases:

- clustering of the features based on a correlation measure of feature similarity;
- compressing each cluster into a single feature.

The authors *suggest an interaction* between the analyst and the data. The analyst investigates clustering for interpretability, the number of features and separation among the pattern classes.

6.3 Accuracy of Performance Estimates

6.3.1 Error Counting Estimates

6.3.1.1 The Hold-Out Method

The hold-out (cross-validation) method is the simplest and most often used error rate estimator for pattern classifiers. In the hold-out error estimation method (HM), the design set is split into the training set (TS) and the validation set (VS).

Let $N_d = N_t + N_v$ be the total number of observations from all classes in the design set, N_t be the number of observations from all classes in the training set, and N_v be the number of observations from all classes in the validation set. Let all observation vectors in the design set be statistically independent. The proportion, $\hat{\varepsilon}_{HM}$, of misclassified observations from the validation set (the test set in certain applications) is the hold-out estimate of the error rate. The estimate $\hat{\varepsilon}_{HM}$ is a *doubly random* variable. Its distribution is conditioned on the TS and VS. For fixed TS, the estimate $\hat{\varepsilon}_{HM}$ is a binomial random variable. Its mean value is equal to $\hat{\varepsilon}_{N_t}$, the conditional PMC (the generalisation error) of the classifier trained on N_t particular observations of the training-set. A variance of $\hat{\varepsilon}_{HM}$ is

$$V[\hat{\varepsilon}_{HM}] = \frac{\varepsilon_{N_t}(1-\varepsilon_{N_t})}{N_v}. \tag{6.27}$$

Here, A, the index of the classifier type, has been omitted. To search for an optimal split of the design set, let us compare $V[\hat{\varepsilon}_{HM}]$ with the variance of the conditional PMC of the linear Fisher DF (Equation (3.12) in Section 3.4.4)

$$V[\varepsilon_N^F] \approx \frac{2(\phi(\delta/2))^2}{\delta^2 N^2}\left(\frac{\delta^4}{16} + \left(1+\frac{\delta^2}{4}\right)^2 (n-1)\right), \tag{6.28}$$

Numerical analysis of (6.27) and (6.28) shows that, for moderate values of the dimensionality, training and validation sets, $V[\hat{\varepsilon}_{HM}] >> V[\varepsilon_N^F]$. One possible explanation for this phenomenon is that the hold-out error counting estimator is a nonparametric method and the linear Fisher discriminant is a parametric one. In the nonparametric hold-out error counting estimate, no prior information concerning the class-conditional densities or concerning the discriminant function $g(\boldsymbol{X})$ is used. To design the Fisher discriminant, one utilises the important additional information which proclaim that the pattern classes are Gaussian and that the covariance matrices of separate classes are equal among themselves. This information reduces the variance.

The values $V[\hat{\varepsilon}_{HM}]$ and $V[\varepsilon_N^F]$ can be utilised to find *the best split* of the design set into the training and validation sets for the standard Fisher linear classifier. Equations (6.27) and (6.28) along with the equation for the expected error (3.10) indicate that the optimal split should depend on the dimensionality n, the distance between the pattern classes δ and the design set size N_d. Note that formula (6.28) is only valid for the standard Fisher linear discriminant function and the GCCM data model. The optimal split found for this classifier can be ineffective when applied to other classifiers.

6.3.1.2 The Resubstitution Estimator

In this method, all the N_d design set observations are used to train the classifier. Hence, the training-set can be called the design set, i.e. $N_t = N_d$. After training, the same vectors are used to estimate the classification performance. Therefore, the classifier adapts to the peculiarities of the design set and results in an optimistic (biased) estimate of the error rate. For example, for the Fisher linear DF a mean value of the resubstitution error counting estimate is

$$E[\hat{\varepsilon}^{F}_{RM}] \approx \Phi\{ -\frac{\delta}{2}\sqrt{T_M T_{\bar{\Sigma}}} \}, \tag{6.29}$$

where $T_M = 1+ \dfrac{2n}{\delta^2 \bar{N}}$ and $T_{\bar{\Sigma}} = 1+\dfrac{n}{2\bar{N} - n}$.

In Equation (6.29) $\bar{N} = N/2 = N_v/2 = N_t/2 = N_d/2$. The terms T_M and $T_{\bar{\Sigma}}$ arise from the approximate sample estimation of the mean vectors and the covariance matrix, respectively. The expected classification error of the Fisher classifier is

$$E[\varepsilon^{F}_{N}] \approx \Phi\{ -\frac{\delta}{2}\frac{1}{\sqrt{T_M T_{\bar{\Sigma}}}} \}. \tag{3.10}$$

With an increase in N, the number of design set vectors, both expected values, $E[\hat{\varepsilon}^{F}_{RM}]$ and $E[\varepsilon^{F}_{N}]$, converge on each other and to the asymptotic error ε^{F}_{∞} The symmetry is obvious between Equations (6.29) and (3.10).

Example 1. In Figure 6.3, we present graphs of dependence of the expected PMC and the expectation of the resubstitution estimator on N, the training-set size. The graphs are calculated for data with the Mahalanobis distance $\delta = 3.76$, $n = 10$ and $n = 30$. For a large number of design samples, the both graphs become symmetrical with respect to the asymptotic classification error ε^{F}_{∞}.

This symmetry is observed for a number of other statistical classifiers. Unfortunately, there are no similar analytical expressions for many of them. Nevertheless, in Chapter 3 we have had a number of the theoretical equations of the expected PMC. These equations characterise the increase in the mean generalisation error $\Delta_N = \bar{\varepsilon}^{A}_{N} - \bar{\varepsilon}^{A}_{N}$. The symmetry suggests that they can be used to evaluate the bias of the resubstitution estimate. Thus, these theoretical results may help to determine conditions when the resubstitution estimator can be used to estimate the asymptotic PMC. From the other hand, the theoretical difference $\Delta_N = \bar{\varepsilon}^{A}_{N} - \varepsilon^{A}_{\infty}$ can be utilised to improve the resubstitution estimate

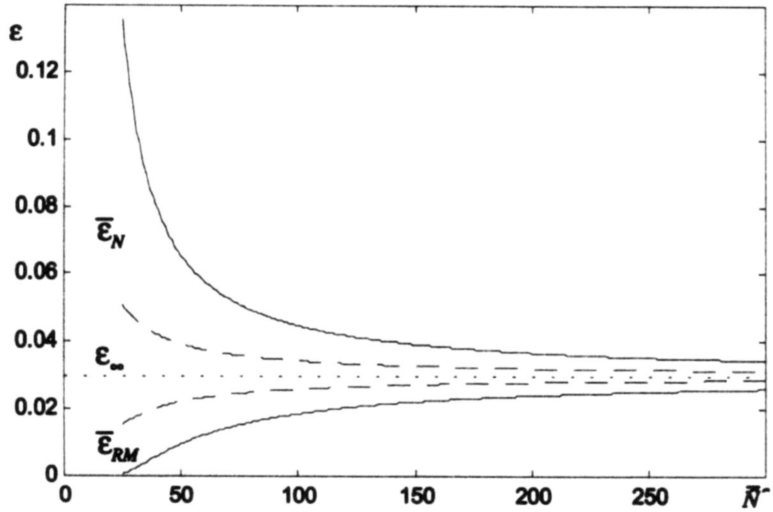

Fig. 6.3. The expected PMC $\bar{\varepsilon}_N$ and resubstitution error $\bar{\hat{\varepsilon}}_{RM}$ of the Fisher linear DF versus the number of training vectors N. The GCCM data model with the Mahalanobis distance $\delta = 3.76$ and dimensionality $n = 30$ (solid lines) and $n = 10$ (dashed lines).

For example, in order to estimate the expected PMC of the Fisher linear classifier instead of $\hat{\varepsilon}_{RM}^{(F)}$ one can use:

$$\hat{\varepsilon}_{RM}^{F*} = \hat{\varepsilon}_{RM}^{F} + (\Phi\{-\frac{\delta}{2}\frac{1}{\sqrt{T_M T_{\bar{\Sigma}}}}\} - \Phi\{-\frac{\delta}{2}\sqrt{T_M T_{\bar{\Sigma}}}\}) \text{ or}$$

$$\hat{\varepsilon}_{RM}^{F+} = \hat{\varepsilon}_{RM}^{F} + 2\,\Delta_N = \hat{\varepsilon}_{RM}^{F} + 2\,(\Phi\{-\frac{\delta}{2}\frac{1}{\sqrt{T_M T_{\bar{\Sigma}}}}\} - \Phi\{-\frac{\delta}{2}\}), \qquad (6.30)$$

where Δ_N denotes an absolute increase in the mean generalisation error.

The resubstitution estimate is a *random variable*. The distribution of the error counting resubstitution estimate is conditioned on $E\hat{\varepsilon}_{RM}$, its expected value. A variance of $\hat{\varepsilon}_{RM}$ is

$$V[\hat{\varepsilon}_{RM}] \approx \frac{E\hat{\varepsilon}_{RM}(1 - E\hat{\varepsilon}_{RM})}{N_d}, \qquad (6.31)$$

where A, an index of the classifier's type, has been omitted.

Comparison of (6.31) with (6.27), the variance of the hold-out estimate, indicates that for $N_d = N_v$ the variance of the resubstitution error is smaller. The difference is caused by the fact that the expected value of the resubstitution estimate, $\bar{\hat{\varepsilon}}_{RM}$, is smaller than the expected value of the hold-out estimate, $\bar{\hat{\varepsilon}}_{HM}$. *Relative variances* $V[\hat{\varepsilon}_{RM}]/(\bar{\hat{\varepsilon}}_{RM})^2$, and $V[\hat{\varepsilon}_{HM}]/(\bar{\hat{\varepsilon}}_{HM})^2$, however, are virtually the same.

6.3.1.3 The Leaving-One-Out Estimator

When the observations in the design set are statistically independent, the leaving-one-out method (N_d-fold cross-validation) is practically the unbiased estimator of the conditional PMC e_N^{A}. The variance of the leaving-one-out error counting estimate is expressed by the following equation

$$V[\hat{\varepsilon}_{LOOM}] = \frac{\varepsilon_{N_d}(1-\varepsilon_{N_d})}{N_d}. \tag{6.32}$$

In Equation (6.32), N_d is used to emphasise that one does not split the design set into the training and validation sets. All vectors are used, instead of a portion.

We emphasise once more that the leaving-one-out estimate is unbiased only if all design set vectors are statistically independent. Statistically dependent vectors more or less duplicate each other. Each omitted vector can be correlated with other vectors used for training. Thus, the leaving-one-out estimate becomes similar to resubstitution estimate which is optimistically biased.

For large N (when $\hat{\varepsilon}_{LOOM}^{\mathsf{A}} / \hat{\varepsilon}_{RM}^{\mathsf{A}} < 2$) the symmetry of the learning curves of the resubstitution estimate and the expected probability of misclassification (the expected value of the leaving-one-out estimate) suggests the following simple, almost unbiased estimate of the asymptotic error

$$\hat{\varepsilon}_{\infty}^{(\mathsf{A})} = \tfrac{1}{2}(\hat{\varepsilon}_{LOOM}^{\mathsf{A}} + \hat{\varepsilon}_{RM}^{\mathsf{A}}). \tag{6.33}$$

In the above estimate, index **A** emphasises that the asymptotic error is specific for each classifier design method. Note, the difference $\hat{\varepsilon}_{LOOM}^{\mathsf{A}} - \hat{\varepsilon}_{RM}^{\mathsf{A}}$ (or the ratio $\hat{\varepsilon}_{LOOM}^{\mathsf{A}} / \hat{\varepsilon}_{RM}^{\mathsf{A}}$ can be utilised to evaluate the training-set size necessary for sufficient training of the classifier **A**.

6.3.1.4 The Bootstrap Estimator

In the small design set case, estimate (6.5) is a slightly biased estimate of the conditional PMC $\varepsilon_N^{\mathsf{A}}$. To overcome the bias, a number of modifications of the bootstrap method have been proposed in the literature. The variance of the first term in the right side of Equation (6.5) is the variance of the bootstrap resubstitution estimate. The expectation of the resubstitution estimate is smaller than the expected probability of misclassification. Therefore, the variance of the resubstitution estimate is smaller than the variance of the leaving-one-out estimate.

The bias term $Bias(\hat{\varepsilon}_{RM})$ in Equation (6.5) is also a random variable. Theoretical and experimental analysis has shown that the bootstrap estimate is more accurate for a small number of design set vectors N_d and for large values of asymptotic error ε_∞^A if compared with the leaving-one-out estimate. The variance of the bootstrap estimate approaches the variance of the leaving-one-out estimate (6.32) with an increase in N_d and a decrease in ε_∞^A

$$V[\hat{\varepsilon}_{BM}] \approx \frac{\varepsilon_{N_d}(1-\varepsilon_{N_d})}{N_d} \approx V[\hat{\varepsilon}_{LOOM}]. \tag{6.34}$$

6.3.2 Parametric Estimators for the Linear Fisher Classifier

The error counting estimators simply count the number of misclassifications and evaluate its proportion among the total number of vectors used. The estimate is nonparametric in nature. In this estimator, no assumptions concerning the distribution of either the pattern vectors or the discriminant function are made.

In order to construct the parametric estimates discussed in Section 6.1.2.3, we have assumed that the classes are multivariate Gaussian and the covariance matrices are common. This assumption provides an important additional piece of information. Suppose this assumption is correct. Obviously, if correctly used, this information can help improve the accuracy of the estimators.

Let us evaluate this gain in the accuracy for the GCCM data model. The sample estimate $\hat{\delta}^2$ of the Mahalanobis distance (6.11) can be represented as a scaled non-central F random variable (6.12). For large N, a variance of the sample estimate δ^2 is

$$V[\hat{\delta}^2] = \frac{\delta^2}{\bar{N}}\left(\frac{T_M}{T_{\bar{\Sigma}}}\right)^2\left\{\frac{\delta^2}{T_\Sigma}+\frac{8}{T_M}\right\}. \tag{6.35}$$

Utilisation of the first terms of the Taylor expansion of the parametric estimate (6.11) and the variance $V[\hat{\delta}^2]$ gives

$$V[\hat{\varepsilon}_D] = \frac{\phi\left(\frac{\delta}{2}\sqrt{T_M T_{\bar{\Sigma}}}\right)^2}{16\bar{N}} T_{\bar{\Sigma}}(\delta^2 T_M T_{\bar{\Sigma}} + 8). \tag{6.36}$$

Numerical calculations show that, for moderate values of δ, n and N, the variance (6.36) is lower than the variance of the resubstitution error counting estimate (6.31). A comparative difference between variances of both the classification error estimates increases with an increase in the distance δ (a decrease in the asymptotic error ε_{∞}^{F}). It means that, for small error rates, the parametric estimate can become much more effective than the nonparametric one.

The estimate (6.12) is derived for multivariate Gaussian distributions with equal covariances. In real situations, the data differs from the theoretically postulated model. Therefore, undesired bias arises in estimating the classification error rates. In principle, the bias can be positive or negative. Its value depends on a difference between the idealised model (GCCM) and the real distributions.

There is one more important general remark concerning all types of estimates: the standard deviations of the estimates are directly related to their mean values. The smaller the mean value, the smaller will be the variance. Therefore, the optimistic bias of the estimate decreases the variance. Consequently, the resubstitution and the bootstrap estimates just seem to be more accurate than the leaving-one-out and the hold-out estimates.

6.3.3 Associations Between the Classification Performance Measures

In the model selection, one can use the error estimates as well as the simplified performance measures. The designer of a pattern recognition system should be aware that there is a great number of types of the classification errors. The simple, easy to calculate, measures often only approximately characterise the real quality of the feature subset or the network architecture. Moreover, a real rank of the feature subset depends on the type of classification rule used later. The features which provide good performance for the nonparametric Parzen window classifier can appear to be poor performers for the parametric linear Fisher classifier. And vice versa, in the small training-set case, uni-modal very highly-correlated features can be poor performers for the Parzen window classifier and very good for the linear Fisher classifier. Figure 6.2 shows two simple illustrative examples of this fact. The highly-correlated features are also poor performers for the Parzen window, the binary decision tree and the Radial basic function neural classifiers. Thus, the features which are good for the perceptron can be bad for the RBF network.

Example 2. The following examples are presented in order to demonstrate associations between different classification performance measures and the classification error. To avoid the finite sample size effects and reveal only similarities and differences between the measures, we utilise the resubstitution performance estimates.

Quadratic DF versus the Fisher linear DF. Figure 6.4 presents a scatter diagram of distribution of 126 values of the probability of misclassification (PMC) of the quadratic DF versus the PMC of the Fisher linear DF. Real-world lung data was used. We examined $C_9^5 = 126$ five-variate subsets of features selected from nine spectral and cepstral original features. For comparison of the two classification error evaluation methods, the resubstitution error counting method was used (the design set size was $N_1 = N_2 = 90$).

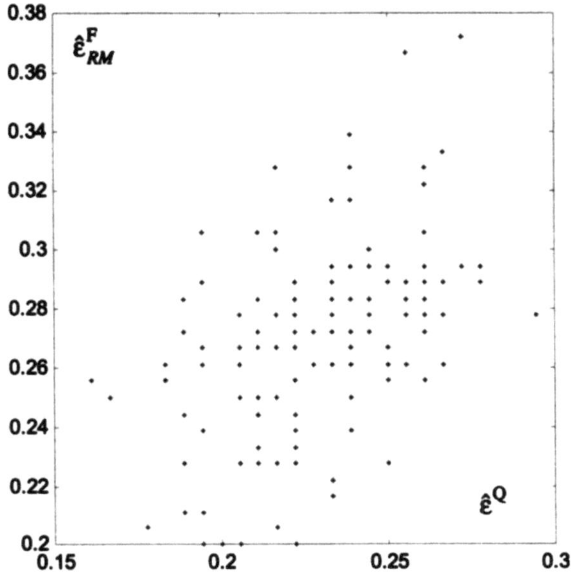

Fig. 6.4. The probability of misclassification of the linear Fisher $\hat{\varepsilon}^{(F)}_{RM}$ versus the probability of misclassification of the quadratic DF $\hat{\varepsilon}^{(Q)}_{RM}$.

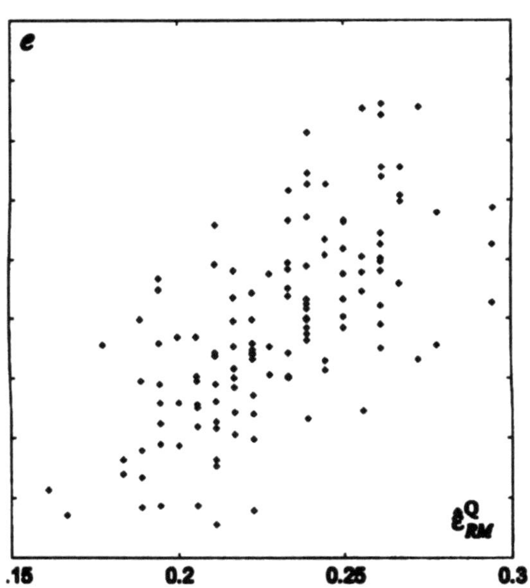

Fig. 6.5. The entropic loss e versus the PMC of the quadratic DF $\hat{\varepsilon}^{(Q)}_{RM}$.

One can see an obvious difference in the quality of the individual feature subsets evaluated by utilisation the standard linear and quadratic classifiers. The correlation coefficient between the performance criteria $\hat{\varepsilon}_{RM}^{(Q)}$ and $\hat{\varepsilon}_{RM}^{(F)}$ is rather small: $\rho = 0.47$. Note that for the GCCM pattern classes, theoretically one should obtain correlation $\rho = 1$. The scatter diagram characterises the differences in the classification errors which are functions of the mean vectors, covariance matrices and deviations of the data from the Gaussian distribution. Thus, the scatter diagrams can be useful as compact descriptions of the multivariate distribution of the pattern classes.

Quadratic classifier versus the entropic loss (6.24). In Figure 6.5, a scatter diagram is presented for 126 feature subsets evaluated from the lung data set. One can see that the performance evaluation measures rank the feature subsets in different ways: the correlation coefficient $\rho = 0.67$. It means that, for this particular lung diagnosis problem with cepstral features, the entropic loss is far from being a very good quality measure for the feature selection if, in future, the quadratic classifier is utilised.

Saliency versus PMC of the perceptron. The saliency (6.25), a popular measure in ANN architecture selection, is also an approximate quantity. Figure 6.6 contains a scatter diagram of the distribution of 54 values of the saliency $s_i = 1/1080 \Sigma s_i(\boldsymbol{X}_j)$ versus the resubstitution estimate of PMC of the non-linear SLP. Both measures are estimated for 53-variate vectors representing short segments of the lung noise.

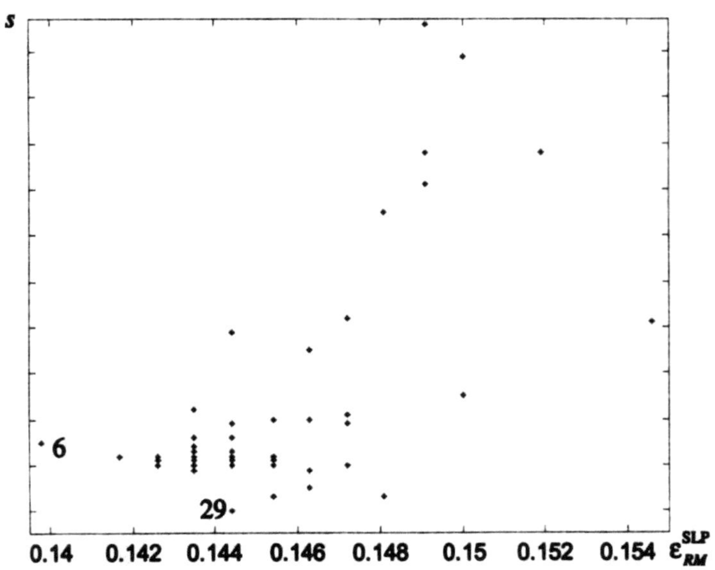

Fig. 6.6. Saliency versus the probability of misclassification $\varepsilon_N^{(SLP)}$ of the non-linear SLP.

The number of the vectors in the design set is 1080 (540 + 540). In this classification problem, we have used the nine-variate data which was mapped into 54-variate space of the new polynomial features. We considered the backward feature selection, where 53-variate feature subsets were selected from the 54 features. Thus, we calculated the saliency for m = 54 feature subsets. In this experiment, after training the SLP with 54 inputs for 1000 iterations in batch mode, the saliency was calculated for each feature. Then this feature was rejected and after 500 additional iterations, the PMC was evaluated.

It is much easier to calculate the saliency than to train the perceptron for the additional 500 iterations and to evaluate the classification error rate afterwards. Figure 6.6 illustrates that in the perceptron architecture selection, the classification error and the saliency suggest the rejection of different features (features 6 and 29). We have a notable difference between the classification error of the feature subsets without feature 6 or feature 29. In multiple application of this procedure, the selection errors accumulate. The difference allows one to assess the computation cost in terms of the classification error that is gained while utilising the proper feature selection criterion.

Low correlation between the simplified performance measures and the classification error is characteristic to most real-world problems. The indirect secondary performance measures are only approximately related to the classification accuracy. Their utilisation provides a foundation for finding new features but sometimes they give little information to minimise the classification error. Thus, if one utilises simple inexact performance measures, there is no need to apply a complex selection strategy to test a large number of models. We will return to this problem in Section 6.5.2.

6.4 Feature Ranking and the Optimal Number of Features

In Section 1.5, the peaking phenomenon was explained in the following situation:

- in the high-dimensional and finite training-set size case, the generalisation error can increase substantially;
- some of the features are almost worthless.

In this section, it will be shown that, in addition to the training-set size, two extra factors affect the peaking phenomenon and the optimal number of features:

- the classifiers' complexity;
- the order in which the features are presented.

6.4.1 The Complexity of the Classifiers

Example 3. In order to understand more clearly the peaking phenomenon in feature selection, let us return to the simple but instructive multivariate GCCM data model, already discussed in Section 1.5. The means $\boldsymbol{M}_1$, $\boldsymbol{M}_2$ are different and the covariance matrix $\overline{\Sigma}$ is common to both pattern classes. Let

$$\boldsymbol{M}_1 - \boldsymbol{M}_2 = (\delta_0, \delta_0, \ldots, \delta_0)^T \text{ and } \Sigma = \begin{bmatrix} 1 & \rho & \ldots & \rho \\ \rho & 1 & \ldots & \rho \\ \ldots & \ldots & \ldots & \ldots \\ \rho & \rho & \ldots & 1 \end{bmatrix}. \tag{6.37}$$

In this data model, all individual features have exactly the same discriminative power i.e. $\delta_i^2 = \delta_0^2$, because $m_{1i} - m_{2i} = \delta_0$. The Bayes error and asymptotic probability of misclassification of the Fisher linear DF are uniquely determined by the Mahalanobis distance $\delta^2 = (\boldsymbol{M}_1 - \boldsymbol{M}_2)^T \overline{\Sigma}^{-1} (\boldsymbol{M}_1 - \boldsymbol{M}_2)$. For the model analysed:

$$\overline{\Sigma}^{-1} = \begin{bmatrix} a & b & \ldots & b \\ b & a & \ldots & b \\ \ldots & \ldots & \ldots & \ldots \\ b & b & \ldots & a \end{bmatrix},$$

$$\text{where } a = \frac{n\rho - 2\rho + 1}{(1-\rho)(n\rho + 1 - \rho)}, \; b = -\frac{\rho}{(1-\rho)(n\rho + 1 - \rho)}, \; \delta^2 = \frac{n\,\delta_0^2}{n\rho + 1 - \rho}. \tag{6.38}$$

All features are equally informative; on the other hand, the features are correlated among themselves. Therefore, with an increase in n the Mahalanobis distance increases quickly at first but later this increase saturates. A limit value of the Mahalanobis distance is $\delta^2 \to \delta_0^2/\rho$, as the number of features $n \to \infty$.

As in Figure 1.8*a*, in Figure 6.7, we have the graph of dependence of the asymptotic classification error $\varepsilon_\infty^F = \varepsilon_B = \Phi\{-\frac{1}{2}\delta\}$ on the dimensionality n (the dotted curve). The data model (6.37) with $\delta_0^2 = 3.0$ and $\rho = 0.5$ was used. In Figure 6.7, we have the expected generalisation errors of the linear Fisher DF, F, and the quadratic DF, Q, versus n calculated from Equations (3.10) and (3.19). We see the optimal dimensionality for the quadratic classifier is smaller.

In Section 1.5, it was demonstrated that the optimal number of features depends on the number of training vectors. Now one can observe that it depends also on the complexity of the classifier. The optimal dimensionality increases with an increase in the training-set size and decreases with an increase in the complexity of the classifier (in strict terms, the complexity of the algorithm used to find the weights).

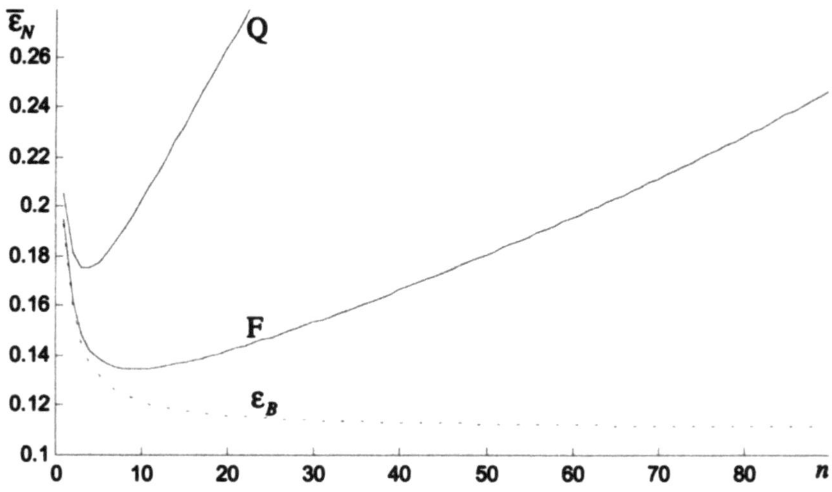

Fig. 6.7. The Bayes error ε_B and expected errors of the linear and quadratic classifiers versus dimensionality n; $N_2 = N_1 = 80$.

6.4.2 Feature Ranking

In Figure 6.7, the graphs were obtained for the model when all features are equally informative. The features have different levels of quality in most real-world problems. There are good and bad uninformative features. Thus, the researcher ranks and selects the best features first. After the feature ranking, the contribution of a single feature into the Mahalanobis distance depends on the feature number: the first features contribute the most and each following feature contributes less than the previous one.

Example 4. Consider a data model where individual features have different discriminative powers. All the features are statistically independent and the contribution of each single feature depends on its order number:

$$\delta_i^2 = (m_{1i} - m_{2i})^2 / \sigma_i^2 = \delta_0^2 \gamma^i \qquad (\gamma < 1).$$

The Mahalanobis distance of all n features is

$$\delta^2 = \delta_0^2 \sum_{j=1}^{n} \gamma^j = \delta_0^2 \gamma (1-\gamma^n)(1-\gamma)^{-1}. \tag{6.39}$$

Utilisation of data model (6.39) with parameters $\delta_0^2 = 0.8$, $\gamma = 0.9$ and the linear Fisher DF for the training-set size $\bar{N} = 80$ gives the two graphs marked 1 in Figure 6.8. In this figure, *dotted curves* represent the asymptotic PMC. *Solid curves* represent the expected PMC. The two curves marked 1 correspond to the optimal and best possible feature ranking (ordering). Here, we use the best feature with the largest δ_i^2 at first, etc.

The curves marked by the number 2 correspond to the worst ordering when the worst features (with smallest δ_i^2) are presented at first. For the parameter values under consideration ($\gamma = 0.9$ and $\bar{N} = 80$) we have no minimum.

Let the features be presented at random. It is natural to assume $\delta_i^2 \approx \delta^2/n$. This situation is illustrated by the curves marked 3 in Figure 6.8. For the linear Fisher DF, $n_{opt} \approx \bar{N}$. It is a much higher value than n_{opt} obtained for the best ordering.

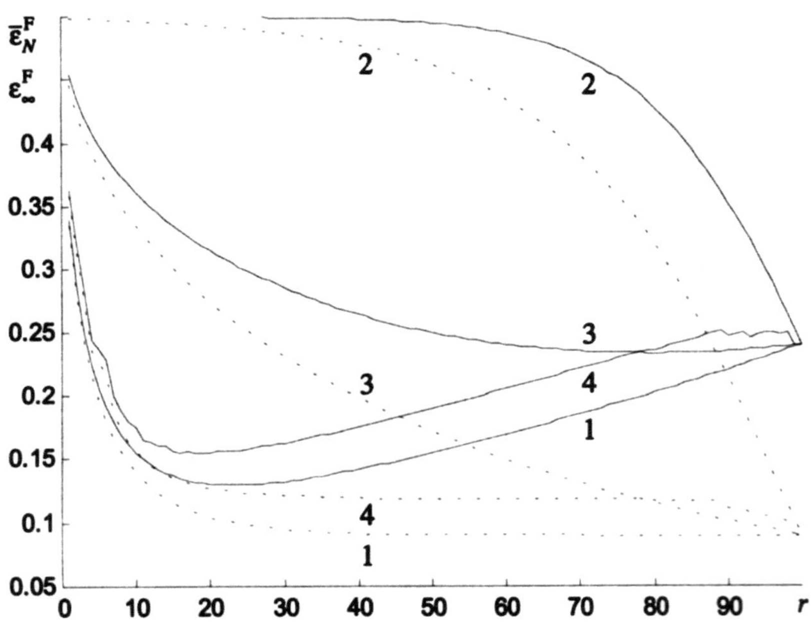

Fig. 6.8. Influence of feature ordering on the character of the curves; the generalisation (solid curves) and asymptotic errors (dotted curves) versus the number of features r: 1 – the best possible ordering, 2 – the worst possible ordering, 3 – random ordering, 4 – ordering according to inaccurate estimates of the individual quality of the features.

In practice, however one never has the best, the worst or random ordering. One performs the feature selection first and then determines the optimal number of features. To illustrate the non-optimal feature ranking in Figure 6.8, there are two curves denoted by 4. The graphs are obtained for inaccurate individual feature ranking based on imprecise estimations of δ_i^2 . In this virtual experiment, to each value of δ_i^2 we artificially added a random zero-mean noise, ξ_i, with variance

$V(\xi_i) = \delta_i^2\,(\delta_i^2 + 8)\,/\,\bar{N}$. Each single feature has a different noise variance. In this example, the noise variance depends on the feature's discriminative power: the noise variance was calculated using Equation (6.35) for a new dimensionality $n = 1$ (in feature ranking, we evaluated only one feature at a time) and $\delta = \delta_i = \delta_0^2\,\gamma^i$. This data was used to imitate imprecise estimates for the feature quality. As a result of inaccurate feature ranking, the asymptotic PMC and expected PMC (curves 4 in Figure 6.8) are higher than in the case of the ideal feature ranking.

For non-optimal feature ranking, the optimal number of features is usually higher than for ideal ranking. However, exceptions are possible. The minimum of the expected PMC for non-optimal ranked features is *always* higher. Thus, the optimal dimensionality and the generalisation error depends on the feature ordering.

The spherical Gaussian distribution of the pattern classes is only one known data model where the training-set based feature ordering and subsequent feature selection do not allow the reduction of the generalisation error of EDC in the Bayes predictive sense (see Section 2.4.2, also Serdobolskij, 1983*b*). For most other models of the data and the classification rules the sample-based feature ranking can be effective.

The limited training-set size is only one factor that causes the peaking effect. Let the certain parametric model (say, the model A) of the distribution densities $p_i(X \mid \Theta^{A})$ be used to design the classification rule and the data model $p_i^{data}(X)$ be different. There exist situations when the asymptotic PMC ε_∞^{A} (but not the Bayes error!) decreases at first and then begins to increase with a further increase in the number of features. This kind of peaking effect has already been illustrated in Chapter 1 (see Figure 1.8 *b*).

6.4.3 Determining the Optimal Number of Features

Summarising the above analysis, the main factors which affect the optimal number of features are:

- the pattern recognition problem to be solved and the order in which the features are presented;
- the assumptions used to design the classifier and a correspondence of the assumptions to the data where the algorithm should be applied;
- the size of the training-set and the individual characteristics of the vectors that compose this set.

The above factors are interrelated. Therefore, *a priori*, it is impossible to determine n_{opt} exactly. An enormous number of possible theoretical models of the true multivariate densities $p_i^{data}(X)$ suggests that the optimal number of features should be determined experimentally by trial and error. After the type of classifier is selected and the features (or the feature subsets) are ranked, one needs to obtain the unbiased estimates $\hat{\varepsilon}_j$ of the generalisation error of the feature subsets containing 1, 2, ..., n-1 features. According to the estimates $\hat{\varepsilon}_1$, $\hat{\varepsilon}_2$, $\hat{\varepsilon}_3$, ..., the subset with the minimal error is selected.

In general, the feature subset selection based on imprecise estimates $\hat{\varepsilon}_1$, $\hat{\varepsilon}_2$, $\hat{\varepsilon}_3$, ..., is inaccurate. One of the possibilities for improving the selection accuracy is to smooth an empirical dependence of the estimates $\hat{\varepsilon}$ versus the number of features r, $\hat{\varepsilon} = f^{\mathsf{A}}(r)$, ($r$ = 1, 2, ..., n) and to determine the optimal dimensionality, n_{opt}, according to a minimum of a smoothed curve $\hat{\varepsilon} = f^{\mathsf{A}}(r)$. Note that, for certain classifiers (A) and data types, the curve $\hat{\varepsilon} = f^{\mathsf{A}}(r)$ can have more than one minimum.

Similar considerations and procedures should be applied to solving the related problems: determination of the optimal smoothing parameter of the PW classifier, the regularisation constant in RDA, an optimal number of nearest neighbours, optimal number of iterations in ANN training, etc. In all these complexity control problems, one needs to obtain independent unbiased performance estimates and to find their minimum. The smoothing of empirical dependencies, accuracy versus the smoothing parameter, is also useful.

6.5 The Accuracy of the Model Selection

A priori, it is impossible to select the best sequence of the feature extraction and the classifier design procedures in order to get a good solution. It is a characteristic of real-world pattern recognition problems. Therefore, the designer is forced to test a number of variants.

There are two fundamental aspects of the accuracy problem:

- the accuracy of performance estimates utilised to evaluate quality of each competing variant,
- the accuracy of the selection process where we select one model on a basis of inaccurate estimates of a number of competing models.

6.5.1 True, Apparent and Ideal Classification Errors

In the selection process, the designer usually applies a certain performance evaluation method to estimate the classifier's accuracy and find the best solution. In addition to the four types of classification error discussed in Section 6.1, three new kinds of the classification error arise in the selection process. This problem is illustrated by the following example.

Example 5. To solve the two-category classification problem, five (m = 5) potential classification algorithms are tested:

A1 – the Fisher linear discriminant function;

A2 – the nonparametric three-nearest neighbour classifier;

A3 – the nonparametric five-nearest neighbour classifier;
A4 – the single layer perceptron with four hidden units;
A5 – the single layer perceptron with eight hidden units.

Suppose that the training-set is composed of $N_{t1} = 200$, $N_{t2} = 200$ vectors and an independent validation set of $N_{v1} = 250$, $N_{v2} = 250$ vectors. Let the validation set's estimates of the probability of misclassification ε_V be:

for classifier A1 $\hat{\varepsilon}_{v1} = 0.042$;
for classifier A2 $\hat{\varepsilon}_{v2} = 0.052$;
for classifier A3 $\hat{\varepsilon}_{v3} = 0.038$;
for classifier A4 $\hat{\varepsilon}_{v4} = 0.048$;
for classifier A5 $\hat{\varepsilon}_{v5} = 0.040$.

Then a natural choice would be to select the classifier A3 with $\hat{\varepsilon}_{v3} = 0.038$ and to recommend this classifier for further use, referring to its generalisation error $\varepsilon_N = 0.038$. The statement that the performance of the best classifier is 0.038, however, is not correct. To explain this, suppose we have an independent very large test set composed from $Nt_1 = 1000$ and $Nt_2 = 1000$ vectors in order to estimate the PMC of all five classifiers. Let the estimates of the probability of misclassification ε_t obtained using 2000 observation vectors be:

for classifier A1 $\varepsilon_{t1} = 0.0405$;
for classifier A2 $\varepsilon_{t2} = 0.0605$;
for classifier A3 $\varepsilon_{t3} = 0.0480$;
for classifier A4 $\varepsilon_{t4} = 0.0465$;
for classifier A5 $\varepsilon_{t5} = 0.0515$.

We assume these estimates are accurate as they are obtained from a very large test set. In Figure 6.9, all five pairs of estimates in a bi-variate $\varepsilon_t - \hat{\varepsilon}_v$ space are presented. From the test set estimates it follows that one should make use of the classifier A1 having an error rate $\varepsilon_{t1} = 0.0405$. However, the decision based on the validation set had suggested the use of the classifier A3. The actual (true) error rate of the classifier A3 is $\varepsilon_{t3} = 0.0480$. Thus, inexact model selection based on the small validation set caused an increase in the classification error:

$$\varepsilon_{t3} - \varepsilon_{t1} = 0.0480 - 0.0405 = 0.0075.$$

The true (test set) classification error of the algorithm selected according to the validation estimates is called the *true PMC in selection* and is denoted by ε_{true}. In our example, $\varepsilon_{true} = 0.0480 = \varepsilon_{t3}$.

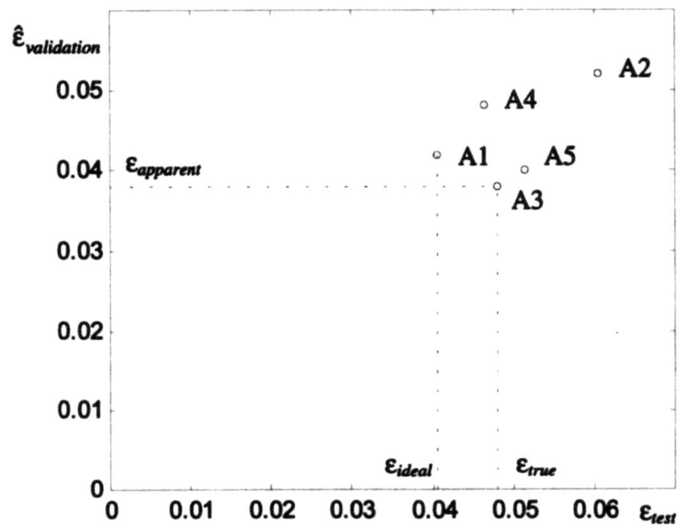

Fig. 6.9. A distribution of five pairs of estimates in the bi-variate ε_t - $\hat{\varepsilon}_v$ space and the apparent, true and ideal error rates in the selection of the best variant.

The validation set estimate of the classification error of the algorithm selected according to the validation estimates is called the *apparent PMC in selection*, and is denoted by $\varepsilon_{apparent}$. In our example, $\varepsilon_{apparent} = 0.0038 = \hat{\varepsilon}_{v3}$.

If the model selection was performed on the basis of the accurate estimates (in the above example, the estimates ε_{t1}, ε_{t2}, ε_{t3}, ε_{t4}, ε_{t5}), then one would select the first algorithm A1. The true (test set) classification error of the classification algorithm selected according to the true (exact) estimates is called an *ideal classification error in selection.* In our example, $\varepsilon_{ideal} = 0.0405 = \varepsilon_{t1}$.

It follows from the definition that $\varepsilon_{ideal} \leq \varepsilon_{true}$. In the case where the estimates are unbiased, most often $\varepsilon_{apparent} < \varepsilon_{ideal}$. For some randomly chosen validation sets, however, this inequality can be violated. The increase in the classification error due to non-ideal model selection

$$\Delta_{selection} = \varepsilon_{true} - \varepsilon_{ideal}$$

is called the *selection loss.*

6.5.2 An Effect of the Number of Variants

In classifier design, these three probabilities crop up all the time and are necessary in the analysis of the accuracy of feature selection, neural networks initialisation, architecture selection, etc. Therefore, in practice, one needs to know the relations between the errors considered and the parameters of a particular pattern-recognition problem to be solved.

Example 6. Figure 6.10 presents a scatter diagram of 200 pairs of the leaving-one-out estimate, $\hat{\varepsilon}$, of the generalisation error of the linear Fisher DF (design set size 25 + 25 = 50 vectors) and the estimate of the conditional PMC obtained on the independent test set (Nt = 500 vectors). The estimates were calculated using 200 independent randomly chosen four-variate subsets of features, selected from a pool of 19 features. Real-world medical data was used.

The leaving-one-out estimate, $\hat{\varepsilon}$, and the conditional PMC rank the feature subsets in different ways. In this example, the feature subset 63 is the best among all 200 subsets according to the leaving-one-out estimate: it results in the smallest error estimate $\hat{\varepsilon}_{63} = 0.14 = \varepsilon_{apparent}$. The test set estimate indicates differently: feature subset 152 is best, with the classification error $\varepsilon_{152} = 0.208 = \varepsilon_{ideal}$. If one selects the subset 63, then its conditional PMC would be $\varepsilon_{63} = 0.228 = \varepsilon_{true}$. The inaccurate feature subset selection increases the classification error from 0.208 to 0.228 ($\Delta_{selection} = 0.02$).

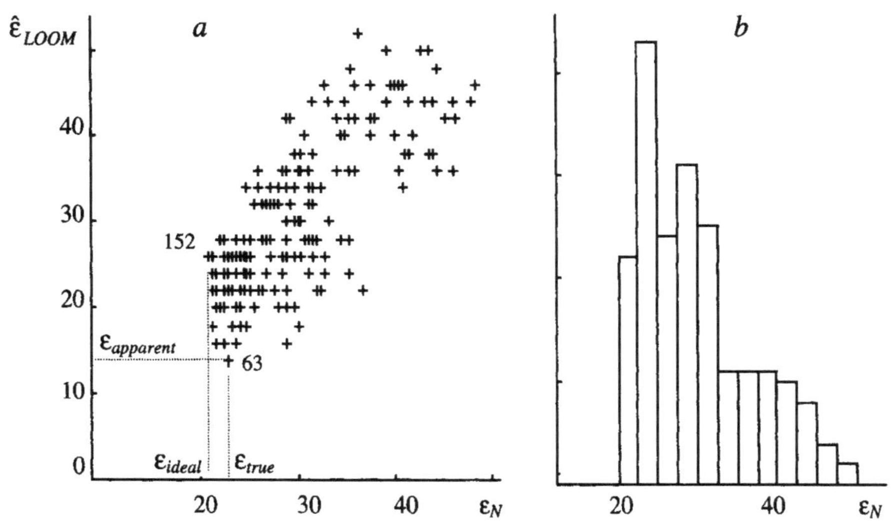

Fig. 6.10. The scatter diagram (a) and a histogram (b) of the distribution of 200 values of the conditional PMC, ε_N, and its leaving-one-out estimates, $\hat{\varepsilon}_{LOOM}$, evaluated for 200 randomly chosen subsets of features; $n = 19$, $r = 4$.

In order to analyse the behaviour of quantities $\Delta_{selection}$, ε_{true}, ε_{ideal} and $\varepsilon_{apparent}$ analytically, one needs to make assumptions that the classifiers (the variants of the classification algorithm or the feature subsets) are chosen randomly. Furthermore, one can assume the estimates $\hat{\varepsilon}_1$, $\hat{\varepsilon}_2$, $\hat{\varepsilon}_3$, ... and the true probabilities of misclassification ε_1, ε_2, ε_3, ... to be *independent* random variables with a *known* joint distribution density function $f(\hat{\varepsilon}_j, \varepsilon_j)$. Then, from m randomly chosen pairs $(\varepsilon_{j1}, \hat{\varepsilon}_{j1})$, $(\varepsilon_{j2}, \hat{\varepsilon}_{j2})$, ..., $(\varepsilon_{jm}, \hat{\varepsilon}_{jm})$, one selects two of the best variants (the first time according to $\hat{\varepsilon}_j$ and the second time according to ε_j) and analyses the expected behaviour of ε_{true}, ε_{idea}, $\varepsilon_{apparent}$ and $\Delta_{selection}$.

Let a distribution density $p(\hat{\varepsilon}_j, \varepsilon_j)$ of bi-variate vector $(\hat{\varepsilon}_j, \varepsilon_j)$ be known. This bi-variate density can be expressed as a product: $p(\hat{\varepsilon}_j, \varepsilon_j) = p(\hat{\varepsilon}_j | \varepsilon_j)\, p(\varepsilon_j)$. We will derive analytical expressions for distribution densities and the statistical moments of ε_{true}, ε_{ideal} and $\varepsilon_{apparent}$. Utilisation of the *theory of the extremes* provides a distribution density of ε_{ideal} that can be expressed as

$$p_{ideal}(\varepsilon) = m(1-P_{\varepsilon}(\varepsilon))^{m-1}\, p(\varepsilon), \tag{6.40}$$

where $p(\varepsilon)$ is the unconditional distribution density of accurate performance values in different models and $P_{\varepsilon}(a) = \int_{-\infty}^{a} p(\varepsilon)d\varepsilon$ is a cumulative distribution function of ε.

Similarly, for the apparent error it can be written

$$p(\varepsilon_{apparent}) = m(1-P_{\hat{\varepsilon}}(\hat{\varepsilon}))^{m-1}\, p(\hat{\varepsilon}) = p_{apparent}(\hat{\varepsilon}), \tag{6.41}$$

where $p(\hat{\varepsilon})$ is the unconditional distribution density of estimates $p(\hat{\varepsilon}) = \int_{0}^{1} p(\hat{\varepsilon}|\varepsilon)p(\varepsilon)d\varepsilon$ and $P_{\hat{\varepsilon}}(a) = \int_{-\infty}^{a} p(\hat{\varepsilon})d\hat{\varepsilon}$ is a cumulative distribution function of the estimate $\hat{\varepsilon}$.

The probability density of ε_{true} is

$$p_{true}(\varepsilon) = \int_{0}^{1} p(\varepsilon|\hat{\varepsilon})\, p_{apparent}(\hat{\varepsilon})d\hat{\varepsilon}, \tag{6.42}$$

where $p(\varepsilon|\hat{\varepsilon}) = p(\hat{\varepsilon}|\varepsilon)\, p(\varepsilon)/p(\hat{\varepsilon})$.

In order to use the above equations to find the expected values of ε_{true}, ε_{ideal} and $\varepsilon_{apparent}$ one needs to specify the joint distribution density function $f(\hat{\varepsilon}_j, \varepsilon_j)$.

The joint density will be defined as a product of conditional $p(\hat{\varepsilon}_j \mid \varepsilon_j)$ and unconditional $p(\varepsilon_j)$ densities:

$$p(\hat{\varepsilon}_j, \varepsilon_j) = p(\hat{\varepsilon}_j \mid \varepsilon_j)\, p(\varepsilon_j).$$

Analysis of artificially generated and real data indicates that, in the case where the original n variables are reasonably selected, often a distribution density $p(\varepsilon_j)$ of the PMC of the various subsets of variables is unimodal, bounded from the left and from the right. If good informative variables dominate over the bad ones the distribution density function has *positive asymmetry* (as in Figure 6.10*b*). If bad uninformative variables dominate over the good ones, the distribution of the values of PMC has *negative asymmetry*. Therefore, we will approximate the unconditional distribution density $p(\varepsilon_j)$ by that of the Generalised Beta distribution (Pearson I type)

$$p(\varepsilon_j) = k_\varepsilon (\varepsilon_j - \varepsilon_{min})^{\gamma-1} (\varepsilon_{max} - \varepsilon_j)^{\eta-1}, \tag{6.43}$$

where k_ε is a normalising constant, parameters ε_{min}, ε_{max} control the minimal and maximal values of ε_j, and γ, η control the shape of the density function $p(\varepsilon_j)$.

The sample based hold-out error counting estimate of the classification error is conditionally a binomial random variable. Let us consider a *hypothetical situation* where we assume that for the estimation of the classification performance of m variants one can have m *different* independent virtual validation sets of size N^*. Then, the conditional distribution $p(\hat{\varepsilon}_j \mid \varepsilon_j)$ is binomial, i.e. probability

$$P(\hat{\varepsilon}_j = \frac{i}{N^*} \mid \varepsilon_j) = C_{N^*}^{i} (\varepsilon_j)^i (1-\varepsilon_j)^{N^*-i}. \tag{6.44}$$

Note, in practice, one utilises only one validation set of size Nv vectors. For that reason, the parameter N^* characterises the evaluation accuracy of the models performance. It is an *effective validation set size*. In principle, the distribution model (6.44) can be applied when the error counting performance estimate or some other performance measure (e.g. divergence, saliency, entropy, etc) is used to evaluate quality of the competing models.

The use of Equations (6.43) and (6.44) in (6.40), (6.41) and (6.42) allows one to calculate the expected values of ε_{true}, ε_{ideal} and $\varepsilon_{apparent}$ by numerical methods. In Table 6.1, we present integration results for the Generalised Beta – Binomial distribution model. We calculated the expected values of the true and apparent error rates for six m values (m is the number of models compared empirically). Here the distribution $p(\varepsilon_j)$ was supposed to be a symmetrical Generalised Beta distribution density with $\gamma = \eta = 4.0$ and $\varepsilon_{min} = 0.01$, $\varepsilon_{max} = 0.2$ (the upper part of Table 6.1), or $\varepsilon_{min} = 0.1$, $\varepsilon_{max} = 0.3$ (the lower part). The conditional distribution $p(\hat{\varepsilon}_j \mid \varepsilon_j)$ is Binomial with the effective virtual set size N^*. Values for $N^* = \infty$ correspond to ε_{ideal}, the expected value of the ideal error rate.

While inspecting Table 6.1, one can notice that the expected values $\bar{\varepsilon}_{true}$ and $\bar{\varepsilon}_{apparent}$ decrease with an increase in N^*. Both of the values approach ε_{ideal}. The expected difference $B_{selection} = \bar{\varepsilon}_{true} - \bar{\varepsilon}_{apparent}$, however, increases with N^*.

Table 6.1. The expected values of the true (the left column for each sample size) and apparent (the right column) error rates in the best model selection (from Raudys, 1981).

$m \backslash N^*$	50		100		200		500		∞
5	.083	.047	.078	.056	.074	.062	.071	.065	.068
10	.076	.032	.069	.043	.064	.050	.060	.054	.057
50	.066	.010	.056	.022	.049	.030	.044	.036	.040
100	.063	.005	.052	.016	.044	.024	.039	.030	.034
500	.061	.000	.046	.006	.037	.014	.031	.021	.026
10^6	.061	.000	.042	.000	.042	.000	.029	.000	.010
5	.180	.127	.175	.141	.170	.150	.165	.156	.161
10	.174	.106	.168	.124	.161	.135	.155	.143	.150
50	.165	.069	.155	.094	.147	.110	.139	.122	.131
100	.162	.057	.152	.084	.143	.101	.135	.114	.126
500	.157	.035	.145	.065	.136	.085	.128	.101	.117
10^6	.149	.000	.132	.014	.123	.041	.115	.067	.100

Similar selection accuracy evaluations can be drawn from the experimental data. Let a number of models investigated experimentally be M. Let we have a set of M bi-variate vectors $(\varepsilon_{j1}, \hat{\varepsilon}_{j1})$, $(\varepsilon_{j2}, \hat{\varepsilon}_{j2})$, ..., $(\varepsilon_{jm}, \hat{\varepsilon}_{jm})$ and want to evaluate accuracy characteristics when the best variant is selected from m randomly chosen models ($m << M$). We investigate all possible collections composed of m models selected from a pool of M models. A number of such collections is

$$J = C_M^m = \frac{M!}{(M-m)!m!}.$$

We consider the model selection characteristics ε_{true}, ε_{ideal} and $\varepsilon_{apparent}$ for each collection. An original algorithm developed by Pikelis (Appendix 4) can be utilised to find mean values and variances of ε_{true}, ε_{ideal} and $\varepsilon_{apparent}$ calculated for J possible collections produced from M bi-variate vectors $(\varepsilon_{j1}, \hat{\varepsilon}_{j1})$, $(\varepsilon_{j2}, \hat{\varepsilon}_{j2})$, ..., $(\varepsilon_{jm}, \hat{\varepsilon}_{jm})$ of the experimental data.

Example 7. In Figure. 6.11, graphs of dependencies of average values of $\varepsilon_{apparent}$, ε_{true} and ε_{ideal} on the size of the collection, m_i (m_i = 2, 3, 5, 10, 20, 50 and 100) are presented. The mean values were calculated from $M = 1000$ bi-variate vectors $(\varepsilon_{ti}, \hat{\varepsilon}_{vi})$ obtained for 1000 randomly selected four-variate subsets of the features from the data considered in Example 6 at the start of Section 6.5.2 (in Figure 6.10*a* we only have 200 bi-variate vectors selected from 1000).

Theoretical values and the experimental graphs show that both the *selection loss*, $\Delta_{selection}$, and the *selection bias*, $B_{selection}$, become large if the effective validation set size, N^*, is small and the number of models, *m*, is large. Therefore, if the number of variants (models) *m* is large and N^* is small, the apparent error of selection (the error estimate of the best variant) can become particularly optimistically biased and can provide little information in determining the real performance of the classification system. It is important to realise that each single performance estimate, $\hat{\varepsilon}_j$, can be unbiased, however, the *estimate of the best variant is biased.*

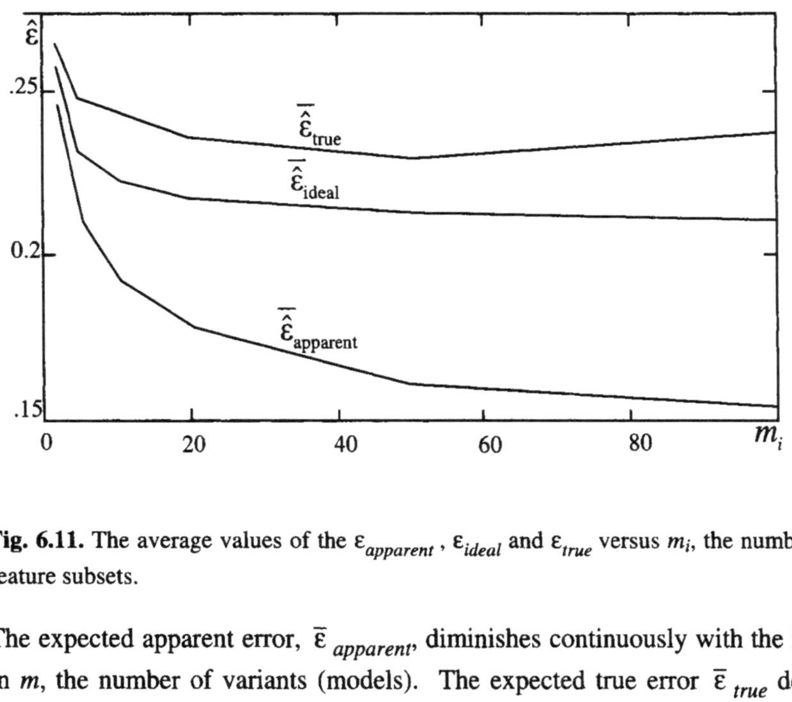

Fig. 6.11. The average values of the $\varepsilon_{apparent}$, ε_{ideal} and ε_{true} versus m_i, the number of the feature subsets.

The expected apparent error, $\bar{\varepsilon}_{apparent}$, diminishes continuously with the increase in *m*, the number of variants (models). The expected true error $\bar{\varepsilon}_{true}$ decreases with *m* at first, however, later it saturates and stops decreasing. An important conclusion follows: in finite validation set size case, it is not worth increasing the number of models investigated. It means one does not need to use sophisticated feature or ANN architecture selection methods, if the performance estimation accuracy is low.

Thus, it is reasonable to fix m_{max}, a maximal number of models, and economise on the computing time when the accuracy of estimates $\hat{\varepsilon}_1, \hat{\varepsilon}_2, \hat{\varepsilon}_3, \ldots$ is low. The last conclusion is based on the assumption that the distribution density $f(\varepsilon_j)$ is fixed *a priori* and does not change practically with an increase in *m*.

6.5.3 Evaluation of the Bias

Previous theoretical considerations about accuracy of the model selection process can help in understanding the accuracy problems in similar situations when one utilises certain inexact simplified performance evaluation methods instead of the exact classification error estimate. The theoretical considerations can be useful also when non-random model selection strategies (e.g., backward selection or pruning the network) are utilised instead of the random search.

In practice, the designer needs to know the difference $\Delta_{selection} = \varepsilon_{true} - \varepsilon_{ideal}$, the loss in the model selection, and $B_{selection} = \varepsilon_{true} - \varepsilon_{apparent}$, the selection bias, or to determine a rational estimate of the maximal number of models m_{max} to be compared experimentally. To solve these tasks one needs to know the distribution densities, $f(\hat{\varepsilon}_j | \varepsilon_j)$ and $f(\varepsilon_j)$.

Our notation "the effective validation size" is a conditional concept used in the previous subsection's formulation of the problem. In theoretical analysis, N^* is the size of m *independent virtual random validation sets* utilised to obtain estimates $\hat{\varepsilon}_1, \hat{\varepsilon}_2, \hat{\varepsilon}_3, ..., \hat{\varepsilon}_m$. While analysing theoretically it was supposed that different validation sets were utilised to obtain the estimates $\hat{\varepsilon}_1, \hat{\varepsilon}_2, \hat{\varepsilon}_3, ..., \hat{\varepsilon}_m$. In actual fact, we use a single validation set. Often other performance measures (such as the divergence, entropic loss or saliency) can be applied instead of the validation set error estimates. Thus, the size of the effective validation set size, N^*, depends on the method used to evaluate performance, the sample size used to obtain the estimates $\hat{\varepsilon}_1, \hat{\varepsilon}_2, \hat{\varepsilon}_3, ..., \hat{\varepsilon}_m$, the pattern recognition problem and a set of models compared experimentally. In practice this accuracy is also unknown.

Without some *additional information* it is impossible to know N^* before the experimentation. In order to evaluate $B_{selection}$ or the number m_{max} precisely, one needs to have a very large test set. Such a situation is unrealistic: one does not have to deal with problems of accuracy in very large test set size cases. We will consider a possible modus operandi when one does not have the test set and use some hypothetical assumptions (hypotheses) about the data.

Let us have M models to be compared. We have some "validation" set (it can be the design set if the leaving-one-out method is used) to estimate the performances of all M competing models.

Procedure 1.

1. Add spherical or coloured noise (see Section 4.6.4.3) to the validation set vectors and form a very large *pseudo-general population* (PGP). From this population, select a random *pseudo-validation set* (PVS) of the size Nv as before in model selection with the error counting estimates, and use both PVS and PGP to produce a set of pseudo-estimates $(\hat{\varepsilon}_1^*, \varepsilon_1^*), (\hat{\varepsilon}_2^*, \varepsilon_2^*), ..., (\hat{\varepsilon}_M^*, \varepsilon_M^*)$. While generating the PGP we assume that the bivariate distribution densities $f(\hat{\varepsilon}, \varepsilon)$ of the

true and pseudo-general populations are similar. This is in fact, our additional information about the data.

2. Subsequently use the pseudo-estimates $(\hat{\varepsilon}_1^*, \varepsilon_1^*), (\hat{\varepsilon}_2^*, \varepsilon_2^*), ..., (\hat{\varepsilon}_M^*, \varepsilon_M^*)$ and the Pikelis algorithm (Appendix 4) to evaluate the average values $\hat{\bar{\varepsilon}}_{apparent}$, $\hat{\bar{\varepsilon}}_{true}$, and $\hat{\bar{\varepsilon}}_{true} - \hat{\bar{\varepsilon}}_{apparent}$ for all $C_M^{m_i^*}$ possible collections of the vectors $(\hat{\varepsilon}_j^*, \varepsilon_j^*)$, say $m_i^* = 2, 5, 10, \ldots, M/5$.

3. Apply the standard statistical procedure to estimate the parameters ε_{min}, ε_{max}, γ, and η from the set $\varepsilon_1^*, \varepsilon_2^*, ..., \varepsilon_M^*$.

4. Select a set of the effective virtual validation set size N^*, say (Nv, $1.2Nv$, $1.4Nv$, …, $4.8Nv$, $5Nv$), and use Equations (6.43) and (6.44) in (6.40), (6.41) and (6.42) to calculate the expected values of ε_{true} and $\varepsilon_{apparent}$ for a number of selected values $m^*_i = 2, 5, 10, \ldots, M/5$ by numerical methods.

5. Select Nv which best fits the empirical differences $\hat{B}_{selection} = \hat{\bar{\varepsilon}}_{true} - \hat{\bar{\varepsilon}}_{apparent}$.

6. Calculate the difference of $B_{selection} = \varepsilon_{true} - \varepsilon_{apparent}$ for $m^*_i = M$ and Nv as determined in the previous step.

This procedure relies on an assumption that the PGP represents the designers problem sufficiently well.

Procedure 2.

Numerous simulation experiments show that it is reasonable to assume $3N < N^* < 5N$, when one uses error counting error estimates in the randomised best variant selection, where N is the number of vectors used to obtain the error estimates. For sketchy estimation of $B_{selection}$ and m_{max}, one can apply the data from Table 6.1 with $N^* = (3\div5)\, N$.

A rule of thumb.

For the error counting cross validation estimation use $B_{selection} = \alpha_s \sqrt{\hat{\varepsilon}(1-\hat{\varepsilon})/Nv}$, where coefficient α_s depends on similarity of the models (the set of features, architecture of ANN, etc.) compared and m, a number of models. For $m = 10 \div 20$ different models with similar classification errors use $\alpha_s = 1$.

Example 8. In the problem of classifying the lung noise data set (66-variate vectors from each of two classes), the training-set was composed of $N = 70 + 70 = 140$ randomly selected vectors, the validation set was composed of $Nv = 40 + 40 = 80$ randomly selected vectors. We utilised the integrated approach to design the linear classification rule and tested 19 CM structurisation models:

Conventional representation

1. No structurisation
2. Circular
3. Toeplitz
4. Tree
5. AR1
6. AR4
7. MA2
8. ARMA11
9. Additive noise

Block diagonal Representation

10. No structurisation
11. Circular
12. Toeplitz
13. Tree
14. AR1
15. AR4
16. MA2
17. ARMA11
18. Additive noise
19.Markov

Structured sample estimates were regularised using four values of regularisation parameter λ = 0, 0.05, 0.1, 0.2. Thus, M = 76 CM estimates were tested for the linear data transformation (decorrelation and scaling) and subsequent training of the SLP classifier. The validation set was used to stop the SLP training optimally. From 76 validation set estimates, we found that the best model is

the block diagonal representation + the tree dependence model and $\lambda = 0.05$.

with apparent error $\hat{\varepsilon} = 0.0875$. To evaluate the bias $B_{selection}$, the Procedure 1 was initially used. 2-*NN* directed noise was added to the validation set and PGP was obtained. The distribution of vectors $(\hat{\varepsilon}_1^*, \varepsilon_1^*), (\hat{\varepsilon}_2^*, \varepsilon_2^*), ..., (\hat{\varepsilon}_{76}^*, \varepsilon_{76}^*)$ is presented in Figure 6.12*a*.

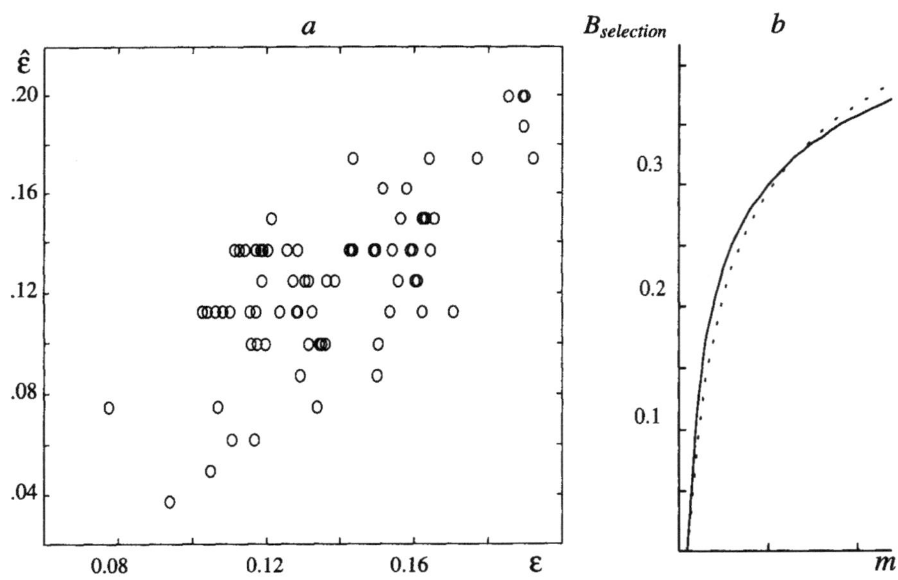

Fig. 6.12. *a)* distribution of the pseudo-validation and the pseudo-test errors, *b)* the bias $B_{selection} = \hat{\bar{\varepsilon}}_{true} - \hat{\bar{\varepsilon}}_{apparent}$ versus the number of models m_{max}: dots – the experimental estimate, solid – the theoretical estimate.

The model selection bias evaluated by utilising the Pikelis algorithm is presented in Figure 6.1*b* (the dotted curve) and the best theoretical fit was obtained for $N^* = 157$ and parameters $\varepsilon_{min} = 0.034$, $\varepsilon_{max} = 0.748$, $\gamma = 14.5$, and $\eta = 86$. As a result, the estimate of the bias was calculated analytically: for $M = 76$ models compared, $B_{selection} \approx 0.045$. Thus, the performance estimate of the model

"the block diagonal representation + the tree dependence model and $\lambda = 0.05$"

$$\hat{\hat{\varepsilon}}_{true} = \hat{\varepsilon} + B_{selection} = 0.0875 + 0.045 \approx 0.12.$$

The rough bias evaluation of Procedure 2 for $Nv = 200$, $\varepsilon_{min} = 0.1$ and the number of variants $M = 100$ resulted in $B_{selection} = 0.044 - 0.024 = 0.02$ (from Table 6.1).

The rule of thumb gives $B_{selection} \approx \sqrt{0.12(1-0.12)/80} = 0.035$.

One needs to have in mind that both estimates rely on the assumptions made and can serve only as a *guide in evaluating the selection bias* $B_{selection}$. Nevertheless, the addition of term $B_{selection}$ to $\varepsilon_{apparent} = \min\{\hat{\varepsilon}_1, \hat{\varepsilon}_2, \hat{\varepsilon}_3, ..., \hat{\varepsilon}_M\}$ serves as an indicator of the adaptation to the validation set. At the same time one needs to remember that the new estimate $\varepsilon_{apparent} + B_{selection}$ is based on a random validation set. Therefore it remains a random variable. If the error counting estimates are used, its variance can be evaluated from Equations (6.27), (6.31), (6.32) or (6.34).

6.6 Additional Bibliographical Remarks

We have reviewed a number of tools and the performance measures which can be useful in selecting the best model, the feature system, and the architecture of the neural network. In order to select the best model correctly we need to use unbiased performance estimates. In practice, however, all performance estimates are inexact. Therefore, while selecting the best model we adapt to the validation set. Consequently, the validation set begins to serve as an additional training-set. In spite of the fact that we use unbiased estimates to evaluate performance of each competing variant, we obtain additional bias. We called it the bias in model selection.

That the partitioning of the classification error estimation methods depends on: the method used to split the design set into the training and validation sets and the type of pattern error function used to determine the contribution of each observation in the aggregate estimation function was suggested by Raudys and Vaitukaitis (1984). The leave-one-out method was suggested by Brailovskij (1964) and popularised by Lachenbruch and Mickey (1968). The fast calculation schemes for standard linear and quadratic classifiers were proposed by Lachenbruch and Mickey (1968) and Fukunaga and Kessel (1971). The first version of the bootstrap estimation approach belongs to Pinsker (1973) and the bootstrap error estimate was formalised by Efron (1982). The recommendation about choosing the number of bootstrap samples $r \geq 20$ and the variance of the bootstrap estimate comes from Raudys (1988).

Glick (1978) introduced the smoothed modification of the error counting estimate. Fukunaga and Kessel (1973) suggested another modification known as the posterior probability estimate that allows one to use unlabeled test-set observation vectors. Lachenbruch and Mickey (1968) suggested parametric and the pseudo-parametric classification error estimates $\hat{\varepsilon}_D$, $\hat{\varepsilon}_{DS}$, PP.

Bryant and Guseman (1979) introduced the distance criterion (6.18) for the linear feature extraction. Two non-linear feature mapping techniques based on the criteria (6.19) and (6.20) are due to Sammon (1969) and Niemann (1980). The optimal discriminant set of vectors was suggested by Foley and Sammon (1975).

The saliency was introduced by Le Cun *et al.* (1990). The entropic loss (6.24) was considered in Vajda (1970) and Amari and Murata (1993), while the heuristic measure (6.26) by Yacoub and Bennani (1997). Other examples of the feature performance measures utilised in the ANN design are a relevance of single weights by Mozer and Smolensky (1989), an estimated sensitivity by Karnin (1990), a saliency by Cibas *et al.* (1996). Utilisation of the MLP for linear and non-linear feature extraction was suggested by Bourland and Kamp (1988).

The symmetry between expectations of the expected and resubstitution errors was shown in Raudys (1973), Pivoriunas and Raudys (1978) and Amari and Murata (1993). The estimate (6.33) of the asymptotic PMC based on a symmetry of the expected and resubstitution errors was recommended by Raudys (1973, 1976). For more information about error estimation methods see McLachlan (1992), Toussaint (1974) and Hand (1986). Useful reviews of feature extraction and selection from Young and Calvert (1974, Chapter 6), Gelsema and Eden (1980), McKay and Campbell (1982*ab*), Devijver and Kittler (1982), Siadliecki, Siadlecka and Sklansky (1988), Mao and Jain (1995), Jain and Zongker (1997), Somol *et al.* (1999), Jain, Duin and Mao (2000) are recommended reading.

The optimal dimensionality problem for pattern classification was first analysed by Allays (1966), Hughes (1965) and Lbov (1966). Relations between the optimal dimensionality and the training-set size for the additive noise model (6.37) were considered by Jain and Waller (1978). A procedure to smooth the empirical curve of the estimate of the generalisation error versus the number of features was proposed in Raudys (1979*b*).

Estes (1965) was the first to pay attention to the adaptation bias in feature selection. The model selection bias was analysed in Meshalkin (1977), Raudys (1979*a*, 1981, 1987), Raudys and Pikelis (1982) and Serdobolskij (1983*b*). The algorithm to estimate the bias in the best variant selection is from Pikelis (1991). The apparent, ideal and true errors in selection were introduced in Raudys (1981). For a specific model of distribution of $f(\hat{\varepsilon}, \varepsilon)$ expected values of these types of classification error were obtained and tabulated. The bias evaluation Procedure 1 is from Raudys, Saudargiene and Povilonis (2000).

Appendices

A.1 Elements of Matrix Algebra

Definitions of vectors and matrices.

$$X = \begin{bmatrix} x_1 \\ x_2 \\ \\ x_n \end{bmatrix}$$ is an n-variate vector column, where $x_1, x_2, \ldots, x_n$ are components of X.

$\mathbf{Z} = (x_1, x_2, \ldots, x_n)$ is an n-variate vector row, $\mathbf{Z} = X^T$; ^{T} denotes a transpose operation; and n is called a dimensionality of the vectors X and $\mathbf{Z}$.

$\mathbf{A} = ((a_{ij})), (i, j = 1, 2, \ldots, n)$ is an $n \times n$ quadratic matrix, a_{ij} are the elements of matrix $\mathbf{A}$. If $a_{ij} = a_{ji}$, the matrix $\mathbf{A}$ is symmetric.

Multiplication of matrices. Let $\mathbf{B} = ((b_{ij})), (i, j = 1, 2, \ldots, n)$ be another $n \times n$ quadratic matrix. Then $\mathbf{AB} = \mathbf{C} = ((c_{ij}))$, is also an $n \times n$ quadratic matrix with elements $c_{ij} = \sum_{s=1}^{n} a_{is} b_{sj}$. If $Y = (y_1, y_2, \ldots, y_n)^T$ is a n-variate vector column,

$$Y^T\mathbf{A}X = \sum_{j=1}^{n}\sum_{i=1}^{n} a_{ij} y_i x_j .$$

A hyperplane is $V^TX + v_0 = 0$, where V is a vector column.

A distance between a vector and the hyperplane $V^TX + v_0 = 0$ is $H = \dfrac{|V^TX + v_0|}{\sqrt{V^TV}}$.

Orthogonal matrices. If $Y^TX = 0$, the vectors Y and X are said to be orthogonal. If, in addition, $Y^TY = 1$ and $X^TX = 1$, the vectors Y and X are said to be orthonormal. A quadratic matrix $\mathbf{T}$ is said to be orthogonal if $\mathbf{TT}^T = \mathbf{D} = ((d_{ij}))$

(diagonal matrix). In the diagonal matrix **D**, $d_{ij} = 0$ if $j \neq i$. If all $d_{ii} > 0$, the matrix **D** is positively defined. Its determinant det(**D**)= $\prod_{i=1}^{n} d_{ii} > 0$. If $\mathbf{T}\mathbf{T}^T = \mathbf{I}_n$ (the identity matrix), the matrix **T** is said to be orthonormal. The identity matrix has ones on its diagonal, and zeros outside the diagonal. For orthonormal matrix **T** one can write $\mathbf{T}\mathbf{T}^T = \mathbf{T}^T\mathbf{T} = \mathbf{I}_n$.

Singular value decomposition. The symmetric matrix **A** can be decomposed into a product: $\mathbf{A} = \mathbf{T}\,\mathbf{D}\,\mathbf{T}^T$, where **T** is an orthonormal $n \times n$ matrix such that

$$\mathbf{T}^T\mathbf{A}\mathbf{T} = \mathbf{D} = \begin{bmatrix} d_1 & 0 & \dots & 0 \\ 0 & d_2 & \dots & 0 \\ \dots & \dots & \dots & \dots \\ 0 & 0 & \dots & d_n \end{bmatrix}. \qquad \text{(A1.1)}$$

Matrix **T** is called an eigenvectors matrix and diagonal elements of matrix **D** are called eigenvalues of matrix **A**. The matrix **A** is positively defined if all $d_i > 0$.

Inverse of the symmetric quadratic matrix. Let **B** be a quadratic positively defined matrix, such that **BA** = **AB** = **I**. Then **B** is called an inverse of **A** and denoted by $\mathbf{B} = \mathbf{A}^{-1}$. The representation (A1.1) shows that

$$\mathbf{A}^{-1} = (\mathbf{T}\,\mathbf{D}\,\mathbf{T}^T)^{-1} = (\mathbf{T}^T)^{-1}\mathbf{D}^{-1}\mathbf{T}^{-1} = \mathbf{T}\,\mathbf{D}^{-1}\mathbf{T}^T. \qquad \text{(A1.2)}$$

Pseudo-inversion. If n-r eigenvalues of matrix **A** are equal to zero, the matrix **A** is not positively defined. Its determinant is equal to zero. Let us write the diagonal matrix **D** in a block layout $\mathbf{D} = \begin{bmatrix} \mathbf{d} & 0 \\ 0 & 0 \end{bmatrix}$ in (A1.1), where **d** is an $r \times r$ diagonal matrix composed from non-zero values of **D**. Thus, we can rewrite Equation (A1.1) in a block layout

$$\mathbf{T}^T\mathbf{A}\mathbf{T} = [\mathbf{T}_1\ \mathbf{T}_2]^T\mathbf{A}\,[\mathbf{T}_1\ \mathbf{T}_2] = \begin{bmatrix} \mathbf{d} & 0 \\ 0 & 0 \end{bmatrix}, \qquad \text{(A1.3)}$$

where we have split the orthogonal matrix $\mathbf{T} = [\mathbf{T}_1\ \mathbf{T}_2]$ into $n \times r$ matrix $\mathbf{T}_1$ and $n \times (n\text{-}r)$ matrix $\mathbf{T}_2$. Then the pseudo-inverse of matrix **A**

$$\mathbf{A}^{+} = \mathbf{T}\begin{bmatrix} \mathbf{d}^{-1} & 0 \\ 0 & 0 \end{bmatrix}\mathbf{T}^T = [\mathbf{T}_1\ \mathbf{T}_2]\begin{bmatrix} \mathbf{d}^{-1} & 0 \\ 0 & 0 \end{bmatrix}[\,\mathbf{T}_1\ \mathbf{T}_2]^T = \mathbf{T}_1\,\mathbf{d}^{-1}\,\mathbf{T}_1^T. \qquad \text{(A1.4)}$$

A.2 The First Order Tree Type Dependence Model

The probability density function of the random vector $X = (x_1, x_2, ..., x_n)$ having the first order tree type dependence between the variables can be written in the following form:

$$p(x_1, x_2, ..., x_n) = \prod_{j=1}^{n} p(x_j | x_{m_j}) \quad (0 \leq m_j \leq n) \tag{A2.1}$$

where a sequence $m_2, ..., m_n$ constitutes a *graph of connections,* $\mathbf{m}$ (an unknown permutation of the integers 1, 2, ..., n), and $p(x_i | x_0)$, by definition, is equal to $p(x_i)$. In a general case, the covariance matrix has $n \times n$ non-zero elements. An inverse of this matrix Σ^{-1} that has to be used in the classifier design, however, has only $2n$-1 diferent non-zero elements. It is a result of the assumption that each component of the vector X depends directly on only one another component.

To depict the dependence relations graphically, the variable is represented by a point on the plane, and if x_i and x_j are two variables such that $j = m_i$, they will be joined by an arrow pointing from x_j to x_i. Figure A2.1 shows an example of a dependence tree with graph $\mathbf{m} = (m_2, m_3, m_4, m_5, m_6) = (1, 2, 2, 2, 5)$.

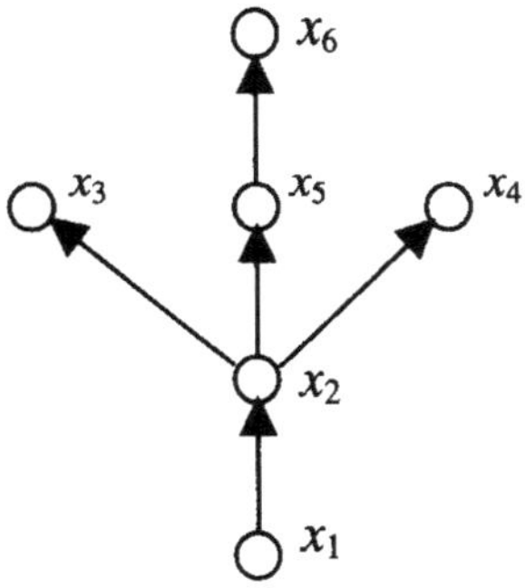

$$p(X) = p(x_1)\, p(x_2|x_1)\, p(x_3|x_2) p(x_4|x_2) p(x_5|x_2) p(x_6|x_5).$$

Fig. A2.1. An example of the first order dependence tree.

We present an analytical expression of the density for the multivariate Gaussian case. The conditional density function for two Gaussian distributed variables is

$$p(x_i | x_j) = N(x_i\,, m_i + (x_j - m_j)\, \sigma_{jj}^{-1} \sigma_{ij}\,,\ \sigma_{ii} - \sigma_{jj}^{-1} \sigma_{ij}^{2}) \tag{A2.2}$$

where σ_{ij} is an element of the covariance matrix Σ.

Using (A2.2) in (A2.1) yields a simple analytical expression for the joint probability density function

$$p(x_1, x_2, ..., x_n) = \prod_{j=1}^{n} N(x_j, m_j + (x_{m_j} - m_{m_j})\, \sigma^{-1}_{m_j m_j} \sigma_{j m_j}, \sigma_{jj} - \sigma^{-1}_{m_j m_j} \sigma^2_{j m_j}) =$$

$$\frac{1}{(2\pi)^{n/2}} \prod_{j=1}^{n} (\sigma_{jj} - \sigma^{-1}_{m_j m_j} \sigma^2_{j m_j})^{-1/2}$$

$$\exp\left(-\frac{1}{2} \sum_{j=1}^{n} \frac{[(x_j - m_j) - (x_{mj} - m_{mj})\sigma^{-1}_{mjmj}\sigma_{jmj}]^2}{\sigma_{jj} - \sigma^{-1}_{mjmj}\sigma^2_{jmj}} \right) \quad \text{(A2.3)}$$

We require that the variables $x_1, x_2, ..., x_n$ be ranked in such a way that $m_j < j$, $j = 2, 3, ..., n$. Then density function (A2.3) may be written in the following form

$$p(x_1, x_2, ..., x_n) = N(\boldsymbol{X}, \boldsymbol{M}, \Sigma),$$

where

$$\Sigma^{-1} = (\mathbf{C}^T\mathbf{C}), \qquad \mathbf{C} = ((c_{ij})), \quad \text{(A2.4)}$$

$$c_{ij} = \begin{cases} \dfrac{1}{\sqrt{\sigma_{ii}(1 - r^2_{im_i})}} & \text{if} \quad j = i \\[2ex] \dfrac{-r_{im_i}}{\sqrt{\sigma_{m_i m_i}(1 - r^2_{im_i})}} & \text{if} \quad j = m_i \\[2ex] 0 \quad \text{if} \quad j = i \quad \text{and} \quad j \neq m_i \end{cases} \quad \text{(A2.5)}$$

$$r_{ij} = \frac{\sigma_{ij}}{\sqrt{\sigma_{jj}\sigma_{ii}}}.$$

Example. Let $\sigma_{21} = 0.7$; $\sigma_{32} = -0.3$; $\sigma_{42} = 0.4$; $\sigma_{52} = 0.2$; $\sigma_{65} = -0.6$, and all variances $\sigma_{11} = \sigma_{22} = \sigma_{33} = \sigma_{44} = \sigma_{55} = \sigma_{66} = 1$. Then

$$\mathbf{C} = \begin{bmatrix} 1 & 0 & 0 & 0 & 0 & 0 \\ -0.9802 & 1.4003 & 0 & 0 & 0 & 0 \\ 0 & 0.3145 & 1.0483 & 0 & 0 & 0 \\ 0 & -0.4364 & 0 & 1.0911 & 0 & 0 \\ 0 & -0.2041 & 0 & 0 & 1.0206 & 0 \\ 0 & 0 & 0 & 0 & 0.7500 & 1.2500 \end{bmatrix},$$

$$\Sigma^{-1} = \begin{bmatrix} 1.9608 & -1.3725 & 0 & 0 & 0 & 0 \\ -1.3725 & 2.2918 & 0.3297 & -0.4762 & -0.2083 & 0 \\ 0 & 0.3297 & 1.0989 & 0 & 0 & 0 \\ 0 & -0.4762 & 0 & 1.1905 & 0 & 0 \\ 0 & -0.2083 & 0 & 0 & 1.6042 & 0.9375 \\ 0 & 0 & 0 & 0 & 0.9375 & 1.5625 \end{bmatrix}, \text{ and}$$

$$\Sigma = \begin{bmatrix} 1 & 0.700 & -0.210 & 0.280 & 0.140 & -0.084 \\ 0.700 & 1 & -0.300 & 0.400 & 0.200 & -0.120 \\ -0.210 & -0.300 & 1 & -0.120 & -0.06 & 0.0360 \\ 0.280 & 0.400 & -0.120 & 1 & 0.080 & -0.048 \\ 0.140 & 0.200 & -0.06 & 0.080 & 1 & -0.600 \\ -0.084 & -0.120 & 0.0360 & -0.048 & -0.600 & 1 \end{bmatrix}.$$

When the graph $\mathbf{m} = (m_2, \ldots, m_n)$ is known, we estimate the inverse covariance matrix from the sample covariance matrix as $\hat{\Sigma}^{-1} = \hat{C}^T \hat{C}$, where $\hat{C}$ is determined by Equation (A2.5) with the elements σ_{ij} substituted by their corresponding sample estimates.

To estimate the graph $\mathbf{m} = (m_2, m_3, \ldots, m_n)$, it is suggested that one uses a stepwise algorithm developed by Kruskal (1956) for the construction of trees of maximum total branch weight. Let $\{|\hat{r}_{12}|, |\hat{r}_{13}|, |\hat{r}_{14}|, \ldots, |\hat{r}_{n-1\ n}|\}$ be the absolute values of the sample correlation coefficients between the variables. Then, the first step is to select a branch with the greatest weight $|\hat{r}_{st}|$, while the i-th step ($2 \le i \le n$-1) is to choose a branch with the greatest weight $|\hat{r}_{vu}|$ that is different from all the branches selected during the previous steps and does not form a cycle with the previously selected branches. If the multivariate normal density may be represented by the branch $\mathbf{m}$ model, then the sample estimate $\hat{\mathbf{m}}$

of the graph asymptotically (as the sample size N_1, $N_2 \to \infty$ and the dimensionality $n \to \infty$) converges to the true graph **m**.

When the above model is used to design the linear discriminant function (for the two category case when it is assumed that $\Sigma_2 = \Sigma_1$) then one has to estimate $4n - 1$ parameters: $2n$ components of the mean vectors, n variances σ_{ii} and $n - 1$ covariances, as well as $n - 1$ numbers that compose the graph **m**.

A.3 Temporal Dependence Models

Let the components $x_1, x_2, ..., x_{n-1}, x_n$ of the multivariate vector be measurements differing in time or in space, and assume they are a stationary random process. Then the covariance matrix has a following structure

$$\Sigma = \begin{bmatrix} \delta_1 & \delta_2 & \delta_3 & \ldots & \delta_{n-1} & \delta_n \\ \delta_2 & \delta_1 & \delta_2 & \ldots & \delta_{n-2} & \delta_{n-1} \\ \delta_3 & \delta_2 & \delta_1 & \ldots & \delta_{n-3} & \delta_{n-2} \\ \ldots & \ldots & \ldots & \ldots & \ldots & \ldots \\ \delta_{n-1} & \delta_{n-2} & \delta_{n-3} & \ldots & \delta_1 & \delta_2 \\ \delta_n & \delta_{n-1} & \delta_{n-2} & \ldots & \delta_2 & \delta_1 \end{bmatrix}. \tag{A3.1}$$

We see only n parameters $\delta_1, \delta_2, \delta_3, ..., \delta_n$ that describe the dependence between the variables and have to be estimated from the training-set. Let $X_1, X_2, ..., X_N$ be N training-set vectors, $X_j = (x_{j1}, x_{j2}, ..., x_{jN})^T$. Then, the sample estimate

$$\hat{\delta}_l = \frac{1}{N(n-l)} \sum_{j=1}^{N} \sum_{t=1}^{n-l} (x_{jt} - \bar{x}_t)(x_{jt+l} - \bar{x}_t).$$

A number of special models, such as autoregression, moving average, ARMA, and circular, reduce the number of parameters even more.

In the *autoregression model*, we have $q + 1$ independent parameters, and here the dependence among variables is determined by the equation

$$x_t + a_1 x_{t-1} + \ldots + a_r x_{t-r} = v_t, \tag{A3.2}$$

where random variables v_t, $v_{t-1\ t}$, ... are supposed to be mutually independent and identically distributed $N(0, 1)$. In this model, the last p-r variables $x_r, x_{r+1}, ..., x_{n-1}$ are linearly dependent on the previous ones. The inverse covariance matrix has a simple form, and can be calculated analytically (Kligiene, 1977)

$$\Sigma^{-1} = \begin{pmatrix} \kappa_{11} & \dots & \kappa_{1r} & \kappa_r & 0 & \dots & 0 & 0 & 0 & \dots & 0 \\ \dots & \dots & \dots & \dots & \dots & \dots & \dots & \dots & \dots & \dots & \dots \\ \kappa_{r1} & \dots & \kappa_{rr} & \kappa_1 & 0 & \dots & 0 & 0 & 0 & \dots & 0 \\ \kappa_r & \dots & \kappa_1 & \kappa_0 & 0 & \dots & 0 & 0 & 0 & \dots & 0 \\ 0 & .. & 0 & 0 & \kappa_0 & \dots & 0 & 0 & 0 & \dots & 0 \\ \dots & \dots & \dots & \dots & \dots & \dots & \dots & \dots & \dots & \dots & \dots \\ 0 & \dots & 0 & 0 & 0 & \dots & \kappa_0 & 0 & 0 & \dots & 0 \\ 0 & \dots & 0 & 0 & 0 & \dots & 0 & \kappa_0 & \kappa_1 & \dots & \kappa_r \\ 0 & \dots & 0 & 0 & 0 & \dots & 0 & \kappa_1 & \kappa_{rr} & \dots & \kappa_{r1} \\ \dots & \dots & \dots & \dots & \dots & \dots & \dots & \dots & \dots & \dots & \dots \\ 0 & \dots & 0 & 0 & 0 & \dots & 0 & \kappa_r & \kappa_{1r} & \dots & \kappa_{11} \end{pmatrix}, \qquad \text{(A3.3)}$$

where $\kappa_l = \sum_{k=0}^{r-l} a_k a_{k+l}$, $\quad \kappa_{st} = \sum_{k=0}^{\min(s,t)-1} a_k a_{k+|s-t|}$, $\quad s, t = 1, 2, \dots, r.$

In the *moving average model*, we have $q + 1$ independent parameters, and here the dependence among variables is determined by the equation

$$x_t = \mu_t + b_0 v_t + b_1 v_{t-1} + \dots + b_q v_{t-q}, \qquad \text{(A3.4)}$$

where the variables v_t, v_{t-1}, ... are supposed to be mutually independent and identically distributed $N(0, 1)$. In this model, we have

$$\delta_{q+1} = \delta_{q+2} = \delta_{q+3} = \dots = \delta_n = 0; \; q < n.$$

The *circular* covariance matrix has $n/2$ independent parameters and has form

$$\Sigma = \sigma_0 \begin{pmatrix} 1 & \rho_1 & \rho_2 & \rho_3 & \cdots & \rho_2 & \rho_1 \\ \rho_1 & 1 & \rho_1 & \rho_2 & \cdots & \rho_3 & \rho_2 \\ \rho_2 & \rho_1 & 1 & \rho_1 & \cdots & \rho_4 & \rho_3 \\ \rho_3 & \rho_2 & \rho_1 & 1 & \cdots & \rho_5 & \rho_4 \\ \rho_4 & \rho_3 & \rho_2 & \rho_1 & \cdots & \rho_6 & \rho_5 \\ \cdots & \cdots & \cdots & \cdots & \cdots & \cdots & \cdots \\ \rho_1 & \rho_2 & \rho_3 & \rho_4 & \cdots & \rho_1 & 1 \end{pmatrix}. \qquad \text{(A3.5)}$$

This matrix can be transformed into a canonical form by means of the following orthonormal matrix $\mathbf{L} = ((l_{mn}))$ with elements

$$l_{ms} = \sqrt{n}\left(\cos\frac{2\pi}{n}(m-1)(s-1) + \sin\frac{2\pi}{n}(m-1)(s-1) \right), \tag{A3.6}$$

such that $\mathbf{L}^T\mathbf{\Sigma}\mathbf{L}=\begin{pmatrix} \sigma_1 & 0 & \dots & 0 \\ 0 & \sigma_2 & .. & 0 \\ \dots & \dots & \dots & \dots \\ 0 & 0 & \dots & \sigma_n \end{pmatrix}$.

Note, the transformation matrix **L** does not depend on **Σ**.

The model of the *additive noise* is typical to physical measurements of the same origin where all variables are influenced by the same systematic Gaussian error N(0, σ_1^2). The original and the inverse covariance matrices are determined only by two parameters:

$$\mathbf{\Sigma} = \begin{pmatrix} \sigma_1^2+\sigma_2^2 & \sigma_1^2 & \sigma_1^2 & \dots & \sigma_1^2 \\ \sigma_1^2 & \sigma_1^2+\sigma_2^2 & \sigma_1^2 & \dots & \sigma_1^2 \\ \sigma_1^2 & \sigma_1^2 & \sigma_1^2+\sigma_2^2 & \dots & \sigma_1^2 \\ \dots & \dots & \dots & \dots & \dots \\ \sigma_1^2 & \sigma_1^2 & \sigma_1^2 & \dots & \sigma_1^2+\sigma_2^2 \end{pmatrix},$$

$$\mathbf{\Sigma}^{-1} = \begin{pmatrix} a & b & b & \dots & b \\ b & a & b & \dots & b \\ b & b & a & \dots & b \\ \dots & \dots & \dots & \dots & \dots \\ b & b & b & \dots & a \end{pmatrix}, \tag{A3.7}$$

where

$a = ((n-1)\sigma_1^2 + \sigma_2^2)/(\sigma_2^2(n\sigma_1^2+\sigma_2^2))$,

$b = -\sigma_1^2/(\sigma_2^2(n\sigma_2^2+\sigma_2^2))$.

A.4 Pikelis Algorithm for Evaluating Means and Variances of the True, Apparent and Ideal Errors in Model Selection

Let $\hat{\varepsilon}_{v1}, \hat{\varepsilon}_{v2}, ..., \hat{\varepsilon}_{vM}$ be M "inaccurate" (e.g. validation set) performance estimates, and $\hat{\varepsilon}_{t1}, \hat{\varepsilon}_{t2}, ..., \hat{\varepsilon}_{tM}$ be m "accurate" (e.g. large test set) performance estimates, corresponding to M variants (models). We investigate all possible collections composed of m models selected from a pool of M models ($m < M$). We need to estimate the mean values E and variances V of the true, apparent, and ideal errors when we select the best variant from an arbitrary collection composed of m randomly chosen vectors ($\hat{\varepsilon}_{vj}, \hat{\varepsilon}_{tj}$).

1. Input data: M – a total number of variants considered in the experiment,
   m – a number of variants in a collection under consideration
   M – two-variate vectors ($\hat{\varepsilon}_{vj}, \hat{\varepsilon}_{tj}$), $j = 1, 2, ..., M$. Note, $m << M$.

2. Rank M values $\hat{\varepsilon}_{v1}, \hat{\varepsilon}_{v2}, ..., \hat{\varepsilon}_{vM}$ in increasing order and find order numbers $i_1, i_2, ..., i_M$ of the ranked data.

3. Calculate a number v_j of cases when the value $\hat{\varepsilon}_{vj}$ was the smallest one in each of $J = C_M^m = \dfrac{M!}{(M-m)!\, m!}$ possible collections composed of r vectors from m ones: $v_1 = m/M$. The following values of $v_2, v_3, ...$ are found using the recursive formula:

$$v_{j+1} = v_j * (M-r-j+1)/(M-j), \quad j = 1, 2, ..., M-m+1.$$

4. Calculate the means and variances:

$$E\varepsilon_{apparent} = \sum_{j=1}^{M-m+1} v_{i_j} \hat{\varepsilon}_{vi_j}, \qquad V\varepsilon_{apparent\,t} = \sum_{j=1}^{M-m+1} v_{i_j} (\hat{\varepsilon}_{vi_j} - E\varepsilon_{apparent})^2,$$

$$E\varepsilon_{true} = \sum_{j=1}^{M-m+1} v_{i_j} \hat{\varepsilon}_{vi_j}, \qquad V\varepsilon_{true} = \sum_{j=1}^{M-m+1} v_{i_j} (\hat{\varepsilon}_{vi_j} - E\varepsilon_{true})^2.$$

The mean and the variance of the ideal error $E\varepsilon_{ideal}$ can be found in an analogous way. We recommend applying this algorithm for a set of values of m ($m << M$).

A.5 Matlab Codes (the Non-Linear SLP Training, the First Order Tree Dependence Model, and Data Whitening Transformation)

```
% A main program to test for the data whitening by the
% first order tree dependence model and subsequent
% training the nonlinear SLP
% This program generates two p-variate Gaussian classes
% with covariance matrix C having a linear tree
% dependence model structure
% The SLP is trained twice: in original and
% transformed feature spaces.

% AUTHOR: Sarunas Raudys   <raudys@das.mii.lt>

% Example:    dimensionality:  p=30;
% training & valdation sizes   nm=30;nv=500;
% N of iterations:             iter=500;,
% regularization:              lambda=0.001;
% correlation:                 ro=0.5;
% increase in learning step:  gama=1.01 (Section 4.6.6)
CI=eye(p);CI1=ro*eye(p+1);
CI=CI+CI1(2:p+1,1:p)+CI1(1:p,2:p+1);C=inv(CI);
[u,d]=eig(C);G=sqrt(real(d))*real(u);

A= randn(nm,p)*G; % training-data
B=randn(nm,p)*G+ones(nm,1)*[ones(1,10),-ones(1,p-10)];
Av=randn(nv,p)*G; % validation-data
Bv=randn(nv,p)*G+ones(nv,1)*[ones(1,10),-ones(1,p-10)];

% conditions E1, E2 (see Section 4.1.2.1):
M=mean([A;B]);A=A-ones(nm,1)*M;B=B-ones(nm,1)*M;
Av=Av-ones(nv,1)*M;Bv=Bv-ones(nv,1)*M;
CM=0.5*(cov(A)+cov(B));Wstart=zeros(1,p+1);

% training SLP in original feature space:
[W,etest]=slp(A,B,iter,0.1,0.00,Wstart,Av,Bv,gama);

[covt,covtI]=gentree(CM);% search for tree structure
[u,d,v]=svd(covt+lambda);% data whitening
T=u*inv(sqrtm(d));a=A*T;b=B*T;av=Av*T;bv=Bv*T;
% training SLP in transformed (whitened) feature space:

[W,et]=slp(a,b,iter,0.1,0.00,Wstart,av,bv,gama);
figure(1);plot([1:iter],etest,'r-',[1:iter],et,'g-');

%       Try to PRINT:
%disp(covtI(1:7,1:7))a part of inverse of structurised CM
% disp ([min(etest),min(et)]) % minima of
% generalisation error without and with
% whitening data transformation
+++++++++++++++++++++++++++++++++++++++++++++++++++++
```

Single layer perceptron

```
% Non-linear single-layer perceptron for 2 classes
% Author S.Raudys  <raudys@das.mii.lt>
% Inputs:
% A, B - training sets from two classes
% rows contains observations, columns - features
% n - number of training iterations
% step - learning step
% target - target value for class A (sigmoid transfer
% function)
% Wstart - initial weight vector
% Aval, Bval - validation set from classes A, B;
% rows contains observations, columns - features
% gama - coefficient to change the learning speed
% after each training  iteration, step=step * gama
% Outputs:  W - weight after the last iteration
% etest - test error after each iteration

function
[W,etest]=slp(A,B,iter,step,target,Wstart,Av,Bv,gama)

[ma k] = size(A);[mb k] = size(B);
[mav k] = size(Av);[mbv k] = size(Bv);

W=Wstart;
stepz=step/(ma+mb);
ta = (1-target) * ones(ma,1);tb = target * ones(mb,1);
oa = ones(ma,1);ob = ones(mb,1);
oav = ones(mav,1);obv = ones(mbv,1);
A=[A,oa];B=[B,ob];Av=[Av,oav];Bv=[Bv,obv];

      for i=1:iter   da = A * W';
db = B * W';
e = (sum(da<0) + sum(db>=0))/(ma+mb);
fa = oa./(oa+exp(-da));
fb = ob./(ob+exp(-db));
za = ((ta-fa).* (fa - fa.*fa))'*A;
zb = ((tb-fb).* (fb - fb.*fb))'*B;
W = W + stepz * (za + zb);
etest(i)=
size([find(W*Av'<0),find(W*Bv'>0)],2)/(mav+mbv);
stepz=stepz*gama;
      end
return
```

```
++++++++++++++++++++++++++++++++++++++++++++++++++++++

% Structurisation of the covariance matrix by
% the first-oder tree-type dependence model
% A main program
% Author: Ausra Saudargiene, ausrsaud@takas.lt
% Department of Data Analysis, Institute of Mathematics
% and Informatics, Akademijos 4, 2600 Vilnius

% Input:   C-covariance matrix
% Outputs: covgen-structured CM, covgenI-inverse of CM

function [covtree,covtreeI]=gentree(C);

[M,S,SS,num]=treev(C);%estimation of the graph,
% weights of the branches, and the new order of
% features

[covtree,covtreeI]=treecov(M,S,SS,num);
%calculation of the tree-type covariance matrix
return

++++++++++++++++++++++++++++++++++++++++++++++++++++++

% First-order tree-type dependence model
% Estimation of the graph, weights of the branches,
% and the new order of the features
% Author: A.Saudargiene, ausrsaud@takas.lt

% Input:   C-covariance matrix
% Output:
% M - graph of the tree
% S - weights of the branches (covariances)
% SS - variances, num - initial order of the features

function [M,S,SS,num]=treev(C);
[p,ms]=size(C);
%Regularization, if covariance matrix is singular
alfa=0.01;%regularization constant
if det(C)<1e-10, C=C+alfa*eye(p,p); end

%Correlation coefficients
for j=1:p
for i=1:p
     A0(i,j)=C(i,j)/sqrt(C(i,i)*C(j,j));
end
end

A=triu(A0);
Mn(1)=0; M(1)=0;S(1)=0;
k=1;
```

```
M_all=zeros((p*p-p)/2,1);

%Estimating graph of the tree
for ind=2:p % number of branches
   max_A=0;
%finding max value for i-th branch
   for i=1:p
      for j=i+1:p
         ski=0;skj=0;sk=0;
% current A(i,j): checking for common points with the
% previously selected branches
% finding max value
         if abs(A(i,j))>abs(max_A)
            for l=1:k
               if i==M_all(l) ski=1; end
               if j==M_all(l) skj=1; end
            end
            sk=ski+skj;
            if ind==2, sk=1; end
            if sk==1
               max_A=A(i,j);ki=i;kj=j;
               if ski==1
                  Mn(ind)=ki; num(ind)=kj;
               else
                  Mn(ind)=kj; num(ind)=ki;
               end
            end
         end
      end
   end

   S(ind)=C(ki,kj);
   A(ki,kj)=0;
   M_all(k)=ki;k=k+1;M_all(k)=kj;k=k+1;

%Finding initial point
   if ind==2
      if M_all(1)<M_all(2)
         Mn(2)=M_all(1);
num(1)=M_all(1);num(2)=M_all(2);
      else
         Mn(2)=M_all(2);
num(1)=M_all(2);num(2)=M_all(1);
      end
   end
end

% Changing the order of the features
for i=1:p
   for j=1:p
      if Mn(i)==num(j) M(i)=j; end
```

```
      C1(i,j)=C(num(i),num(j));
   end
end
SS=diag(C1)';

return
++++++++++++++++++++++++++++++++++++++++++++++++++++
% First-order tree-type dependence model
% Calculation of the covariance matrix (CM)
% Author: A.Saudargiene, ausrsaud@takas.lt
% Inputs: are outputs of  treev.m:
% Outputs: covgen - CM,covgenI - inverse of CM
function [covgen,covgenI]=treecov(M,S,SS,num)

[s1,s2]=size(M);p=s2;
for i=2:p
   r(i)=S(i)/sqrt(SS(i)*SS(M(i)));
end
for i=1:p
   for j=1:p
      C(i,j)=0;
      if j==i
         C(i,j)=1/sqrt(SS(i)*(1-r(i)^2));
      end
      if j==M(i)
         C(i,j)=-r(i)/sqrt(SS(M(i))*(1-r(i)^2));
      end
   end
end

KI=C'*C;d=diag(C);
K=inv(KI);

%Initial order of the features
for i=1:p
   k=find(num==i);
   numret(i)=k;
end

for i=1:p
   for j=1:p
      covgen(i,j)=K(numret(i),numret(j));
      covgenI(i,j)=KI(numret(i),numret(j));
   end
end

return
```

References

Abramson N, Braverman D (1962) Learning to recognize patterns in a random environment. *IRE Transactions Information Theory* IT-8(5):58–63.

Abend K, Harley TJ (1969) Comments "On mean accuracy of statistical pattern recognizers". *IEEE Transactions on Information Theory* IT-15:420–421.

Aivazian S, Buchstaber V, Yeniukov I, Meshalkin L (1989) *Applied Statistics: Classification and Reduction of Dimensionality*. Reference edition. Finansy i statistika, Moscow (in Russian).

Allais DC (1966) The problem of too many measurements in pattern recognition. *IEEE International Convention Record* 7:124–30.

Amari S (1967) A theory of adaptive pattern classifiers. *IEEE Transactions Electronic Computers* EC-16:299–307.

Amari S (1987) Differential-geometrical methods in statistics. *Lecture notes in statistics*, 28. Springer, New York.

Amari S (1993) A universal theorem on learning curves. *Neural Networks* 6:161–66.

Amari S, Fujita N, Shinomoto S (1992) Four types of learning curves. *Neural Computation* 4:605–18.

Amari S, Murata N (1993) Statistical theory of learning curves under entropy loss criterion. *Neural Computation* 5:140–53.

An G (1996) The effects of adding noise during back propagation training on generalization performance. *Neural Computation* 8:643–74.

Anderson TW (1951) Classification by multivariate analysis. *Psychometrika* 16:31–50.

Anderson TW (1958) *An Introduction to Multivariate Statistical Analysis*. John Wiley, New York.

Anderson TW (1971) *The Statistical Analysis of Time Series*. John Wiley, New York.

Anderson TW, Bahadur RR (1962) Classification into two multivariate normal distributions with different covariance matrices. *Annals of Mathematical Statistics* 33: 420–31.

Anoulova S, Fisher P, Polt S, Simon HU (1992) PAB-Decisions for boolean and real-valued features. *Fifth Annual Workshop on Computational Learning Theory* 5:353–62. Morgan Kaufman, San Mateo, CA.

Atick JJ, Redlich AN (1990) Towards a theory of early visual processing. *Neural Computation* 2:308–20.

Babu CC, Chen WC (1971) An optimal algorithm for pattern classification. *International Journal of Control* 3:577–86.

Barsov DA (1982) Optimal ridge estimates of the covariance matrix in highdimensional discriminant analysis. *Theory of Probability and Applications* N4:820–21.

Bishop CM (1995) *Neural Networks for Pattern Recognition*. Clarendon Press, Oxford.

Boser B, Guyon I, Vapnik V (1992) A training algorithm for optimal margin classifiers. *Fifth Annual Workshop on Computational Learning Theory* 5: 144–52. Morgan Kaufman, San Mateo, CA.

Bourland H, Kamp Y (1988) Auto-association by multilayer perceptrons and singular value decomposition. *Biological Cybernetics* 59:291–4.

Box GEF, Jenkins GM (1976) *Time Series Analysis. Forecasting and control*. Holden-Day, San Francisco, CA.

Brailovskij VL (1964) An object recognition algorithm with many parameters and its applications. *Engineering Cybernetics* N2:22–30 (in Russian).

Breiman L, Friedman J, Olshen R, Stone C (1984). *Classification and Regression Trees*. Chapman & Hall, New York,

Broomhead DS, Lowe D (1988) Multivariable functional interpolation and adaptive networks. *Complex Systems* 2: 321–55.

Bryant J, Guseman LE Jr (1979) Distance preserving linear feature selection. *Pattern Recognition* 11:347–52.

Bryson AE, Ho YC (1969) *Applied Optimal Control*. Blaisdell, New York.

Buchsbaum G, Gottshalk A (1983) Trichromacy opponent colours coding and optimum colour information transmission in the retina. *Proceedings of Royal Society*, London, 220: 1221-3.

Bunke O, Fisher K (1983) Some fundamentals and procedures of distribution free and discrete discriminant analysis. *Preprint N 51, Neue Folge*. Humbolt Universitat zu Berlin, Sektion Matematik, Berlin.

Chandrasekaran B, Jain AK (1979) On balancing decision functions. *Journal of Cybernetics and Information Science* 2(2):12–15.

Cheng B, Titterington D (1994) Neural networks: a review from a statistical perspective. *Statistical Science* 9: 2–54.

Cherkassky V, Mulier F (1998) *Learning from Data: Concepts, theory, and methods*. John Wiley, New York.

Chow CK, Liu CN (1968) Approximating discrete probability distributions with dependence trees. *IEEE Transactions on Information Theory* IT-14:462–7.

Cibas T, Fogelman-Soulie F, Gallinari P, Raudys S (1996) Variable selection with neural networks. *Neurocomputing* 12:223–48.

Cochran WD, Hopkins C (1961) Some classification problems with multivariate qualitative data. *Biometrics* 17:11–31.

Cortes C, Vapnik V (1995) Support-vector networks. *Machine Learning* 20: 273–97.

Cover TM (1965) Geometrical and statistical properties of systems of linear inequalities with applications in pattern recognition. *IEEE Transactions on Electronic Computers* EC-14:325–34.

Cybenko G (1989) Approximation by superpositions of a sigmoidal function. *Mathematics of Control, Signals, and Systems* 2:303-14.

Day NE (1969*a*) Estimating the components of a mixture of normal distributions. *Biometrika* 56:463–74.

Day NE (1969*b*) Linear and quadratic discrimination in pattern recognition. *IEEE Transactions on Information Theory* IT-15:419–20.

Day NE, Kerridge DF (1967) A general maximum likelihood discriminant. *Biometrics* 23:313–23.

Deev AD (1970) Representation of statistics of discriminant analysis and asymptotic expansions in dimensionalities comparable with sample size. *Reports of Academy of Sciences of the USSR* 195(4):756–62 (in Russian).

Deev AD (1972) Asymptotic expansions for distributions of statistics W, M, W* in discriminant analysis. In Y Blagoveschenskij (editor), *Statistical Methods of Classification,* 31: 6–57. Moscow University Press, Moscow (in Russian).

Deev AD (1974) Discriminant function designed on independent blocks of variables. *Engineering Cybernetics* N12:153–6 (in Russian).

Denoeux T, Langelle R (1993) Initialising back-propagation with prototypes. *Neural Networks,* 6(3): 351-361.

Devijver PA, Kittler J (1982) *Pattern Recognition: A statistical approach.* Precentice-Hall, London.

Devroye L, Giorfi L, Lugosi G (1996) *A Probabilistic Theory of Pattern Recognition*, Springer, New York.

Di Pillo PJ (1979) Biased discriminant analysis: evaluation of the optimum probability of misclassification. *Communications in Statistics: Theory and methods* A8(14):1447–57.

Dong DW (1993) Associative decorrelation dynamics in visual cortex. *Lawrence Berkeley Laboratory Technical Report* LBL-34491. Berkeley, CA.

Dong DW (1994) Associative decorrelation dynamics: a theory of self organization and optimization in feedback networks. In G Tesauro, DS Touretzky and TK Leen (editors), *Advances in Neural Information Processing Systems,* 7:925–32. MIT Press, Cambridge, MA.

Do-Tu H, Installe M (1978) Learning algorithms for nonparametric solution to the minimum error classification problem. *IEEE Transactions on Computers* C-27:648–59.

Duda RO, Hart PE, Stork DG (2000) *Pattern Classification and Scene Analysis.* 2nd editionn. John Wiley, New York.

Duin RPW (1978) *On the Accuracy of Satistical Pattern Recognizers.* Ph.D. dissertation. Delft University of Technology, Delft.

Duin RPW (1993) Nearest neighbour interpolation for error estimation and classifier optimisation. In KA Hogda, B Braathen, K Heia (editors) *Proceedings of the 8th Scandinavian Conference on Image Analysis,* 5-6. Tromso, Norway.

Duin RPW (1995) Small sample size generalization. In G. Borgefors (editor), *Proceedings of the 9th Scandinavian Conference on Image Analysis*, 2:957-64.

Duin RPW (1996) A note on comparing classifiers. *Pattern Recognition Letters* 17:529–36.

Efron B (1975) The efficiency of logistic regression compared to normal discriminant analysis. *Journal of the American Statistical Association* 70:892–8.

Efron B (1982) *The Jacknife, the Bootstrap and Other Resampling Plans*. SIAM, Philadelphia.

Estes SE (1965) *Measurement Selection for Linear Discriminant used in Pattern Classification*. PhD dissertation. Stanford University, Stanford, CA.

Fisher RA (1936) The use of multiple measurements in taxonomic problems. *Annals of Eugenics* 7(2):179–188.

Fix E, Hodges JLJr (1951) Discriminatory analysis, nonparametric discrimination: consistency properties. *Report No. 4, Project 21-49-004*. USAF School of Aviation Medicine, Randolph Field, TX.

Fogelman-Soulie F, Vinnet E, Lamy B (1993) Multimodular neural network architectures: application in optical character and human face recognition. *Pattern Recognition and Artificial Intelligence* 5:721–55.

Foley DH, Sammon JWJ (1975) An optimal set of discriminant vectors. *IEEE Transactions on Computers* C-24: 281–9.

Friedman JM (1989) Regularized discriminant analysis. *Journal of American Statistical Association* 84:165–75.

Fukunaga K (1990) *Introduction to Statistical Pattern Recognition*. 2nd edition. Academic Press, New York.

Fukunaga K, Hayes RR (1989) The reduced Parzen classifier. *IEEE Transactions Pattern Analysis and Machine Intelligence* PAMI-11:423–5.

Fukunaga K, Kessel D (1971) Estimation of classification errors. *IEEE Transactions on Computers* C-20:151–7.

Fukunaga K, Kessel D (1973) Nonparametric Bayes error estimation using unclassified samples. *IEEE Transactions on Information Theory* IT-19:434–9.

Geisser S (1964) Posterior odds for multivariate normal classifications. *Journal of the Royal Statistical Society Series B* 21(1):69–76.

Gelsema ES, Eden G (1980) Mapping algorithms in ISPAHAN. *Pattern Recognition* 12(3):27–36.

Geman SL, Bienenstock E, Doursat R (1992) Neural networks and bias/variance dilemma. *Neural Computation* 4:1–58.

Glick N (1978) Additive estimators for probabilities of correct classification. *Pattern Recognition* 10(3):211–22.

Glucksman H (1966) On improvement of a linear separation by extending the adaptive process with a stricter criterion. *IEEE Transactions on Electronic Computers* EC-15:941–4.

Goldin SV, Poplavskij NN (1970) Methods to increase a robustness of discriminant function. *Mathematcal Methods in Oil Gology and Geophysisics. Proceedings of Siberian NIGNI* 36:129–55. Tiumen (in Russian).

Güler C, Sankur B, Kahya Y, Skurichina M, Raudys S (1996) Classification of respiratory sound patterns by means of cooperative neural networks. In: G.Ramponi, G.L.Sicuranza, S. Carrato, S.Marsi (editors), *Proceedings of 8th European Signal Processing Conference* (isbn 88-86179-83-9). Edizioni Lint, Trieste.

Gyorgyi G, Tishby N (1990) Statistical theory of learning a rule. In K Thuemann and R Koeberle (editors), *Neural Networks and Spin Glasses,* 31–6. World Scientific, Singapore.

Griskevicius D, Raudys S (1979) On the expected probability of the classification error of the classifier for discrete variables. In S Raudys (editor), *Statistical Problems of Control,* 38:95–112. Institute of Mathematics and Informatics, Vilnius (in Russian).

Gupta AK (1977) On the equivalence of two Classification Rules. *Biometrical Journal* 19(5): 365–7.

Halkaaer S, Winter O (1996) The effect of correlated input data on the dynamics of learning. In MC Mozer, MI Jordan and T Petsche (editors), *Advances in Neural Information Processing Systems,* 9:169–75. MIT Press, Cambridge, MA.

Han CP (1968) A note on discrimination in the case of unequal covariance matrices. *Biometrika* 55:586–7.

Han CP (1970) Distribution of discriminant function in circular models. *Annals of Institute of Statistical Mathematics* 22(1):117–25.

Hand DJ (1982) *Kernel Discriminant Dnalysis.* Research Studies Press, Chichester.

Hand DJ (1986) Recent advances in error rate estimation. *Pattern Recognition Letters* 22:335–46.

Harley TJ (1963) Pseudoestimates versus pseudo-inverses for singular sample covariance matrices. Section 2 in *Report No 5, Contract DA-36-039-SC-90742, AD427172* (Sept, 1963); also MS thesis, Moore School of Electrical Engineering, University of Pennsylvania (1965).

Haussler D, Kearns M, Seung HS, Tishby N (1994) Rigorous learning curves from statistical mechanics. *Proceedings of the 7th Annual ACM Workshop on Computational Learning Theory* 7:76–87. Morgan Kaufman, San Mateo, CA.

Haykin S (1999) *Neural Networks: A comprehensive foundation.* 2nd edition. Prentice-Hall, Englewood Cliffs, NJ.

Hertz J, Krogh A, Palmer RG (1991) *Introduction to the Theory of Neural Computation.* Addison Wesley, Reading, MA.

Hills M (1967) Discrimination and allocation with discrete data. *Applied Statistics* 16(3): 237–50.

Hinton GE (1989) Connectionist learning procedures. *Artificial Intelligence* 40:185–234.

Ho TK, Basu M (2000) Measuring the complexity of classification problems. *Proceedings of 15th International Conference on Pattern Recognition* 2:43–7. IEEE Computer Society Press, Los Alamitos, CA.

Hoerl AE, Kennard RW (1970) Ridge regression: Biased estimation for orthogonal problems. *Technometrics* 12:55–67.

Holmstroom L, Hamalainen A (1993) The self organizing reduced kernel density estimator. *Proceedings of the 1993 IEEE International Conference on Neural Networks* 1:417–421. San Francisco, CA.

Hornik K, Stinchcombe M, White H (1989) Multilayer feedforward networks are universal approximators. *Neural Networks* 2:359-66.
Huber PJ (1981) *Robust Statistics.* John Wiley, New York.

Hughes GF (1965) On the mean accuracy of statistical pattern recognizers. *IEEE Transactions on Information Theory* IT-14:55–63.

Ibaraki T, Muroga S (1970) Adaptive linear classifier by linear programming. *IEEE Transactions on Systems Science and Cybernetics* SSC-6:53–62.

Jain AK and Chandrasekaran B (1982) Dimensionality and sample size considerations in pattern recognition practice. In PR Krishnaiah and LN Kanal (edotors), *Handbook of Statistics*, 2:835–85. North-Holland, Amsterdam.

Jain AK and Dubes R (1978) Feature definition in pattern recognition with small sample size. *Pattern Recognition* 10:85–97.

Jain AK, Duin RPW and Mao J (2000) Statistical pattern recognition: a review. *IEEE Transactions on Pattern Analysis and Machine Intelligence* PAMI-22:4– 37.

Jain AK, Mao J and Mohiuddin M (1996) Neural networks: a tutorial. *IEEE Computer* 29:31–44.

Jain AK and Waller WG (1978) On the optimal number of features in the classification of multivariate Gaussian data. *Pattern Recognition* 10:367–74.

Jain AK and Zongker D (1997) Feature selection: evaluation, application, and small sample performance. *IEEE Transactions on Pattern Analysis and Machine Intelligence* PAMI-19:153–8.

John S (1961) Errors in discrimination. *Annals of Mathematical Statistics* 32:1125–44.

Kanal L, Chandrasekaran B (1971) On dimensionality and sample size in statistical pattern classification. *Pattern Recognition* 3:238–55.

Karnin ED (1990) A simple procedure for pruning back-propagation trained neural networks. *IEEE Transactions on Neural Networks* 1:239–42.

Keehn D (1965) A note on learning for Gaussian properties. *IEEE Transactions on Information Theory* IT-11:126–31.

Kharin YS (1996) *Robustness in Statistical Pattern Recognition*. Kluwer Academic Publishers, Dordrecht.

Kligiene N (1977) Asymptotic estimate of the probability of misclassification of autoregressive sequences. In L Telksnys (editor), *Statistical Problems of Control*, 19:81–102. Institute of Mathematics and Informatics, Vilnius (in Russian).

Koford JS, Groner GF (1966) The use of an adaptive threshold element to design a linear optimal pattern classifier. *IEEE Transactions on Information Theory* IT-2:42–50.

Kohonen T (1986) Learning vector quantisation for pattern recognition. *Technical Report TKK-F-A601*. Helsinki University of Technology, Helsinki.

Kowalczyk A (1996) Model of generalisation error in learning systems with training error selection. In S Amari, L Xu, LW Chan, I King and KS Leung (editors), *Progress in Neural Information Processing: Proc ICONIP'96*, 180–7. Springer, Hong Kong.

Kraaijeveld MA, Duin RPW (1994) The effective capacity of multilayer feedforward network classifiers. *Proceedings of 12th International Conference on Pattern Recognition* 2: 99–103. IEEE Computer Society Press, Los Alamitos, CA

Kruskal IB Jr (1956) On the shortest spanning subtree of a graph and the travelling salesman problem. *Proceedings of American Mathematical Society* 7:48–50.

Kubat M (1998) Decision trees can initialize radial-basis function networks. *IEEE Transactions on Neural Networks* 9:813–21.

Lachenbruch PA, Goldstein M (1979) Discriminant analysis. *Biometrics* 5(3):9–85.

Lachenbruch PA, Mickey RM (1968) Estimation of error rates in discriminant analysis. *Technometrics* 10(1):1–11.

Lbov GS (1965) A selection of an efficient system of statistically dependent variables. In NG Zagoruiko (editor), *Computing Systems,* 19:21–34. Institute of Mathematics, Novosibirsk (in Russian).

Lbov GS (1966) On representativeness of the sample size while choosing the effective measurement system. In: NG Zagoruiko (editor), *Computing Systems,* 22:39–58. Institute of Mathematics, Novosibirsk (in Russian).

Lbov GS (1981) *Methods of Processing Experimental Data with Mixed Variables*. Nauka, Novosibirsk (in Russian).

Le Cun Y (1986) Learning process in an asymmetric threshold network. In E Bienenstock, F Fogelman-Soulie and G Weisbuch (editors), *Disordered systems and biological organizations*, 233–240. Proceedings of NATO Workshop, Les Houches, March 1985. Springer.

Le Cun Y (1987) *Modeles Connexionistes de l'Apprentissage*. Ph D thesis. University Paris 6.

Le Cun Y, Denker JS, Solla S (1990) Optimal brain damage. In D Tourecky (editor), *Advances in Neural Information Processing Systems,* 598–605. Morgan Kaufmann, San Mateo, CA.

Le Cun Y, Kanter I, Solla S (1991) Eigenvalues of covariance matrices: application to neural-network learning. *Physical Review Letters* 66(18):2396–9.

Levin E, Tishby N, Solla SA (1990). A statistical approach to generalization in layered neural networks. *Proceedings of the IEEE* 78:2133-50.

Linhart G (1959) Techniques of discriminant analysis with discrete variables. *Metrika* 2:116, 138–40.

Lim TS, Loh WY, Shih YS (2000) A comarison of prdiction accuracy, complexity, and training time of thirty-three old and new classification algorithms. *Machine Learning* 40(3):203–28.

Lipskaya VA (1981) An optimal decision rule for a problem of identification. *Theory of Probabilities and Mathematical Statistics*, 24:91–102. Visha Shkola Publishers, Kiev (in Russian).

Malinovskij LG (1979) *Objects Classification by Means of Discriminant Analysis.* Nauka, Moscow (in Russian).

Mao J, Jain A (1993) Regularisation techniques in artificial neural networks. *Proceedings of the World Congress on Neural Networks*, IV:75–9. IEEE Computer Society Press, Portland.

Mao J, Jain A (1995) Artificial neural networks for feature extraction and multivariate data projection. *IEEE Transactions on Neural Networks* 6:296–317.

Mazurov VD (1971) Committees of systems of inequalities and recognition problem. *Cybernetics* N3:140-7 (in Russian).

McCulloch WS, Pitts W (1943) A logical calculus of the ideas immanent in nervous activity. *Bulletin of Mathematical Biophysics* 5:115-33.

McKay RJ, Campbell NA (1982*a*) Variable selection techniques in discriminant analysis. I. Description. *British Journal of Mathematical and Statistical Psychology* 35: 1–29.

McKay RJ, Campbell NA (1982*b*) Variable selection techniques in discriminant analysis. II. Allocation. *British Journal of Mathematical and Statistical Psychology*, 35: 30–41.

McLachlan GJ (1992) *Discriminant Analysis and Statistical Pattern Recognition.* John Wiley, New York.

Meshalkin LD (1976) Assignment of numerical values to nominal variables. In S Raudys and L Meshalkin (editors), *Statistical Methods of Control,* 14: 49–56. Institute of Mathematics and Informatics, Vilnius (in Russian).

Meshalkin LD (1977) Theory of Statistical Analysis of Chronical Progressing Diseases. USSR Dr Sc dissertation. Moscow State University, Moscow (in Russian).

Meshalkin LD, Serdobolskij VI (1978) Errors in classifying multivariate observations. *Theory of Probabilities and Its Applications*, 23:772–81(in Russian).

Michie D, Spiegelhalter DJ, Taylor CC (editors) (1994) *Machine Learning, Neural and Statistical Classification.* Ellis Horwood, New York.

Miyake A (1979) Mathematical aspects of optimal linear discriminant function. COMPSAC'79. *Proceedings of the IEEE Computer Society's 3rd International Computer Software and Applications Conference* 161–6.Chicago, Ill.

Mozer MC, Smolensky P (1989) Skeletonization: a technique for trimming the fat from a network via relevance assessment. In DS Touretzky (editor), *Advances in Neural Information Processing Systems* 1:107–115. Morgan Kaufmann, San Mateo, CA.

Nieman H (1980) Linear and nonlinear mapping of patterns. *Pattern Recognition* 12(2):83–8.

Norusis A (1991) Construction of logical (decision tree) classifiers with the top-down search. In S Raudys (editor), *Statistical Problems of Control,* 93:131-158. Institute Mathematics and Informatics, Vilnius (in Russian).

Okamoto M (1963) An asymptotic expansion for the distribution of linear discriminant function. *Annals of Mathematical Statistics* 34:1286–301, 39:1358–9.

Opper M, Haussler D (1991) Calculation of the learning curve of Bayes optimal classification algorithm for learning perceptron with noise. *Proceedings of Fourth annual ACM Workshop on Computational Learning Theory* 4:75–87. Morgan Kaufman, San Mateo, CA.

Parker DB (1985) Learning logic. *Technical Report 47*, Center for Computational Research in Economic and Management Science, MIT Press, Boston.

Parzen E (1962) On estimation of probability function and mode. *Annals of Mathematical Statistics* 33:1065–76.

Patrick EA, Shen LYL (1971) Interactive use of problem knowledge for clustering and decision making. *IEEE Transactions on Electronic Computers* EC-10(2):216–22.

Patterson DW, Mattson RL (1966) A method of finding linear discriminant functions for a class of performance criteria. *IEEE Transactions on Information Theory* IT-12:380–7.

Pietrantonio H, Jurs PC (1972) Iterative least squares development of discriminant functions for spectroscopic data analysis by pattern recognition. *Pattern Recognition* 4:391–400.

Pikelis V (1974) *Analysis of Learning Speed of Three Linear Classifiers*. Ph.D. dissertation. Institute of Physics and Mathematics, Vilnius (in Russian).

Pikelis V (1976) Comparison of methods of computing the expected classification errors. *Automatic and Remote Control* N5:59–63 (in Russian).

Pikelis V (1991) Calculating statistical characteristics of experimental process for selecting the best version. In S Raudys (editor) *Statistical Problems of Control*, 93:46–56. Institute of Mathematics and Informatics, Vilnius (in Russian).

Pinsker IS (1973) Estimation of learning method and learning sample. In IS Pinsker (editor) *Simulation and Automatic Analysis of Electrocardiograms*, 13–23. Nauka, Moscow (in Russian).

Pivoriunas V (1978) The linear discriminant function for the identification of spectra. In S Raudys (editor), *Statistical Problems of Control*, 27:71–90. Institute of Mathematics and Informatics, Vilnius (in Russian).

Pivoriunas V, Raudys S (1978) On the accuracy of "leaving-one-out" estimate. In S Raudys (editor), *Statistical Problems of Control*, 27:53–70. Institute of Mathematics and Informatitics, Vilnius (in Russian).

Plaut, DC, Nowlan SJ, Hinton GE (1986) Experiments on learning by back propagation. *Technical Report CMU-CS-86-126*. Carnegie-Mellon University, Pittsburg, PA.

Quinlan JR (1993) *C4.5: Programs for Machine Learning*. Morgan Kaufmann, San Mateo, CA.

Randles RH, Brofitt JD, Ramberg IS, Hogg RV (1978) Generalized linear and quadratic discriminant functions using robust estimates. *Journal of the American Statistical Association* 73(363):564–8.

Rao CR (1949) On some problems arising of discrimination with multiple characters. *Sankya* 9:343–65.

Rastrigin LA, Erenstein RCh (1981) *Method of Collective Recognition.* Energoizdat, Moscow (in Russian).

Raudys A (2000) Interactive initialisation of the multilayer perceptron. *Pattern Recognition Letters*, 21907-16.

Raudys A, Long A (2000) MLP based linear feature extraction for nonlinearly separable data. *Pattern Analysis and Applications* (accepted).

Raudys S (1967) On determining training sample size of linear classifier. In NG Zagoruiko (editor) *Computing Systems,* 28:79–87. Institute of Mathematics, Novosibirsk (in Russian).

Raudys S (1970) On the problems of sample size in pattern recognition. In VS Pugatchiov (editor) *Detection, Pattern Recognition and Experiment Design,* 2:64–76. Proceedings of the 2nd All-Union Conference Statistical Methods in Control Theory. Nauka, Moscow (in Russian).

Raudys S (1972) On the amount of a priori information in designing the classification algorithm. *Engineering Cybernetics* N4:168–74 (in Russian).

Raudys S (1973) Estimation of probability of misclassification In L Telksnys (editor), *Statistical Problems of Control,* 5:9–44. Institute of Mathematics and Informatics, Vilnius (in Russian).

Raudys S (1976) Limitation of sample size in clasification problems. *Statistical Problems of Control*, 18:1-186. Institute of Mathematics and Informatics, Vilnius (in Russian).

Raudys S (1979*a*) Classification errors when features are selected. In S Raudys (editor), *Statistical Problems of Control*, 38:9–26. Institute of Mathematics and Informatics, Vilnius (in Russian).

Raudys S (1979*b*) Determination of optimal dimensionality in statistical pattern classification. *Pattern Recognition* 11: 263–71.

Raudys, S. (1981) Influence of sample size on the accuracy of model selection in pattern recognition. In S Raudys (editor), *Statistical Problems of Control,* 50:9–30. Institute of Mathematics and Informatics, Vilnius (in Russian).

Raudys S (1987) On the accuracy of model selection in data analysis. *Proceedings of the III-rd International Conference on Data Analysis and Informatics* 1:91–100. INRIA Press, Paris.

Raudys S (1988) On the accuracy of a bootstrap estimate of the classification error. *Proceedings of 9th International Joint Conference on Pattern Recognition*, 1230–2. IEEE press, Los Alamitos, CA.

Raudys, S (1991) On the efectiveness of Parzen window classifier. *Informatica* 2:434–54. Institute of Mathematics and Informatics, Vilnius.

Raudys S (1993) On shape of pattern error function, initializations and intrinsic dimensionality in ANN classifier design. *Informatica* 4:360–83. Institute of Mathematics Informatics, Vilnius.

Raudys S (1994) Why do ANN classifiers have favourable small sample properties? In: ES Gelsema and LS Kanal (editors), *Pattern Recognition in Practice* IV: 287-298. Elsevier Science, Amsterdam.

Raudys S. (1995*a*) Generalization of linear and non-linear adaptive classifiers. *Proceedings ICANN'95* 1:183–90.EC2 & Cie Press, Paris.

Raudys S (1995*b*) A negative weight decay or antiregularisation, *Proceedings ICANN'95* 2:449-54. EC2 & Cie Press, Paris.

Raudys, S (1996) Linear classifiers in perceptron design. *Proceedings of 13th International Conference on Pattern Recognition* 4(D):763–7. IEEE Computer Society Press, Los Alamitos, CA.

Raudys S (1997) On dimensionality, sample size and classification error of nonparametric linear classification algorithms. *IEEE Transactions on Pattern Analysis and Machine Intelligence* PAMI-19:669–71.

Raudys S (1998*a*) Use of statistical hypothesis in neural network design. In: SA Aivazian, YS Kharin (editors), *Computer Data Analysis and Modelling,* 2:55–63. Minsk University Press, Minsk.

Raudys S (1998*b*) Evolution and generalization of a single neurone. I. SLP as seven statistical classifiers. *Neural Networks* 11: 283–96.

Raudys S (1998*c*) Evolution and generalization of a single neurone. II. Complexity of statistical classifiers and sample size considerations. *Neural Networks* 11:297–313.

Raudys S (2000*a*) How good are support vector machines? *Neural Networks* 13:9-11.

Raudys S (2000*b*) Evolution and generalization of a single neurone. III. Primitive, regularized, standard, robust and minimax regressions. *Neural Networks* 13(4-5):507-23.

Raudys S (2000*c*) Scaled rotation regularization. *Pattern Recognition* 33:1989–98.

Raudys S (2000*d*) Classifier's complexity control while training multilayer perceptrons. In: F Ferri, JM Inest, A. Amin and P Pudil (editors), *Advances in Pattern Recognition,* 32–44. Springer Lecture Notes in Computer Science, 1876.

Raudys S, Amari S (1998) Effect of initial values in simple perception. In *Proceedings 1998 IEEE World Congress on Computational Intelligence* IJCNN'98:1530–5. IEEE Press.

Raudys S, Duin RPW (1998). On expected classification error of the Fisher classifier with pseudoinverse covariance matrix. *Pattern Recognition Letters* 19:385–92.

Raudys S, Jain AK (1991) Small sample size effects in statistical pattern recognition: recommendations for practitioners. *IEEE Transactions on Pattern Analysis and Machine Intelligence* PAMI-13:252–64.

Raudys S, Pikelis V, Juskevicius K (1975) Experimental comparison of thirteen classification algorithms. In S Raudys (editor), *Statistical Problems of Control,* 11:53-80. Institute of Mathematics and Informatics, Vilnius (in Russian).

Raudys S, Pikelis V (1980) On dimensionality, sample size, classification error and complexity of classification algorithm in pattern recognition. *IEEE Transactions on Pattern Analysis and Machine Intelligence*, PAMI-2:242–52.

Raudys S, Pikelis V (1982) Collective selection of the best version of a pattern recognition system. *Pattern Recognition Letters* 1:7–13.

Raudys S, Saudargiene A (1998) Structures of the covariance matrices in the classifier design. In: A Amin, D Dori, P Pudil, H Freeman (editors), *Advances in Pattern Recognition*, 583–92. Springer Lecture Notes in Computer Science, 1451.

Raudys S, Saudargiene A (2001) Tree type dependency model and sample size - dimensionality properties. *IEEE Transactions on Pattern Analysis and Machine Intelligence* 23(1).

Raudys S, Saudargiene A, Povilonis E (2000) The bias evaluation in the model selection. *Pattern Analysis and Applications* (submitted)

Raudys S, Skurichina M (1994) Small sample properties of ridge estimate of the covariance matrix in statistical and neural net classification. In EM Tiit, T Kollo, H Niemi (editors), *New Trends in Probability and Statistics: Multivariate statistics and matrices in statistics,* 3:237–45. TEV, Vilnius and VSP, Utrecht.

Raudys S, Skurichina M (1992) The role of the number of training samples on weight initialisation of artificial neural net classifier. In *Neuroinformatics and Neurocomputers. Proceedings of RNNS/IEEE Symposium,* 343-353. IEEE Press.

Raudys S, Skurichina M, Cibas T, Gallinari P (1995) Ridge estimates of the covariance matrix and regularization of artificial neural network classifier. *Pattern Recognition and Image Processing* N4:633–50. International Journal of Russian Academy of Sciences, Moscow.

Raudys S, Vaitukaitis V (1984) Methods to estimate the probability of misclassification. In: S Raudys (editor), *Statistical Problems of Control,* 66:43–65. Institute of Mathematics and Informatics, Vilnius (in Russian).

Reed R (1993) Pruning algorithms: a survey. IEEE *Transactions on Neural Networks,* 4:740–7.

Reed R, Marks RJ, Oh S (1995) Similarities of error regularization, sigmoid gain scaling, target smoothing, and training with jitter. *IEEE Transactions on Neural Networks* 6:529–38.

Ripley B, (1994) Neural networks and related methods for classification. *Journal of Royal Statistical Society Series B56*: 409–56.

Rosenblatt F (1958) The Perceptron: A probabilistic model for information storage in the brain. *Psychological Review* 65:386-408.

Rosenblatt M (1956) Remarks on some nonparametric estimates of a density function. *Annals of Mathematical Statistics* 27:832–37.

Rumelhart DE, Hinton GE, Williams RJ (1986) Learning internal representations by error propagation. In: DE Rumelhart, JL McClelland (editors), *Parallel Distributed Processing: Explorations in the microstructure of cognition* I:318–62. Bradford Books, Cambridge, MA.

Sammon JW (1969) A non-linear mapping for data structure analysis. *IEEE Transactions on Computers* C-18:401–9.

Saudargiene A (1999) Structurization of the covariance matrix by process type and block diagonal models in the classifier design. *Informatica* 10(2): 245–69.

Schalakoff RJ (1992) *Pattern Recognition: Statistical, structural and neural approaches*. John Wiley, New York.

Schuermann J (1977) *Polynomklassifikatoren fur Zeichenerkennung*. Oldenbourg, Verlag, Munchen-Wien.

Schuermann J (1996) *Pattern Classification: A unified view of statistical and neural approaches*, John Wiley, New York.

Scott D (1992) *Multivariate Density Estimation: Theory, practice, visualization.* John Wiley, New York.
Sebestyen GS (1962) *Decision-Making Process in Pattern Recognition.* Macmillan, New York.

Serdobolskij VI(1979) The moments of discriminant function and classification for a large number of variables. In S Raudys (editor), *Statistical Problems of Control*, 38:27–51. Institute of Mathematics and Informatics, Vilnius (in Russian).

Serdobolskij VI (1983*a*) On minimal error probability in discriminatnt anlysis. *Reports of Academy of Sciences of the USSR* 270:1066–70 (in Russian).

Serdobolskij VI (1983*b*) The influece of selecting components of random variable on classification. *Izvestija VUZOV USSR, series Mathematics* N9:46–55. Moscow (in Russian).

Sethi I and Jain AK (editors) (1991) *Neural Networks and Statistical Pattern Recognition*, North-Holland, Amsterdam.

Seung HS, Sompolinsky H, Tishby N (1992) Statistical mechanics from examples. *Physical Review* A45(8): 6056–91.

Shlesinger M (1968) Interrelation between learning and self-learning in pattern recognition. *Cybernetics* (translated from Russian Consult Bureau, NY) 4(2):81–8.

Siadliecki, W, Siadlecka K, Sklansky J (1988) An overview of mapping techniques for exploratory pattern analysis. *Pattern Recognition* 21:411–29.

Silverman BW (1986) *Density Estimation in Statistics.* Chapman and Hall, New York.

Sitgreaves R (1961) Some results on the distribution of the W-classification statistics. In H Solomon (editor), *Studies in Item Selection and Prediction,* 241–61. Stanford University Press, Stanford, CA.

Sjoberg J, Ljung L (1992) Overtraining, regularization, and searching for minimum in neural networks. *Technical Teport S-581 83.* Department of Electrical Engineering, Linkoping University, Sweden.

Skurichina M (1991) Effect of the kernel functional form on the quality of nonparametic Parzen window classifier. In S Raudys (editor), *Statistical Problems of Control,* 93:167–81. Institute Mathematics and Informatics, Vilnius (in Russian).

Skurichina M, Raudys S, Duin RPW (2000) K-nearest neighbors directed noise injection in multilayer perceptron training, *IEEE Transactions on Neural Networks*, 11 504–11.

Smith FW (1971) Design of minimum-error optimal classifiers for patterns form distributions with Gaussian tails. *IEEE Transactions on Information Theory* IT-17:701–7.

Smith FW (1972) Small-sample optimality of design techniques for linear classifiers of Gaussian patterns. *IEEE Transactions on Information Theory* IT-18:118–26.

Sohn SY (1999) Meta analysis of classification algorithms for pattern recognition. *IEEE Transactions on Pattern Analysis and Machine Intelligence* PAMI-21:1137–44.

Solomon H (1956) Probability and statistics in psychometric research. In IJ Neyman (editor), *Proceedings of 3rd Berkley Symposium on Mathematical Statistics and Probability,* 169–84. University California Press, Berkley, CA.

Somol P, Pudil P, Novovočova J and Paclik P (1999) Adaptive floating search methods in feature selection. *Pattern Recognition Letters* 20:1157-63.

Takeshita T, Toriwaki J (1995) Experimental study of performance of pattern classifiers and the size of design samples. *Pattern Recognition Letters* 16:307–12.

Tax DMJ, Breukelen M, Duin RPW, Kittler J (2000) Combining multiple classifiers by averaging or by multiplying? *Pattern Recognition* 33:1475–85.

Tou JT, Gonzales RC (1974) *Pattern Recognition Principles.* Addison-Wesley, Reading, MA.

Toussaint GT (1972) Polynomial representation of classifiers with dependent discrete-valued features. *IEEE Transactions on Computers* C-21(2):205–8.

Toussaint GT (1974) Bibliography on estimation of misclassification. *IEEE Transactions on Information Theory* IT-20(4):472–9.

Tsypkin Ya Z (1966) Adaptation, learning and self-learning in automatic systems. *Automatic and Remote Control* N1:23–61 (in Russian).

Tsypkin Ya Z (1973) *Foundations of the Theory of Learning Systems.* Academic Press, New York.

Tubbs JD, Coberley WA, Young DM (1982) Linear dimension reduction and Bayes classification with unkown parameters. *Pattern Recognition* 14(3):167–172.

Vajda I (1970) Note on discrimination information and variation. *IEEE Transactions on Information theory* IT-16:771-773.

Valiant LG (1984) A theory of the learnable. *Communications of ACM*, 27:1134–42.

Van der Smagt PP (1994) Minimization methods for training feedforward neural networks. *Neural Networks* 7: 1–11.

Vapnik VN (1976) A method of minimization of sum risk in problem of pattern recognition. In S Raudys and L Meshalkin (editors), *Statistical Problems of Control*, 14:174–7. Institute of Mathematics and Informatics, Vilnius (in Russian).

Vapnik VN (1982) *Estimation of Dependencies Based on Empirical Data.* Springer, New York

Vapnik VN (1995) *The Nature of Statistical Learning Theory*. Springer, Berlin.

Vapnik VN, Chervonenkis DYa (1968) On uniform convergence of relative frequencies of events to their probabilities. *Soviet Math Doklady* 9:915–8.

Vapnik VN, Chervonenkis DYa (1974) *Theory of Pattern Recognition: Statistical learning problems.* Nauka, Moscow (in Russian).

Vidyasagar M (1997) *A Theory of Learning and Generalization.* Springer, London.

Wald A (1944) On a statistical problem in the classification of an individual into one of two groups. *Annals of Mathematical Statistics* 15:145–62.

Wald A (1950) *Statistical Decision Functions.* John Wiley, New York.

Wand M, Jones M (1995) *Kernel Smoothing.* Chapman & Hall, New York.

Warmack RE, Gonzales RC (1973) An algorithm for optimal solution of linear inequalities and its application to pattern recognition. *IEEE Transactions on Computers* C-22:1065–75.

Welch BL (1939) Note on discriminant functions. *Biometrica* 31:218–20.

Werbos PJ (1974) *Beyond Regression: New tools for prediction in the behavioral sciences.* Ph.D. Thesis, Harvard University Cambridge, MA.

Widrow B, Hoff ME (1960) Adaptive switching circuits. *WESCON Convention Record*, 4:96–104.

Wolf AC (1966) The estimation of the optimum linear decision function with a sequential random method. *IEEE Transactions on Information Theory* IT-12:312–5.

Wolpert DH (editor) (1995) *The Mathematics of Generalization*. Proceedings of the SFI/CNLS workshop on formal approach to supervised learning (Santa Fe (Studies in the Sciences of Complexity). Santa Fe Institute, Santa Fe, NM.

Wolverton CT, Wagner TJ (1969) Asymptotically optimal discriminant functions for pattern classification. *IEEE Transactions on Information Theory* IT-15:258–65.

Wyman F, Young D, Turner D (1990) A comparison of asymptotic error rate expansions for the sample linear discriminant function. *Pattern Recognition* 23:775–83.

Yacoub M, Bennani Y (1997) A heuristic for variable selection in multilayer artificial neural network classifier. In C Dagli, M Akay, O Ersoy, B Fernandez and A Smith (editors) *Intelligent Engineering Systems Through Artificial Neural Networks* 7:527–32. ASME, New York.

Yau SS, Schumpert JM (1968) Design of pattern classifiers with the updating property using stochastic approximation techniques. *IEEE Transactions on Computers* C-17:908–1003.

Young TY, Calvert TW (1974) *Classification Estimation and Pattern Recognition*. Elsevier Science, New York.

Zarudskij VI (1979) The use of models of simple dependence problems of classification. In S Raudys (editor), *Statistical Problems of Control* 38:33–75. Institute of Mathematics and Informatics, Vilnius (in Russian).

Zarudskij VI (1980) Determination of some graph connections for normal vectors in large dimensional case. In SA Aivazian (editor) *Algorithmic and Programic Supply of Applied Multivariate Statistical Analysis*, 189-208. Nauka, Moscow (in Russian).

Zhezel YN (1975) A minimal essentially complete class of discriminant rules when the higher moments are unknown. *Theory of Probability and Applications* 19:832–4

Index

FSC
www.fsc.org
MIX
Papier aus verantwortungsvollen Quellen
Paper from responsible sources
FSC® C105338

If you have any concerns about our products,
you can contact us on
ProductSafety@springernature.com

In case Publisher is established outside the EU,
the EU authorized representative is:
Springer Nature Customer Service Center GmbH
Europaplatz 3, 69115 Heidelberg, Germany

Printed by Libri Plureos GmbH
in Hamburg, Germany